SAMS Teach Yourself

Mac® OS X Panther™

Robyn Ness and John Ray

SAMS   800 East 96th Street, Indianapolis, Indiana 46240 USA

Sams Teach Yourself Mac OS X Panther All in One

International Standard Book Number: 0-672-32603-5

Library of Congress Catalog Card Number: 2003094094

Printed in the United States of America

First Printing: December 2003

06 05 04 03   4 3

Trademarks

All terms mentioned in this book that are known to be trademarks or service marks have been appropriately capitalized. Sams Publishing cannot attest to the accuracy of this information. Use of a term in this book should not be regarded as affecting the validity of any trademark or service mark.

Warning and Disclaimer

Every effort has been made to make this book as complete and as accurate as possible, but no warranty or fitness is implied. The information provided is on an "as is" basis. The author and the publisher shall have neither liability nor responsibility to any person or entity with respect to any loss or damages arising from the information contained in this book.

Bulk Sales

Sams Publishing offers excellent discounts on this book when ordered in quantity for bulk purchases or special sales. For more information, please contact:

U.S. Corporate and Government Sales
1-800-382-3419
corpsales@pearsontechgroup.com

For sales outside of the U.S., please contact:

International Sales
+1-317-428-3341
international@pearsontechgroup.com

Acquisitions Editor
Betsy Brown

Development Editor
Lorna Gentry

Managing Editor
Charlotte Clapp

Senior Project Editor
Matthew Purcell

Copy Editor
Geneil Breeze

Indexer
Heather McNeill

Proofreader
Leslie Joseph

Technical Editor
Terrence Talbot

Team Coordinator
Vanessa Evans

Designer
Gary Adair

Page Layout
Julie Parks

Contents at a Glance

Table of Contents

Part II: Common Applications

Authors

John Ray is an award-winning developer and security consultant with more than 17 years of programming and administration experience. He has worked on projects for the FCC, the National Regulatory Research Institute, The Ohio State University, Xerox, and the State of Florida. He has written or contributed to more than 10 books currently in print, including *Mac OS X Unleashed, Special Edition Using TCP/IP, Sams Teach Yourself Dreamweaver MX Application Development in 21 Days*, and *Maximum Mac OS X Security*. He bought his first Macintosh in 1984 and remains a strong proponent for the computer and operating system that revolutionized the industry.

Robyn Ness holds a master's degree in psychology with a specialization in judgment and decision making from The Ohio State University. She currently works as a Web developer, focusing on issues of usability and content design. In her spare time she tests the bounds of iPhoto by taking a ridiculous number of digital photographs, the best of which can be seen at www.shadesofinsanity.com.

Dedication

For those responsible for Aqua Teen Hunger Force, Sealab 2021,
and Home Movies. And for our dogs.

Acknowledgments

We would like to acknowledge the dedicated people at Sams Publishing who worked to make this book possible. Specifically, Betsy Brown, Kathryn Mohr, Lorna Gentry, Matt Purcell, and Geneil Breeze were instrumental in bringing *Sams Teach Yourself Mac OS XPanther All in One* to press. We offer a sincere thank you as well to Terrence Talbot for his thorough technical review. Through the tireless effort of this team, we're able to bring you, our readers, this helpful guide to Mac OS X Panther.

We Want to Hear from You!

As the reader of this book, *you* are our most important critic and commentator. We value your opinion and want to know what we're doing right, what we could do better, what areas you'd like to see us publish in, and any other words of wisdom you're willing to pass our way.

You can email or write me directly to let me know what you did or didn't like about this book—as well as what we can do to make our books stronger.

Please note that I cannot help you with technical problems related to the topic of this book, and that due to the high volume of mail I receive, I might not be able to reply to every message.

When you write, please be sure to include this book's title and author as well as your name and phone or email address. I will carefully review your comments and share them with the author and editors who worked on the book.

Email: consumer@samspublishing.com

Mail: Mark Taber
         Associate Publisher
         Sams Publishing
         800 East 96th Street
         Indianapolis, IN 46240 USA

Reader Services

For more information about this book or others from Sams Publishing, visit our Web site at www.samspublishing.com. Type the ISBN (excluding hyphens) or the title of the book in the Search box to find the book you're looking for.

Introduction

Our goal in creating this book is to give you, the reader, the most information possible about Mac OS X 10.3 (also known as Panther) in as friendly and straightforward a manner as possible. Although we've included tips that even seasoned Mac users can benefit from, this book is especially written for the following:

▶ People who have recently switched to the Mac who want to learn the basics of the operating system, as well as some of the best Mac programs available.

▶ Long-time Mac users who want to learn the new Mac OS X operating system, as well as work more productively with common OS X applications.

▶ People who are already familiar with some aspects of Mac OS X but want a helpful reference for those parts they haven't yet mastered.

How This Book Is Organized

The chapters of this book are categorized into seven sections:

Part I, "Mac OS X Basics," explores fundamental elements of the operating system, including the Finder, the Dock, and System Preferences. It also explains the basics of how to work with windows, files, and applications.

Part II, "Common Applications," introduces several programs that come bundled with OS X, including Calculator, Preview, QuickTime, and DVD Player, as well as software installation and other applications you may want to add to your system.

Part III, "Internet Applications," covers how to connect to the Internet and several applications from Apple that use a network connection, including the Safari Web browser, the email program Mail, and the instant messaging client iChat.

Part IV, "Hardware and Related Settings," focuses on peripheral devices, including monitors, printers, and USB and FireWire devices, as well as some of the settings needed to run them.

Part V, "Apple's iLife Applications," explores Apple's digital media applications—iTunes, iPhoto, iMovie, and iDVD.

Part VI, "System Administration and Maintenance," explains several topics—such as setting up your Mac for multiple users, securing your system, recovering from crashes, and backing up your data—that can make your system run smoother or, at least, help in times of trouble.

Part VII, "Advanced Topics," introduces some aspects of Mac OS X that the average user may not be aware of, including using the Unix command line, running AppleScript, and working with various system utilities.

An Invitation from the Authors

If you have questions or comments about Mac OS X or this book, please feel free to email us.

Thanks for reading!

Robyn Ness (robynness@mac.com)
John Ray (johnray@mac.com)

PART I

Mac OS X Basics

CHAPTER 1

Introducing Mac OS X

This chapter begins with a quick look at the initial setup of Mac OS X and at the components that give Mac OS X its power. We then examine basic desktop controls, System Preferences, and some of the applications included with 10.3, which are examined in depth in later chapters.

Setting Up Mac OS X

The first time Mac OS X starts, it runs Setup Assistant, which helps you set up the basic features of the operating system. During the setup procedure, your network settings are configured, and your registration details are sent back to Apple.

Creating Your Account

Mac OS X requires you to create an account for one user during the setup process. You can add other user accounts later, but. the original account is an administrator account, which is used to control access to the system and to prevent unauthorized changes from being made to your software.

> Mac OS X is a multiuser operating system that allows you to create multiple user accounts. This allows each user to have his own files and system preferences and requires each user to access the system with a username and password. Passwords provide a measure of security. On the other hand, if you're the only user and don't want to log in each time, you can configure your system to start without a login. We'll discuss the options further in Chapter 33, "Sharing Your Computer with Multiple Users."

Did you Know?

The account setup fields are explained here:

- ▶ Name—Enter your full name.

- ▶ Short Name—The short name is the name of your account. It should be composed of eight or fewer lowercase letters or numbers. Spaces and punctuation aren't allowed.

▶ Password—The Password field is used to enter a secret word or string of characters that Mac OS X uses to verify that you are who you say you are.

▶ Verify—The Verify field requires you to type the same string you entered in the Password field. This step ensures that the password you typed is actually what you intended.

▶ Password Hint—Type a phrase or question that reminds you of your password. If you attempt to log in to your system three times without success, the hint is displayed.

After you fill in this user information, click Continue to proceed.

Additional Settings

After you create a user account, you can set up your Internet connection. If you already have Internet access, but don't have all the information required to connect to your network or dial in to your ISP, skip this step for now. We cover specifics about Internet access in Chapter 11, "Connecting to the Internet."

The next step is to specify the time zone for your computer. After you choose the appropriate zone and set the date and time, click Continue.

Congratulations! You've reached the last step of the configuration process. When prompted, click the Done button, and Mac OS X takes you to the desktop. Now let's briefly explore the structure of Mac OS X.

A Peek Under the Hood of Mac OS X

Mac OS X consists of 11 separate pieces that work together and complement each other (as represented in Figure 1.1). Let's take a brief look at the components that make up Mac OS X. We'll also examine how they influence its features.

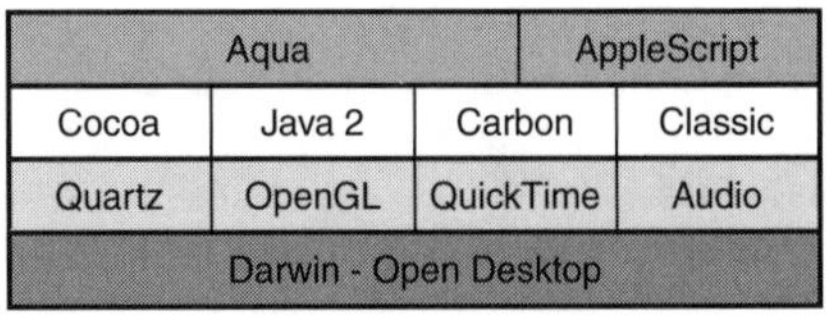

FIGURE 1.1
This layered model represents the complex architecture of Mac OS X.

Aqua			AppleScript
Cocoa	Java 2	Carbon	Classic
Quartz	OpenGL	QuickTime	Audio
Darwin - Open Desktop			

Mac OS X is made up of several components that work together to run applications, generate images, and provide a cutting-edge user experience:

- ▶ Aqua —Apple's graphical user interface (GUI) system, which controls the appearance of windows, buttons, and other onscreen controls.

- ▶ AppleScript —A language that enables users to write scripts that interact with other software on the computer.

- ▶ Cocoa— A programming environment that enables applications for Mac OS X to be built from scratch quickly.

- ▶ Java 2—Mac OS X supports the development and deployment of Java-based programs.

- ▶ Carbon—An interface for developing programs that run on Mac OS 8/9 as well as Mac OS X.

- ▶ Classic—The environment that enables some applications written for Mac OS 9, the older Mac operating system, to run under Mac OS X.

- ▶ Quartz—Apple's 2D imaging framework and window server, which is based on the Portable Document Format (PDF).

- ▶ OpenGL—The industry standard for 3D graphics.

- ▶ QuickTime—Apple's award-winning multimedia technologies are built into the graphics foundation of Mac OS X.

- ▶ Audio—Mac OS X continues Apple's tradition of providing world-class audio support for musicians and audiophiles.

- ▶ Darwin—The Unix-based core operating system.

Let's start at the bottom with Darwin and work our way up.

Darwin

Darwin is a Unix-based system that gives OS X all the power and stability of other forms of Unix. If Mac OS X were a building, Darwin would be the rock-solid foundation on which the other elements stand.

Unix (pronounced YOU-nix) is an operating system developed at Bell Labs during the 1970s. Unix was created to be a development platform for computer programmers. However, it has traditionally been run in the form of text commands typed at a command line, which can be a bit intimidating for casual computer users. Mac OS X preserves the power of Unix while adding the usability of a Mac interface.

Darwin itself is composed of two parts: the Mach kernel and the BSD subsystem. A *kernel* is a small piece of controlling code that serves as a gatekeeper for all other processes and programs. In Mac OS X, only the Mach kernel can directly access hardware, such as the keyboard, the monitor, and even the memory. By allowing only a single piece of software to perform these critical activities, individual applications can no longer crash or corrupt the system. (As any user familiar with Mac OS 9 and earlier knows, this is not how the Macintosh operating system worked in the past.)

Above the Mach kernel is the Berkeley Software Distribution (BSD) subsystem, which is a collection of software that makes up a Unix operating system. In many respects, Mac OS X is a composite of two operating systems. The BSD system is a completely functional environment in its own right that can be accessed through text commands. Mac OS X, however, is known for its user-friendly graphical environment. Together they form a system that's suitable for use by people with a broad range of computer experience.

Although this might seem complex, the good news is that Mac OS X shields all these technical details from your view—unless you choose to know more. Although software developers can create new modules that operate at the kernel level, the rest of us need do nothing more than sit back and reap the benefits. Those who want to access the BSD subsystem can learn more about it in Chapter 38, "Using Basic Unix Commands."

The Imaging Layer

The second layer of the Mac OS X foundation is the imaging layer. It comprises the tools that your applications call on to create onscreen images.

The first of these tools is the QuickTime Application Programming Interface (API). To many people, QuickTime is a media player that's used to listen to music or watch video clips, but it's far more than that. QuickTime forms the heart of all multimedia operations in Mac OS X. Using QuickTime, applications can support reading and writing dozens of image file formats.

Three-dimensional imaging is performed by another component: OpenGL. Used to create realistic special effects in games and productivity applications, OpenGL produces effects ranging from texture mapping to motion blur.

By the
Way

Mac OS X, with the help of OpenGL, performs a variety of eye-catching visual effects, such as seamlessly fading between screensaver images and scaling icons. However, some computers that can handle the other demands of Mac OS X have a graphics card that isn't capable of producing these effects. If you find that transitions between images are jerky, your graphics card might be to blame. However, rest assured that the other less-cosmetic aspects of Mac OS X are unaffected.

The final piece of Apple's imaging framework is Quartz, which is based on a standard developed by Adobe called PDF, the Portable Document Format.

By the
Way

You might recognize PDF as a common file type for forms and documents available on the Internet. PDFs are especially useful for distributing forms because they reproduce the page layout regardless of the type of computer receiving the information. If your Internet browser has called for you to downloaded Adobe's Acrobat Reader, you've already encountered PDFs.

Quartz, like all PDFs, renders images precisely and makes it easy to resize them. These qualities allow Mac OS X to display dramatic desktop visuals. Double-click the Finder icon, which looks like a smiling face, in the row of icons along one edge of your screen to launch a window and then double-click on the window's title bar. You'll see that the window you viewed in full-size has shrunk into a tiny version of itself to fit in the *Dock* (which, by the way, is the name for the row of icons on your screen).

Mac OS X also uses a variation on Quartz called Quartz Extreme. Quartz Extreme pairs the image manipulation capabilities of Quartz with the powerful graphic transformation features of OpenGL. (Although powerful for 3D rendering, OpenGL can also manipulate 2D images with ease.) Using Quartz Extreme, video cards, such as the Radeon and GeForce, can perform the work of OpenGL rendering using the card's dedicated graphics processing unit (GPU), virtually eliminating the burden of Quartz from your computer's processor.

Application Programming Layer

The next layer of Mac OS X consists of APIs under which applications are created.

The first of these APIs is called Classic. It was created because Apple knew people upgrading to OS X would want to use their favorite (and essential) programs from the older Mac operating system. Using Classic, almost any application that's functional in Mac OS 9 can run inside Mac OS X. (This is truly astounding because Mac OS X's foundation is in no way similar to the traditional Mac operating system.)

If you install and open a "Classic" application, your computer actually starts up a version of Mac OS 9.After Mac OS 9 boots, you'll notice subtle changes in the desktop—including a multicolored Apple icon at the upper left instead of the blue Apple icon of OS X! For more detail about using applications in the Classic environment, see Chapter 4, "Working with Folders, Files, and Applications."

In addition to Classic, there are three other development platforms for creating software that will run under Mac OS X: Carbon, Cocoa, and Java 2.

Carbon is a rewrite of the traditional Macintosh development toolbox to take advantage of the new technologies in Mac OS X. When an application is written in Carbon, it can run on both Mac OS X and Mac OS 8/9.

Cocoa provides a compelling development environment for Mac OS X. Compared to traditional programming methods, Cocoa offers the ability for a single programmer to create full-scale applications in a fraction of the time required for other approaches.

The final programming environment included in Mac OS X is Java 2. Java applications can be developed easily to run on a variety of operating systems, broadening the range of applications available for use under OS X.

Aqua and AppleScript

The final layer, composed of Aqua and AppleScript, provides a user interface to the Mac OS X operating system and a scripting language to control it. With translucent colors, transparent windows, and graphics that morph in and out of position, Aqua does for the computer desktop what the iMac did for the aesthetics of computer design.

In Aqua, all the standard Mac OS user interface elements—scrollbars, buttons, window shapes, and every other control—are now represented with the translucent theme. We'll take a closer look at the interface elements of Aqua in the section "Interface Elements" later in this chapter so that you can become familiar with how they look and operate.

AppleScript provides a way for a user to control all the layers underneath it by writing simple scripts or programs. You learn about AppleScript's capabilities in Chapter 39, "Introducing AppleScript."

Now that you have an idea of what Mac OS X is made of, let's take a look around.

Applications Included with Mac OS X

As you've already learned, Mac OS X was built to allow the continued functioning of many applications written to operate under Mac OS 9. However, in the time since Mac OS X was unveiled, many fun and helpful programs have become available for use with Mac OS X.

Here are just a few of the applications that come bundled with Mac OS X:

▶ iTunes—stores and playHelps you store and play music files and burn custom CDs as well as listen to Internet radio stations. Figure 1.2 shows iTunes' Visualizer, which displays colors and patterns in time with the music. You learn more about iTunes in Chapter 22, "Using iTunes."

FIGURE 1.2
Here's a glimpse of iTunes.

▶ iPhoto—Helps you import and organize digital photographs as well as adjust photo quality and share your work. You find out more of the details in Chapter 23, "Using iPhoto."

▶ iMovie—Enables you to edit digital video. It also includes features that let you add titles and visual effects to your movies. You learn more about it in Chapter 24, "Exploring the iMovie Interface," through Chapter 29, "Exporting iMovies."

▶ Safari—This Web browser comes bundled with Mac OS X. In Chapter 12, "Using Safari," you find out about accessing the Web.

▶ Mail—Sends and receives email, including text and image attachments. Chapter 15, "Using Mail," explores email and related settings.

If your favorite applications weren't mentioned, remember that many other applications are included with Mac OS X and still more are available for purchase or download. We discuss additional software that you might want to add in Chapter 9, "Installing Additional Software."

Now let's move on to exploring the desktop!

The Mac OS X Desktop

One of the best features of the Macintosh operating system has always been its interface filled with pictorial icons and easy-to-access menus. The Mac OS X desktop, shown in Figure 1.3, continues that tradition.

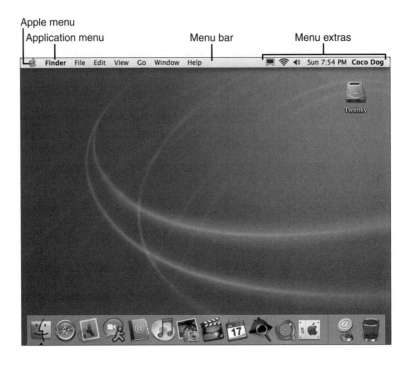

FIGURE 1.3
The Mac OS X desktop.

As you may already know, the Mac desktop is part of the Finder, which manages your computer's tasks and organizes your files. The desktop is a neat and orderly place with a row of menus across the top (called the menu bar), a row of icons along one edge (called the Dock), and plenty of wide open space to hold all the application windows you'll soon be working with.

Let's take a look at several elements of the Mac OS X environment and their basic use. We continue our exploration in greater depth with discussion of the Finder in Chapter 2, "Using the Finder," and the Dock in Chapter 3, "Exploring the Dock."

The Apple Menu

The Apple menu provides access to system controls. You open the Apple menu by clicking the Apple icon in the menu bar. It remains accessible, and its options are unchanged regardless of which program is in use. Figure 1.4 shows this menu.

FIGURE 1.4
Systemwide preferences and information are located under the Apple menu.

These options are available in the Apple menu:

▶ About This Mac—Displays information about the computer, such as the current version of the operating system, the amount of available memory, and the type of processor that the system is using.

▶ Software Update—Launches the Software Update feature, where updates to currently installed Apple software are listed as they become available for your download.

▶ Mac OS X Software—Launches the user's preferred Web browser and loads the URL http://www.apple.com/downloads/macosx/. At that Web page, you can download third-party applications from Apple's list of available Mac OS X software.

▶ System Preferences—The equivalent of the traditional control panels, the System Preferences selection launches the application used to control almost all aspects of the Mac OS X configuration.

▶ Dock—One of the most visible additions to Mac OS X. The Apple menu provides quick access to common Dock preferences, such as the ability to hide the Dock. We discuss Dock preferences further in Chapter 3.

▶ Location—Enables you to quickly adjust the Mac OS X network settings for your current location. This is the equivalent of the Location Manager Control Strip module.

▶ Recent Items—Displays the most recently launched applications and documents.

▶ Force Quit —Opens a list of applications and allows you to select which to quit. This is equivalent to pressing Command-Option-Esc to exit an application that has frozen.

By the Way

Traditional Mac users know that Command-Option-Esc is an example of a *key command*, which is a kind of shortcut activated by holding down a set of keys. For those new to the Mac, the Command key shows outlines of an apple and a cloverleaf.

▶ Sleep—Places your computer in a sleep state that requires very little power and can be restarted in a matter of seconds without the need for a full reboot.

Did you Know?

Although the Sleep option is convenient for momentarily powering down and allowing a quick start, PowerBook/iBook users might want to prevent battery drain by shutting down their computers completely instead of putting them to sleep for long periods.

▶ Restart—Quits all applications, prompts the user to save open files, and gracefully reboots the computer.

▶ Shut Down—Quits all applications, prompts the user to save open files, and shuts down the computer.

▶ Log Out—Quits all applications, prompts the user to save open files, and then returns to the Mac OS X login screen.

The Application Menu

Immediately to the right of the Apple menu is the application menu, which provides functions specific to the application currently in use. When an application launches in Mac OS X, a menu based on its own name appears to the right of the Apple icon. For example, if you start an application named TextEdit, the TextEdit application menu is the first menu item after the Apple icon.

The application menu contains items that act on the entire application rather than on its files. Figure 1.5 displays the application menu for Mail—an application included with Mac OS X.

Seven default items make up an application menu:

▶ About—Reveals information about the running program.

▶ Preferences—An application menu provides a standardized location for application preferences.

▶ Services—An interesting feature of Mac OS X. When a service is installed by an application, it can act on a selected item on the system. For example, if you want to have a portion of an email message read aloud by your computer, you could select the text in your Mail window and then choose Start Speaking Text from the Speech submenu under Services. This would automatically have your computer read you the chosen text.

▶ Hide—Hides all windows of the active application.

▶ Hide Others—Hides the windows of all applications other than the frontmost application. This effectively clears the screen except for the program you're currently using.

▶ Show All—Shows all hidden applications.

▶ Quit—Quits the current application. Command-Q is the universal Quit shortcut.

The remaining menus vary widely by application, so we'll cover them for specific applications in later chapters as needed.

Windows

One of the most obvious places in which you interact with the Mac OS X interface is through onscreen windows, as illustrated in Figure 1.6. Let's take a brief look at the controls for a Mail window.

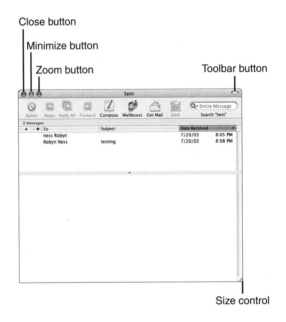

Close button

Minimize button

Zoom button

Toolbar button

Size control

Close/Minimize/Zoom

In the upper-left corner of each window are the Close (red X), Minimize (yellow –), and Zoom (green +) buttons. Differentiated only by color and position, the corresponding symbol appears in each button when the mouse cursor nears.

The Close, Minimize, and Zoom buttons in the currently active window will have color, whereas those in windows that don't have the system's focus won't have color.

Clicking the Close button closes the open window. The Mac OS X Minimize button shrinks the window into an icon view and places it in the Dock. This icon is a miniature of the original window—down to the items it contains. In some cases, the icon even updates its appearance when the parent application generates new output. Clicking the icon in the Dock restores the window to its original position and size on the screen.

Did you
Know?

There is a preference option that makes double-clicking the title bar of a window have the same effect as clicking the Minimize button. This option can be found in the Appearance section of the System Preferences, which can be open from the Apple menu.

The Zoom button (usually) opens the window to the size necessary to display the available information. Most Windows PC users expect the maximized window to fill the entire screen. However, if there are only three icons to be shown, Mac OS X doesn't waste space by filling up your window with blank area.

Did you
Know?

Holding down Option while clicking the Minimize or Close button results in all the windows in the current application being minimized or closed.

Toolbar Button

In the upper-right corner of some windows (including the Finder and Mail windows) is an elongated button, called the Toolbar button, that can be used to quickly show or hide special toolbars in the top of some windows. Figure 1.7 shows the result of hiding the toolbar in the Mail application.

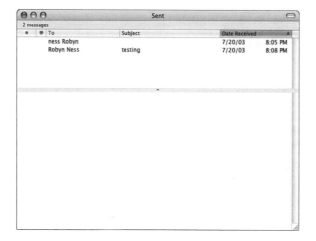

FIGURE 1.7
With the task toolbar hidden, the window occupies less screen space.

Apple advocates the use of toolbars in applications to increase usability and efficiency. However, because individual programmers must write their programs to support the toolbar button, you shouldn't expect all applications with toolbars to have the Toolbar button.

Window Moving and Resizing

Another characteristic of some Mac OS X windows is the borderless content area. As shown in Figure 1.8, the display in most Mac OS X application windows (except those with a metal appearance) stretches to the of the content window. In contrast, some operating systems such as Mac OS 9 and Windows offer window borders for dragging.

FIGURE 1.8
The content in a window goes right to the edge.

To drag a window, you must grab it by its title bar. For windows with a metal appearance, you can grab them by any "metal" area.

To resize a window, click and drag the size control in the lower-right corner of each window. Many applications in Mac OS X take advantage of live resizing; that is, as you resize the window, its contents adjust in real-time (such as Web pages in Safari).

It is possible to resize a window so large that you can't reach the size control. If you can't reach the size control, how do you make the window smaller? Click the green Zoom button, which makes a window only as large as it needs to be to show its contents or makes the window fit within the viewable screen area.

In Chapter 4, we'll talk about a feature called Exposé, which allows you to temporarily view the full windows of everything open on your desktop all at once. The settings for this feature are accessed in the System Preferences, discussed in the section "System Preferences" later in the chapter.

There are a few other neat tricks you can use when working with Mac OS X windows. If you hold down the Command key, you can drag inactive windows located behind other windows. If fact, holding down Command enables you to click buttons and move scrollbars in many background applications.

Another fun trick is holding down the Option key while clicking on an inactive application's window. This hides the frontmost application and brings the clicked application to the front.

Finally, instead of switching to another window to close, minimize, or maximize it, positioning your cursor over the appropriate window controls highlights them—enabling you to get rid of obtrusive windows without leaving your current workspace.

Did you Know?

Sheet Windows and Window Drawers

Two other unique interface elements in Mac OS X are *sheet windows* and *window drawers*. Sheets are used in place of traditional dialog boxes. Normally, when a computer wants to get your attention, it displays a dialog box containing a question such as, "Do you want to save this document?" If you have 10 open documents on your system, how do you know which one needs to be saved?

Sheet windows connect directly to the title bar of an open window. As shown in Figure 1.9, these messages appear inside the window they're associated with.

Sheet windows are used just like regular dialog boxes, except that they're attached to a document. Unlike many dialog boxes, which keep you from interacting with the rest of the system until you interact with them, sheet windows limit access only to the window in which they appear.

A window drawer is used to store commonly used items, such as settings or additional content, that might need to be accessed while a program is running. Figure 1.10 shows the Mac OS X Mail application's window drawer holding a list of active mailboxes.

To use active drawers in applications that contain them, you typically click a button in the toolbar. After a drawer is open, you can often drag its edge to change the drawer's size.

FIGURE 1.9
The sheet window appears to drop from an open window's title bar.

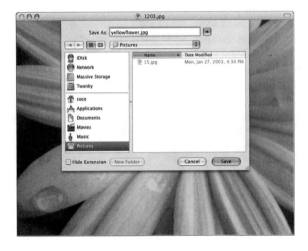

FIGURE 1.10
Window drawers hold options that are needed often during use of a program.

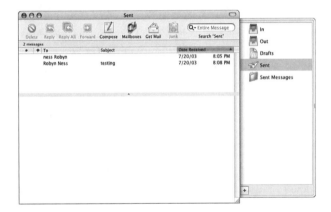

Did you Know?

Although only a few applications use the Mac OS X window drawer feature, there are already two standards for how it operates. By default, the drawer slides out from a single side, left or right, of the main window after you click a button to activate it. If the window is too close to that side of the screen, the drawer is either forced out on the other side of the window, or the main window moves over to make room.

Interface Elements

Other functions of the interface are activated by *graphical interface elements*. Figure 1.11 shows samples of many of the Mac OS X interface elements.

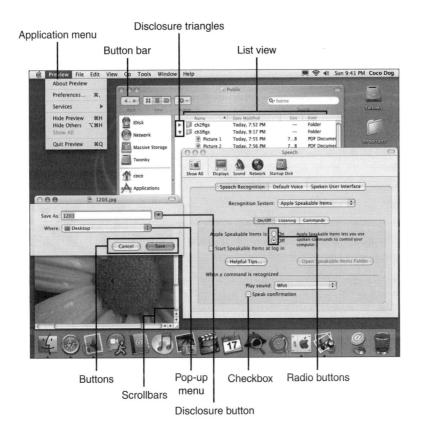

Application menu

Disclosure triangles

Button bar

List view

Buttons

Scrollbars

Pop-up menu

Checkbox

Radio buttons

Disclosure button

FIGURE 1.11
These are (most of) the Mac OS X interface elements.

Aqua interface elements include the following:

▶ Pushbuttons—These are rendered as translucent white or aqua ovals or as square-ish buttons with appropriate label text. They're typically used to activate a choice or to respond to a question posed by the operating system or application. The default choice, which is activated by pressing the Return key, pulses for easy visual confirmation.

▶ Check boxes/radio buttons—Check boxes are used to choose multiple attributes (AND), whereas radio buttons are used to choose between attributes (OR).

▶ List views—Clicking a category, such as the Date Modified heading shown in Figure 1.11, sorts by that selection. Clicking the category again reverses the direction of the sort (ascending to descending or vice versa). To resize category headings, click the edge of the heading and drag in the direction you want to shrink or expand the column.

▶ Pop-up menus/system menuspop-up menus>—Single-clicking a menu drops down the menu until you make a selection. The menu can stay down indefinitely. With Mac OS X's multitasking system, other applications can continue to work in the background while the menu is down.

▶ Disclosure trianglesThese continue to work as they always have. Click the triangle to reveal additional information about an object.

▶ Disclosure pushbuttons—Like disclosure triangles, these pushbuttons are used to reveal all possible options (a full, complex view) or to reduce a window to a simplified representation. They are used in the new File Save sheets.

▶ Scrollbars—Scrollbars visually represent the amount of data in the current document by changing the size of the scrollbar slider in relation to the data to display. The larger the slider, the less data there is to scroll through. The smaller the slider, the more information there is to display.

▶ Button bar—Button bars, made up of several buttons, are used to move between separate settings within a single window when you can only choose one available option at a time. By breaking up long lists in this way, windows with many options are less overwhelming, but you might have to click between sections to find the settings you're looking for.

System Preferences

Mac OS X enables you to control many aspects of your system, from desktop appearance to user access. Conveniently, you can tailor these settings to your own needs from one centralized place, System Preferences, as shown in Figure 1.12.

To access System Preferences, simply click the Dock icon that resembles a light switch; it should be located in the row of icons at the bottom of your screen. Or choose System Preferences from the Apple menu. As you can see in Figure 1.12, the items in System Preferences are organized by function. You'll learn more about System Preferences in Chapter 5, "Setting System Preferences and Universal Access Options," and throughout this book as we discuss different topics.

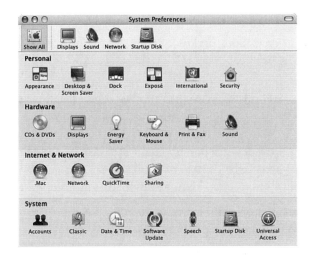

FIGURE 1.12
Many system settings are accessible through System Preferences.

Menu Extras

Mac OS X offers a feature that gives users quick access to common system settings: menu extras. They appear as icons at the upper right of the menu bar. Figure 1.13 shows a number of menu extras.

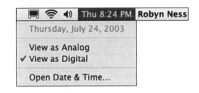

FIGURE 1.13
Menu extras provide quick access to system settings.

Each extra is added to the menu bar through individual System Preferences panes that correspond to an item's function. You can activate or deactivate an extra by clicking the Show <option> in Menu Bar check box for the corresponding option. For example, under Displays in the Hardware group, you can turn on the Displays Menu Extra.

A few of the menu extras available under Mac OS X include

- ▶ Date & Time—Displays the time and date graphically as a miniature clock or by using the standard text format.

- ▶ Displays—Adjusts the resolution and color depth of the display from the menu bar.

- ▶ Volume—Changes the sound volume.

- ▶ Battery—For PowerBook and iBook users, this option tracks battery usage and recharge time.

- ▶ AirPort—Monitors AirPort signal strength and quickly adjusts network settings. (The AirPort is a device that enables computers to be connected to the Internet without wires. It's discussed further in Chapter 11.)

Clicking a menu extra opens a pop-up menu that displays additional information and settings. Items such as Battery and Date & Time can be modified to show textual information rather than a simple icon status representation.

You can alter the order of menu extras by holding down the Command key and dragging an icon to a different position.

Summary

A lot of care went into making Mac OS X the versatile, powerful, and attractive system that's available today. In this chapter, you learned about the structure of Mac OS X as well as some basic features to help you find your way around the Mac OS X desktop. The focus was on elements such as the Apple and application menus and window controls. We also briefly discussed some of the applications bundled with Mac OS X and the System Preferences, which are covered in more detail in later chapters. In Chapter 2, you explore the Mac OS X file system and some useful shortcuts to your favorite applications.

CHAPTER 2

Using the Finder

You're now ready to take a closer look at Mac OS X and its operation as we focus on the Finder. The Finder is the application that Mac OS X uses to launch and manipulate files and applications. Unlike other tools and utilities that you activate, the Finder starts immediately after you log in to the system and is always active. In addition to helping you locate your files, the Finder handles all common tasks, such as creating, deleting, moving, and copying files and folders, which we'll talk about in Chapter 4, "Working with Windows Folders, Files, and Applications.")

You can interact with the Finder in several different ways. There's a menu bar for the Finder, but there's also the Finder window, which has several different modes and view options. The Finder window is perhaps the easiest way to understand and move through the Mac OS X file system, so let's look at it first.

The Finder Window

To help people manage their files, the Finder includes a specialized window, which is accessed by double-clicking the icon for the Mac OS X hard drive on the desktop.

Mac OS X introduces two modes of operation in the Finder window. In the first of the two window modes , shown in Figure 2.1, a sidebar appears along the left, and a toolbar appears at the top. Content area takes up the rest of the window. In this mode, which we'll call the toolbar mode, double-clicking a folder displays its contents in the content area of the current window, replacing what was there before.

The second mode, a toolbar-less version of the Finder window, can be entered by clicking the Hide/Show toolbar button in the upper-right corner of the Finder window. In this mode, shown in Figure 2.2, double-clicking folders opens additional windows to display their contents while leaving the original window as it was.

FIGURE 2.1
The toolbar version of the Finder window enables you to move forward and back through the contents of your hard drive—and even your local network.

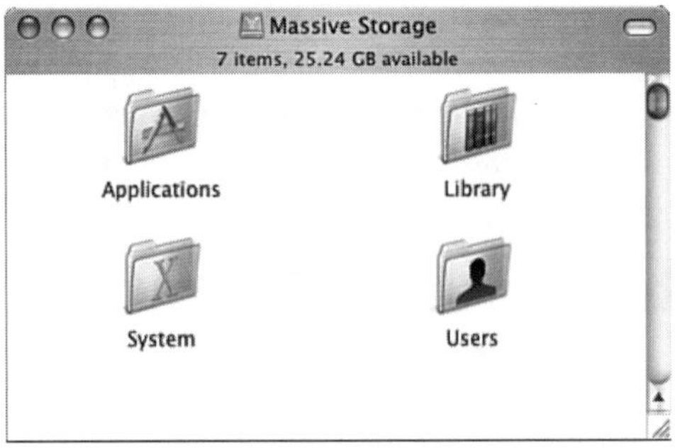

FIGURE 2.2
The toolbar-less version of the Finder window provides no navigation tools because the previous window remains open.

By the Way

At the top of the toolbar-less version of the Finder window is the status bar, which shows the number of items in a folder and the amount of space available on the drive. The status bar can be toggled on and off by using the Show/Hide Status Bar command in the Finder's View menu.

The Finder Window Toolbar

The toolbar version of the Finder window provides several useful controls for viewing and navigating your files.

In the upper-left corner of the toolbar is the Back arrow—click it to return to the previous folder. Using this technique, you can dig many levels deep into the file system and then quickly back out by using this button. The Forward arrow enables you to follow the same path back to inner levels.

By default, there are several other elements in the toolbar, as shown previously in Figure 2.1. From left to right, you see the View selector, the Action pop-up menu, and the Search text entry field. We talk more about using the Finder to find files in the section "Performing File and Content Searches" later in this chapter.

You can customize your Finder toolbar by adding other predefined Mac OS X shortcuts or by removing the default items in this way:

1. Choose View, Customize Toolbar from the menu.

2. From the sheet window containing all the available shortcuts (shown in Figure 2.3), locate the items you want to add.

FIGURE 2.3
Finder shortcuts give you single-click access to special features.

3. Add a shortcut by dragging it from the window to wherever you want it to appear on the toolbar.

When you modify your toolbar, it's modified for all Finder windows in your workspace, not just the currently open folder. However, the changes that you make to your toolbar don't affect other user accounts on the same computer.

While the Customize Toolbar sheet window is visible, you can also rearrange or remove any toolbar shortcuts. To rearrange, simply drag a shortcut to a new location—the others will move aside. To remove, drag the shortcut icon outside the toolbar area. It disappears with a whoosh and a puff of smoke.

Now that you've seen the Finder window, let's explore the Finder's file system.

The File System

After you double-click the icon for your Mac OS X drive, you see a collection of permanent folders, as shown previously in Figure 2.1. These folders contain preinstalled applications, utilities, and configuration files for your system, known collectively as *system folders*. You cannot modify these system-level directories or move them from their default locations. However, you can create folders and files *within* these locations.

The following list describes the folders at this level, which are the starting point for accessing most of your system's functions:

▶ Applications—Contains all the preinstalled Mac OS X applications, such as iTunes, Mail, Safari, and many others. Within the Applications folder is the Utilities folder, which contains the tools necessary to set up your printers, calibrate your display, and other important (if sometimes unglamorous) tasks.

Watch Out!

Unlike most other system-critical folders, the Utilities folder *can* be modified by a Mac OS X user. You can move, rename, or delete the folder if you want, but such changes should be made only with great caution because the performance of some applications could be disrupted.

▶ Library—Although it doesn't have a strict definition, Library mostly stores systemwide application preferences, application libraries, and information that should be available to anyone using the computer. Some of the folders in Library are used by applications to store data such as preferences, whereas others hold printer drivers or other system additions made by the user.

▶ System—Next on the list is the Mac OS X System folder. By default, the System folder contains only a folder called Library—a more specific version of the other Library folder. Within the System's Library folder are the components that make up the core of the Mac OS X experience. These files and folders shouldn't be changed unless you're aware that any modifications you make could cause your computer not to start up or otherwise operate as expected.

▶ Users—As mentioned in Chapter 1, "Introducing Mac OS X," Mac OS X is a true multiuser operating system in which each user has a private account and password to access the operating system. The Users folder contains the home directories of all the users on the machine. (We'll talk about "home" directories next.)

Let's take a closer look at the Users directory, where folders are created for use by each individual user on your system. Figure 2.4 shows the Users folder in List view for a system with three users: robyn, jray, and coco.

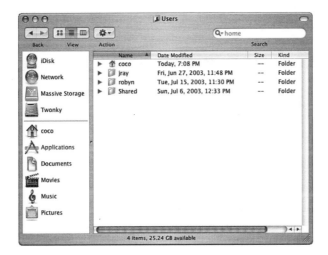

FIGURE 2.4
All users have their own home folder, but they cannot access the contents of each other's home folder.

Your home folder can be considered your workplace. It's yours alone because most of the files and folders stored there are protected from other users. Even though you can see the folders for every user, you can access only the Public and Sites folders in another user's home folder. (Chapter 33, "Sharing Your Computer with Multiple Users," further discusses setting up additional user accounts.)

The Home Directory

Your home directory, as shown in Figure 2.5, is the start of your personal area on Mac OS X. There, you can save your own files, and no one can alter or read them.

FIGURE 2.5
The default folders
in a user's home
directory.

Your home directory is named with the short name you chose when you created your Mac OS X user account. Several default folders are created inside your home directory. Those folders and their purposes are as follows:

▶ Desktop—Contains all the files, folders, and applications that you've saved to your desktop.

▶ Documents, Movies, Music, and Pictures—These four folders are generic store-all locations for files of these kinds. You don't have to use these folders; they're merely recommended storage locations to help you organize your files. (Applications such as iPhoto, iTunes, and iMovie store their files in the appropriate folders by default.)

▶ Library—Serves the same purpose as the top-level Library folder and the Library folder in the System folder, except what is stored there is available for your use only. Within the subfolders in this folder, you can store fonts, screensavers, and many other extensions to the operating system—especially those you don't want to share with other users of the computer.

▶ Public—Provides a way for you to share files with other users on your computer without granting total access. Also, if you plan to share your files over a network, you can do so by placing them in the Public folder and activating file sharing in the Sharing System Preferences panel. This is discussed further in Chapter 33.

▶ Sites—If you want to run a personal Web site, it must be stored in the Sites folder. To share your site with the outside world, you also have to enable Personal Web Sharing, which we discuss in Chapter 33 and Chapter 34, "Sharing Files and Running Network Services."

Although folders for different file types exist by default, you can do nearly anything you want with your home folder. The only folders that should treated with caution are the Desktop and Library folders. They are critical to system operation and must not be renamed or removed. (Also, you shouldn't remove any of the items in the Library folder unless you put them there to start with.)

The Sidebar

Now that you've seen the file structure, let's take a look at the default items in the sidebar along the left side of the toolbar version of the Finder window, as shown previously in Figure 2.5.

Although you can choose to display your computer's hard drive on the desktop, it is also visible in the top portion of the sidebar. Any additional FireWire or USB drives (and other types of removable media, including CDs) currently recognized by the system will also appear.

In the bottom portion of the sidebar are icons for the home directory of the current user, the applications folder, and several folders within the current user's home directory.

Clicking any drive or folder in the sidebar fills the content space of the Finder window with a view of the files it contains.

Customizing the Sidebar

Just as you can customize the toolbar, you also can add your own shortcuts to favorite folders, files, and applications by adding them to the sidebar.

> If you want to change the width of the content area or the sidebar, you can click and drag the narrow strip separating the two areas. Double-clicking the strip toggles the sidebar open and closed.

By the Way

When folders and applications are added to the sidebar, a single click on the icon opens or launches the selected item. You can also drag documents onto an application icon or folder icon in the toolbar to open the file by using the application or to move the file into a folder.

To add something to the sidebar, locate the item's icon and drag it to the list. A blue insert bar appears, as shown in Figure 2.6, to show you where the file will be added. If you drag an item onto an existing folder or storage device (including your hard drive) in the sidebar, that folder will be outlined in blue, as shown in Figure 2.7, to let you know the item you are dragging will be placed inside it.

FIGURE 2.6
Create a sidebar to a file.

FIGURE 2.7
Place a file inside an item in the sidebar.

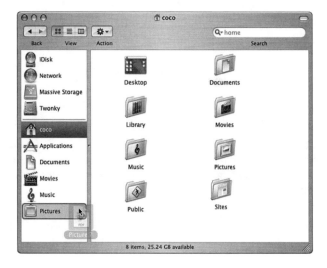

Finder Window View Options

In addition to the options to switch between the toolbar and toolbar-less versions of the Finder window, there are other display options from the Finder window. Three View buttons in the toolbar enable you control the way information is displayed in the Finder window.

Icon View

The first time you log in, the Finder is in toolbar mode and using Icon view. If you've already been using the Finder and are no longer in Icon view, you can quickly switch to Icon view by choosing As Icons from the menu or by clicking the first of the View buttons in the toolbar. (Refer to Figure 2.5 to see the Finder window in Icon view.) In Icon view mode, you navigate through the folders on your drive by double-clicking them.

List View

The next view to explore is the Finder's List view. You can switch to List view by clicking the middle button in the Finder's View selector or, if the toolbar isn't present, by choosing View, As List from the Finder's menu. Demonstrated in Figure 2.8, the List view is a straightforward means of displaying all available information about a file or folder in tabular form.

The columns in the List view represent the attributes for each file. Clicking a column highlights it and sorts the file listing based on that column's values. For example, if you want to locate the most recent files in a folder, you can view the folder contents in List view and click the Date Modified header. By default, the column values are listed in descending order. Clicking a column header again reverses the sorting order. An arrow pointing up or down at the right of each column indicates the current sort order.

You can change the width of the columns by placing the mouse cursor at the edge of the column and click-dragging to the left or right. You can reposition the columns by clicking and dragging them into the order you want. However, the first column, Name, cannot be repositioned.

When a folder appears in the file listing, a small disclosure triangle precedes its name. Clicking the triangle reveals the file hierarchy within that folder. As with Icon view, double-clicking a folder in this view either opens a new window (if you're in toolbar-less mode) or refreshes the contents of the existing window with the contents of the selected folder. (Double-clicking applications or files opens them in any view.)

FIGURE 2.8
List view packs a
lot of information
into a small
amount of space.

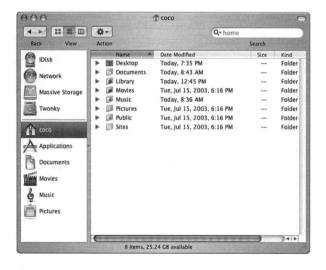

Column View

Unlike other views, which can either overwhelm you with information or require multiple windows to move easily from point to point, the Column view is designed with one thing in mind: ease of navigation.

The concept is simple: Click an item in the first column of the content area, and its contents are shown in the next column. Click a folder in this new column, and its contents are shown in the next column, and so on. Figure 2.9 shows a multi-column display that reaches down two levels.

FIGURE 2.9
Using the Column
view, you can easily
navigate through
the folders on your
hard drive.

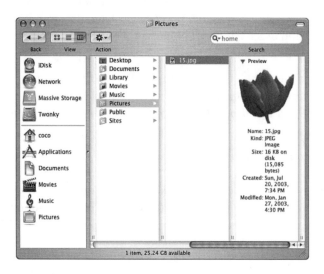

Did you
Know?

If you use the horizontal scrollbar to move back along a path, the folders you've chosen remain highlighted in the columns. You can, at any time, choose a different folder from any of the columns. This refreshes the column to the right of your choice. There's no need to start from the beginning every time you want to change your location.

One big bonus of using Column view is the ability to instantly see the contents of a file without opening it. If you choose a file or application, a preview or description of the selected item appears in the column to the right. For an example, take a look at the far right column in Figure 2.9, where a representation of an image file is displayed. When you choose an application or a file that cannot be previewed, only information about the file is displayed, such as the creation/modification dates, size, and version.

Show View Options

For each of the three Finder window views, there are additional settings that you can customize by choosing View, Show View Options from the menu. For Icon and List views, you can also choose whether your changes apply to the current window only or to all Finder windows.

For Icon view, you can scale icons from the smallest to largest size by dragging the Icon Size slider from the left to the right. You can choose how the icon is labeled, including the font size and label placement. You can set how the icons are arranged and what color the window background is.

List view enables you to choose small or larger icons, text size, and which columns of information to display with the filenames. You can also choose to show relative dates, such as "Today" and "Yesterday," or to calculate the sizes of all files. (Be warned, however, that calculating files sizes does consume some system resources.)

Column view gives you options for text size and whether to show icons or the preview column. There are no global settings for this view.

Now that you understand how to navigate within the Finder window and alter your view options, let's move on to exploring the desktop. (We'll save discussion of the Action pop-up menu that appears in the Finder window toolbar until Chapter 4.)

The Desktop

The desktop is, for all intents and purposes, a global Finder window that sits behind all the other windows on the system. The primary difference between the desktop and the other window modes we've discussed is that the desktop is always in Icon view mode.

As with other Finder windows, the desktop layout is controlled by the View Options in the View menu. Use the Icon Size slider, text, and arrangement settings exactly as you would adjust any other window in Icon view mode.

By the Way

> You can change the background image of your desktop in the Desktop & Screen Saver pane of System Preferences. There you'll find many background images from which to choose, and you can even add images of your own!

The Desktop and Exposé

Besides being a window-like object that displays icons, the desktop is also your workspace. As you open Finder and application windows, they cover the desktop; as you open more and more windows, they cover each other. To help you find buried windows, or even just focus your attention, Apple has introduced a feature called Exposé, which rearranges and resizes the windows currently open so that you can see them all at one time, as demonstrated in Figure 2.10. From this view of open windows and applications, you can then choose what you want to work on.

You set up Exposé from the System Preferences pane shown in Figure 2.11. There you can choose what activates the various states of Exposé. Those states are

- ▶ All Windows—Displays all open windows, as shown previously in Figure 2.10. You can then move your mouse cursor over the window you want to bring to the front and select it. The other windows on the desktop will reappear in their original locations behind it.

- ▶ Application Windows—Displays all open windows for the application that's currently active and dims the rest of the desktop. When you select a window, it appears in front of all the other windows for that application.

- ▶ Desktop—Moves all open windows aside to reveal the desktop. You can open Finder windows to locate files or applications you want to launch, and Exposé maintains its state. If you double-click a file or application to open it, the file or application window opens, and the other windows on the desktop reappear in their original locations behind it.

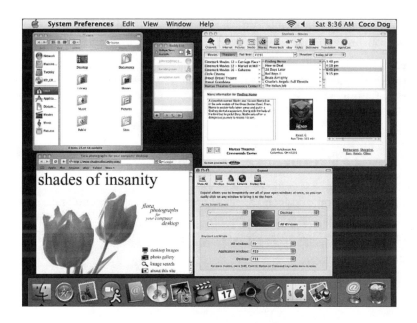

FIGURE 2.10
Exposé can display all open windows while dimming the desktop.

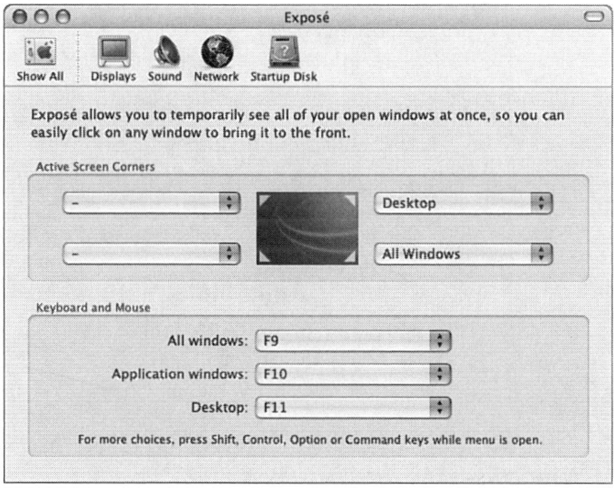

FIGURE 2.11
The Exposé pane of System Preferences allows you to set screen corners or keyboard and mouse commands as triggering actions.

> You can also temporarily de-clutter a busy workspace by choosing either Hide [current application] or Hide Others from most application menus, but availability of this feature is at the discretion of each application's developer.

By the Way

If you would prefer using keyboard commands to activate Exposé, you can set those options instead. (Or even set both screen corners and keyboard options.)

> To dismiss Exposé without making a choice, simply repeat the triggering action that called it. For example, if you've set an active screen corner, move the cursor back to that corner, and your screen returns to normal.

The Finder Preference Options

The Finder Preferences can be used to adjust settings that control how you interact with your desktop and icons. Open these settings by choosing Preferences from the Finder application menu. Figure 2.12 shows the options available in the General pane of the Finder preferences.

FIGURE 2.12
The Finder's General preferences control what's visible on the desktop and how new Finder windows behave.

> You can change the appearance of Finder windows, and systemwide elements, from the Appearance pane of the System Preferences. There, you can choose the color of highlighted items and the interface elements (as discussed in Chapter 1).

Among the General preference settings are whether to display icons for the hard drive, removable media, or connected servers on the desktop and the default content displayed by new Finder windows. *Spring-loading* is the desktop behavior that occurs when you drag a file or folder on top of another folder and it springs open to let the dragged item move inside and then closes again to return the desktop to its previous state.

The Label settings relate to a feature discussed in Chapter 4, so we'll discuss this pane further in the section "Adding Color Labels" in Chapter 4.

The Sidebar section allows you to choose which items appear in the sidebar of the Finder window while it is in toolbar mode. Check and uncheck the boxes in front of the options, which include computer, hard disks, network, removable media, desktop, and applications.

The Advanced section pertains to a variety of Finder features and functions. You can set whether to show file extensions. Traditionally, Mac users have paid little attention to whether a filename ends in .doc or .txt, but Windows users are used to seeing these extensions. (That's because the Windows operating system uses these extensions when determining which application can open a given file; Macs, on the other hand, rely on hidden information stored in the file itself to make that determination.) Checking this option reveals file extensions.

The option to show hidden files will make visible files used by your system that normally users don't know are there. There's also an option to display a warning that appears when you empty the Trash to give you a second chance to reconsider.

The final option in the Finder's Advanced preferences allows you to choose the languages of which files to index for file searching. (Indexing is a process of cataloging all the content in a location so that searches can be performed faster.) If you don't plan to read many documents in other languages, it's best to limit the checked options to your native language because indexing additional options requires additional time and storage space.

Close the Finder Preferences pane when you're satisfied with your settings.

Performing File and Content Searches

In addition to organizing your files, the Finder enables you to search for applications and folders by name, and documents by filename or by content. But the best part is that the search results are interactive. You can launch located programs and applications by double-clicking their icons in the results window. Also, dragging a file or folder to the desktop or a Finder window moves that object to a new location. This is a quick way to clean up when you accidentally save a file to the wrong folder.

An easy way to search for a file by name only is through the Finder window. To do this, open a Finder window by double-clicking the folder or drive containing the file you want to find. Then type your search term in the Search box in the toolbar. Remember, if the toolbar isn't visible, you can show it by clicking the oblong button at the upper right of the window's title bar. If the search box isn't visible, you might have to enlarge your window by dragging from the diagonal lines in the bottom-right corner.

If you want to do a search of file contents or search more than a defined folder, choose File, Find (Command-F) from the menu. Figure 2.13 shows the Find dialog box.

When the screen in Figure 2.13 appears, follow these steps:

1. Choose where to search. Your options are

   ▶ Everywhere—Examines all local and network drives, including user accounts.

   ▶ Local Disks—Examines all local drives and all user accounts on them.

   ▶ Home—Examines only the home directory of the person currently logged in.

   ▶ Specific Places—Displays a list of available drives for you to choose from. You can also click the Add/Remove button to insert or remove specific folders.

2. Pick whether to search by filename, content, dates created or modified, kind, label, size, file extension, visibility, type, or creator. (Use the + button to add more types of search criteria.) Enter your search term into the appropriate field(s).

   Although filename, content, size, and date created or modified are obvious, some of these search criteria require a bit of explanation.

   ▶ Kind refers to whether the item sought is an application, folder, document, audio file, image, movie, or an alias (or shortcut) to a real file.

   ▶ Label refers to a color-coding system you can apply to your files to help you organize and prioritize them. (We'll discuss labels further in Chapter 4.

   ▶ Extension, as you'll recall from earlier in the chapter, refers to an ending added to filenames to identify their file type (such as .JPG or .PDF) or the program that created the file (such as .PSD for PhotoShop Document, as created by Adobe PhotoShop).

▶ Visibility may seem like a strange option—you probably don't know of any invisible files on your system. However, as you learned in Chapter 1, Mac OS X is a Unix-based system, and under Unix (and many other operating systems) files meant to be used by the system alone may not be visible under normal circumstances.

▶ Creator is a somewhat more advanced option. Previously, you learned that file extensions are used by some operating systems, such as Windows, to identify which files go to which applications. However, Macintosh systems have always stored that information as hidden data in a document. The Creator criterion lets users search the data about the application that made a document. Note that special codes are used, so this field only holds four characters. (You can find Microsoft Word documents by typing MSWD.)

▶ Type, like Creator, is an advanced option that searches a file's hidden data about the kind of file, such as text or image.

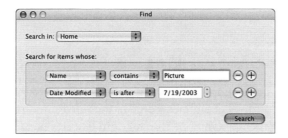

FIGURE 2.13
Use the Find dialog box to locate files by name, content, or other criteria.

3. If you want to refine your search further, add further search criteria by clicking the + button. (To remove an unwanted search criterion, click the − button.)

4. Click the Search button to start the search.

In a few moments, the search results are displayed, as shown in Figure 2.14. For each result, Find lists the filename, the parent folder that contains it, the date it was modified, its size, and the kind of file it is. After an item is highlighted, the path required to reach it on your hard drive is shown at the bottom of the window. (You can drag the divider line up or down to show a large or an abbreviated path map.) Double-clicking any portion of the path opens the file, folder, or application.

Searching for file contents requires that the directory containing the file be indexed or cataloged. You can index a folder, or check for the last date of last indexing, using the Get Info command, which is discussed shortly.

FIGURE 2.14
Scroll through the results to choose the file you were looking for!

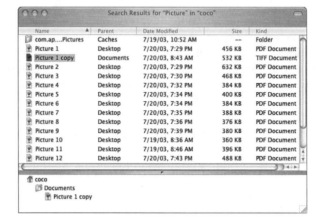

The Finder Menu Bar

We've talked about the Finder window, but there's also a Finder menu bar, which provides access to a range of features. Some of those features are standard and shouldn't require much description. The standard features include options in the Edit menu to Undo/Redo, Copy, Paste, and Select All and an option in the Window menu to access all open Finder windows.

Some menu bar options offer other ways to perform actions that we've already discussed. For example, several of the View options duplicate settings in the Finder window toolbar. We'll cover some of the unique options in the following sections.

The File Menu

The options in the File menu mostly have to do with creating, opening, duplicating, and getting information about an item. We'll talk about these in Chapter 4.

The Find function, discussed earlier, is also accessed from the File menu.

However, there is an unexpected, and useful, feature in the Finder File menu—Burn Disc.

Burn a Disc

Mac OS X makes writing a CD similar to moving files to any other storage device. To make the process as simple as possible, Mac OS X stores applications, files, and folders that you want to write to CD in a special folder until you tell the system to burn the CD. Files are transferred to the CD only after the burn starts.

> To choose File, Burn Disc from the menu, the active Finder window must be the CD's window. If the CD is not the active window, the menu item will be disabled.

These are the steps to write your own data CD using the Finder:

1. Insert a blank CD into the CD writer. The Mac OS X Finder prompts you to prepare the CD, as shown in Figure 2.15. (This doesn't actually write anything to the CD yet, but it tells the computer what your intentions are for the disc.)

FIGURE 2.15
When you insert a blank CD, your computer asks what you intend to use it for.

> If you want to insert a CD in the drive but don't want to prepare it (for use in another CD-burning application), click Ignore rather than OK in the window that appears when you first insert a CD.

Did you Know?

2. Choose the Open Finder option from the Action pop-up menu. (We talk about burning from iTunes in Chapter 22, "Using iTunes.")

3. Enter a name for the CD you're writing. The disc appears with this name on the desktop.

4. Click OK to start using the CD on your system. An icon representing the CD appears on your desktop. At this point, you can interact with it as you would any other folder or storage device under Mac OS X. You can copy files to it, delete files, and so on.

5. When you create the CD layout you like, you can start the burn process by choosing File, Burn Disc from the menu (or by clicking the Burn toolbar shortcut if you've added it). In addition, dragging the CD to the Trash also prompts burning to begin. This process takes a few minutes and is tracked by the Finder much like a normal Copy operation.

If you decide against writing the CD, you can choose File, Eject from the menu and then click the Eject button in the CD burning dialog box to remove the media and erase the CD layout you created.

The Go Menu

If you want to navigate quickly to several commonly used folders or drives, you can use the folder shortcuts in the Go menu. This menu enables you to jump to one of several predefined locations. These options are the same ones that can be set in the Finder window's sidebar.

The Go menu also enables you to manually enter the name of a directory to browse. This quick-navigation option is the Go to Folder dialog box (Shift-Command-G). Here, you can tell the Finder where you want to be, based on the pathname you enter. Figure 2.16 shows the Go To Folder dialog box.

You can type any folder pathname in the Go to the Folder field. Folder names are separated by the / character (think of a pathname as being similar to a Web URL). For example, if you want to open the Documents folder in your home directory, you would type the following:

```
/Users/[your Home directory name]/Documents
```

FIGURE 2.16
The Go To Folder dialog box lets you enter your destination by hand!

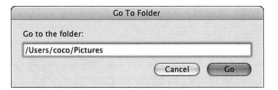

Also in the Go menu is the option Connect to Server for connecting to remote computers, which we discuss in Chapter 34.

Summary

The Mac OS X Finder is a powerful tool for managing your files and folders. It offers a high degree of customization to help you work efficiently. In addition to the expected file search capabilities, the Finder also provides some special functions, including CD burning, that make it more than just a filing system.

CHAPTER 3

Exploring the Dock

Along one edge of your screen (either the bottom, left, or right) is a colorful banner of icons known as the Dock. The Dock, shown in its default state in Figure 3.1, acts as a taskbar, to show open applications and minimized or reduced versions of a document window. It also offers quick access to favorite applications, shows feedback from open applications, and provides a resting place for the Trash.

FIGURE 3.1
The Dock is useful for organizing your desktop.

Here's a fast overview of the Dock's arrangement:

- ▶ Left (or Top) portion—At left (or top) are icons for applications. The ones you've opened have a triangle next to them.

- ▶ Right (or Bottom) portion—At right (or bottom) are document icons representing the documents you've reduced or minimized.

> Remember: To minimize a document, you can click the yellow (center) button at the top left of each window, or simply double-click the window's title bar.

▶ Trash—At the extreme right (or bottom) is the Trash, the place to drag files that you want to throw away.

> You can also drag URLs into the right (or bottom) side of the Dock. A single click launches your default Web browser and opens it to the saved address.

▶ Separator bar—The separator bar splits the Dock into the application and file/folder areas.

> To make the icons in the Dock larger or smaller, click the separator bar and then move the mouse up to increase the size or down to reduce it if positioned horizontally, or move it left and right if your Dock is positioned vertically.

Applications and the Dock

The left (or top) portion of the Dock contains all docked and currently running applications.

To launch an application whose icon is in the Dock, just click its icon once, and the Dock takes it from there. When you launch an application that isn't in the Dock, its icon will appear in the Dock.

As the application launches, you'll see the icon bounce. When opened, a small triangle appears next to its icon to show that it is running—as you can see with the first icon on the left in Figure 3.1. When you quit or close the application, the triangle disappears. (For applications that haven't been set to remain in the Dock, the icon also disappears from the Dock.)

To switch between active applications, just click the icon in the Dock that you want to become the active application. You can also switch between open applications by holding down Command-Tab. This moves you through active applications in the Dock in the order in which they appear. When you reach the item you want to bring to the front, release the keys to select it.

By the Way

Dropping is a shortcut for opening document files in a specific application. To drop a file, you can drag and drop the document icon on top of the icon of the application you want it to open in. In Mac OS X, you can use the application's Dock icon instead of having to locate the real application file on your hard drive.

Also, to force a docked application to accept a dropped document that it doesn't recognize, hold down Command-Option when holding the document over the application icon. The application icon is immediately highlighted, enabling you to perform your drag-and-drop action. (Keep in mind, however, that many applications can only work with files in certain formats—forcing an application to open something it doesn't have the capacity to read won't get you very far!)

Adding and Removing Docked Applications

You can add applications to the left side (or top) of the Dock to create a quick launching point, no matter where the software is located on your hard drive. Dragging an application icon to the Dock adds it to that location in the Dock.

By the Way

When the Dock expands to the full width of the screen, it'll automatically get smaller as you open more applications or add more icons to it.

To make an open application a permanent member of the Dock, simply do the following:

1. Locate the application's icon appears in the Dock. (If it's not in the Dock, the application isn't open!)

2. Click and hold on the icon to pop up a menu, as shown in Figure 3.2.

3. Choose the option Keep in Dock. (If the application already has a place in the Dock, you won't be given this option.)

After you've placed an application on the Dock, you can launch it by single-clicking the icon.

By the Way

Moving an icon to the Dock doesn't change the location of the original file or folder. The Dock icon is merely an alias to the real file. Unfortunately, if a docked application has been moved, the Dock can no longer launch that application.

To remove an application's icon from the Dock, make sure that the application isn't running and drag it out of the Dock. It will disappear in a puff of smoke (try it and see).

FIGURE 3.2
Click and hold on
an application's
icon in the dock.

Getting Information from the Dock

In addition to providing easy access to commonly used applications, the Dock also gives you feedback about the functioning of applications through their icons.

The icon of an application that's opening will bounce in the Dock (unless configured not to) and continues bouncing until the software is ready. Also, if an open application needs to get your attention, its icon bounces intermittently until you interact with it.

The Dock also signals which applications are running by displaying a small triangle, or arrow, next to those application icons. This is a good way to see which applications are open, even if you've hidden them or closed all their windows.

Besides telling you which applications are open, icons can also offer quick access to documents open in them. For example, when you have multiple Finder windows open, you can view a list of those windows by clicking and holding on the Finder icon in the Dock. From the list shown in Figure 3.3, you can easily choose the one you want.

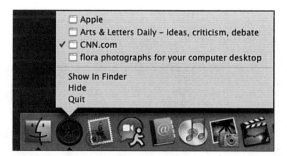

FIGURE 3.3
Click and hold on
the Dock icon of an
open application
for a list of open
windows.

Some applications, such as System Preferences and Sherlock, take "Dock menuing" even further. If they are open, you can choose from among all their sections, whether those sections are open or not, by click-holding on their icons in the Dock.

Did you Know?

Some applications even have customized Dock's icons to display information about events occurring in the application itself. For example, the Mail program displays the number of unread email messages in a red seal displayed in the Mail icon in the Dock, as shown in Figure 3.4. (We'll cover Mail in detail in Chapter 15, "Using Mail.")

FIGURE 3.4
The Mail icon tells
you when there's a
new message.

Docked Windows, Files, and Folders

Now, let's talk about the left, or bottom, portion of the Dock. You can drag commonly used documents to this area of the Dock, and a link to them is stored for easy access, as shown in Figure 3.5.

You can also drag commonly used folders to this portion of the Dock. Click-holding (or right-clicking) a docked folder displays a list of its contents and the contents of the subfolders in that folder, as shown in Figure 3.6.

Minimized application windows are also placed in this portion of the Dock. They are labeled with the icon for their associated application for easy identification, as shown in Figure 3.7.

FIGURE 3.5
Add an important
document to the
Dock.

FIGURE 3.6
View the contents
of docked folders
with ease!

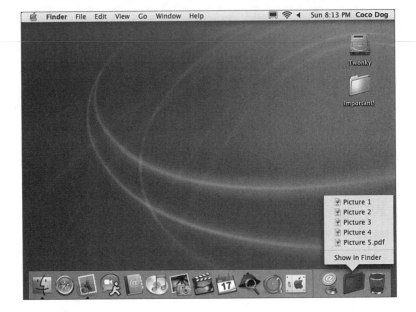

FIGURE 3.7
Temporarily store your work-in-progress in the Dock.

In addition to reducing desktop clutter, these window miniatures can serve another useful purpose. Depending on the application, minimized windows might continue to update as their associated applications attempt to display new information. QuickTime Player, for example, continues to play movies.

Trash Can

Another important resident of the Dock is the Trash (see Figure 3.8). The Trash is where you drag files, folders, or applications when you want to delete them from your computer. Figure 3.8 shows the Trash when empty. Figure 3.9 shows the Trash filled with one or more files.

FIGURE 3.8
This trash can is empty.

FIGURE 3.9
The trash contains items, and the files are ready to be permanently deleted.

The Trash is also used for ejecting disks, CDs, or DVDs. (It is also used to unmount external hard drives that you may attach to your computer for extra storage.) To avoid user fears that this might hurt the contents of the item being ejected, Mac OS X changes the Trash icon into the Eject symbol when you drag a disk icon to it, as shown in Figure 3.10.

FIGURE 3.10
Ejecting a disk.

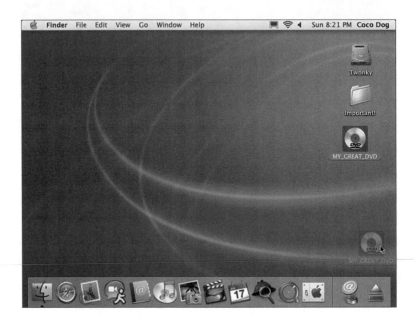

> You don't have to use the Trash when ejecting disks. Ctrl-clicking a mounted volume opens a contextual menu with an Eject option. Alternatively, you can highlight the disk to remove and choose File, Eject (Command-E) from the Finder's menu or press the Eject key on some models of the Macintosh's keyboard.

By the Way

Deleting Files

To get rid of unwanted files, simply follow these steps:

1. Click and drag a program's icon onto the trash can icon, which will be highlighted as soon as the icon is brought atop it. See Figure 3.11 for the effect.

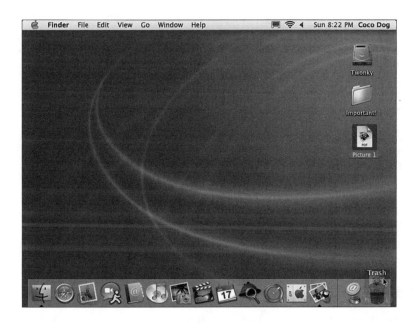

FIGURE 3.11
When you release
the mouse, the file
is placed inside the
trash can.

2. Choose Empty Trash from the Finder's application menu, which opens the request for confirmation, as shown in Figure 3.12.

When you click and hold the trash icon, you'll see an Empty Trash command, which is a fast way to delete its contents. But be forewarned: There is no second chance, no warning. When you choose this command, there's no opportunity to change your mind.

Did you
Know?

FIGURE 3.12
Do you really want
to delete the files
in the Trash?

When you click OK, the file is deleted.

Did you Know?

The Trash works like a folder. If you're not sure what's inside, just double-click it to open a window displaying its contents. If you change your mind and decide to keep something, click and drag that icon out of the Trash window onto the desktop.

Secure Empty Trash

The files you delete using the normal Empty Trash command are no longer available for use. However, special software exists for the purpose of recovering deleted files. If you want to ensure that your deleted files can't be recovered, choose File, Secure Empty Trash from the menu.

Secure Empty Trash works by deleting a file and then filling the space it occupied on a drive with meaningless data to obscure any traces of the file that may still be readable.

Customizing the Dock

After you've used the Dock for a while, you'll probably want to customize it to better suit your needs.

If you have a small monitor, you might want to resize the Dock icons to cover less area. The easiest and fastest way to resize them is to click and hold on the separator bar that divides the Dock areas. As you click and hold on the separator bar, drag up and down or left and right (if your Dock is placed vertically). The Dock dynamically resizes as you move your mouse. Let go of the mouse button when the Dock reaches the size you want.

After playing with different Dock sizes, you might notice that some sizes look better than others. That's because Mac OS X icons come in several native icon sizes, and points between those sizes are scaled images. To choose only native icon sizes, hold down the Option key while using the separator bar to resize.

Dock Preference Options

For more fine-tuning of the Dock, open the Dock pane of the System Preferences panel. This pane, shown in Figure 3.13, includes settings for adjusting the Dock's size and icon magnification and for making it disappear when not in use.

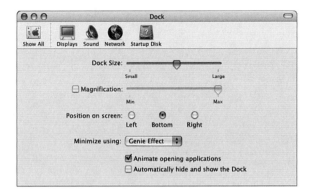

FIGURE 3.13
Configure your
Dock to the size
you want, or make
it disappear when
not in use.

> Even if you choose the option to hide the Dock, it's not really gone; it reappears for your use when you bring your mouse cursor to the Dock's edge of your screen.

By the Way

You can also shut off the animation effects that occur when document windows are minimized and stored in the Dock.

When you've made your selections, choose Quit (Command-Q) from the System Preferences application menu, or click the close button at the top of the window.

Summary

The Dock is an important part of the OS X interface. In this chapter you learned how to use it to launch applications as well as receive feedback about them as they run. You also learned how to store files, folders, and document windows in the Dock—and to use the Trash to delete files, folders, and applications you no longer need.

CHAPTER 4

Working with Folders, Files, and Applications

In the first three chapters, you learned how to work with the desktop and windows and how to navigate the file system. Along the way, you encountered folders, files, and applications. In chapter, we'll take a closer look at using them productively. Let's begin with a brief explanation of each.

Folders, Files, and Applications

Folders, files, and applications appear as icons on the desktop and in the Finder window, as shown in Figure 4.1.

The folders on your computer are like folders in an office—they hold collections of (hopefully) related items, including other folders. (Most folders look alike, but some are customized with an icon.) To look inside a folder, double-click its icon, and a Finder window opens to reveal the contents.

Files, on the other hand, contain information of some kind. File icons reflect their type or the application that will be used to open them. (In Figure 4.1, for instance, the bottom item in the column of icons on the right is a PDF that would be opened by the Preview application, whose icon is displayed upper right in the open Finder window.) If you double-click a file icon, the application that made (or one that recognizes) the file is launched, and the file opens in a window on your screen.

To move a folder or file, click its icon and drag to a new location. You can even drag files into folders if you feel like getting organized.

As you may have gathered from the discussion in the previous chapters, applications are computer programs designed for various purposes. Double-clicking an application's icon (in a window or the Dock) launches the application so that you can use it.

Folders

Applications

Hard drive

FIGURE 4.1
A variety of folder,
file, and application
icons.

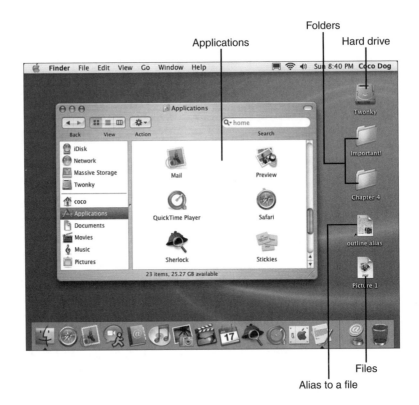

Files

Alias to a file

Creating Aliases

Aliases are shortcuts that point to a folder or file. They let you have access to
things you need from anywhere you need them—without making redundant
copies or moving the original from its current location.

> You can't make an alias for an application, but you can add an application to the
> Dock where its icon will act as an alias.

Figure 4.1 shows an alias icon. The little arrow at the lower left indicates that this
is not the actual folder or file, but a pointer to it (hence the arrow). Double-click
the alias icon for a folder, and you'll see the contents of the original folder.

To create an alias for an original file or folder, press Command-L when you select
an icon. You can also choose File, Make Alias from the menu, or hold down
Command-Option while dragging a folder, to accomplish the same thing.

If you move the alias of a file to the trash, the original is not deleted, just the alias. If you really want to delete the original, too, you need to drag both icons to the trash. If you trash the original and not the alias, the latter becomes nonfunctional, although the Finder usually gives you the chance to pick another file for it to point to when it's double-clicked.

Renaming, Copying, and Deleting

To rename a file or folder in the Finder, click once to select the file, pause, and click a second time on the file's name. The filename becomes editable in a few seconds, as shown in Figure 4.2.

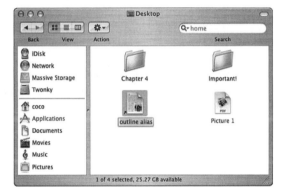

FIGURE 4.2
Clicking the name of a selected icon's label makes it editable.

In Chapter 2, "Using the Finder," you learned about file extensions, which you can choose to make visible under the Finder Preferences. If you change a file extension when renaming a file, OS X shows a dialog box asking you to confirm the change.

It's best not to rename applications.

Copying

Copying a file or folder creates an exact duplicate of an original. (Note that this is different from creating an alias to a file, which is just a pointer and not a separate object.) The new file contents and creation/modification dates are identical to those of the original. There are a number of ways to create a copy in Mac OS X:

▶ Drag a file to a different disk—Dragging a file to a disk other than the one it is currently stored on creates a copy with the same name as the original.

▶ Drag a file while holding down the Option key—If you drag a file icon to a folder on the same disk it is currently located in while holding down the Option key, a duplicate of that file is created in the new location. The copy has the same name as the original. (As you drag the file icon, a + appears next to your cursor.)

▶ Choose Duplicate from the contextual or Finder menu—If you want to create an exact duplicate of a file within the same folder, highlight the file to copy and then choose Duplicate from the Finder's File menu (Command-D), or Ctrl-click the icon and choose Duplicate from the pop-up contextual menu. A new file is created with the word *copy* appended to the name.

As the file is copied, the Finder displays an alert box in which you can see the progress of the copy operation. If multiple copies are taking place at the same time, the statuses of the operations are shown stacked on one another in the Copy alert box.

If you attempt to copy over existing files of the same name, the Finder asks whether you want to replace the files. Also, if you attempt to replace existing files to which you don't have access, the copy operation fails.

Deleting

Your Mac allows you to delete folders, files, and applications from the desktop, and consequently from your hard drive. It is important to remember that deletion permanently removes these things from your system.

Like copying a file, there are a number of ways to delete one:

▶ Drag to Dock Trash—Dragging an icon from a Finder window into the Dock's Trash is one of the most obvious and easy ways to get rid of a file.

▶ Finder toolbar—A Delete shortcut can be added to the Finder's toolbar (refer to the section "The Finder Window Toolbar," in Chapter 2 for details). Any items selected can be quickly moved to the Trash by clicking the Delete shortcut. Delete is *not* one of the default toolbar icons.

As you learned in Chapter 3, "Exploring the Dock," moving an item on your desktop to the Trash does not delete it permanently. Instead, it places the item inside the trash folder. To completely remove a file from your system, choose Empty Trash from the Finder's application menu or press Shift-Command-Delete.

If you want to rescue a file you've accidentally moved to the Trash, you can click the Trash icon and drag the file's icon out of the window.

The Finder Window Action Menu

In Chapter 2, during our look at the Finder window, we postponed our discussion of the Action pop-up menu in the toolbar. We'll return to it now to see how it can be used to make working with folders, files, and applications more convenient.

The items in the Action menu are context-dependent, which means they will differ depending on whether a folder, file, or application is selected. The Action menu for files, shown in Figure 4.3, contains the most options, so we'll start by listing those options.

FIGURE 4.3
This is the Action menu when a file is selected.

▶ Open—Opens the selected item.

▶ Open With—Allows you to choose which application installed on the system will be used when the selected file is opened. A list of recommended applications is presented along with the option Other, which allows you to select any application on your hard drive or connected to it. When you select an application, the file will be opened in it.

▶ Get Info—Opens the Info window for the selected item. (We'll talk about the Info window in greater detail later in the chapter.)

The Get Info option appears in the Action menu when you select your hard drive. If you select a removable drive, such as an external hard drive, Get Info and Eject appear in the Action menu.

By the Way

- ▶ Color Label—Allows you to color-code the selected file for easy identification. Also, if you recall from Chapter 2, you can perform file searches for items marked with a specific color. (We'll talk about using Color Labels in just a moment.)

- ▶ Move to Trash—Provides another way to place an item in the Trash for deletion from your system.

- ▶ Print—Allows you to print a file without having to open it.

- ▶ Duplicate—Provides another way to copy an item. When Duplicate is used, the copy appears in the same place as the original with the word "copy" appended to its name.

- ▶ Make Alias—Provides another way to make an alias of an item.

- ▶ Archive—Creates a compressed, or "zipped," version of an item that takes up less space than the original.

- ▶ Copy/Paste—Provides yet another way to copy an item. When Copy is used, the file is copied but not pasted. You can then navigate to the location where you want the copy and choose Paste from the Action pop-up menu. (The Paste option is visible only after an item has been copied.)

The options available for a folder are similar to those for a file, except that the options Open With and Print are not given.

For applications, the list of available options includes Open, Get Info, Move to Trash, Archive and Copy/Paste. (Color Label also appears in the menu but is grayed out to indicate unavailability.) There is also the option Show Package Contents, which opens a second Finder window to display the supporting files associated with the selected application.

> Applications on your drive are often really folders of items that work together. When you choose Show Package Contents, you can see elements "inside" the application that are normally hidden from view. Although it's interesting to see how things work, you shouldn't rename or remove any of the items needed by a program unless you are prepared to deal with the consequences.

Adding Color Labels

Previously, you learned that one of the items in the Action pop-up menu is Color Label, which can be used to color-code your files and folders. There are seven colors from which to choose. Besides helping you visually locate important documents, the colors can be used as search criteria in the Find window.

By the Way

You can change the names of the color labels from simply their colors to more meaningful terms, such as "work" or "book project," in the Labels section of the Finder preferences. You can access the Finder preferences under the Finder application menu.

To apply color labels to a selected file or folder, do the following:

1. Locate the item you want to label in the Finder window and select it.

2. Click the Action pop-up menu to open it and reveal the Color Label options, as shown previously in Figure 4.3.

3. Click one of the seven colors to apply it to the selected file or folder.

The color appears as a background behind the file or folder's label, as shown in Figure 4.4.

FIGURE 4.4
Eye-catching color labels can make finding important documents easy.

To remove a color label, select the item, open the Action pop-up menu, and choose the "x" under the Color Label option.

Now, let's take a close look at the Info window that can be launched from the Action pop-up menu.

Getting Info

The Info window displays detailed information, such as graphical previews and user permissions, about your folders, files, and applications. TheInfo window can be displayed by selecting the file you want to examine in the Finder, and then choosing Get Info from the Action pop-up menu in the Finder toolbar. Alternatively, you can select an item and choose File, Get Info (Command-I) from the menu.

Like the options in the Action pop-up menu, the Info window is context-dependent, with slightly different options depending on what it's giving information about. Let's examine the information available in the Info window.

General

As shown in Figure 4.5, the General section supplies basic facts about the selected resource, including the kind, size, and date of creation.

FIGURE 4.5
General information includes basic size, location, and type information about a file.

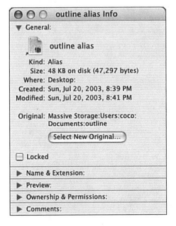

If the item you're viewing is an alias file (remember, an *alias* is a shortcut to the place where the real file is stored), the General section shows the location of the original file along with a Select New Original button that enables you to pick a new file to which the alias should be attached.

In the General section of the Info window is a check box labeled Locked—and for files, one labeled Stationary Pad. If an item is locked, a small lock appears in its icon that shows you won't be able to move or delete it. If you try, your system displays a message that it can't comply because the item is locked. You also won't be able to rename an item.

Stationary Pad is an option only for files—and only if they aren't already locked. Checking this box makes a file into something of a template. If you double-click a file set as stationary pad, it won't open, but an exact copy of it will be made in the same place so that you can make changes to the copy while the original remains untouched.

Although an identifying icon appears for locked items, there is no indication that a file is a template—except that a duplicate file automatically appears whenever you try to open the file. It's a good idea to title stationary pad files to indicate their purpose so that you'll know which files are affected this way.

Name & Extension

As you've learned, a filename can contain an extension—a period followed by several letters at the end of a name that indicates what kind of file it is. Common examples of file extensions are .doc for Microsoft Word documents and .html for Web pages. Many other operating systems rely on file extensions to identify file types. The Name & Extension section, shown in Figure 4.6, enables you to choose whether to view the filename with or without its extension. If you plan to exchange files with other systems (Windows), you might want to verify that your files include the extensions before sending them through email and so on.

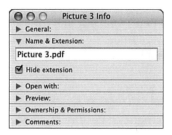

FIGURE 4.6
Change a file's name and choose whether to hide or show its file extension.

For folders and applications, the Name & Extension section simply shows the name of the item.

Open With

If you select a file icon (not an application or a folder), you can access the Open With section in the Info window, which is similar to the Open With item in the Action menu discussed previously. If you download a file from a non–Mac OS X system, your computer might not realize what it needs to do to open the file. The Open With section enables you to configure how the system reacts.

> If there are multiple files you want to have open with a different application than is currently configured, you can select them all by holding down the Command key as you click the files' icons. Then, you can open the Info window and change the Open With settings for all of them at once.

To use this feature, click the disclosure triangle next to Open With. The default application name is shown as the current choice in a pop-up menu containing alternative application choices. Use the pop-up menu to display options and make a selection. If the application you want to use isn't shown, choose Other, and then use the standard Mac OS X Open dialog box to browse to the application you want to use.

If you have a group of files that you want to open with a given application, you can select the entire group and follow the same procedure, or use the Change All button at the bottom of the window to update all files on your system simultaneously.

Content Index

When you view the Info window for a folder, the Content Index option enables you to index the folder's contents or check the last time it was indexed. As discussed in Chapter 2 in the section on file searches, indexing allows searches on a folder to be performed on the text within files, not just on the filenames.

Preview

If you select a QuickTime-recognized document, Preview enables you to quickly examine the contents of a wide variety of media files, including MP3s, CD audio tracks (AIFFs), JPEGs, GIFs, TIFFs, PDFs, and many more (see Figure 4.7).

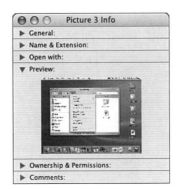

FIGURE 4.7
View an image file
with the Preview
feature.

If you're previewing a video or audio track, the QuickTime Player control appears and enables you to play the file's contents.

If you select a folder or an application, the Preview section displays its icon.

Languages

For an application, the Info window includes a section called Languages that enables you to see which languages the application recognizes. If you uncheck the currently active language, the application's menus are presented in another available language the next time you open it.

Ownership & Permissions

Mac OS X is a multiuser system, and by default all the files and folders on your system identify themselves with the user who created them. That means only the owner can move or modify them. Applications have different permissions depending whether they are shared or stored in a personal account. The Ownership & Permissions section, shown in Figure 4.8, enables you to change who owns a file, what other groups of users can access it, and what actions can be performed on it. You learn more about working with multiple user accounts and administrative access in Chapter 33, "Sharing and Securing Your Computer and Files."

You can select a group of items and change the ownership and permissions for them all at once. Hold down the Command key as you click to select multiple items; then open the Info window and change the settings.

Did you Know?

FIGURE 4.8
Determine, or alter,
who has access to
an item on your
system.

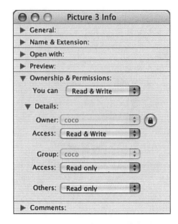

Comments

The Comments section enables you to create notes attached to specific files, folders, and applications. Adding Comments can be helpful if you want to note where a file came from.

Additional Tips for Using Applications

In later chapters, we will explore specific applications ranging in complexity from your system's Calculator to iMovie. For now, however, let's talk about some fairly common practices for working with applications.

Using Open and Save Dialog Boxes

Although you can launch an application by double-clicking a file created by it, sometimes you are already in an application and want to open additional files. To open existing files in an open application, choose File, Open from the menu. This launches the Open dialog box, as shown in Figure 4.9.

The Open dialog box is a modified Finder window where the toolbar has been replaced with a pop-up menu to help you quickly navigate to a different level of the file system. There's also a pair of buttons, Cancel and Open, at the bottom of the window so that you can cancel the dialog box or open a selected file.

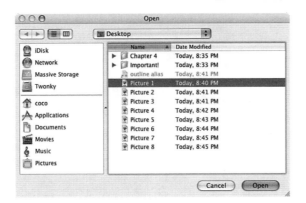

FIGURE 4.9
In the Open dialog
box, the shortcut
list and content
area should look
familiar.

> In addition to Open and Save, other common dialog boxes and helpers are the Page Setup and Print windows and the Font panel, which we discuss in Chapter 20, "Printing, Faxing, and Working with Fonts."

By the Way

You can use the shortcut list and content area to move through the file system to locate a specific file. Applications, which can't be opened in another application, will be grayed out to show that they are unavailable. You can, however, click folders to open them. The Open button at the bottom of the Open dialog box will be grayed out until you select a file.

> You can select more than one document to open in the current application by holding down the Command key on your keyboard. If you want to select a long list of files all in a row, you can hold down the Shift key and select the first and last file in the list—all the files in between will also be selected.

Did you Know?

When you are using an application, you will likely create new documents that you want to save. To save a document, choose File, Save or File, Save As from the menu. This opens a Save sheet window attached to the current document, as shown in Figure 4.10.

> The first time you save a new document, Save and Save As cause the same outcome. Later, however, there is a difference. Save saves changes to the file you've already saved with that name. Save As allows you to rename your document and save—which is especially useful if you want to keep the original intact for comparison later.

By the Way

FIGURE 4.10
The "short" version
of the Save sheet
window.

If you want to save your document in its current location, as indicated by the
Where pop-up menu, you can simply enter a title and click the Save button. (Use
the Cancel button if you've changed your mind about saving.)

If you want to save the document to another location (or if aren't sure where the
Where pop-up is putting your document), click the disclosure triangle button to
the right of the Save field. An expanded version of the Save sheet window
appears, as shown in Figure 4.11.

FIGURE 4.11
Navigate to the
location where
you want to save
your file.

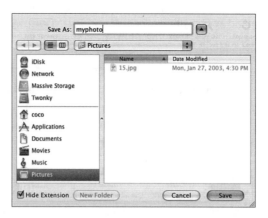

The expanded Save sheet window is like the Open dialog box, with a few additional options. You can use it to move to any folder on your hard drive, or even to

connected storage devices. The New Folder button allows you to create and name a new folder into which to save your document. You also have the option to show or hide the file extension, as discussed previously.

When you've chosen the location and given your file a name, click the Save button to store your file.

Force-Quitting Applications with the Process Manager

Occasionally, applications fail to work as expected. A feature that's sometimes necessary when using applications is Force Quit, which exits a program that has stopped responding. In Mac OS X, the Option-Command-Esc keyboard shortcut brings up a process manager, shown in Figure 4.12, that contains a list of running applications. Applications that the system deems to have stopped responding are marked in red. To force an application to close, choose it in the list and click the Force Quit button.

FIGURE 4.12
Choose the application you want to force-quit.

> Forcing an application to quit does not save any open documents. Be sure that the application is truly stalled, not just busy, before you use this feature.

You can also access the Force Quit feature from the Apple menu, or by opening the pop-up Dock menu for a running application and pressing the Option key to toggle the standard Quit selection to Force Quit. If the system deems that an application has stopped responding, a Force Quit option automatically appears in the Dock pop-up menu.

If the Finder (which is also an application!) seems to be misbehaving, you can choose it from the application list. The Force Quit button becomes the Relaunch button, enabling you to quit and restart the Finder without logging out.

Running Classic Applications

As briefly discussed in Chapter 1, "Introducing Mac OS X," the Classic environment is a way for you to operate some older Mac software while still using the Mac OS X operating system. Using Classic, almost any application that was functional in Mac OS 9 can run inside Mac OS X.

You must have at least 128MB of memory to use Classic. Also, a 400MHz G3 (or faster) computer is recommended. Why? Classic is a process running under Mac OS X. When it's in use, your computer is really supporting two operating systems simultaneously. As you can imagine, this is resource intensive.

Launching Classic

The Classic environment needs to be launched only once during a Mac OS X login session, and it can be launched manually or automatically. After it's running, Classic remains active (but mostly unnoticeable) until you log out or manually force it to shut down.

How can you find out whether a piece of software on your hard drive is indeed a Classic application? You can always ask the Finder. Simply select the icon for the program in question and choose File, Get Info (or press Command-I) from the Finder's menu. A Kind of Classic Application indicates that the software requires Classic to operate.

There are two ways to launch the Classic environment: through the Classic pane in System Preferences or by double-clicking a Classic application.

First, let's start Classic from the System Preferences pane. Here's what to do:

1. Locate the System Preferences icon in the Dock and double-click it (the icon looks like a wall-mounted light switch) or choose System Preferences from the Apple menu.

2. In System Preferences, click the Classic icon to open its Preferences pane, shown in Figure 4.13.

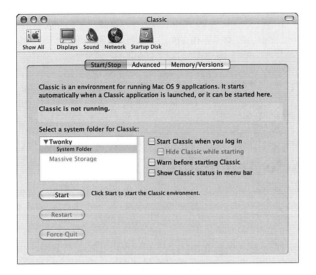

FIGURE 4.13
The Classic pane
allows you to
start/stop, restart,
or force-quit the
Classic
Environment.

3. Click the Start/Stop view of the Classic Preferences pane. Here you see several options, including a Stop or Start button for manually turning Classic off or on, Restart for when you want to reboot Classic, and Force Quit for when the Classic system is unresponsive after a crash.

4. Click the Start button to launch Classic. Mac OS 9 takes a few minutes to boot and then you're ready to run your older applications.

The first time you start Classic, your system requests permission to make some changes that allow Classic to operate.

By the Way

Let's try the second way to launch Classic:

1. Locate an older, non–Mac OS X application and double-click it.

Yes, there's only one step. If Classic isn't already running, it boots automatically before the application you've chosen is launched. It may take a little while for both Classic and the application you've launched to open and be ready for use. Remember that, after it's started, Classic remains in the background until you log out of Mac OS X or manually stop Classic. Even when you log out of all Classic applications, Classic itself is still running.

The Classic System Preferences pane shows the status of the Classic environment—that is, whether or not it's running. Because Classic does not appear as an active task in the Dock, this is one way to check its status.

Although it's true that in most cases Classic will run until you log out or manually stop the process, it's still (like Mac OS 9 was) susceptible to crashes. If Classic crashes, so do any applications running within it. You must restart the Classic process to continue working.

Using Classic Applications

The first time you open a Classic application, you'll notice that several interesting things happen.

Be careful not to alter settings in a Mac OS 9 control panel! When running Classic, the Mac OS X menu bar is replaced by the Mac OS 9 menu bar with a rainbow apple at the upper left in place of the solid-color one you usually see. Using the Mac OS 9 Apple menu, you can access all the earlier system's control panels and associated functionality. Settings in control panels such as Appearance and Sound are harmless enough, but it's possible to accidentally disrupt your network connections by working with the TCP/IP and AppleTalk control panels. It's best to avoid the Mac OS 9 control panels altogether.

Visually, Classic applications look different from applications that run under OS X. These older applications appear just as they would under Mac OS 8 and 9. The appearance of Mac OS X interface elements does not carry over to their windows or buttons, but the Mac OS X Dock and Process Manager do recognize Classic applications, as shown in Figure 4.14.

After it starts, Classic is easy to use without extra detail about how it interacts with Mac OS X. You simply operate programs as you normally would. However, there are a few exceptions that might be confusing for you:

▶ Copy and paste/drag and drop—Two of the most common means of moving data in the Mac OS suffer when working between native and Classic applications. It can take several seconds before data copied from one environment is available for pasting into another. Dragging and dropping text and images between native and Classic applications fails altogether.

▶ Open and Save dialog boxes—Mac OS X applications are aware of the special folders and files used by the system and take care to hide them. The same cannot be said for Classic applications. The Open and Save dialog boxes clearly show the invisible items. Although normal, these invisible files could be alarming to users not accustomed to seeing them.

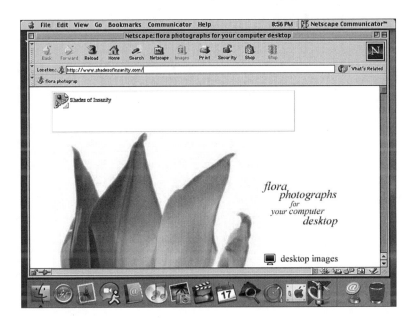

FIGURE 4.14
A mixture of OS X and OS 9 interface elements appears.

Note that when using the Classic environment, applications still need to access all hardware through Mac OS X, so software trying to access hardware directly will fail for devices not compatible with Mac OS X.

By the Way

Summary

In this chapter, we covered many of the basics of interacting with folders, files, and applications. We examined options in the Finder window's Action menu and the Get Info window. You also learned how to rename, copy, delete, and create aliases for files, folders, and applications. Finally, we discussed some more special techniques for working with applications, including running older Mac applications in Classic mode.

CHAPTER 5

Setting System Preferences and Universal Access Options

System preferences are settings that control aspects beyond a single application and that might even affect the entire system. We've already covered some of Mac OS X's system preferences while addressing specific topics. However, some settings don't apply elsewhere. In this chapter, we fill in the remaining gaps in system configuration and let you know where to find the system preferences discussed in other chapters. We pay special attention to the accessibility features available in System Preferences.

As you've seen in previous chapters, System Preferences items are categorized into four groups, as shown in Figure 5.1. They are Personal, Hardware, Internet & Network, and System.

FIGURE 5.1
The System Preferences panes are loosely categorized.

Within those sections, each button may have many features (accessible after clicking it) and contain buttons or pop-up menus that organize its features into smaller units. This could mean that you have to click through several options before you locate the setting you want to change. Use the button labels and explore pop-up menus to help guide you. Also, if you want to view all the system preferences again after selecting a specific one, click Show All at the upper left in the System Preferences window.

Personal System Preferences

The options in the Personal section of System Preferences affect your personal desktop. Each user can decide individual settings without interfering with the settings of others.

Appearance

The Appearance Preferences pane enables you to choose between Blue and Graphite for a general color scheme for menus, buttons, and windows on your desktop. You can also pick the highlight color for selected items. Other settings are the placement of arrows in the scrollbars, the number of listings for recent applications and documents, and activation of font smoothing for optimal font appearance on different screens.

Desktop & Screen Saver

The Desktop Preference pane, shown in Figure 5.2, allows you to choose the background on which all the items on your desktop will be displayed.

FIGURE 5.2
Choose a desktop background to brighten your day—or to minimize distraction.

You can choose from among the images in the Nature, Abstract, or Desktop folders provided by Apple, or use your own images stored in your Pictures folder or elsewhere on your system. You can also choose a solid color. To set a new background, simply select a folder from the left-hand column and click a thumbnail image that appears at the right.

If you like variety, select a folder, check the Change Picture box, and set a frequency for the change. Your desktop background will phase between all the images in that folder. You can also check the Random Order box if you want.

Under Screen Saver Preferences, you can choose among several preinstalled screensavers. The preview window shown in Figure 5.3 enables you to view your selection before applying it.

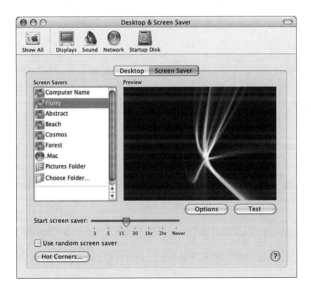

FIGURE 5.3
Choose a screensaver and how it activates.

You can also choose how the screensaver activates by setting the time until activation and whether to require a password to return to the desktop. The Hot Corners button enables you to pick corners of the screen that activate or prevent activation of the screensaver when your mouse enters a given corner. We'll talk more about using your own photos for desktop backgrounds and screensavers in Chapter 23, "Using iPhoto."

Dock

The setting under Dock enable users to customize the appearance of the Dock by resizing it or positioning it on the left, bottom, or right edge of the screen. Other options include graphic effects that occur when documents are minimized into the Dock or when applications are launched. The Dock is discussed in greater detail in Chapter 3, "Exploring the Dock."

Exposé

Exposé allows you to configure the feature that temporarily shifts the windows on your desktop so that you can view them all at one time. You can set Active Screen Corners or keyboard and mouse combinations to trigger different modes of Exposé. Exposé is covered in Chapter 2, "Using the Finder."

International

The International settings control the language displayed, as well as date, time, and number conventions. You can also choose keyboard layouts to support different languages from the Input Menu section.

Security

Under Security preferences, shown in Figure 5.4, you can choose to activate a feature called FileVault to encrypt your entire Home folder to ensure that no one will be able to read your files. This feature operates in the background, so you can use your files a usual. However, if someone steals your computer or connects to your computer remotely and doens't know your passwords, , your files will be undecipherable. To turn on this feature, click the Turn On FileVault button. Note that you will need spare room on your hard drive for the encryption to take place.

> Encryption, when done right, isn't easy to crack. If you forget both your account password and the Master password, which was set when you first set up your account, your files will remain securely encrypted even from you! For this reason, FileVault is a serious security option, not a toy—use it wisely.

Under the Security preferences, you can also set whether a password is required to wake your computer from sleep or from screensaver, to log in to user accounts, or to unlock secure system preferences.

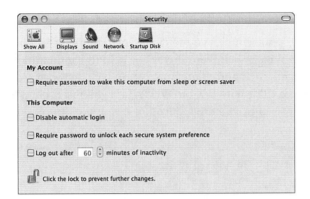

FIGURE 5.4
Security features
range from encrypt-
ing your entire
account to requiring
a password to
wake your comput-
er from sleep.

Secure system preferences, such as the Security settings shown in Figure 5.4, are marked by a lock icon in the lower left of the pane. If the lock is "locked," you must type the username and password of an "administrator" to make changes to the preferences. An administrator is a user with special privileges—the account you created the first time your computer ran OS X is automatically an adminis-trator. Other accounts can be set up to be administrators as well, which we'll dis-cuss in Chapter 33, "Sharing Your Computer with Multiple Users."

If you can't remember your login name, you can find it in the Accounts Preferences pane as your "short name," which we'll discuss later in this chapter. If you can't remember your password, you can reset it using your OS X installation disk as described in Chapter 37, "Recovering from Crashes and Other Problems."

By the Way

You can also choose to have the computer log out any user after a specific period of inactivity to prevent passersby from using an unattended workstation.

Hardware System Preferences

Hardware preferences, such as those for monitor, keyboard, and mouse, are found in the Hardware section of System Preferences.

For those with compatible graphics tablets, the Ink preferences also appear in this section, as discussed in Chapter 8, "Working with Address Book, Keychain Access, iSync, and Ink."

By the Way

CDs & DVDs

The CDs & DVDs pane enables you to direct your computer in what to do when CDs and DVDs are inserted in your drive. The default configuration, shown in Figure 5.5, launches the appropriate application included with Mac OS X when you insert a music CD, photo CD, or DVD. When you insert blank media, the Finder prompts you to choose an application to suit your purpose.

FIGURE 5.5
Choose which application is activated when you insert a CD or DVD.

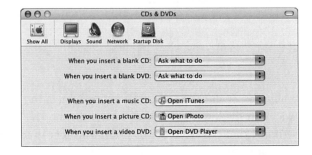

Displays

The Display section of the Displays preferences allows you to set your monitor's resolution, brightness, and the number of colors displayed. You can also choose to show Displays in the menu bar as a menu extra for convenient access to resolution settings. In the Color pane, you can choose a display profile, which is a specific color balance setting, or recalibrate your display. Both the Displays and Color panes are examined further in Chapter 18, "Working with Monitors and ColorSync."

Energy Saver

The Energy Saver pane, shown in Figure 5.6, enables you to set Sleep and Wake options for your machine. Laptop users also have the option to show the battery status in the menu bar. Notice that separate settings exist for the display and the hard disk.

By the Way

Laptop users will see two additional options in the Energy Saver preferences: Optimize Energy Settings and Settings For. Changing the options for these pop-up menus switches the Sleep settings between preset configurations.

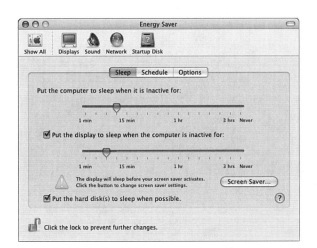

FIGURE 5.6
Energy Saver lets your system conserve power in response to monitor and hard drive inactivity.

After you've set Sleep options, use the Options tab of the Energy Saver pane to set Wake options.

The Schedule pane allows you to set your computer to start up and shut down at a given time on weekdays, weekends, everyday, or a specific day.

> When performing functions that require lengthy periods of keyboard inactivity, such as CD burning or digital video rendering, it's best to set the Sleep option to Never to avoid disruption to the process that can result in skips in the output.

Watch Out!

Keyboard & Mouse

In the Keyboard pane, you can set the repeat rate of the keyboard and the delay before keys start to repeat when you hold them down. The Keyboard Shortcuts pane, shown in Figure 5.7, can be used to customize keyboard shortcut settings that enable users to control menus, windows, and other interface elements from the keyboard.

Just as the Keyboard pane enables you to control keyboard sensitivity, the Mouse pane enables you to control tracking and double-click speeds. You might need to test the options a bit to find the most comfortable settings for your system.

> For laptop users, who don't have a mouse on their system, the Mouse pane appears under the label Trackpad.

By the Way

FIGURE 5.7
Use keyboard controls in addition to your mouse in changing system focus and navigation.

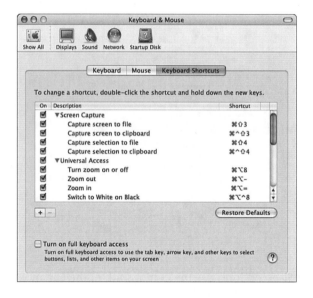

Laptop users will be delighted to find an Ignore Trackpad While Typing option. This disables the trackpad temporarily while the keyboard is being used. No more messed-up sentences because you accidentally hit the trackpad with your thumb while typing.

The Bluetooth section of the Keyboard & Mouse preferences relates to a standard for wireless connection that is now being used in some devices, including keyboard and mice. The Bluetooth preferences allow you to set up this kind of keyboard and mouse to work with your computer and also show the battery levels of these devices after they've been set up.

Print & Fax

The Printing pane gives you access to an application called Printer Setup Utility where you can set up printers. You can also choose the selected printer that will appear in the Print dialog box and a default paper size. Finally, you can choose whether to share your printer with other computers over the network.

Under Faxing, you can check the box to receive faxes on your computer and enter the phone number of the phone line connected to your computer. You can also choose how received faxes will be handled. Finally, you can allow others on your network to send faxes through your computer.

Printing and Faxing are discussed further in Chapter 20, "Printing, Faxing, and Working with Fonts."

Sound

The Sound pane, shown in Figure 5.8, contains Sound Effects options and volume controls for alerts and the main system, as well as the option to choose your sound output and input devices. You can also change the overall volume levels from the keyboard sound controls.

If you have multiple sound input and output devices (such as an iSub speaker) connected to your computer, you can choose between them in the Output and Input panes. For output devices, set the balance between left and right speakers. For Input devices, set the Input volume. In addition, you can use the Show Volume in Menu Bar check box to add a volume control menu extra to your menu bar.

FIGURE 5.8
The Sound Preferences pane enables you to pick error alerts and select from which audio output they emanate.

Internet & Network System Preferences

The next grouping of preferences, Internet & Network, determines how your machine talks to other computers on the network and works with your Internet services, such as email and Web.

.Mac

Pronounced "dot Mac," the .Mac preferences allow you to set up a for-pay account with Apple that offers an email account and storage space referred to as iDisk. We'll discuss the .Mac services and these preferences in detail in Chapter 14, "Exploring the .Mac Membership."

Network

The Network preferences are used to set up your computer's Internet connection. This is explained in Chapter 11, "Connecting to the Internet."

QuickTime

QuickTime, which is often used as a browser plug-in, requires information about your Internet connection. We will cover the QuickTime preferences in Chapter 7, "Using QuickTime and DVD Player."

Sharing

Sharing refers to giving other users access to resources and files on your system. Chapter 33, "Sharing Your Computer with Multiple Users," Chapter 34, "Sharing Files and Running Network Services," and Chapter 35, "Securing Your Computer," explain various aspects of the Sharing preferences.

System Preferences

The System section of System Preferences controls settings relating to your overall system rather than to a single user or to a specific application.

Accounts

The Accounts pane allows you to create additional user accounts so that others can have their own place to store files and keep their own desktop preferences without interfering with yours. You can also edit a user's information, including login picture. We'll discuss options for setting up additional user accounts in Chapter 33.

In an earlier note, you learned that you have to use a system installation disk to reset your password. That's because, although you can change your password from the Accounts pane, you have to enter your password to authorize that change!

The Startup Items section of the Accounts Preferences, shown in Figure 5.9, allows you to choose applications or files to open automatically whenever your account is active. To add an item, simply click the "+" button and navigate to it in the window that appears.

FIGURE 5.9
You can choose to have Mail automatically start up whenever you log in.

Be careful not to start too many applications at startup, or you may have to wait a long time for your system to be ready for use!

Watch Out!

Classic

In Chapter 4, "Working with Windows Folders, Files, and Applications," we talked about running Classic applications, which were written for the previous Mac operating system. The Classic preferences allow you to start Classic for use with those applications and to restart or force-quit Classic if it misbehaves. The Advanced pane of the Classic preferences allows you to fine-tune some aspects of Classic if you are a frequent user, whereas the Memory/Versions pane displays applications running in Classic and the memory used by them.

Date & Time

Not surprisingly, you set the system date and time in the Date & Time section of the Date & Time Preferences. If your computer remains connected to the Internet, you can choose Set Date & Time automatically and select a network time server to control your system clock. You can also set your time zone in the Time Zone pane. Finally, in the Clock pane you can choose whether to show the date and time in the menu bar or as a window on your desktop, as shown in Figure 5.10. You also can choose what form it should take—digital like a stop watch or analog like a pocket watch.

FIGURE 5.10
Put a clock on your desktop—and even give it a second hand.

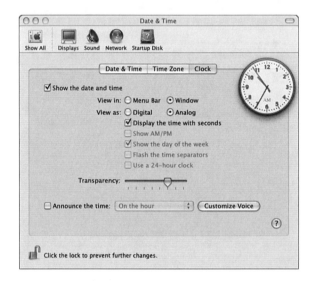

Software Update

As software updates become available, use the settings in the Software Update preferences to install them. You can also view what updates have been installed. We'll talk about this further in Chapter 36, "Maintaining Your System."

Speech

The Speech pane controls two separate, but related, elements: speech recognition and text-to-speech conversion.

Speech Recognition

In the Speech Recognition pane, shown in Figure 5.11, the primary option is to turn the Speakable Items feature on or off. As the name suggests, Speakable Items is a group of commands; when you speak one of these commands, your computer reacts to it. You can specify whether you want this option enabled at login. You can also open a panel of helpful speech-recognition tips and choose a feedback sound to inform you when your commands have been recognized.

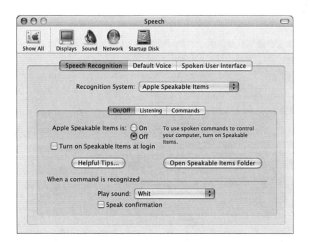

The Listening section of the Speech Recognition pane, visible in Figure 5.12, enables you to choose how you interact with the computer when speaking commands to it. The first option is whether you must press the Esc key before voicing your command or whether you can address the computer without using the listening key.

If you choose not to interact with the keyboard before your commands, you have the option to give the computer a name so that it knows when you're directing it, or you can simply hope that it recognizes the commands without warning by setting the Name Is pop-up menu to Optional Before Commands.

Keep in mind that addressing your computer by a name means that it is always listening unless you manually toggle listening with the chosen key. No, this statement isn't meant to stir up paranoia. But it does mean that your computer has to determine which sounds are directed toward it and which ones are environmental or incidental. Depending on the circumstances, this might be difficult, and your computer is simply unable to obey. To avoid undue frustration, we recommend using Speakable Items with the Listening Key option enabled.

The final option on the Listening section gives you information on which microphone, if more than one is available, is receiving your spoken input.

In the Commands section of the Speech Recognition pane, you can choose which system features will be accessible by spoken commands.

If you turn on speech recognition, the circular Speech Feedback window appears on your screen, as shown in Figure 5.12.

This unusual windoid shows the level of sounds detected by the microphone by filling in the lines in the lower portion of the window. The Speech pane of System Preferences and the Speech Commands window are accessible by clicking the arrow at the bottom of the window. The Speech Commands window shows the commands that you may speak to the computer. It also displays a log of all recognized commands and the system response enacted.

Default Voice

The Default Voice pane of the Speech preferences lets you set the voice and rate of speech used by applications that speak. For example, this feature is used by the Finder to read alerts when they haven't been responded to after a reasonable amount of time has passed. To test each voice, just click the different voice names. Mac OS X automatically plays a short sentence using the selected voice.

Spoken User Interface

The Spoken User Interface tab is where you enable features in applications that speak. You can activate spoken alerts and choose an introductory phrase to announce them. You can also have your computer speak to get your attention or have your computer read the text under your cursor or selected text.

Startup Disk

Some computers have multiple operating systems available on them, which are installed on a different section of the hard drive or attached via external drives. In the Startup Disk preferences pane, you can choose which system to use when you next start up your computer.

Did you Know?

If multiple operating systems are available to your computer, such as when you have an operating system installed on an external drive, you can choose which to use by holding down the option key as you turn on your computer. As the computer starts up, a special screen appears where you can select the bootable drive you want to run.

Now, let's look at the accessibility features built into Mac OS X under the Universal Access Preferences.

Universal Access

The Universal Access Preferences enable you to interact with your computer in alternative ways to provide greater accessibility for those with disabilities. The Seeing and Hearing panes contain special settings for users with low vision or poor hearing. If you have difficulty using the keyboard and the mouse, Universal Access also enables you to customize their sensitivity.

By the Way

While you're in the Universal Access pane of System Preferences, your computer reads you the items under your cursor as if you've enabled the Text Under the Mouse option of the Spoken User Interface section of the Speech pane.

Seeing

The options under the Seeing preferences, shown in Figure 5.13, affect the size or contrast of the elements onscreen.

Turn Zoom On activates a feature that enlarges the area of the display near the mouse cursor. Using key commands, you can zoom in (Command-Option-=) several levels to examine text or detail in any application, and then zoom back out (Command-Option—). To toggle zoom on or off, use the key command Command-Option-8. In Zoom Options, features such as degree of magnification can be configured.

FIGURE 5.13
The Seeing settings control zoom and contrast options.

Switch to White on Black (Command-Option-Control-8) displays white detail on a dark background. You can also toggle the display between color and grayscale, which shows only white, black, and shades of gray. A slider control allows you to vary the contrast between light and dark areas on your screen from a normal level to a maximum. (Key commands Command-Option-Control-, and Command-Option-Control-. decrease and increase contrast, respectively.)

Hearing

The Hearing pane enables you to have your computer notify you of alert sounds by flashing the screen. You can also open the Sounds Preferences pane to adjust volume.

Keyboard and Mouse

The Keyboard pane is shown in Figure 5.14. The Sticky Keys option helps with typing key combinations, such as Command-C, so that you can press only one key at a time. After Sticky Keys is set, you can turn the feature on or off by pressing the Shift key five times in succession. You can also use the Set Key Repeat button to open the Keyboard pane settings to minimize accidental multiple key presses.

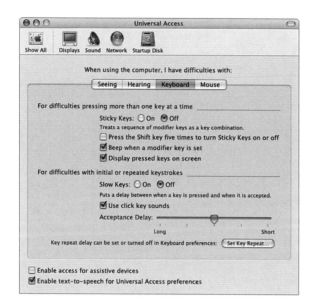

FIGURE 5.14
Change keyboard and mouse sensitivity in Universal Access.

For those who would rather use the numeric keypad than the mouse to direct the cursor, you can turn on Mouse Keys under the Mouse pane. Like Sticky Keys, Mouse Keys can be turned on or off by pressing the Option key (instead of Sticky Keys' Shift key) five times. The Mouse pane also contains settings to control the speed and delay of mouse cursor movement.

Summary

This chapter gave a synopsis of System Preferences options that aren't discussed elsewhere in this book. These preferences adjust settings for system functions ranging from the individual user's desktop settings to overall hardware configurations. They also include features that make Mac OS X accessible to a wide range of users with different physical abilities. To help you realize the range of their effect, Mac OS X has arranged them into four groups based on their spheres of influence. Also, preference panes with a larger number of settings have been broken into multiple panes or sections available via pop-up menus.

PART II

Common Applications

CHAPTER 6

Using Calculator, Stickies, Preview, and TextEdit

Mac OS X includes a number of utilities and applications that enable you to start working as soon as your Mac is up and running. This software includes a calculator, an application called Stickies to place short notes on your desktop, a PDF viewer called Preview, and a basic text editing program called TextEdit,. Because they require no installation or additional setup, we recommend giving each of these applications a try as a way to familiarize yourself with the Mac OS X desktop.

Calculator

The Mac's system Calculator, shown in Figure 6.1, is located in the Applications folder. You can toggle between basic view and advanced view, which supports trigonometry functions and exponents, under the View menu.

FIGURE 6.1
The Calculator in basic view supports common arithmetic functions.

You can operate the Calculator by clicking the buttons in the window or by using your numeric keypad. The number keys on your keypad map directly to their Calculator counterparts, and the Return key is equivalent to clicking the equal button.

If you want to view a record of your calculations, choose View, Show Paper Tape. This opens a separate window to display inputs, as shown in Figure 6.2. You can print the tape by choosing File, Print Tape (or even save it by choosing File, Save Tape As) from the menu.

FIGURE 6.2
Keep records of your calculations by saving or printing the Paper Tape.

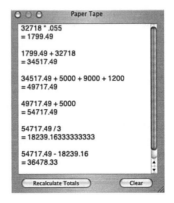

Another useful, if unexpected, feature is the Calculator's Conversion function. It enables you to easily perform conversions of currency, temperature, weight, and a variety of other measurement units. Simply enter a value in the Calculator and then choose the desired conversion type from the Convert menu.

Watch Out!

Currency exchange rates fluctuate over time—be sure to check the time they were last updated, and update as needed, in the Convert menu before making your calculations.

In the sheet that appears from the top of the Calculator, choose the units to convert from and those to convert to and click OK. Figure 6.3 depicts a currency conversion.

FIGURE 6.3
You can update currency rates when choosing monetary units in the currency conversion sheet.

Stickies

Stickies, also located in the Application folder, is a digital version of a Post-It notepad. You can store quick notes, graphics, or anything you might want to access later. Stickies offer several formatting features, such as multiple fonts, colors, and embedded images. The screen displayed in Figure 6.4 is covered with sticky notes.

The Stickies application installs a service that's accessible from many other applications running in OS X. Through this service, you can quickly store selected text from an application in a sticky note. To do this, select the desired text and then look in the application menu for the Services submenu and choose the option Make New Sticky Note. (Alternatively, select the desired test and use the key command Shift-Command-Y.) The Stickies application will become active and you will see your new sticky onscreen along with any other notes that had previously existed.

By the Way

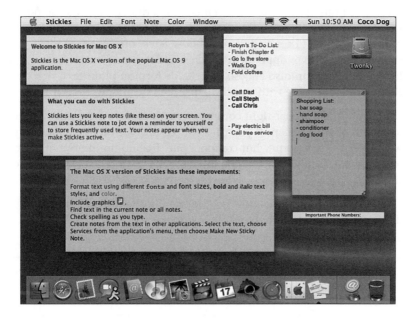

FIGURE 6.4
Sticky notes can contain any information you want.

To make a new Sticky, choose File, New Note from the menu. You can then type anything you want in it—or even drag in images, as shown in Figure 6.5.

FIGURE 6.5
Drag image files
from your hard
drive into a sticky
to illustrate your
notes.

The Stickies application does not use the standard Mac OS X window. Instead, each window appears as a colored, borderless rectangle when it isn't selected. When a window is active, three controls appear:

▶ Close box—The close box in the upper-left corner of the sticky note closes the active note. If the note has been edited, a dialog appears asking whether you want to save the note. If you choose Don't Save, the contents of the sticky won't be saved; if you choose Save, an Export window, as shown in Figure 6.6, appears in which you can name and choose a location for the file. You can also choose a basic file format: plain text, rich text file (RTF), or rich text file with attachments, such as images (RTFD).

▶ Cleanup—In the upper-right corner is a triangle that moves the box to the lower left of your screen. If you click this control for all open Stickies, you will end up with a somewhat compact pile, freeing up the rest of your desktop. Figure 6.7 shows the change in Figure 6.4 if all the stickies are moved to the left corner.

▶ Grow box—Dragging the grow box, located in the lower-right corner, dynamically shrinks or expands the window.

By the Way

If you move your mouse cursor over the title bar of a selected Sticky, it displays the creation and modification dates for the active note. To dismiss this information, click outside the current note.

In addition to the three visible controls, Mac OS X Stickies also supports window-shading. Double-clicking the title bar of an active window shrinks it to the size of the title bar. Double-clicking the title bar a second time returns the window to its previous size. When in windowshaded mode, the sticky note displays the top line of text from its contents in the title bar of the collapsed window. An example is visible at the lower right in Figure 6.4.

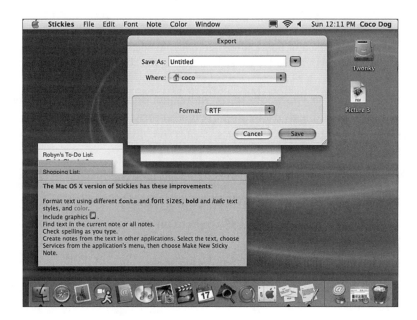

FIGURE 6.6
When closing a sticky note, save the contents of a sticky to a file—or lose the information forever!

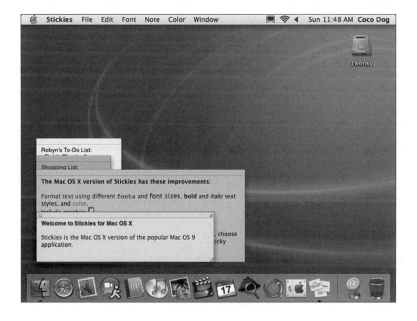

FIGURE 6.7
Move the sticky notes to the lower left so that you can see more of the desktop.

Strangely enough, you cannot minimize Stickies into the Dock. Choosing Window, Minimize Window from the menu windowshades the active note.

The Stickies and Calculator applications are unusual because they have no application preferences, which would typically be located under their application menus.

Sticky notes are not, as you might think, individual documents. All the notes are contained in a single file that's written to your Library folder. The File menu in Stickies enables you to create new notes, export individual notes to text files, and print the contents of notes:

- ▶ New Note (Command-N)—Creates a new blank note.

- ▶ Close (Command-W)—Closes the active sticky note.

- ▶ Save All (Command-S)—Saves changes to all notes.

- ▶ Import Text—Imports a text file into a new note. Text can be in plain text or rich text format (RTF). Font style information is retained if you use rich text format.

- ▶ Import Classic Stickies—Imports note files from Mac OS 8/9.

- ▶ Export Text—Exports the active note to a text file in plain text, rich text (.rtf), or rich text with images (.rtfd) formats.

- ▶ Page Setup—Configures printer page setup.

- ▶ Print Active Note (Command-P)—Prints the active note.

- ▶ Print All Notes—Prints all notes.

In addition to the normal Edit menu items are three components you might not expect in a simple Post-It application: Find, Spelling, and Speech. The Find option helps you to search for specific words or phrases in your notes, and the Spelling option checks your spelling. Under the Speech submenu, you can start, and then stop, your system from speaking the selected sticky aloud.

The Font menu offers control over the text formatting in each note, including font and text formatting and colors. Copy Style is an unusual selection that copies the font style from the current text selection (size, font face, color, and so on) so that you can easily apply it elsewhere by using the Paste Style command.

> When choosing font colors, you will be working with the Colors window, a common element of OS X shown later in Figure 6.10.

By the Way

In the Note menu, Floating Window enables you to set the chosen note to float in front of all other windows, even when other applications are active. Translucent Window makes the selected note transparent so that whatever is behind it will show through. The Use as Default option enables you to apply the current setting as the default for new notes.

What would a sticky note be without a bright-colored background? The Color menu contains the common Post-It colors for your enjoyment (yellow, blue, green, pink, purple, and gray).

The Window menu lists all active notes using the first several words that appear on them.

Stickies, unlike many of the applications we'll be discussing in upcoming chapters, has no application preferences.

Preview

For viewing PDF files and images of all sorts, Mac OS X comes with the Preview application, which can be found in the Applications folder.

> Since version 10.2, the standard graphic file format in Mac OS X has been the PDF. One nifty result is that you can make a PDF of nearly any document on your system. Simply choose File, Print from the menu and click the Save As PDF button at the bottom of the Print sheet window.

By the Way

Preview can be launched in a number of ways. First, you can double-click the application icon. Doing so starts Preview, but doesn't open any windows. You must then choose File, Open from the menu to select a file to view.

> Another common application for viewing PDF documents is Adobe Acrobat.

By the Way

Second, you can open Preview by dragging the image or PDF files onto the Preview icon in the Finder or Dock.

Third, Preview is integrated into the Mac OS X printing system, so clicking Preview in any Print sheet window starts it.

> If you want to view a series of images in one Preview window, select them all and drag the set on top of the Preview icon in the Applications folder or in the Dock.

When you open an image or PDF document in Preview, it shows up in a window with a toolbar across the top, as shown in Figure 6.8. The following options are located in the toolbar:

▶ Drawer—Opens and closes a drawer, shown in Figure 6.8, which displays either a list of page headings or or a series of thumbnail images representing the pages or files open in the current Preview window. Clicking a page heading or thumbnail image shows that page the main viewing area. (For text documents, you can choose whether the drawer contains text or thumbnails using the view buttons at the top of the drawer.)

> You can search text-based PDFs using the search box at the top of the drawer. Just start typing your search term, and pages containing the string you've typed will appear in the drawer for your convenience.
>
> You'll know whether a document is text-based by whether search box appears at all. Not all documents that contain text are encoded as text; some are more like "pictures" of a page. In those cases, you'll have to search without Preview's assistance (There is an exception to using the appearance of the search box to determine whether a PDF is text-based—if you use the selection tool as discussed later, the resulting PDF won't be text-based, but the search box will be present.)

▶ Back/Forward—If you've viewed several pages in a multipage file out of sequence, you can page back and forth through in the order you visited using the Back/Forward arrows.

▶ Page—When you're viewing a multipage PDF file, Page Number enables you to enter a page number to jump directly to that page.

▶ Page Up and Page Down—If you're viewing a multipage file, you can move through the pages sequentially using the Page Up and Page Down arrows.

▶ Zoom In and Zoom Out—These two options enable you to view a larger or smaller version of the selected image or PDF. If the image is larger than the Preview window, scrollbars appear.

Did you
Know?

If you open a document and find it's sideways or upside down, you can rotate the document using the Rotate Left and Rotate Right commands from the View menu. If you want to see a mirror image (either left-to-right or top-to-bottom), choose View, Flip Horizontal or View, Flip Vertical.

▶ Tool Mode—This set of buttons, which varies depending on whether you are viewing a text or image file, contains the following tools:

  ▶ Scroll Tool—Allows you to scroll within a selected page by clicking and dragging in the main viewing area. To move between pages, you still need to use the Page Up/Page Down controls or select another page in the drawer. (The mouse cursor appears as a hand icon while in this mode.)

  ▶ Text Tool—Allows you to select text in a PDF. When selected, the text can be copied and pasted to another document using standard commands under the Edit menu. (Note, this tool is available only in text-based documents.)

  ▶ Select Tool—Allows you to select a portion of a page, which you can then copy using Edit, Copy command from the menu. When copied, you can create a new PDF document containing only the selected area by choosing File, New from Clipboard from the menu. Unlike the Text Tool, you can select either text or images with the Select Tool, but the result when copied will be an image-based PDFformat, not editable or searchable text.

Just as you can for Finder windows, you can hide the Preview toolbar by using the toolbar button at the upper right of the window's title bar. Note, however, that you can't simply scroll to reach another page of the PDF unless you activate Continuous Scrolling from the View menu.

By the
Way

In addition to viewing files, you can use Preview to convert a file to one of several common file types and export it to a new location. To do this, choose File, Export from the menu and enter a filename. Then choose a location to save in and a file format. The Options button reveals additional settings for color depth and filter options.

FIGURE 6.8
The Preview window includes a toolbar where you can easily alter the viewing style of your files or move between pages.

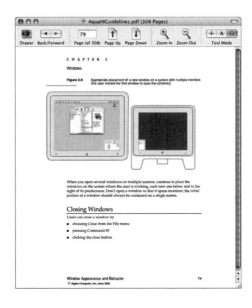

Preview Preference Options

As you learned in Chapter 1, "Introducing Mac OS X," one of the standard items in an application menu is Preferences, which allow you to customize some aspects of how an application responds.

The General pane of the Preview Preferences, shown in Figure 6.9, allows you to choose how Preview uses the thumbnails it displays. You can choose a size, whether to show thumbnail images and/or their names, and whether to load all thumbnails or wait until they are needed.

FIGURE 6.9
The Preview Preferences pane.

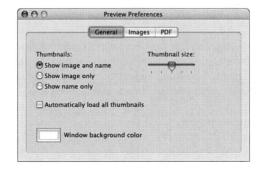

You can also choose a background color for the window using the Colors window, as shown in Figure 6.10.

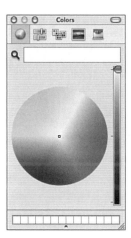

FIGURE 6.10
The Colors window is a standard part of OS X.

In the Images and PDF preference panes, you can choose the default size at which images and PDF documents are opened—fit to screen or some other size. You can also choose some aspects of how images or text are rendered on screen.

TextEdit

Mac OS X comes with the text editor TextEdit installed in the Applications folder. TextEdit can save files in plain text or the RTF format and uses many built-in Mac OS X features to give you advanced control over text and fonts. Its RTF files can be opened in popular word processing programs, such as Microsoft Word, and display all formatting attributes. Even better for some, the current version of TextEdit can open, edit, and save Word documents, which allows documents to be traded back and forth between Word and TextEdit users.

About Unicode

TextEdit also handles Unicode editing. *Unicode* is a character-encoding format that uses 16 bits (as opposed to the traditional 8) for storing each character. This allows more than 65,000 characters to be represented, which is necessary for some languages such as Japanese and Greek. Eventually, Unicode is expected to entirely replace ASCII encoding (which can represent a total of only 255 characters).

When you start it, TextEdit opens a new Untitled.rtf document for you to begin working, as shown in Figure 6.11.

FIGURE 6.11
The basic TextEdit workspace.

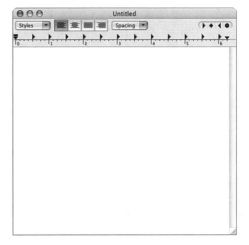

If you want to open an existing document, choose File, Open (Command-O) from the menu. To read a file, however, it must be a supported document type, such as plain text, Hypertext Markup Language, Microsoft Word documents, or RTF. Figure 6.12 demonstrates TextEdit's rich text editing capabilities.

FIGURE 6.12
TextEdit can edit styled text documents stored in RTF.

By the
Way

By default, TextEdit opens HTML documents and displays the styled information similar to the way a Web browser would display it. To open an HTML file and edit the
source code, you must adjust the Application preferences to ignore rich text commands in HTML files.

You will find the options to change the size or font style of text using TextEdit
under the Font item of the Format menu. Choose Show Fonts to launch the OS X
Font window, where you can choose between any of the fonts installed on your
system. (We'll talk more about fonts in Chapter 20, "Printing, Faxing, and
Working with Fonts.")

To change the text color, choose Format, Font, Show Colors from the menu. This
launches the Colors window shown previously in Figure 6.10.

If you change your mind about all the fonts and color modifications you've made
and just want to stick with simple, unadorned text, choose Format, Make Plain
Text from the menu. Figure 6.13 shows the plain text version of the document displayed in Figure 6.12. (Also notice that the ruler at the top of the document window has disappeared; to bring it back, choose Format, Make Rich Text from the
menu.)

By the
Way

The ruler is only available for Rich Text Documents. Using the ruler, you can visually
adjust tabs and other layout features of the active document. You can also use it to
easily and visually change formatting and placement of text.

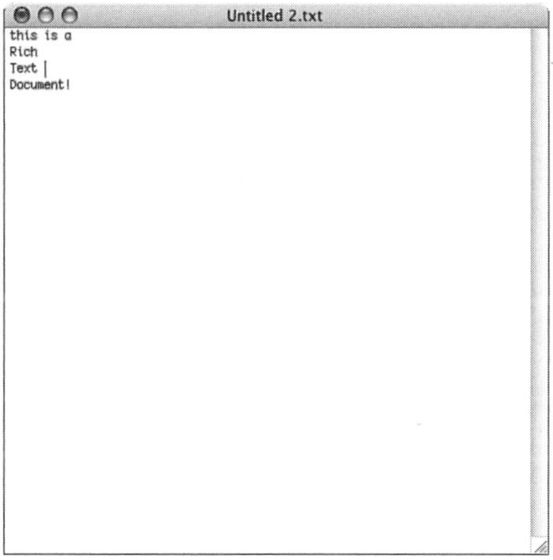

Untitled 2.txt

this is a
Rich
Text |
Document!

FIGURE 6.13
This document is
not a rich text doc-
ument!

For the most part, you should be able to open TextEdit and start creating and editing text documents. However, you can use a number of preferences and features to customize its appearance and functionality.

Preferences

The TextEdit Preferences window, shown in Figure 6.14, controls the default application preferences. Most of these options can be chosen from the menu bar and stored on a per-document basis as well as for the entire application.

FIGURE 6.14
The TextEdit Preferences enable you to control a range of features.

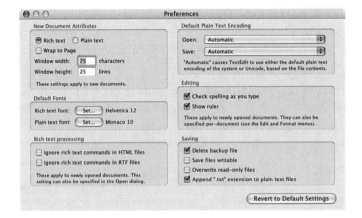

The New Document Attributes section of the preferences includes an option for Rich Text or Plain Text. It enables you to select the Wrap to Page check box so that lines will fit the page width. You can also choose the default width in characters and height in lines of new windows.

Use the Set buttons in the Default Fonts section to choose new default fonts for rich text and plain text documents. The default fonts are Helvetica 12 and Monaco 10, respectively.

To disable rich text commands in HTML and RTF files, click the corresponding check box in the Rich Text Processing section. Ignoring the style information opens the document as a plain text file, showing all the control codes and tags used to embed the original styles. This is required for editing HTML tags within a Web page.

The options for Default Plain Text Encoding require a bit of explanation. By default, TextEdit attempts to read style information in whatever file it opens. Allowing automatic detection enables TextEdit to open files created on other operating systems, such as Windows, and transparently translate end-of-line characters. When opening or saving a document, TextEdit gives you the opportunity to override automatic detection of the appropriate file encoding type to use. To choose an alternative encoding, such as Unicode, use the pop-up menus in the Default Plain Text Encoding section.

To have TextEdit automatically check your spelling as you type, select the Check Spelling as You Type check box in the Editing section. Misspelled words will be underlined in red. Ctrl-click the misspelled word to open a contextual menu that enables you to choose from a list of corrections, ignore the word, or add it (the Learn option) to the Mac OS X dictionary. You can also choose to show the ruler in the TextEdit window.

The options in the Saving section include

▶ Delete Backup File—Removes the TextEdit backup file after a document is successfully saved.

▶ Save Files Writable—Saves read-only files with write permissions turned on; that is, they can be edited later.

▶ Overwrite Read-only Files—Overwrites files, even if their permissions are set to read-only.

▶ Append ".txt" Extension to Plain Text Files—Adds a .txt extension to the end of plain text files for cross-platform compatibility and ease of recognition.

To save your settings, close the TextEdit Preferences panel. To revert to the original configuration, click the Revert to Default Settings button.

Menus

As you learned earlier, the TextEdit menus provide control over fonts. They also control other document-specific information. Most of the application preferences can be overridden on a per-document basis from the main menus.

You can open, save, and print documents by using the File menu.

The Edit menu contains the basic copy and paste functions, along with the find, replace, and spell-checking features introduced in Stickies.

The Format menu enables you to control your font settings, colors, and text alignment. In addition, you can toggle wrapping modes, rich text and plain text, and hyphenation.

The Window menu allows you to choose among open TextEdit windows or bring all to the front.

Summary

Mac OS X includes a wealth of applications and utilities, ranging from the simple (but not so simple!) Stickies to a versatile PDF viewer. The experience of using one application applies to others you will encounter. This is especially true for TextEdit, which uses the Mac OS X system-level color-picker, spell-checking, and font controls.

CHAPTER 7

Using QuickTime and DVD Player

In the previous chapter, you learned to use several practical applications that come with Mac OS X. In this chapter, we'll try out some more entertainment-oriented applications—QuickTime and DVD Player.

QuickTime

You learned in Chapter 1, "Introducing Mac OS X," that QuickTime is one of Mac OS X's built-in imaging components. By using its technology, system applications can support reading or writing many different image formats.

You might also know that QuickTime is a popular media player used to enjoy media, both from within a Web browser and as an application on your desktop. In the first half of this chapter, we look at using QuickTime 6.

QuickTime supports most common digital media formats, including those for movies, MP3 files, WAV files, images, and interactive applications. QuickTime 6 also supports MPEG-4, the global standard for multimedia, which is designed to deliver high-quality video using smaller file sizes.

You can learn more about the supported formats by visiting Apple's QuickTime specification page at www.apple.com/quicktime/whyqt/.

Did you Know?

Watching QuickTime movies play in your Web browser window is one of the most common uses for QuickTime, so let's take a look at the controls of the QuickTime browser plug-in. Figure 7.1 shows a QuickTime movie playing in the Safari Web browser.

If you're a movie fan, you'll love Apple's movie trailers Web page, located at www.apple.com/trailers/.

By the Way

FIGURE 7.1
Many users experi-
ence QuickTime
through their Web
browsers.

The movie controls are located across the bottom of the video. There's a volume
control at the far left, with a play/pause button immediately to its right. The
progress bar takes up the middle. At the right are buttons to rewind or fast-
forward and a downward pointing arrow to get information and change settings.

If you've used a VCR or other media player, you've certainly seen these before.
However, you might want to know a few shortcuts.For example, clicking the
speaker icon on the far left can instantly mute the volume. You can also control
the volume level using the up-arrow and down-arrow keys on the keyboard.

**Did you
Know?**

To increase the volume beyond its normal limit, hold down the Shift key while dragging the volume control.

Playback controls also can be activated from the keyboard, saving the need to
mouse around on your screen. To toggle between playing and pausing, press the
Spacebar. To rewind or fast-forward, use the left-arrow and right-arrow keys,
respectively.

If the movie being played is streaming from a remote server, some of these controls might not be available. For example, on-demand streaming video can't be
fast-forwarded or rewound, but static files can be. The available controls depend
entirely on the movie you're viewing.

The QuickTime Player

In addition to the QuickTime plug-in, there's also the QuickTime Player. The QuickTime Player application provides another means of viewing movies and other QuickTime-compatible media, including digital images and music files, directly from your desktop.

> Minimizing a QuickTime Player movie while it is playing adds a live icon to the Dock. The movie (with sound) continues to play in the minimized Dock icon. Even if you don't have a use for this feature, give it a try—it's extremely cool!

To use QuickTime Player, open it from its default home in the Dock or from the Applications folder. After the default QuickTime window opens, click the QuickTime icon button at the lower right to launch the Apple QuickTime view, as shown Figure 7.2.

FIGURE 7.2
The Apple QuickTime view enables you to choose from several categories of content.

The left side of this view lists several categories from which you can choose what to view or listen to. Clicking a category launches your default Web browser and brings up a page listing the available content. Selecting a listed item does one of two things: It either launches a new Apple QuickTime window in your desktop to play the item, as shown in Figure 7.3, or opens a new Web browsing window where you can view the QuickTime element using the QuickTime plug-in.

When QuickTime starts to load a streaming video clip, it goes through four steps before displaying the video:

1. Connecting—Makes a connection to the streaming server.

2. Requesting data—Waits for acknowledgement from remote server.

FIGURE 7.3
Watch a streaming
movie in QuickTime
player.

3. Getting info—Retrieves information about the QuickTime movie.

4. Buffering—QuickTime buffers several seconds of video to eliminate stutter-
ing from the playback.

If the player stalls during any of the four steps that precede the video display, there
might be a problem with the remote server or your transport settings (how your computer talks on the Internet). Try another streaming source, and if it still fails, use the
QuickTime System Preferences pane to change your settings. (We'll discuss
QuickTime preferences in the "QuickTime Preferences" section later in this chapter.)

If you have a streaming server URL, you can choose File, Open URL in New Player
(Command-U) from the menu to directly open the stream.

Using QuickTime Player to Play Other Media

You can use QuickTime Player to play information from other sources besides
those from the Web. QuickTime refers to every media type as a movie. For example, you can open and play CD audio tracks and MP3s by selecting File, Open
Movie command from the menu. Even though there aren't any visuals, these
media types are referred to as *movies* in QuickTime's vocabulary.

You can open local movie files by choosing File, Open Movie in New Player
from the menu (Command-O) or by dragging a movie file onto the QuickTime
Dock icon.

QuickTime Preferences

The Preferences submenu, found in the QuickTime Player application menu in
your menu bar contains three different choices: Player Preferences, QuickTime
Preferences, and Registration.

The Player Preferences settings are preferences for the QuickTime Player application itself, whereas the QuickTime Preferences settings refer to the QuickTime System Preferences pane. If you're interested in registering QuickTime (which we highly suggest), the Registration option provides an input area for entering your registration code.

Figure 7.4 shows the Player Preferences dialog box.

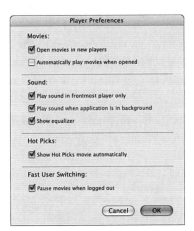

FIGURE 7.4
Choose how QuickTime Player reacts to opening and playing movies.

Use the following options in the Player Preferences dialog box to control how the application handles multiple movies and playback:

▶ Open Movies in New Players—By default, QuickTime Player reuses existing windows when opening new movies. To open new movies in new windows, select this check box.

▶ Automatically Play Movies When Opened—Does what it says! When checked, QuickTime Player starts playing a movie immediately after it's opened.

▶ Play Sound in Frontmost Player Only—By default, sound is played only in the active player window. To hear sound from all playing movies simultaneously, uncheck this option.

▶ Play Sound When Application Is in Background—If this option is checked, sound continues to play even when QuickTime Player isn't the active application.

▶ Show Equalizer—Displays the sound levels to the right of the progress bar.

▶ Show Hot Picks Movie Automatically—Automatically fetches and plays Apple's Hot Pick movie when QuickTime Player is started.

▶ Pause Movies When Logged Out—Pauses active movies, switching from one user account to another using Fast User Switching. (We'll talk more about setting up and working additional user accounts in Chapter 33, "Sharing Your Computer with Multiple Users.")

Click OK to save the application preferences.

The QuickTime System Preferences pane (located in the Internet & Network section of System Preferences) enables you to change QuickTime's settings for better quality playback and to make other modifications. Let's discuss some of the more useful settings.

The first section, Plug-In, is shown in Figure 7.5. (Remember, plug-ins are used when movies are viewed in a Web browser.)

FIGURE 7.5
Use QuickTime's System Preferences to optimize display for your system.

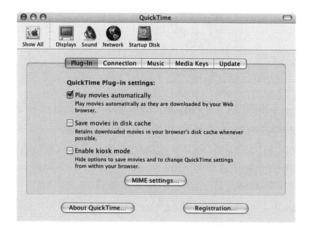

The Play Movies Automatically option directs QuickTime to start playing a movie after enough of it has been buffered. This option applies to movies that aren't streamed. Select the Save Movies in Disk Cache option to temporarily store a clip to speed up repeated viewings. The Enable Kiosk Mode option makes it possible for movies to run continuously unattended for demonstrations and presentations.

Click the MIME Settings button to open a list of all the MIME types that QuickTime can handle and everything it's currently configured to display. MIME stands for Multipurpose Internet Mail Extension and defines a set of document types, such as text, HTML, and so on.Some items (such as Flash) are intentionally disabled because they're better handled by other browser plug-ins.

The Connection section, shown in Figure 7.6, configures the type of network access QuickTime can expect your computer to have. This information helps QuickTime choose the appropriate type of media to display, depending on how fast it can be received.

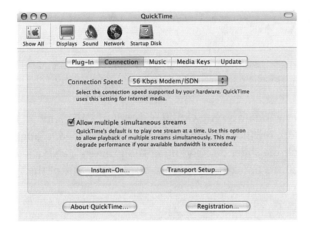

FIGURE 7.6
Choose your connection speed and transport type for best movie quality.

The Transport Setup button is used to choose the protocol used for streaming. By default, QuickTime attempts to choose the best transport based on your network type. It's best not to change these settings unless you're having difficulty viewing media.

Watch Out!

By default, QuickTime allows only a single media stream. If your bandwidth enables you to do so, click the Allow Multiple Simultaneous Streams option to stream many sources at once. This option is automatically selected when you specify a high-speed connection method.

DVD Player

Included with Mac OS X is DVD Player, an application for displaying DVD content on computers equipped with internal DVD drives. To start DVD Player, simply insert a video DVD into your system, or double-click the application icon in the Applications folder.

By default, Mac OS X launches DVD Player automatically when it detects a DVD in the drive. At startup, the DVD begins to play, and a playback controller appears onscreen. Figure 7.7 shows the playback controller.

FIGURE 7.7
DVD Player's controller window keeps all the needed controls in one convenient place.

By the Way

> Unlike for QuickTime movies, if you minimize a DVD Player window, the picture won't play in the Dock. However, the sound continues to be audible.

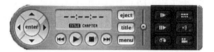

Use the controller window as you would a standard DVD remote. Basic playback buttons (play, stop, rewind, and fast-forward) are provided, along with a selection control and a volume slider directly under the primary playback controls. Also available are buttons to access the menu, display the title of the current scene, and eject the DVD.

Did you Know?

> Typically, viewers navigate through DVD menus with arrow keys on their DVD controllers. Because your DVD Player is run on your computer, you have additional options. To navigate onscreen selections without the use of the controller, you can simply point-and-click at a DVD menu item to select it. To navigate with the keyboard, use the arrow keys and press Return.

Six additional advanced controls are accessible by clicking the far right edge of the controller window. In Figure 7.7, the controller window is shown with the window tray extended. This opens a window drawer containing two columns of buttons that control playback or special features of DVDs. Those controls, from top to bottom, left to right, are Slow, Step, Return, Subtitle, Audio, and Angle buttons.

If you prefer a vertically oriented player control, as shown in Figure 7.8, choose Control, Use Vertical Control (Option-Command-C) from the menu. You can switch back to the horizontal layout at any time by choosing Controls, Use Horizontal Control (Option-Command-C) from the same menu. To hide or show the Control regardless of its orientation, use the key command Command-Shift-C.

FIGURE 7.8
Same controls, different arrangement.

Keyboard Commands

Although the onscreen controller can be used for most everything, DVD Player also provides keyboard commands for controlling playback.

The following options are available under the Controls menu:

▶ Use Horizontal/Vertical Controloer—Toggle between Horizontal or Vertical orientation (Option-Command-C) .

▶ Play/Pause—(Spacebar) Play or pause the video.

▶ Stop—(Command-.) Stop the current video from playing.

▶ ScanForward—(Command-right arrow) Speed through the video playback.

▶ Scan Backwards—(Command-left arrow) Move backward through the video playback.

▶ Volume Up—(Command-up arrow) Increase the volume.

▶ Volume Down—(Command-down arrow) Decrease the volume.

▶ Mute—(Command-K) Mute the sound.

▶ Closed Captioning—(Option-Command-T) Display captioning on DVDs for which it is available. (It can be set to appear either over the video as it plays or in a separate window under the Closed Captioning item of the Controls menu.)

▶ Eject—(Command-E) Eject the current DVD.

When fast-forwarding or rewinding, the view is displayed at an accelerated rate. Use the Scan Rate option under the Controls menu to set the speed to two, four, or eight times faster than normal.

These useful commands are available under the Go menu for DVD Player or through key commands:

▶ DVD Menu—(Command-`) Stop playback and load the menu for the active DVD.

▶ Previous Chapter—(Right arrow) Skip to the previous chapter on the DVD.

▶ Next Chapter—(left arrow) Skip to the next chapter on the DVD.

DVD Player Preferences

The preferences for DVD Player are split into four sections. The Player pane, shown in Figure 7.9, enables you to set how DVD Player reacts on system startup and insertion of a DVD. You can also choose the viewer size, whether to enable closed captioning when muted, and whether to mute audio when connecting to an audio or video chat in iChat, an application discussed in Chapter 16, "Using iChat AV."

FIGURE 7.9
Change how DVD
Player is activated
and the size of the
viewing window.

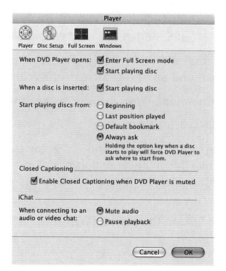

The Disc Setup pane contains settings for default language and the option to enable DVD@ccess, which allows DVD Player to recognize and react to embedded hot spots that link to Internet Web sites. You can also change audio output settings.

The Full Screen pane allows you to set a viewer size (maximum, normal, half, or current) and to decide whether the viewer can be resized. Options are also available for dimming other windows while DVD Player is active, remaining in full screen when DVD Player is inactive, and disabling the menu bar (kiosk mode) so that viewers can't exit the program.

If you disable the menu bar, you can exit the DVD Player by ejecting the DVD.

By the Way

The Windows pane controls whether the controller fades away or just disappears when it is hidden and turns on and off status information, which appears while a movie is playing. You can also choose the color and transparency of these messages, as well as the color and transparency of closed captioning.

Gradual fade of the controller upon hiding and transparent text are features enabled through the use of Quartz Extreme, which allows some graphics cards to take some of the graphics-processing load off Mac OS X.

By the Way

Summary

In the first half of this chapter, you learned to use QuickTime, both as a plug-in for your Web browser that can be used to view movies online and as a standalone player that runs on your desktop. In the last half, we looked at DVD Player, which allows you to view DVDs on your desktop.

CHAPTER 8

Working with Address Book, Keychain Access, iSync, and Ink

Chapter 6, "Using Calculator, Stickies, Preview, and TextEdit," and Chapter 7, "Using QuickTime and DVD Player," explored several basic applications that come with OS X. This chapter continues in that vein. However, the applications discussed here can be considered "helper" applications because they typically work with other applications rather than run on their own. Address Book and Keychain Access store information that other programs can access. iSync synchronizes information between different computers—for example, it can be used to synchronize Address Book between your work and home computers. Finally, Ink allows you to interact with your computer and applications by writing rather than typing; note, however, it does require additional hardware to accomplish this.

Address Book

The Mac OS X Address Book is more than a simple contact manager or a mailing label printer. It is a systemwide database that stores all your contact information and is accessible from other applications that require you to "contact people." So, you, ask, what are these "other applications"; email is the only the place where it could be useful, right? Wrong. Address Book data is available in the Safari Web browser, the search utility Sherlock, the scheduling program iCal, your system's Fax function, and the instant messaging program iChat! A properly maintained Address Book can organize your data and streamline how you use your computer.

Using Address Book

The main Address Book window, shown in Figure 8.1, has two view modes—Card and Column view and Card Only view. To toggle between them, use the View buttons at the upper left. You will do most of your work with Address Book in Card and Column view. The Card Only view displays only a single contact at a time, making the usefulness debatable.

FIGURE 8.1
The Address Book,
shown here in Card
and Column view,
keeps track of your
contact information
with a simple
uncluttered
interface.

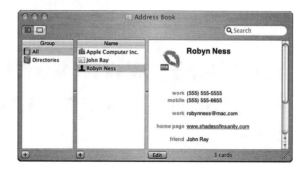

The Card and Column view displays a three-column view of the Address Book with these columns:

▶ Group—A list of all the groups of contacts on your system. There three pre-defined groups: All, which shows the contents of all your group, Directories (LDAP Servers), and Last Import, which contains the last card/cards you imported via LDAP or from an external source.

▶ Name/Directory—The contacts (or available directory servers) within the selected group.

▶ Contact Card—A "business" card view of the currently selected contact.

At the bottom of the Group and Name columns are "+" buttons that add new Groups and Contacts to the system. Under the Contact Card panel is an Edit button that switches the current contact to Edit mode.

You can browse through your contacts much like using the Finder's column view. Choose a group, choose a contact within the group, and then view their information in the contact panel. The search field at the top of the Address Book window searches the currently selected group for a string of your choice.

Working with Cards

Because Address Book maintains contact information, the base "unit" of information is a single person or organization stored in an Address Book card. Address cards can store multiple addresses, phone numbers, and contact information for an individual, making it unnecessary to maintain multiple cards for a single person.

Adding/Editing Cards

To add a card, select the group that should contain the contact and then click the + button below the Name column. This opens a blank card in the right column where you can type what information you want to save.

There are fields for name, work and mobile phone, email address, home page, names of friends/relatives, AIM handle, and addresses, as well as a space at the bottom for notes. You can tab between fields or click into the ones you want to insert. You can add as much or as little information as you want, but an email address is required if you plan to use the card with Mail and AIM handle for iChat.

> vCards are a standard across multiple platforms and are often included in email messages. You can drag vCard attachments from within the Mail application into Address Book to add them.

By the Way

If the label to the left of the field doesn't match the information you want to add, you can adjust it by clicking the up/down arrows icon. This opens a pop-up menu with several common labels as well as an option to customize. In some cases, such as adding a phone number, you may want (or need) to add multiple values. When you're editing a field that supports multiple entries, plus and minus buttons appear to the left of the field. Clicking plus adds a new field of the same type; minus removes the field. To add completely new fields, choose Card, Add Field; then select from any of the available fields.

> The default template for creating new cards can be changed in the Address Book application preferences, or by choosing Card, Add Field, Edit Template.

Did you Know?

In the upper-left corner of the card column is the card picture well. If you want to add a custom picture, you can paste it into the well, or double-click the picture well (Card, Choose Custom Image) to open a window where you can drag an image file and zoom/crop the image, or even take a video snapshot. To clear a custom image, choose Card, Clear Custom Image.

When you're finished adding information, click the Edit button again, and the unfilled fields disappear.

To edit a card you've already created, select the name of the individual from the Name column and click the Edit button below the card column, or choose Edit, Edit Card (Command-L) from the menu.

To delete a card, select it and press the Delete key on your keyboard or choose Edit, Delete Person from the menu. You are asked to confirm the action before it is carried out.

Special Card Settings and Functions

When editing a card, a few special properties and functions can be applied. The first—Card, Make this My Card—sets the current card so that it represents *you*, the owner of the active system account. Your Address Book card is represented with a "head" icon in Address Book listings, unlike other cards.

A second property, set by choosing Card, This Is a Company, or by clicking the Company check box when editing a card swaps the Company and Contact information in the card display and alters the card icon in the listing to resemble a small building.

If you are displeased with the first/last name ordering in a card, choose Card, Swap First/Last Name, and they will be reversed in the card view. To reset to the default ordering, choose Card, Reset First/Last Name to Default.

A final option, Card, Merge Cards (Command-|) is useful if you've accidentally created multiple cards for the same person. You can merge information in two or more cards by selecting them in the Name column and then choosing the Merge Cards option.

Viewing Cards

When a card is not in edit mode, many of the labels in the card view provide links to useful functions. Clicking a "friend/relation" name displays the option to jump to that person's contact card, if it exists.

A unique feature Apple provides is the ability to display a Web-based map of any street address in your Address Book. Click the label to the right of any address field and choose Map Of from the pop-up menu. Your Web browser opens to a map of the location. You can also choose to copy the URL of the map, or copy an address label form of the address to the Clipboard.

If you have the Apple BlueTooth adapter, you can click the button in the Address Book to locate paired BlueTooth phones within range. You can then click a phone number within an address card and choose Dial from the pop-up menu to dial your phone.

In addition, BlueToothpaired phones automatically trigger Address Book to display the Address card (if available) for incoming calls and provide the ability to answer the call or send the call to voice mail.

Adding/Editing Groups

You can arrange your cards into your own custom groups, which, besides creating organization, can be used to send email to a common collection of people.

> If you have many cards to work with but no need for mailing to custom groups, you can enter keywords in the Notes section of the cards and then use the search function, located at the upper right of the Card and Column view, to see only those cards that contain your chosen keyword.

Did you Know?

To create a group, click the "+" button under the Group column and type a name for it. You can then start adding contacts to the group, either by adding them using the method discussed previously, or by selecting another contact group (such as All) and dragging contacts from the Name column to populate the new group. You can hold down the Command key to select more than one addressee at a time.

> The "+" button is a common feature in many of Apple's applications, including iPhoto and Safari, and is used to create a new collection. The column arrangement and method of dragging items into a newly created collection also carries over to these applications.

Did you Know?

Distribution Groups

An Address Book group can be used with Mail to send messages to a group of people simultaneously by dragging the group into the Address field in Mail. When used in this manner, the group is considered a *distribution group*. All Address Book groups can be used as distribution groups, but before using them, you may want to choose which email address each contact in the group will use when the message is sent. To do this, highlight your group in Address Book; then choose Edit, Edit Distribution List. A window similar to that in Figure 8.2 appears.

Use the pop-up menu in the upper-right corner of the Distribution List window to switch all contacts in the group to their work, home, or other addresses. To switch on a person-by-person basis, simply click the correct contact address in the list to highlight it.

FIGURE 8.2
Choose the address to use if a group is used to send email.

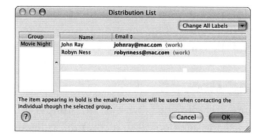

When all the correct addresses are selected, click OK. You can now use your Address Book group as a mailing distribution list.

Printing Lists and Mailing Labels

Built into OS X 10.3's Address Book is the capability to easily print labels. To print labels, first select the group you want to print; then Choose File, Print. Address Book displays the dialog box shown in Figure 8.3.

FIGURE 8.3
Print lists and mailing labels with ease.

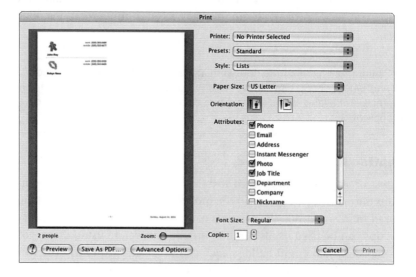

Use the Style pop-up menu to choose between a mailing label layout and a simple list of names. When printing lists, as shown in Figure 8.3, you'll be given the option of choosing which attributes are printed in the list and what font to use.

Mailing labels provide settings for controlling your paper layout under the Layout Button bar option and includes several label standards, such as Avery. The Label button displays settings for choosing between which Address Book addresses are printed (Home or Work), sorting, font options, and an image that can be printed beside each address.

Make your setting choices and view the results in the preview on the left side of the window; then click Print to start printing.

Preferences

The Address Book preferences, accessible from the application menu, are used to choose sorting display and vCard preferences and to configure LDAP servers for use with the Address Book directory services.

General

The General pane, shown in Figure 8.4, allows you to choose the Display order for names (first or last name first), how the contacts should be sorted, the Address format, and the display font.

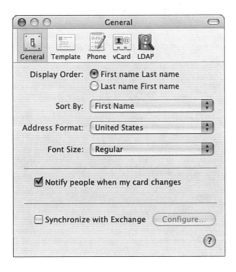

FIGURE 8.4
The Address Book General Preferences.

To automatically send updates that are made to your personal card to a group of people in your Address Book, click the Notify People When My Card Changes check box. When you change any piece of information in your card, you will be prompted if you want to email the update to your contacts. You can choose the groups to send email to, and type a brief message to them, as shown in Figure 8.5.

FIGURE 8.5
Have Address Book
automatically notify
other people when
updates take place.

Template

The Template preferences pane provides control over the "default" Address Card format. Using the same controls available when creating a card entry, you can create your own custom template, as shown in Figure 8.6.

FIGURE 8.6
Define a custom
Card template.

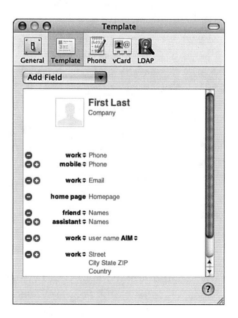

Use the Add Field pop-up menu to add fields to the template.

Phone

The Phone preferences pane, shown in Figure 8.7, enables you to create and choose custom phone layouts and activate/deactivate automatic formatting of phone numbers in Address Book.

FIGURE 8.7
Add or choose custom telephone formats.

Use the Formats menu to choose from one of the predefined formats, or click the disclosure button to display the format editor (visible in Figure 8.7). To use the format editor, Click "+" to add a new format and type the number format as you want it to appear, substituting the pound (#) sign for the actual phone number digits.

Use the "-" button to remove phone number formats or the Edit button to edit existing formats. The formats can also be dragged in the listing to change their order.

vCard

vCards are a common way to attach contact information to email in a standardized format. Use the vCard pane to choose the default format of your own vCard "address card."

> To attach your own vCard, you can drag your card from the Address Book into a new message window in most email programs.

By the Way

You can also ensure the privacy of your personal card by enabling the Enable Private 'Me' Card option. This keeps everything but your *work* contact data from being exported with your card.

Use the Export Notes in vCards option to include the notes field when exporting cards. Because notes are typically personal information, they are not exported by default.

LDAP

LDAP (Lightweight Directory Access Protocol) defines a means of querying remote directory systems that contain personnel data. The Address Book can use LDAP server connectivity to retrieve contact information from network servers. This pane of the Address Book preferences is used to set up Address Book for LDAP queries. Speak to your network administrator if you want to know more about this option.

Keychain Access

Keeping track of passwords for email servers, file servers, Web sites, and other private information can be difficult. That's why Apple has included a security application called Keychain Access to make managing your collection of passwords and PIN numbers much easier.

Think of Keychain Access as a database of your most sensitive information, all accessible through your Mac OS X account password. The Keychain Access software automatically stores passwords from Keychain Access-aware applications such as Mail and the .Mac Internet services. That means that you don't have to enter your password every time you check your email.

Not all applications have been constructed to interact with Keychain Access. In those instances, you can manually add your own passwords or even store credit card information for convenient lookup when you need it.

Automated Access

If you open Keychain Access from the Utilities folder within the system Applications folder, you can see the contents of your default keychain. For an account that has set up email and enabled the Safari Web browser to store Web logins, the Keychain Access window should look similar to the one shown in Figure 8.8.

The obvious question is, "How did these items get here?" They were added by Mac OS X applications. Typically, when an application wants to store something in Keychain Access, you're given the option of storing it. Choosing the Remember Name and Password option automatically adds the entered password to the default keychain. Over time, your keychain could become populated with items, and you might not know it!

FIGURE 8.8
The Keychain Access window displays a list of accounts with stored passwords.

Manual Access

You can manually add new information to a keychain (or view what's already there) through the Keychain Access program. Each item listed in the Keychain Access window can be viewed by selecting it in the upper pane.

> If Keychain Access is something you want easy access to, you can add a menu extra to your menu bar by selecting View, Show Status in Menu Bar from the menu in Keychain Access. A lock icon, open or locked, appears in the menu bar to show the status of your keychains, whether or not Keychain Access is running. Clicking it gives you options to lock or unlock all keychains and to launch the Keychain Access application.

Attributes

Two sections of information for each Keychain Access entry are Attributes and Access Control. The Attributes settings provide basic information about the stored item, as shown in Figure 8.8. You can also add any additional comments about the item by typing them in the Comments field. Check the Show Password button to display your password. To authorize revealing your saved password, you're prompted for your Keychain Access password.

When authorizing Show Password, you're asked for your password to access Keychain Access itself. At that time, you have the option to Allow Once, Always Allow, or Deny Permission. Because Keychain Access isn't listed as having unlimited access to stored items, it asks each time it needs to retrieve the information unless you choose the Always Allow option.

Access Control

When a Keychain Access-aware application wants to access information from your keychain, it must first make sure that the keychain is unlocked. Your default Mac OS X keychain is automatically unlocked when you're logged in, making its passwords accessible to the applications that stored them.

You can manually lock or unlock the entire keychain by clicking the Lock button in the toolbar of the Keychain Access window. After the keychain is locked, you're asked to enter a password—which, for the default keychain, is your account password—whenever an application attempts to access keychain information. Also, the details of keychain items within Keychain Access won't be shown until a password is entered. (However, the name of the items and when they were created are displayed.)

The Access Control settings, shown in Figure 8.9, enable the user to choose which applications can use information from Keychain Access. Click Allow All Applications to Access This Item to allow access the resource with no user interaction. If you prefer to monitor use of your passwords by programs on your system, click the Confirm Before Allowing Access radio button to be prompted to decrypt each password when needed.

You can further specify how individual applications deal with passwords in the Always Allow Access by These Applications section. Use the Add and Remove buttons to add and remove applications from the list.

Adding New Entries to Keychain Access

New pieces of information can be added to Keychain Access by clicking the Password button in the toolbar in the Keychain Access window or by choosing New Password Item from the New submenu of the File menu. This action opens a new window, shown in Figure 8.10, in which to enter the data to be stored.

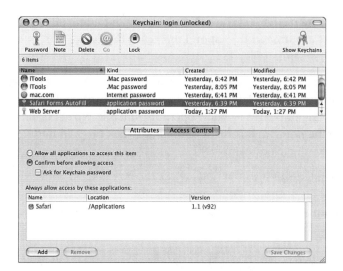

FIGURE 8.9
Access Control enables you to choose which applications can apply your passwords.

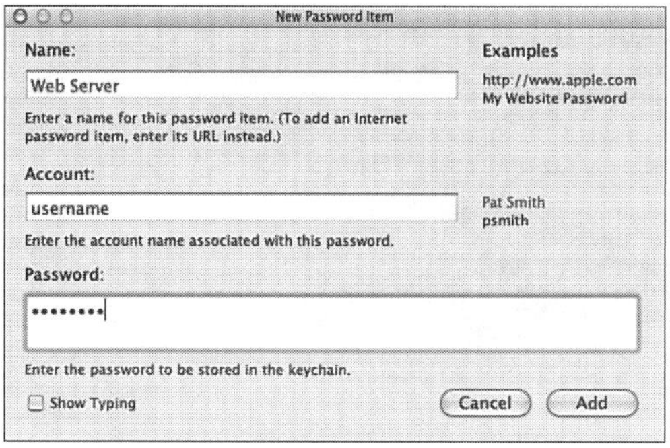

FIGURE 8.10
New items can easily be added manually to an existing keychain.

To add a new item, follow these steps:

1. Enter the name (or for password-protected Web sites, the URL) of the new item into the Name field.

2. Enter the account name associated with the data into the Account field.

3. Enter the account password into the Password field. By default, the password is hidden as you type. To display the password as it's typed, click the Show Typing check box.

4. When you've completed these fields, click Add.

To remove any item from Keychain Access (either automatically or manually entered), select its name in the list and then click the Delete icon or choose Edit, Delete from the menu.

In addition to adding new passwords to your keychain, you can also create Secure Notes. To do this, click the Note icon in the toolbar or choose File, New Secure Note from the menu. A new window opens in which to type your note. When you've typed the name and content of the note, click the Add button to save. The note is added to the list of items.

To view the contents of a secure note, check the box labeled Show Note and enter your password for authorization—make sure that you are in the Attributes section of the Keychain Access window. You can then edit the note and save changes (see Figure 8.11).

FIGURE 8.11
Private information can be stored as a secure note within Keychain Access.

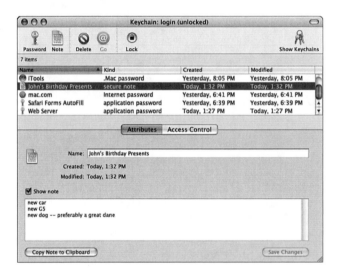

Adding and Managing Keychains

Each user has a default keychain that's unlocked with the system password, but you can have as many keychains as you want. Sensitive information can be placed into a secondary keychain with a different password so that someone with your account password won't have access to all your information.

To add a new keychain, do the following:

1. Choose File, New Keychain from the menu.

2. You are prompted for a name and save location for the keychain. The default save location is Library folder in your home folder. When you've set these options, click Create.

3. A dialog box appears, prompting you to enter and verify the password that unlocks the new keychain. (It's best to choose something different from your account password to prevent people who might gain access to your account from seeing your most sensitive information.)

4. Click OK.

To switch between different keychains, click the Show Keychains icon in the toolbar to reveal a drawer containing the available options, as shown in Figure 8.12.

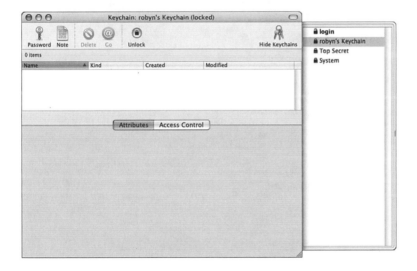

FIGURE 8.12
Choose a keychain from the tray—notice that a locked keychain shows nothing in the Attributes section until its password is entered.

iSync

Most people's lives extend beyond their home to their workplace (or vice versa). Information should be available wherever you go, on whatever device you use. To this end, Apple has created the iSync software. Since its initial introduction, iSync has grown to support dozens of mobile phones, Palm devices, your iPod, iCal, Safari, Address Book, and more.

If you have a .Mac account, no matter what Macintosh you're using, your critical information is only a "sync" away. (See Chapter 14, "Exploring the .Mac Membership," for more details about .Mac membership; see the section "Setting Up .Mac Synchronization" later in this chapter for how-to information.)

The iSync Interface

The iSync window, shown in Figure 8.13, provides control over what you're syncing and when you're syncing it. On the left side of the window are the devices (data sources) that have been "registered" with iSync, and on the right is the Sync Now button to start the synchronization process. Clicking a device icon in the iSync window opens a pane with all available synchronization settings for that device.

FIGURE 8.13
Devices to sync and a big shiny button.

Adding Portable Devices to iSync

To add devices such as iPods and PDAs to iSync, choose Devices, Add Device from the menu. Click Scan if nothing is initially detected. iSync scans for any iPods, PDAs, and Bluetooth-paired devices within the range of your computer, as shown in Figure 8.14.

By the Way

If you're a Palm user, you *must* have Palm Desktop 4.0 or later installed, and then install the iSync Palm Conduit (available at at the bottom of the page www.apple.com/isync/download) for iSync to work.

Pocket PC users can use the excellent The Missing Sync application in conjunction with iSync to synchronize their handheld devices with Mac OS X. (www.markspace.com/pocketpc.html)

FIGURE 8.14
Scan for other iSync capable devices.

Double-click the found devices to add them to the iSync window and "register" them with the iSync process. Choosing a registered device in the iSync window displays the synchronization options specific to that device. For example, Figure 8.15 shows sync options for my iPod.

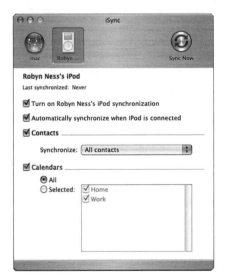

FIGURE 8.15
Synchronization options are unique for each device.

For the iPod, you can choose to automatically synchronize each time your iPod is connected as well as choose what contacts and calendars should be synced. The options for your devices are likely to vary from what you see here. It simply depends on the type of device and the features it supports.

Setting Up .Mac Synchronization

By default, only one item is available for synchronizing—your .Mac account. This is a "special" device in that it provides a holding area for multiple computers to send and then retrieve information. If you have a .Mac account, it can be used with each of your Macintosh workstations to synchronize Bookmarks and other data. If you do not have a .Mac account, you will *not* be able to synchronize machines and devices over the network.

By the Way

For each computer that will be synchronized through the .Mac account, you must "register" that computer with the iSync service. To do this, first make sure that you've successfully added your .Mac account information to the .Mac control panel (discussed in Chapter 14). Assuming that your .Mac settings are in order, highlight the .Mac icon, click the Register button, choose a unique name for the computer, and click the Continue button (see Figure 8.16).

Configuring Device Sync Options

Each time you register a device, you must also choose what happens on the first "sync"—whether information should be copied from the computer to the device, or whether information should be merged with what is currently stored on .Mac.

For the .Mac sync options, you also can choose what items are being synchronized (Safari Bookmarks, Address Book Contacts, and iCal information).

At the bottom of the .Mac sync pane are a list of all computers that have been registered with through iSync with your .Mac account. You can select a computer in the list and click the Unregister Selected Computer button to remove it.

By the Way

Removing a selected computer does not delete any information from it. It *does* effectively disable its capability to sync until it is re-registered, but you won't lose any information.

FIGURE 8.16
Register each computer to be synchronized with .Mac.

To automatically synchronize your chosen items with .Mac every hour, click the Automatically Synchronize Every Hour check box. Click the .Mac icon to close the configuration pane.

Synchronizing

After choosing the sync options for each of the devices you want to use, click the Sync Now button, or choose Devices, Sync Now (Command-T) from the menu to synchronize all of them. iSync often displays a confirmation message with the changes it is about to make, allowing you to stop or apply the modifications (this warning is configurable in the iSync Preferences). Figure 8.17 shows the synchronization process.

FIGURE 8.17
iSync gathers information from your devices and software and then synchronizes it.

After a few seconds, all your devices will have a copy of the latest calendars and contacts.

Safety Features

To safeguard your data (in case of accidental or malicious synchronizing), Apple built in a few features that can help you recover from an "oops" situation. Using Devices, Revert to Last Sync, you can revert to the information stored on your computer *before* the last time it was synchronized.

Perhaps even more useful is the ability to take a "snapshot" of your computer's synchronization data using Devices, Backup My Data. You can do this at any time—presumably when you have your computer setup in a critical state that you wouldn't want to lose. To revert to the backed-up state if something goes awry, you simply choose File, Revert To Backup.

Resetting All Devices

The Devices, Reset All Devices option can come in handy in two situations.

If you've been working on your computer and have it configured the way you want it and *don't* want to sync for fear of messing up your settings, Reset All Devices allows you to override the information stored on your other devices with what is contained on your local computer.

Alternatively, if your local machine isn't the way you want it, and you don't want its configuration to mess up anything else, you can use Reset All Devices to reset its data with what is currently stored in your .Mac account, overriding anything that would have been synchronized with other devices.

The iSync Log

To view a log of what iSync has done, when it was done, and the result, choose Window, Show Logs. The log window, shown in Figure 8.18, appears.

Use the disclosure triangles in front of each log line to expand or collapse details about each entry.

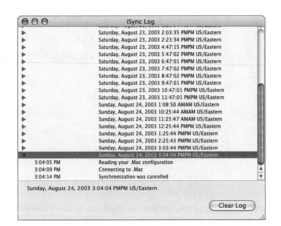

FIGURE 8.18
iSync logs each synchronization.

Preferences

The iSync application preferences, shown in Figure 8.19, allow you to add an iSync menu extra to your menu bar. From the menu extra, you can synchronize your devices, open iSync, or view any warnings that occurred during the last synchronization process.

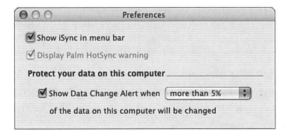

FIGURE 8.19
Use the iSync preferences to add a menu extra to your menu bar.

Within the preferences, you can also choose the amount of data that has to change for iSync to display a warning message.

Ink

Mac OS X includes a handwriting recognition feature called Ink, which enables you to write input to any application including word processing programs, email applications, and even Web browsers. Built on Apple's Recognition Engine, Ink requires no special alphabet, although people with messy handwriting might require practice to understand how Ink interprets characters. Figure 8.20 shows Ink being used with Mail, Mac OS X's built-in email program.

FIGURE 8.20
Ink enables you to set your keyboard and mouse aside.

To run Ink, you must have a Wacom graphics tablet with a USB connector, or another compatible graphics tablet. You must also install the Wacom tablet driver for Mac OS X, available for download from www.wacom.com/. A wizard guides you through the installation steps. When finished, restart your computer. (If you need more information about downloads or software installation, read Chapter 9, "Installing Additional Software.")

When a graphics tablet is plugged into one of your computer's USB ports, the Ink icon shows up under the Hardware section of System Preferences. The Ink preferences, shown in Figure 8.21, give you options to turn handwriting recognition on or off and to change several settings.

If you plan to use Ink regularly, check the Show Ink In Menu Bar check box in the Settings pane of the Ink preferences. This adds a menu item from which you can turn Ink on and off as needed. It also allows you to toggle Allow Me to Write Anywhere on and off, which determines whether you write directly into applications or use the InkPad, which we'll discuss next, as an intermediary.

FIGURE 8.21
To activate Ink, you need to go to the Ink preferences in the System Preferences.

Turning on handwriting recognition launches the InkBar, a toolbar that floats on top of all other application windows. From the InkBar, you can toggle between handwriting recognition mode and pointer mode, select common menu command and keyboard shortcut characters, and open the InkPad, as shown in Figure 8.22. With the InkPad open, you can switch between the writing and drawing modes using the buttons at the lower left.

FIGURE 8.22
InkPad appears below the InkBar to provide a space for you to write or draw.

The text or drawings you create in InkPad can be inserted into other documents. Simply create the content of your choice in the workspace and click the Send button to add it to the active document at the current insertion point. For instance, when you finish composing the text of an email message, you could sign your name in the drawing view of InkPad and insert your signature at the bottom of your message. Note, however, that you cannot insert pictures into applications that don't support image display.

Although InkPad enables you to compose your additions before you add them to a document, you can also write directly into a program. To add text directly to an application, touch the stylus to the tablet to open a writing space with guiding lines in which to form characters and begin writing words. An example of this is shown in Figure 8.20. If a writing space doesn't appear, try touching the stylus to the graphics tablet in a different place. Because your stylus can also act as a mouse, some areas of the screen, such as window controls or menus, activate commands rather than opening a writing space.

Although Ink doesn't require you to learn special letter forms, you must write linearly—as if you were using paper—instead of writing letters on top of one another as you would on a personal digital assistant (PDA). When you pause, your markings are converted to text at the top of the writing space. To correct a mistake, draw a long horizontal line from right to left and pause to see the last character disappear. If you have larger sections to delete, switch to pointer mode in the InkBar, select the part you want to redo, and switch back to writing mode to try again.

By the Way

Some applications that don't use standard Mac OS X text controls behave unpredictably with Ink's text recognition. If you're using an application in which spaces don't appear between words as needed, try writing your content in InkPad and using Send to insert it in the other application.

Ink Preferences

Now that you know a little about what Ink is and how it works, let's take a closer look at the Ink preferences panes. The following adjustments can be made under the Settings section (shown previously in Figure 8.21):

▶ My Handwriting Style Is—Move the slider to describe your handwriting as closely spaced, widely spaced, or somewhere in between.

▶ Allow Me To Write—Choose whether you can write to all programs or only InkPad.

- ▶ InkPad Font—Set a font for InkPad. For greatest accuracy, Apple recommends keeping the font set to Apple Casual, which contains letter shapes that are the most similar to those recognized by Ink so that you can model your writing after it.

- ▶ Show Ink Window—Brings up the Ink window when Ink is activated.

- ▶ Show Ink in Menu Bar—Adds a menu extra to turn Ink on and off.

Clicking the Options button opens a sheet window with additional handwriting recognition options, including the amount of delay before writing is converted to type, how much the stylus must move before a stroke is recorded, how long the pen must be held still to act as a mouse, and several other options. If you change your mind about configurations you've made in either the Settings pane or the Options sheet, choose Restore Defaults to revert to the originals.

The Gestures pane displays shapes that have special meaning in Ink, such as vertical or horizontal spaces, tab, and delete. Click on an item to see both a demonstration of drawing the shape and a written description of it. You can also activate or deactivate Gesture actions using the check box in front of each item. Apple recommends that you provide extra space in front of a Gesture shape and exaggerate the ending stroke so that the system does not confuse it with a letter.

The Word List pane enables you to add uncommon words that you use frequently. Ink uses a list of common words to help decipher people's input. If you come across a word that Ink doesn't know, click the Add button and type the new word in the text box.

Summary

In this chapter, we explored four "helper" applications—Address Book, Keychain Access, iSync, and Ink—that work with other applications rather than run on their own. Address Book integrates with several applications that use contact information, whereas Keychain Access stores private information (such as passwords) securely. iSync synchronizes information between different computers and portable devices. With the addition of a compatible graphics tablet, Ink can be used as an input device in place of your keyboard and mouse.

CHAPTER 9

Installing Additional Software

Although Mac OS X comes with many programs and tools offering a wide range of features, at some point you'll probably want to add additional software to your system. In this chapter, we talk about how to install additional software in Mac OS X. (Even though software installation is not difficult, Mac OS X supports several different methods of doing so.) We'll also look at some software issues for multiuser systems and present some interesting applications available for your system.

Software Sources

When it comes to expanding your collection of software, your first question might be "What are my options?" You'll be pleased to hear that, despite being a relatively new operating system, Mac OS X already has many available applications. The only tricky part is knowing where to find them.

Fortunately, a number of good online libraries feature Mac OS X software. (If you need to learn more about how to get online or how use a Web browser, those topics are discussed in Chapter 11, "Connecting to the Internet," and 12, "Using Safari.")

The following sites present the latest and greatest Mac OS X programs available for download or on CD-ROM (by purchase):

- ▶ VersionTracker—www.versiontracker.com/macosx/—Updated continually, VersionTracker's Web site is often the first to carry new Mac OS X software. As a nearly comprehensive catalog, it also works as a handy reference guide. To find what you need, just type the name or a keyword for a product into the search field.

- ▶ MacUpdate—www.macupdate.com/index.php?os=macosx—Similar to VersionTracker, MacUpdate lists a broad selection of Mac software.

- ▶ Mac OS X Apps—www.macosxapps.com/—This site features in-depth discussions about new software and uses.

▶ Apple's Mac OS X Downloads—www.apple.com/downloads/macosx/—
Although less up-to-the-minute than the previous two sites, Apple's software
compendium is well documented and easily navigated.

Later in this chapter, we recommend several interesting applications on these sites
that you might want to try.

Downloading and Installing Software

Although there's no single installation technique for all software available for the
Mac OS X, let's look at two common methods. Obviously, you should read the
documentation that comes with your software if you want to be certain of the
results, but for those who are anxious to double-click, this section offers a basic
description of what to expect.

By the Way

> If you would rather purchase your software from a mail-order or in-store vendor, just
> make sure to read the product information to ensure compatibility with Mac OS X, or
> with Mac OS 9 if you need to run the application in Classic mode, as discussed in
> Chapter 4, "Working with Windows Folders, Files, and Applications." The installation
> process for disc images (explained later in this section) still applies.

Go to one of the sites mentioned previously and look for trial versions or freeware
that you want to try. After you locate something interesting, you're ready to
begin:

1. On the software download page, determine which version your system
   requires and click that link. Remember to choose a version that's made for
   Mac OS X.

2. As your system begins downloading your selection, a Downloads window,
   similar to that shown in Figure 9.1, appears on your screen.

FIGURE 9.1
In Safari and most
Web browsers, you
can monitor the
status of an item
as it downloads.

3. When the download is finished, several icons appear on your desktop, similar to Figure 9.2. The icon with the extension .dmg represents a special file that has been encoded as a disk image for easy storage and download. Other common types of download files end with a .gz, .zip, or .sit extension and contain the files in encoded or compressed form. We'll talk more about this in the "Opening Compressed Files with StuffIt Expander" section later in this chapter.

4. The final installation step may differ, depending on the application you're working with. Here are the three major variations:

If a folder icon appears on your desktop, you must open it to reach the application file. The folder also usually contains a ReadMe file that explains what to do next. This kind of install exists only for very small programs. (If you download new fonts, as discussed in Chapter 20, "Printing, Faxing, and Working with Fonts," they often appear in this way.)

If a file icon with the extension .pkg or .mpkg appears, double-clicking starts the Apple Installer, which provides a simple step-by-step guide to installation.

Finally, if a disk image icon appears, as with the Camino disk icon shown second from the bottom in Figure 9.2, double-clicking it mounts the disk image, which you can then double-click to open a Finder window containing instructions. Disk images have the .dmg file extension.

For example, when installing the Camino Web browser, opening the disk icon results in the screen shown in Figure 9.3, which contains an application icon for you to drag to the Applications folder on your hard drive.

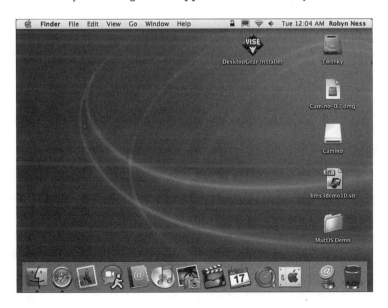

FIGURE 9.2
When you download software, several new icons appear on the desktop. (There are three different files: one disk image [.dmg], one compressed as a .sit file, and one in VISE format, which means it is packaged to use an installation wizard.)

When you've placed the file or folder where you want it, your application is ready for use. You can drag all the files that appeared on your desktop during download and installation to the Trash.

FIGURE 9.3
To install Camino, simply drag the application icon to a folder in a Finder window—preferably the Applications folder.

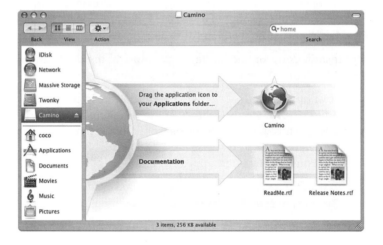

By the Way

You cannot eject a disk image from your computer while running the software contained on that disk.

If you try to drag a disk image to the Trash and receive an error message, it is likely that you didn't copy the contents of the disk image to your hard drive and are instead working off the disk image. To be able to eject the disk image, you need to close the application, and then copy the disk image to the Mac OS X drive.

To uninstall most software, simply locate the application file or folder and drag it to the Trash. Under Mac OS X, you should find most application folders in the systemwide Applications folder.

Opening Compressed Files with StuffIt Expander

You might have noticed that the downloaded file launches another application whose icon appears briefly in the Dock, as shown in Figure 9.4. That application is StuffIt Expander.

You use StuffIt for work with compressed files. Because applications tend to be large files, they come in a compressed form that takes up less space and makes downloading them faster and easier. These compressed files are also referred to as *archive files* because they're compact and easily stored.

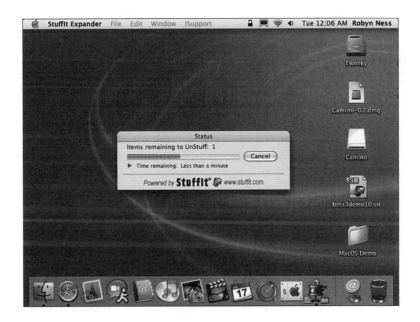

FIGURE 9.4
When the download is finished, StuffIt Expander goes to work.

Compression can be done in several different ways. Mac OS X can compress and uncompress .zip files, which is a common format used on Windows machines. (Recall that you can "zip" a file or folder using the Archive option of the Action menu in the Finder window, as discussed in Chapter 4.) It also can handle the same methods used on the Macintosh system for the past decade, including .sit (StuffIt) files. In addition, it supports Unix standards, such as .tar and .gz files.

To install applications that come as archive files, you must return them to their original state. Recovering a full-sized file from its archive file is known as *extraction*. That's where StuffIt Expander, a tool included with Mac OS X, comes into play.

StuffIt Expander uncompresses most common archive types and makes it simple for anyone to start downloading software. Most of the time, StuffIt Expander opens automatically when it's needed and leaves uncompressed folders on the desktop along with the original archive file.StuffIt Expander is located on your system at Applications/Utilities/StuffIt Expander. You might never need to start it manually, but you can configure a number of settings in its Preferences dialog box to control actions, such as how StuffIt deals with files after extraction.

Software Considerations in a Multiuser System

Mac OS X is a multiuser system. When it comes to installing software, this seemingly small detail really matters. For one thing, not all users might have the same privileges on the system. When you set up user accounts, as will be explained in Chapter 33, "Sharing Your Computer with Multiple Users" you have the option to prevent others from modifying the system in any way. That includes installing additional software.

Also, when you install applications, keep in mind that other users don't necessarily have access to your home directory. If you install a large application in your home directory, you might be the only person who can use it, which could lead to other users installing copies of this same application on the same machine. To best utilize disk space and resource sharing, major applications should be installed in the system's Applications folder or in a subdirectory of Applications rather than inside your home directory.

One other issue: Be sure to read your software license agreements regarding operation by multiple users. If an application is licensed for only a single user (rather than a single computer), it should not be placed in the Applications folder where other users of your system can have access.

Some Software Suggestions

For the rest of the chapter, we look at some interesting applications available for Mac OS X. These programs have been selected based on their unique features and immediate availability (either in full or demo form) over the Internet.

Although we recommend the following software, keep in mind that many other fine programs are available, and that number grows daily. The following should serve only as a starting point for exploring the possibilities.

Web Browsing Applications

Even before Mac OS X was released, developers were looking forward to exploiting its advanced networking, multitasking, and graphics capabilities. The following sections describe a few interesting applications. Some you might have heard of, whereas others are entirely new to the Mac platform.

Mozilla

Mozilla (www.mozilla.org) is a Web browser related to Netscape Communicator—in fact, it's the open source project from which recent versions of Netscape were developed. The Mozilla software developers emphasize standards compliance and stability, and their product includes many new features before they appear in Netscape. (A beta version of Camino, a browser related to Mozilla but built especially for Mac OS X, is also available. Figure 9.5 shows a sample photo.)

FIGURE 9.5
Camino is an attractive Web browser, made especially for OS X.

> *Open source* means that software is developed by a community of programmers and isn't owned by a specific company. Rather, open source software is meant to be distributed freely and improved by anyone who can make improvements.

By the Way

> *Beta software* is software that's in a public test phase—the quality of betas varies greatly, so you might not want to depend on beta software for work-related projects!

By the Way

OmniWeb

OmniWeb, by the Omni Group (www.omnigroup.com/), is an alternative Web browser that supports standards-compliant Web technologies. Omniweb will update you when the URL of a bookmarked site has changed. It also allows you to search your history files for any word you recall from a Web page so that you can find your way back to a site without knowing the name.

PDF Browser Plugin

If you've ever used a PC for Web browsing, you may have noticed that PDF documents open within the Web browser instead of downloading to the desktop as they do on the Mac. If you want this opportunity to preview PDF content in Safari (and several other Web browsers) before downloading, install the widely praised PDF Browser Plugin by Manfred Schubert. It's available at `www.schubert-it.com/pluginpdf/`.

Productivity Applications

Here are a few practical applications for your word processing, image editing, and computer programming needs.

Nisus Writer Express

Nisus Writer Express is a word processing program with an interface worthy of Mac OS X. Also, one of its special features is support for noncontiguous selection, so you can copy and paste bits and pieces of information easily. It's available for a free 30-day trial at `www.nisus.com/Express/`.

OmniGraffle 3

OmniGraffle 3, from the makers of OmniWeb (`www.omnigroup.com`), is a charting/diagramming program that you can use to draw organizational structures and flow charts. (It may not sound exciting, but it does these things so well!) Without a license, you're limited to use of 20 objects per document.

Graphic Converter X

If you've been looking for a program that can open and save images files of just about any format, Graphic Converter is for you. It's available as shareware from Lemke Software (`lemkesoft.com/en/graphcon.htm`).

Desktop "Helpers"

A host of small programs have been written to make working with your desktop more efficient. Here are a couple of the most well-loved.

- ▶ WindowShade X—If you find yourself double-clicking the title bars of windows expecting the window to collapse to a title bar as it did in OS 9, try WindowShade X from Unsanity (`www.unsanity.com`).

By the Way

WindowShade and Graphic Converter are *shareware*, which means that the developer makes software available for your use (at least in a limited trial) but requests a small payment in return. If you try any shareware applications and like them, paying the fee is the right thing to do!

▶ Drop Drawers X—Drop Drawers, available as shareware from Sig Software (www.sigsoftware.com/dropdrawers/), adds "drawers" to the edge of your screen where you can store notes, URLs, or files for easy access. Simply double-click their handles, and the drawers open. Figure 9.6 shows an example.

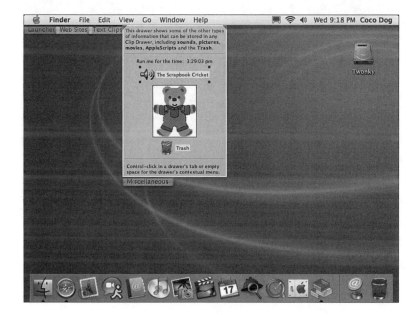

FIGURE 9.6
Add storage to your screen with Drop Drawers.

Games

If you're looking for recreation, try one of these:

▶ Burning Monkey Solitaire (www.freeverse.com/bms.mgi), available as shareware, offers several versions of the Solitaire card game, including Klondike, Freecell, and 52 Card Pick-up, delivered in an interface filled with taunting monkeys. A limited demo is available without purchase of a license code.

▶ Battle Cocoa (eng.osxdev.org/battlecocoa/), which was written especially for Mac OS X, is a smooth-playing Tetris clone with network play capacity.

▶ Enigmo, available as shareware from Pangea Software (www.pangeasoft. net/enigmo/), is a challenging puzzle/strategy game with a fun interface and catchy music. See Figure 9.7 for a glimpse. A limited demo is available without purchases of a license code.

FIGURE 9.7
The objective of Enigmo is to direct droplets of water (and sometimes fire) into containers using only the tools provided.

Screensavers

Mac OS X comes with several attractive screensavers, but many people delight in finding new and interesting ones. Spice up your system by downloading one of these excellent replacements:

▶ Mac OS X Screensavers 3.0 (www.epicware.com/macosxsavers.html) is a collection of popular screensavers that have been transplanted from another platform. Although several years old, this set is still pleasing to the eye.

▶ Neko.saver
(homepage.mac.com/takashi_hamada/Acti/MacOSX/Neko/index.html) turns one or more animated cats loose on your desktop to play, sleep, and scamper across your screen.

To install a screensaver, simply place its application file in the system folder Library/Screen Savers or in your own ~/Library/Screen Savers folder, depending on whether you want public or private access. After you've installed a new screen-saver, you still must choose it in the Screen Saver section of the Desktop & Screen Saver pane of the System Preferences to activate it.

Customizing Desktop Icons

In addition to downloading and installing new and interesting screensavers, you can customize your desktop by downloading and installing new icons for your files, folders, and applications—and even your hard drive icon. One popular source for free, custom icons is the Icon Factory (www.iconfactory.com/), which both develops and holds yearly open contests for new icon sets.

To customize an icon, start by locating a set of icons you like and downloading it. (The Icon Factory offers icons in a couple of different formats—be sure to download icons made for the Macintosh.) When downloaded, the icon set uncompresses with help from StuffIt Expander and is ready for use.

Next, open the folder containing the icon set, select the icon you want, and open the Info window for it by choosing Get Info from the Action menu at the top of the Finder window. When the Info window opens, select the icon displayed in the General section so that a highlight appears around it (as shown in Figure 9.8); then choose Edit, Copy from the menu.

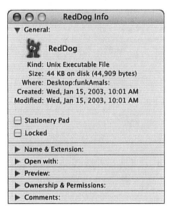

FIGURE 9.8
Select the icon in the General section of the Info window to copy it.

Then open another Finder window and navigate to a point where you can see the folder, file, or application icon you want to customize. Select the item and open the Info window as you did for the custom icon. Select the icon that appears in the General section of the Info window, and choose Edit, Paste from the menu.

The custom icon now appears in place of the standard icon both in the Info window and on your desktop. (Note, however, that items in the sidebar of the Finder window retain their standard icons.)

If you decide you'd rather use the standard icons, simply select the item with the icon you've switched, open the Info window, and select and delete the custom icon. The original icon will appear as if it had never been gone.

If you decide you want to replace all your system icons with one custom icon set, download CandyBar from the Icon Factory Web site. This application works with specially packaged icon sets to change all your icons at once.

Summary

In this chapter, we discussed the basics of adding new software—from finding what you need to downloading and installing it. Although we focused on easy-to-obtain, downloadable software, the issues we discussed also apply to purchased software discs. Remember that, in Mac OS X, it matters where you place new applications on your system if you want to share with other users of the computer.

CHAPTER 10

Using AppleWorks and Keynote

This chapter briefly introduces two additional applications from Apple that that you may want to purchase for use with Mac OS X. The first, AppleWorks, is a versatile application for office-type documents. The other, Keynote, is specifically for creating stylish presentations containing animations, graphs, and even QuickTime movies.

AppleWorks

AppleWorks is an all-in-one business solution that can act as a word processor, spreadsheet, database, drawing or painting program, and presentation developer.

By the Way

Rumor has it that an update of AppleWorks is on the way, but rumor doesn't say when it will arrive! The version discussed in this chapter 6.2; if your version doesn't match up, check to see whether it's a newer or later version.

By the Way

Figure 10.1 shows only one tab of the Starting Points window. Other sections include Assistants, which walks you through creation of various kinds of documents, and Templates, which offers several common document setups for you to base your document on.

Did you Know?

By default, all documents saved by AppleWorks end with the extension .cwk regardless of their type. However, when you open a document, a two-character code appears in its title bar to let you know which type of document it is. Those codes are WP for word processing, SS for spreadsheet, DB for database, DR for drawing, PT for painting, and PR for presentation.

FIGURE 10.1
Choose a type of
document from
the Starting Points
window.

Here are the available file types and their basic use:

▶ Word processing—Used to create documents containing mostly text. The Save-as options allow you to save files in formats compatible with several common word processors, including Microsoft Word.

▶ Spreadsheet—Provides a grid for entering data, especially numerical data or information best presented in rows and columns. Spreadsheet also performs calculations and develops charts from data. The Save-as options allow you to save files in formats compatible with several common spreadsheet programs, including Excel.

▶ Database—Allows you to create more structured collections of data than in a spreadsheet by setting up information fields and their associated types (text, number, data, and so on). The Save-as options allow you to save files as ASCII so that data can be read by other applications.

▶ Drawing—Allows you create lines, curves, and closed polygons (such as rectangles and ovals). The Save-as options allow you to save files in several common image formats, including JPEG, TIFF, and BMP, so that they can be opened by other applications.

By the Way

Technically, the difference between drawing and painting documents is about how the objects are created. In drawing programs, graphics are usually created with vectors, or formulas, for describing their shape. In painting programs, objects are usually composed of all the points inside them, each individually colored, which is called *bitmap*. The implications of this difference matter a bit later when we talk about the AppleWorks Tools window.

▶ Painting—Similar to drawing, except with finer control for filling objects with colors and patterns. As with drawing documents, the Save-as options allow you to save files in several common image formats so that they can be opened by other applications.

▶ Presentation—Allows you to build an onscreen presentation with text and images. Presentations created in AppleWorks are accessible only by AppleWorks.

If you export drawings or paintings in other image formats, you won't be able to edit those files as you would an AppleWorks file, so be sure to keep the original AppleWorks versions saved in case you have to make changes.

All the AppleWorks document types have a similar workspace, with minor variations between the options available in the Tools window, Button Bar, and at the top of the document window. A word processing window and supporting tools are shown in Figure 10.2. (If you don't see the Button Bar or Tools window, the Window menu gives the option to shown them.)

Button bar

Document window

Tools window

FIGURE 10.2
The basic AppleWorks interface.

You can change what controls appear in the Button Bar for each AppleWorks document type by choosing Button Bar under Preferences in the AppleWorks application menu.

AppleWorks Tools

Now let's a take a quick look at each of the tools in the Tools window, shown with labels in Figure 10.3.

By the Way

The Tools window can appear vertically, as it does in Figures 10.2 and 10.3, or horizontally. To switch between these states, simply drag the Tools window up to the menu bar (to switch to horizontal) or drag it down away from the menu bar (to switch to vertical).

FIGURE 10.3
The AppleWorks
Tools window.

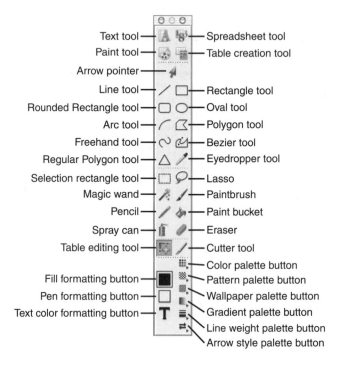

At the top of the Tools window are options used to bring in the functionality of another type of AppleWorks document to the current document:

- ▶ Text tool—Used to create a frame object in which to type text

- ▶ Spreadsheet tool—Used to create a frame object for spreadsheet data

- ▶ Paint tool—Used to create a frame object in which to use painting tools

- ▶ Table creation tool—Used to create a frame object to hold a table for tabular data.

The next set of tools consists of drawing tools:

▶ Arrow pointer—Used to select a frame object created with the Text, Paint, Spreadsheet, or Table Creation tools or any other objects in a window.

In the painting documents, the Arrow pointer doesn't allow you to select items after they are created. Instead, it switches to the Pencil tool. That's because a painting object is a bitmap, or conglomeration of points, rather than a single thing that can be selected.

▶ Line tool—Draws a straight line from the place where you first click to the point where you stop dragging your mouse cursor.

▶ Rectangle tool—Draws a rectangle from the place where you first click to the point where you stop dragging your mouse cursor.

▶ Rounded Rectangle tool—Draws a rectangle with rounded corners from the place where you first click to the point where you stop dragging your mouse cursor.

▶ Oval tool—Draws an oval from the place where you first click to the point where you stop dragging your mouse cursor.

▶ Arc tool—Draws an arc from the place where you first click to the point where you stop dragging your mouse cursor; the area "inside" the arc is filled with the currently selected color.

▶ Polygon tool—Draws adjoining line segments that start and stop on mouse clicks.

▶ Freehand tool—Draws a line following the path of your mouse cursor.

▶ Bezier tool—Draws a fluid curve that flexes with the position of your mouse; click to add points where the curve changes directions.

▶ Regular Polygon tool—Draws a regular polygon, or shape with uniform sides.

By the Way

To set the number of sides for a regular polygon while drawing, double-click the Polygon tool and then choose Edit, Polygon Sides from the menu. For painting, double-click the Polygon tool and enter the desired number of sides in the window that appears.

▶ Eyedropper tool—Samples an object's fill settings (drawing) or color (painting).

As you learned in an earlier note, objects in the painting mode are bitmap objects. The next set of tools is specifically for working with bitmap objects and applies only in painting documents or painting frames:

▶ Selection rectangle tool—Selects a rectangular area.

▶ Lasso—Selects an irregularly shaped object by shrinking to fit the border of enclosed objects.

▶ Magic wand—Selects contiguous regions of a specific color.

▶ Paintbrush—Creates a line along the cursor path in the current fill color and pattern; double-click the Paintbrush tool to change brush size and style.

▶ Pencil—Creates a fine line along the cursor path in the color and fill style currently selected.

▶ Paint bucket—Fills an area with the current fill color and pattern; select this tool and then click an object.

▶ Spray can—Creates a circle of "spray paint" in the current fill color (or a path by dragging your cursor); double-click the Spray can tool to change the size of the circle and the spray rate.

▶ Eraser—Removes the portions of objects it passes through.

> Double-clicking the Eraser tool erases everything on the canvas! If you do this accidentally, you can undo as long as you don't do anything else immediately after erasing.

Table-specific tools are next:

▶ Table editing tool—Allows you to edit cells or data in a table.

▶ Cutter tool—Allows you to split cells in a table; simply select this tool and drag your cursor through cells horizontally (to split into rows) or vertically (to split into columns).

The last grouping of tools controls the style of filled objects, the pen stroke around objects, and text color:

▶ Fill formatting button—Displays the current fill option; to set a fill, click the Fill formatting button and then click the color, pattern, wallpaper, or gradient palette buttons to choose a style.

▶ Pen formatting button—Displays the current pen stroke option; to set a stroke style, click the Pen formatting button and then click the color, pattern, line weight, or arrow style palette buttons to choose a style.

▶ Text color formatting button—Displays the current text color option; to set a text color, click the Text color formatting button and then click the color palette button to choose a color.

▶ Color palette button—Displays a palette of colors for object fill, pen stroke, and text color.

▶ Pattern palette button—Displays an assortment of geometric patterns for object fill and pen stroke.

▶ Wallpaper palette button—Displays an assortment of cute patterns for object fill.

▶ Gradient palette button—Displays an assortment of color and black/white gradient object fill options.

▶ Line weight palette button—Displays an assortment of sizes for pen stroke to outline object or draw lines.

▶ Arrow style palette button—Displays arrow options that can be applied when using the Line tool.

Now that we've run through AppleWorks' features and tools, let's take a quick look at Keynote.

Keynote

Although AppleWorks includes a presentation module, it doesn't have many of the advanced features people have come to expect in a professional-quality presentation application. Apple's response to this performance gap was the development of Keynote.

> Avid Mac fans know that Steve Jobs, CEO of Apple Computer, makes several public addresses each year to announce new products and computer advancements available from Apple. These events are known as *keynotes*.
>
> When Steve Jobs introduced Keynote during a keynote, he said it was originally written just for him to use for his keynote presentations.

By the Way

Keynote is a flexible tool for creating elegant presentations involving slide animations, charts and graphs, and even QuickTime movies. Figure 10.4 shows the
Keynote interface.

FIGURE 10.4
The Keynote inter-
face in Navigator
view.

Slide
organizer

Slide

Figure 10.4 shows the Keynote interface in Navigator view, with the current slide
and slide organizer visible. Under the View menu, you can choose to view only
the slide or to show the outline (all the text you've added to your slideshow) in
place of the slide organizer.

The Keynote Toolbar

Let's run through all the parts in the toolbar and their functions. (We'll discuss
them in order, left-to-right, as they appear in Figure 10.4.)

By the Way

When you aren't using the toolbar, you can hide it as you would the toolbar in a
Finder window—by clicking the clear toolbar button on the right side in the title bar!

The first grouping of buttons affects the slides in your presentation. Here are the buttons in this group:

▶ New—Adds a new slide after the currently selected slide.

▶ Delete—Removes the currently selected slide.

▶ Play—Plays the slideshow as it currently exists in full-screen mode. (To exit a slideshow and return to Keynote, press the Esc—or Escape key—on your keyboard.)

The next three items relate to slide setup and how you view the content of your presentation.

▶ Themes—Opens the Themes sheet window (shown in Figure 10.5), where you can choose a template to apply to your presentation.

The themes with the word "book" in their titles include a "cover," or title page, with a different look than the inside pages.

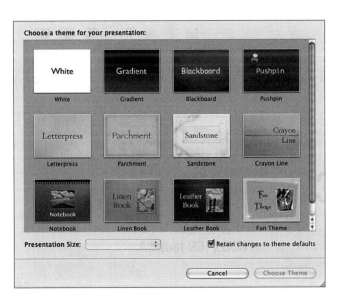

FIGURE 10.5
Choose a theme to give all the slides in your presentation a unified appearance.

▶ View—Changes the viewing mode between Navigator (shown in Figure 10.4), Outline, and Slide Only. You can also view the slide masters for each slide, which we'll discuss next, or open a Note pane at the bottom of the

Keynote window in which to type comments that won't appear inside the presentation.

▶ Masters—View a list of "master" slide layouts for the current theme. Masters show the placement and style of all the elements on a slide; you can edit the masters to change the appearance of your slideshow in a uniform manner.

The next group of buttons allows you to add objects and text to your slide:

▶ Text—Creates a text object. The text object appears in the center of the screen with the word "Text" in it; you can drag it where you want and double-click to type your own text.

▶ Shapes—Creates a shape object. The options are line, rectangle, circle, triangle, right triangle (which has one 90-degree angle), and arrow. Shapes appear in the center of the screen; you can drag them where you want and customize them by selecting them and dragging one of their selection handles.

You can resize, reshape, or change the direction a shape faces with the selection handles. To change a shape's direction, click on a selection handle and drag in the direction you want the shape to flip.

▶ Table—Creates a table in which to organize information. Resize tables as you would a shape. By default, tables are created three rows tall and three columns wide; we talk about customizing table dimensions in our look at the Table pane of the Inspector window later in this chapter.

▶ Chart—Opens a Chart Data Editor window in which to enter information you want to display in a graph. You can customize a chart using the Chart pane of the Inspector window, which we'll examine later in the chapter.

The next set of tools is used to position objects:

▶ Group—Used to link two or more objects that you want to treat as one item; this is useful if you've carefully positioned a set of shapes or text boxes and want to move them on the slide.

To select more than one object in a slide, hold down the Command key as you click.

▶ Ungroup—Used to separate objects that you've grouped.

▶ Front—Puts the selected object on top of all other objects in a slide while leaving it where it was positioned.

▶ Back—Puts the selected object underneath all other objects in a slide while leaving it where it was positioned.

The grouping of options at far right opens additional windows you may need to customize your slides:

▶ Inspector—Opens the Inspector window, which contains specific tools for various slide elements. (See the section "The Keynote Inspector," coming up next in this chapter, for more information.)

▶ Colors—Opens the Mac OS X Colors window, where you can choose colors to apply to objects and text.

▶ Fonts—Opens the Mac OS X Fonts window, as discussed in Chapter 20, "Printing, Faxing, and Working with Fonts."

Now, let's move on to the Inspector window, which contains additional sets of useful tools.

The Keynote Inspector Window

The Inspector window allows you to perform fine customization of elements in a presentation. After you've added a slide or an object (such as text, a shape, chart, or table), you can select it, open the Inspector window, and choose the pane containing the settings you want to customize.

> Make sure that you've opened the proper pane for the selected object, or none of the settings will be active. If all the settings appear grayed out, or faded, you may need to try a different object or different pane to make the changes you intend.

Watch Out!

The panes of the Inspector window are

▶ Slide Inspector—Allows you to change the slide master for a selected slide or choose whether title or slide body text are visible. The Background settings allow you to make the background a color, gradient, or image fill—or to leave the background empty. Under Transitions, decide which animation effect to use to transition from the current slide to the next one.

> You can change the background image of a selected slide by dragging any image file into the image well in the Background section of the Slide Inspector pane.

Did you Know?

▶ Graphic Inspector—Related to the characteristics of the object currently selected. The sections in this pane include Fill, Stroke, Shadow, and Opacity, which is used to change the transparency of an object to allow objects and the background behind it to show through.

▶ Metrics Inspector—Controls the size and placement of objects. The sections in this pane are File Info, Size, Position, Rotate, and Flip. (The Size and Position settings are set in pixels, which are a standard measure for onscreen graphics. Also, the Position is given by x (horizontal) and y (vertical) coordinates relative to the top-left corner of the slide.)

▶ Text Inspector—Controls color and alignment, spacing, and bullets and Numbering of text. (We'll take a closer look at bullets later in this chapter in the section "Using Keynote in Conjunction with PowerPoint.")

▶ Build Inspector—Controls animation effects used to make objects appear (Build In) and disappear (Build Out) from a slide. Sections, as shown in Figure 10.6, include Build Style, Order, Direction, Delivery, and Speed.

FIGURE 10.6
The Build pane allows you to make slide elements appear and disappear.

▶ Table Inspector—Changes the characteristics of tables. Use the Rows and Columns sections to set the number of each. Further customize table appearance using the Alignment, Cell Border, and Cell Background options.

▶ Chart Inspector—Changes the characteristics of a chart, including the chart type and details of data display.

▶ QuickTime Inspector—Sets various aspects of an inserted QuickTime movie, including repeat status and volume.

Using Keynote in Conjunction with PowerPoint

Before we end our look at Keynote, let's address some of the issues that arise when using Keynote in conjunction with another popular presentation-building application, Microsoft PowerPoint.

If you export a Keynote slideshow for use in PowerPoint, subtle changes in the look of the slides will be apparent, including in font sizes and letter spacing and the placement and alignment of objects. But for the most part everything will carry over so that you can edit and present your work in PowerPoint.

By the Way

If you export a slideshow for PowerPoint and then reopen it in Keynote, the slides will appear as they do PowerPoint, including slight differences in font and theme. If you want to restore the Keynote theme to its original state, you will need to choose the theme again from the themes sheet window. (If you use the menu option Reapply Master to Slide, you will not restore the Theme to the look it has in Keynote; it's as if the changes made for PowerPoint don't register as changes to the Master, so nothing is reapplied.)

If you want to collaborate with a PowerPoint user, you can open a regular PowerPoint document, add slides and edit text, and save the document—no need to save specially for the changes you've made to be visible in PowerPoint.

If you need to display using Keynote a slideshow originally created in PowerPoint, you may have to do a bit of cleanup. Sometimes, the changes in object sizing cause elements to overlap. Also, some of the bullet characters used in PowerPoint lists appear incorrectly in Keynote. To fix them, simply select the affected text area and open the Text Inspector pane of the Inspector window. Under the Bullets & Numbering section, shown in Figure 10.7, you can enter a new character for the bullet and change its size.

Did you Know?

If you want to apply a standard bullet, press Option-8 in the text field for Text Bullets (as shown in Figure 10.7). You can then adjust the size percentage to make the bullet any size you want.

FIGURE 10.7
When using Text
bullets, you can
choose a character
and set its
size, color, and
alignment.

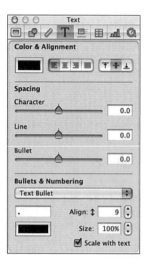

Summary

AppleWorks and Keynote are two applications from Apple that can be purchased separately. AppleWorks is a multipurpose office-type application that can be used to write documents, organize data, or create simple graphics. Keynote is an easy-to-use presentation builder, with a built-in set of charming templates. Both applications offer ways for sharing their files to other users who may not have these applications.

PART III

Internet Applications

CHAPTER 11

Connecting to the Internet

Mac OS X is easy to configure for dial-in, ethernet, AirPort, cable modem, and DSL service. If you have a connection to the Internet, this chapter helps you set up your Mac to access it. Specifically, you learn what tools exist for setting up your network, where to configure your connections, and how to manage multiple locations.

Creating an Internet Connection

The first step in connecting to any network (including the Internet) is determining what, exactly, is being connected. Mac OS X supports a number of technologies out of the box, such as standard wired (ethernet) networks, wireless AirPort networks, and, of course, broadband and dial-in ISPs. For each different type of network, you must collect connection information before continuing. Your network administrator or ISP should be able to provide the details of your network access, including

- ▶ IP address—An Internet Protocol address that's used to uniquely identify your computer on the Internet

- ▶ Subnet mask—A filter that helps your computer differentiate between which machines are on the local network and which are on the Internet

- ▶ Router—A device address used to send and receive information to and from the Internet

- ▶ Domain name server—A computer that translates the name you see in your Web browser, such as www.poisontooth.com, into the corresponding IP address

- ▶ ISP phone number—A number used when creating a dial-in connection

- ▶ Account name—A username for your ISP Internet account

- ▶ Password—A password for your ISP Internet account

- ▶ Proxy—A computer that your Macintosh goes through to reach the Internet

If you're using a dial-in connection, chances are good that all you need are a phone number, an account name, and a password. You should be absolutely positive that you have all the necessary information before you continue; otherwise, your computer could behave strangely when attempting to connect with incomplete or inaccurate information.

Under no circumstances should you *ever* attempt to guess an IP address for your computer. Entering invalid information could potentially disrupt your entire network or cause intermittent (and difficult to diagnose) problems for other users.

With connection information in hand, open System Preferences, and click the Network button in the Internet & Network section. The Network pane is the control center for all your network connections. Figure 11.1 shows the Network Status section of that pane.

FIGURE 11.1
See the status of potential network connections.

By the Way

At the bottom of all the sections in the Network Preferences pane is the Assist Me button. Clicking it launches the Network Setup Assistant, which asks you a series of questions to try to help you set up your Internet Connection. Basically, it collects the same information we'll be discussing in the rest of this chapter If you aren't sure which option is for you, the Setup Assistant's questions may help you decide.

Near the top of the panel is the Show pop-up menu. Use this menu to choose between the different types of connections that your computer uses, such as Internal Modem, Built-in Ethernet, and AirPort. Let's look at each one and how it can be set up for your ISP.

If you use different types of connections (for example, a modem at home and AirPort at work), don't worry. In the section "Setting Network Port Priorities and Locations" later in the chapter, you'll see how several different connection types can get along without any conflicts.

Internal Modem

If you use a modem to connect to the Internet, choose the appropriate Modem option in the Show pop-up menu. The lower portion of your screen changes slightly to reflect the type of connection you're configuring. You see four buttons that lead to four individual setting panes:

▶ PPP—The most important pane, shown in Figure 11.2, the PPP settings enable you to set your username, password, and ISP phone number.

▶ TCP/IP—TCP/IP settings are rarely needed for dial-in connections. Unless you know otherwise, I recommend not touching anything found here.

FIGURE 11.2
The PPP options are usually the only things you need to make a connection.

▶ Proxies—If your ISP has provided proxy servers for your use, you might want to enter them here. A *proxy* manages requests to Internet resources on behalf of your computer to either increase speed or security.

▶ Modem—Settings specific to your computer's modem. If you don't like hearing the annoying connection sound, you can shut off the speaker here. Most important, you can activate the option to Show Modem Status in Menu Bar, which provides a menu extra that enables you to easily connect and disconnect from the Internet.

In the PPP section, enter the username and password you were given for your ISP, along with the phone number for the ISP's servers. If you want to keep your password stored with the machine, click the Save Password check box.

There are a number of settings you might want to look at by clicking the PPP Options button. You can configure settings in a sheet to give you the ability to redial a busy connection, automatically connect when starting TCP/IP applications, and automatically disconnect if you choose Log Out from the Apple menu.

Click Apply Now to save the PPP settings. If you chose the PPP option to connect automatically when needed, you should be able to start Safari (see Chapter 12, "Using Safari") and begin surfing the Web.

By the Way

If you didn't choose to connect automatically, you can choose Show Modem Status in Menu Bar to activate the modem menu extra (this option is in the Modem section) to add a quick-control icon to your menu bar. Alternatively, the Internet Connect application can start and stop a dial-in setting. We talk more about that in "Using Internet Connect" toward the end of this chapter.

Built-in Ethernet

The next type of connection we look at is the built-in ethernet connection. If you have a wired 10BASE-T LAN or a DSL/cable modem hookup, this is where you'll need to focus your attention. Choose Built-in Ethernet in the pop-up menu. Again, several sections enable you to fine-tune related areas.

The sections for the Ethernet settings are

▶ TCP/IP—Unlike the modem TCP/IP settings you saw earlier, the Ethernet TCP/IP pane, displayed in Figure 11.3, offers more configuration options than are typical of a wired network.

▶ PPPoE—PPP over ethernet is a common way for DSL-based services to connect. They generally require a username and password as a modem-based PPP connection does, but operate over a much faster ethernet wire.

▶ AppleTalk—The AppleTalk section is used to control whether you become part of a local AppleTalk network. AppleTalk is Apple's traditional file-sharing protocol and is discussed further in Chapter 34, "Sharing Files and Running Network Services."

▶ Proxies—If your ISP has provided proxy servers for your use, you might want to enter them here.

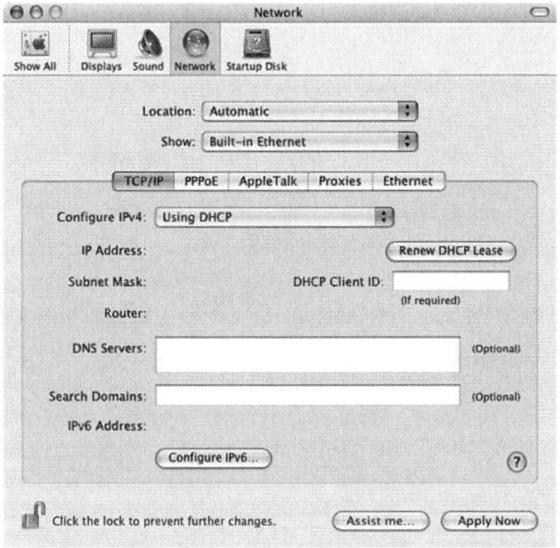

FIGURE 11.3
TCP/IP settings are important for ethernet-based connections.

▶ Ethernet—If you need to look up your Ethernet ID, this is the place to look. Although IP addresses are identifying numbers assigned by your network that can be used to associate a computer with an action, Ethernet ID numbers are unique identifiers associated with the hardware of your computer. (The Configure pop-up menu can be used to access advanced settings, but it may be best to leave them unchanged without help from your system administrator.)

As you can see in Figure 11.3, you definitely need a few items before you can successfully operate an ethernet connection. Fill in the information that you collected from your network administrator or ISP now. If you're lucky, at least a portion of these settings can be configured automatically by a BOOTP (boot protocol) or DHCP Dynamic Host Configuration Protocol) server on your network.

BOOTP and DHCP often provide automatic network setup on corporate and cable modem networks. If your network supports one of these services, you can use the Configure IPv4 pop-up menu in the TCP/IP section to select the appropriate protocol for your connection. Again, it's important that you do not *guess* what you need to connect—using invalid settings could disrupt your entire network.

The TCP/IP section of the Built-in Ethernet settings has button labeled Renew DHCP Lease. This is used to "refresh" the IP address assigned to you by your local network. Sometimes, if your connection is misbehaving, renewing your IP address can correct the problem.

By the Way

If you're required to use PPPoE, click the PPPoE button. In this pane, you can supply a username and password for your connection and enter optional identifying data for the ISP.

Near the bottom of the pane is a check box that enables you to view your PPPoE status in the menu bar. Clicking this check box adds a new menu extra that displays activity on your connection and gives you quick control over your settings.

Click the Apply Now button when you're satisfied with your ethernet setup. You should be able to immediately use the network software on your computer, such as Mail and Safari.

AirPort

The next connection method, AirPort, is available only if you've added an AirPort card to your system and are within range of a wireless base station. AirPort is Apple's 802.11b-based wireless networking device that enables you to connect to the Internet without the burden of running network wires or phone lines.

To configure your AirPort connection, choose AirPort in the Show pop-up menu. AirPort setup, surprisingly, is identical to ethernet. The same TCP/IP, AppleTalk, and Proxies sections apply. There is, however, one additional section that's essential to configure properly: the AirPort section, shown in Figure 11.4.

FIGURE 11.4
Choose the AirPort network you want to connect to or set criteria so that your system can choose.

In the AirPort section, you can direct your computer to Join Automatic, which is whatever network is available, or Join a Specific Network.

AirPort networks are identified by a network name. When the Join a Specific Network radio button is selected, you can use the Network pop-up menu to choose one of the detected AirPort (or AirPort-compatible) networks, or manually type the name into the Preferred Network text field.

As with the modem and PPPoE settings, you can activate yet another menu extra—the AirPort signal strength—by clicking Show AirPort Status in Menu Bar. This menu extra also gives you the ability to instantly switch between the different available wireless networks and even shut down AirPort service if you want.

By the
Way

The Allow This Computer to Create Networks check box allows computers with AirPort cards to create computer-to-computer networks with other AirPort-enabled computers even if no official network is present. To create a computer-to-computer network, check this option and the option to Show AirPort status in menu bar; then click on the AirPort status menu extra and choose Create Network. In the window that appears, enter a name for your network and click OK. (If you want to be sure that only specific people join your network, click the Show Options button and enter a five-digit password that will be required to join your network.) Others in your vicinity will be able to join your network as if it were another AirPort-based network by choosing it from their AirPort status menu extra.

Click Apply Now to start using your wireless network.

Setting Network Port Priorities and Locations

That wasn't so bad, was it? Everything that you need to get yourself connected to the Internet is all located in one System Preferences panel. Unfortunately, not all users' network setups are so easy. Many of us use our PowerBooks at home to dial in to the network, and then go to work and connect via ethernet, and, finally, stop by a coffee shop on the way home to relax and browse the Web via AirPort.

In Mac OS X, all your different network connections can be active simultaneously! This means that if it is possible for your computer to find a way to connect to a network, it will! Obviously, you don't want it trying to dial the phone if it has already found a connection, and, true to form, Mac OS X is smart enough to understand that if it *is* connected, it doesn't need to try any of the other connection methods. In fact, you can alter the order in which it tries to connect to the network by choosing Network Port Configurations in the Network Preferences panel's Show pop-up menu. Figure 11.5 shows this configuration pane.

Here you can see four port configurations: one modem, one ethernet, one AirPort, and one called IrDA, which we'll discuss in the following note. You can drag these different configuration settings up and down in the list to determine the order in which Mac OS X attempts to use them. If you prefer that the computer *doesn't* attempt to connect using one of these configurations, deselect the check box in front of that item.

By the Way

> IrDA is an infrared wireless communication protocol that can be used to transfer files between compatible devices.(Some models of the Macintosh, especially laptops, have infrared ports; you'll have to check your computer's documentation to see whether yours is one of them.) Like the computer-to-computer networks discussed in the earlier "AirPort" section, this allows enabled devices and computers to interact even when no formal network is available.

FIGURE 11.5
Adjust which connection settings take precedence over the others.

Using the New, Delete, and Duplicate buttons on the right side of the pane, you can create alternative configurations for each of your built-in connection methods. These new configurations appear in the Show pop-up menu and are set up just as you set up the modem, ethernet, and AirPort connections earlier.

Locations

Mac OS X creates collections of port settings called *locations* that you can easily switch between. So far you've been dealing with a location called Automatic, shown in the Location pop-up menu of the Network Preferences panel.

To create a new location, choose New Location from the Location pop-up menu. After you create a new location, you can edit the port configurations and priorities just as you have under the default Automatic location. To manage the locations that you've set up, choose Edit Locations in the Location pop-up menu.

Switching from one location to another is simply a matter of choosing its name in the Location pop-up menu or the Location submenu under the systemwide Apple menu.

> Choosing a new location immediately makes the new network settings available and could disrupt any connections currently taking place.

By the Way

Using Internet Connect

The Internet Connect application, which you can launch from the Applications folder, is the final stop in your tour of Mac OS X network utilities. This is a rather strange application that offers a shortcut to several of the same features found in the Network Preferences panel. It can be used for both modem and AirPort connections to quickly log in to different configurations in your current location.

Figure 11.6 displays the Modem side of the Internet Connect application.

FIGURE 11.6
The Internet Connect application enables you to easily log in to your ISP.

To log in to your ISP via modem, follow these steps:

1. Choose the modem configuration you created earlier in the Configuration pop-up menu at the top of the window.

2. Enter the phone number for your ISP or choose from those listed in the pop-up menu.

3. The login name should already be set as configured in the Network Preferences panel. If you didn't save your password in the panel, you must enter it here.

4. Click the Show Modem Status in Menu Bar check box to add the modem menu extra to your screen.

5. Click Connect to start using your dial-in connection.

After you've connected to your ISP, the Connect button changes to Disconnect, giving you a quick way to break the modem connection.

AirPort users also stand to benefit from the Internet Connect application. Along with modem configurations, AirPort settings are also shown in the Configuration pop-up menu. Choosing an AirPort-based configuration displays the status of the connection and signal strength, as shown in Figure 11.7.

FIGURE 11.7
Internet Connect can also control your AirPort settings.

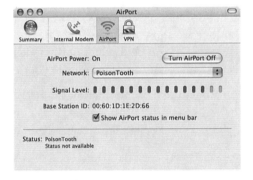

Use the Turn AirPort Off (and subsequent Turn AirPort On) button to disable or enable the AirPort card in your computer. To switch to another wireless network, use the Network pop-up menu.

Finally, to see a readout of the signal strength at all times, check the Show AirPort Status in Menu Bar check box.As you can see, many features of the Internet Connect application are already accessible through the Network Preferences panel. However, Internet Connect has one more setting that we haven't seen before: VPN, which stands for Virtual Private Network. VPN allows remote users to connect to a specially configured network securely and interact as if they were within the local network. Your system administrator will know whether this would apply to you.

Regardless, the Internet Connect application offers a quick means of viewing your connection status and changing common settings.

Summary

In this chapter, you learned how to set up your Mac OS X computer for network access through traditional wired networks, wireless AirPort connections, and, of course, dial-up ISPs. Mac OS X networking has a number of advantages, including the ability to automatically configure itself to whatever type of network is currently available. This feature, combined with a simplified locations manager, makes it easy to adapt your computer to any sort of network environment.

CHAPTER 12

Using Safari

Many people are purchasing computers just to access information over the Internet. As you saw in Chapter 11, "Connecting to the Internet," it's easy to configure Internet settings in OS X. In this chapter, you'll learn how easy it is to use Safari, Apple's own Web browser, to explore the World Wide Web.

The Safari Interface

Figure 12.1 shows Safari's default configuration. Figure 12.2 shows all available interface options. For the most part, these options are turned on and off under the View menu in the application menu bar. (In Figure 12.2, a feature called *tabs* is also activated; we will discuss them later in the section "Using Tabs.")

FIGURE 12.1
Apple's Safari Web browser with a "typical" set of interface options.

By the Way

> If you were using another Web browser on your computer prior to installing Safari, Safari will have set its home page to match that browser.

FIGURE 12.2
The elements of the Safari interface.

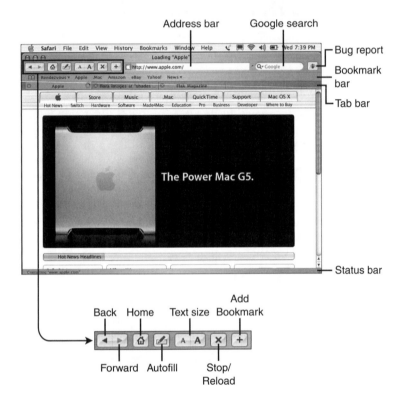

Address Bar

The top row of controls in the Safari window is the Address bar. It contains the basic tools you need to move between Web pages, as well as a few tools to make your use of the Internet easier.

▶ The Back and Forward buttons work together. You use the Back button to return to the Web page you viewed previously. After you've gone back, you can use the Forward button to move ahead to where you were. If you haven't gone back through any pages you've already viewed, the Forward button is grayed out to show that it is not currently an active option.

▶ The Home button returns you to the page set as your default startup page. Think of it as a shortcut for connecting to a site you visit frequently.

> To change the page that comes up automatically when Safari is launched, choose Preferences from the Safari application menu, and click the General option from the toolbar. (If you don't see a toolbar, click the transparent oval-shaped button at the upper right of the Preferences window.) You can type a new Web address in the field labeled Home Page or, if your Safari window is open to the page you want to use, simply click the button marked Set to Current Page.
>
> Also, if you prefer, you can have windows open with your list of bookmarked pages instead of seeing a default page when you open a new window. Simply change the setting in the New Windows Open With pop-up menu from Home Page to Bookmarks.

By the Way

▶ The Autofill button activates a service that helps you complete online forms, such as registration and login pages, where you have to provide basic personal information. It works by storing information you've previously entered in Web page text fields so that it can repeat them on later visits.

▶ The Text Size button allows you to easily increase or decrease the font size in the current page.

▶ The Stop/Reload button changes depending on whether the current page identified in the Address field has been loaded or is loading. If a page has been loaded, you will see the Reload button, as shown in Figure 12.1, which allows you to refresh the page. This can be useful if you view a page that is updated frequently throughout the day and you want to make sure that you are viewing the most current version. The Stop button, shown in Figure 12.2, appears as a page is loading to allow you to stop it from loading. In cases where a page takes a long time to load, and you'd rather give up than wait, the Stop button lets you return Safari to an idle state so that you can enter the address for a new page.

▶ Clicking the Add Bookmark button, which looks like a "+", adds the current page to your bookmark list so tat you can easily visit it again without writing down the address. We'll discuss bookmarks more later in this chapter in the section "Working with Bookmarks."

▶ The Address field is where you can type Web addresses of sites you want to visit. It also shows the addresses of pages you reach through links in other pages or through pages you've bookmarked. In addition to showing addresses, the Safari Address field also shows the status of pages as they are loading. As shown in Figure 12.2, a blue-shaded bar moves from left to right across the Address field as information for displaying the current page is received.

If the Status bar stops moving, there may be a problem loading the page. Use the Stop button to tell Safari to stop trying to load the page. You can try to connect again by clicking the Refresh button.

▶ The Google Search field allows you to type a word or phrase of interest and search the powerful Google search engine for relevant sites. The results listing appears in your browser window.

Google, located at www.google.com, is a popular search engine with a reputation for strong performance. However, just because a site isn't in Google doesn't mean that it doesn't exist. Search engines work by cataloging sites, not by actually searching all Web sites at the moment you request the information. Sometimes newer or more obscure sites haven't been cataloged, or a technical glitch results in a site "disappearing" temporarily from the listing.

▶ Because Safari was only recently released, the Report Bugs button was included to allow people to report any problems they experience in viewing pages. If you attempt to view a page in Safari and you know that the page works in other browsers, you may want to submit a bug report to help Apple locate problem areas in Safari. Although hopefully you won't need to use the Bug button, isn't it nice to know they care?

Bookmarks Bar

Earlier, you were introduced to the Add Bookmark button in the Address bar, which allows you to add the current page to a list of bookmarked pages. The Bookmarks bar holds links to sites you want to keep close at hand.

You can add sites to the Bookmarks bar by clicking the icon in front of the address in the Address field and dragging it into the Bookmarks bar. A sheet window appears where you can enter a name to identify the site, as shown in Figure 12.3. Remove a site by dragging the address outside the Safari window. If you drag addresses within the Bookmarks bar area, you will be able to rearrange them.

Because only a limited number of items will remain visible in the Bookmarks bar, there is also an expanded Bookmark view where you can store and organize favorite addresses. This is where addresses go when you click the Add Bookmark button. You can open it by clicking the icon that looks like an open book at the far left of the Bookmarks bar. We'll talk more about managing bookmarks later in the chapter in the section "Working with Bookmarks."

FIGURE 12.3
Keep the page's official title or enter one you'll remember better.

Tab Bar

Tabs are an option in Safari that allows you to have several Web pages open at one time without all the clutter of extra browser windows. The Tab bar shown previously in Figure 12.2 has three open pages that you can click between. We'll talk about this morein the section "Using Tabs" later in the chapter.

Status Bar

The Status bar, which you can choose to include at the bottom of the Safari window, displays information about a page as it loads. For example, in Figure 12.2, the page has been reloaded, so the Status bar reads "Contacting 'www.apple.com.'"

The Status bar also provides information about hyperlinked elements on a page as you move your mouse cursor across them. For example, if you run your mouse across a text link or a linked image, the address to which the link goes appears.

Don't underestimate the value of the Status bar. In some cases, seeing the linked address can help you decide whether you want to click. You may decide not to following links that lead outside the current site, or not to click on links that lead to documents in PDF format.

Web Browsing in Safari

Now that you know what the parts of the Safari interface can do, let's do some Web browsing.

To visit a Web site for which you know the address, type the address in the Address field in the Button bar and press Return on your keyboard. You see a blue shaded bar move across the Address field as the page loads, and, if you've chosen to view the Status bar, a countdown of the page elements that are loading.

By the Way

Web pages aren't a single object—typically, they are composed of a page file and separate image files. (In some cases, there may be additional supporting files containing page content or formatting information as well.) The countdown in the Status bar as a page loads tells you just how many files it requires!

When a page has loaded, you can click text links, linked images, or buttons to move to other pages, or click in the Address field to type a new address.

Did you Know?

Web sites don't always work. If you try to visit a site and receive a "Server Not Found" message, as shown in Figure 12.4, the problem is not likely to be Safari. Such a message occurs when there are technical difficulties for the computer hosting the Web site or when a site is no longer available. Your best option is to double-check the address you've entered. If the address is correct, you may need to wait before trying the site again, in case there's some kind of temporary site outage. If the site doesn't return, you may want to try a Google search on the name of the site to see whether a "cached" version of the content is still available.

FIGURE 12.4
The Server Not Found sheet window lets you know when an address can't be reached. (In this example, that's because there is a misspelling in the intended address.)

If you begin to type in an address you've visited recently, Safari tries to autocomplete it. A drop-down menu of addresses for pages you've been to that match what you've typed so far appears. Also, Safari's best guess of which address you're typing appears, high-lighted in blue, in the text field. If the page you want to view is listed in the drop-down menu, use your mouse cursor to select it. If it isn't listed, continue to type the rest of the address in the Address field.

By the Way

Shopping online has become a popular time (and money) saver in recent years, but it's important to use caution when sending personal information (such as credit card numbers) over the Internet. To make sure that the site accepting your data is configured to transfer data securely, look for a lock icon at the upper right in the Safari window (as in Figure 12.6). (Note however, that even a secure site may fall prey to a persistent criminal.)

Using Snap-Back

As you use Safari, you may notice an icon displaying a "return" arrow in an orange circle at the far-right side of the Address field. That's the Snap-Back button. It appears in any page you navigate to through links within other Web pages. If clicked, the Snap-Back button takes you back to the last address you physically typed in the Address field.

You can also manually set a page to be the one to which Snap-Back returns. Simply choose History, Mark Page for Snap-Back from the menu, or use the keyboard shortcut Command-Option-M. This is a convenient way to mark a specific page while you continue following links.

Using Tabs

As you saw previously, Safari's tabs allow you to have several Web pages open at one time without the clutter of extra browser windows.

If you want to use tabs, choose Preferences from the Safari menu, open the Tabs pane (shown in Figure 12.5), and the Enable tabbed browsing box. You can also decide whether tabs containing freshly loaded pages will automatically be selected or whether they will wait for you to click them. Finally, you can choose whether to show the Tab bar even when only one tab exists.

After you've enabled tabs under the preferences, you're ready to try them out. Tabs are easy to use. When you want one, simply choose File, New Tab from the menu (or use the keyboard shortcut Command-T). You then see a row of boxlike buttons, or tabs just below the Address bar. Each tab is labeled with the name of the Web page it contains, as shown in Figure 12.6, so you can easily click between them. If you want to close a tab, click the close icon on its far-left side.

FIGURE 12.5
The Tabs preference pane contains a few options as well as a list of keyboard shortcuts.

Watch Out!

If tabbed browsing isn't enabled in the Safari preferences, you will not see the option to open a tab under the File menu.

FIGURE 12.6
A row of tabs, each representing a Web page ready for view.

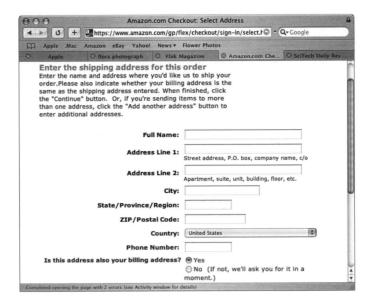

Did you Know?

If you want to open a linked page in a new tab, hold down the Control key on your keyboard as you click the link. A contextual menu appears under your mouse cursor, as shown in Figure 12.7, from which you can choose Open Link in New Tab.

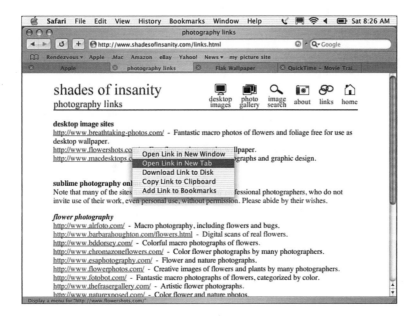

FIGURE 12.7
You can also create tabs through a contextual menu, opened by Control-clicking a link.

Downloading Files

In addition to viewing Web pages with Safari, you can also use it to download files linked from Web pages.

Downloadable files commonly linked from Web pages include PDF files, word-processing or spreadsheet documents, and compressed (or "zipped") files and folders. Compressed files and folders include software applications, such as those discussed in Chapter 9, "Installing Additional Software."

By the Way

When you click a link for certain types of documents, Safari automatically opens a Downloads window, as shown in Figure 12.8. Depending on your preference settings, this window may list other files you've downloaded as well as showing status of the current download.

When the download is complete, the file will be on your local computer. By default, Safari stores downloaded files on your desktop, but you can change these preferences options in the General pane of the system preferences, which we'll discuss in the "Safari Preference Options" section later in this chapter.

There is a potential for downloaded files to transfer malicious code, such as computer viruses or cleverly written software that spies on your keystrokes, to your computer. PDFs, images, sounds, text documents, and compressed files are usually safe, but it is smart to exercise caution and download materials only from reputable sources.

Working with Bookmarks

Earlier, you learned to drag a Web address from the Address field into the Bookmarks bar to quickly store it for later reference. As useful as that feature is, there's limited space for all the pages you want to keep. However, there is plenty of room in the Bookmarks window, shown in Figure 12.9, which you can open by clicking the Show All Bookmarks button in the Bookmarks bar.

By the Way

In addition to any pages you've bookmarked, Safari also stores all the pages you've visited in the past seven days. You can view them under the History menu or in the History category of the Bookmarks window.

By default, Safari comes with several common Web sites already stored as bookmarks, but you can add your own simply by clicking the Add Bookmark button in the Address bar when you are viewing a page you want to add. (If the Add Bookmark button is not visible, go to the View menu to select it.) Safari displays a sheet window, shown in Figure 12.10, where you can name your bookmark and select a folder in which to store it.

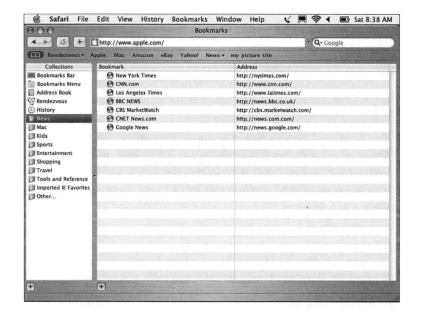

FIGURE 12.9
A special window to view and organize lists of your favorite Web sites. (When opened, it displays the last section you visited.)

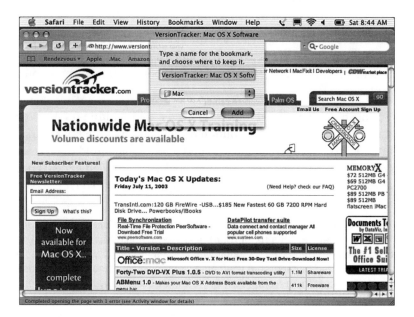

FIGURE 12.10
Name and categorize the site.

If you had another Web browser, such as Internet Explorer, on your computer at the time Safari was installed, Safari may have created a folder of the bookmarks saved for its use.

To return to a page you've bookmarked, open the Bookmarks window and choose the folder where you stored it.

If you decide another category would be more appropriate for something you've already bookmarked, you can drag it from one folder into another. If you want to remove a page all together, select it and press the Delete key on your keyboard. (You can also drag unwanted items to the Trash in the Dock.) Be careful when deleting folders and bookmarks, however, because you don't get a second chance to confirm your choices.

If the new category was added to the main folder list, you can drag exiting bookmarks into it easily. However, if you created a subfolder, you may have to drag bookmarks into its parent folder first and then drag them into place. Alternatively, you could select bookmarks from elsewhere, choose Edit, Copy from the menu, and paste them into the new folder.

Although Safari's preset category folders are straightforward, you may want to rearrange them or add new ones. You can move a folder by selecting it and dragging it to a new location in the list. An insertion bar appears to show you where it will be placed.

You can create more specialized folders (or even a folder within a folder) by clicking the Create a Bookmarks Folder button at the bottom of the Bookmarks window. Use the button at the bottom-left to add a main folder and the one at bottom-center to add a subfolder to the current folder. An untitled folder is added where you can type your new category, as shown in Figure 12.11.

Bookmarks are useful things, but what happens if you use more than one computer? How can you have access to all your bookmarks? Apple has a solution—using iSync (discussed in Chapter 8, "Working with Address Book, Keychain Access, iSync, and Ink") and a .Mac membership you can synchronize your bookmarks across computers and even view them from nearly any browser over the Web. We'll cover the details in Chapter 14, "Exploring the .Mac Membership."

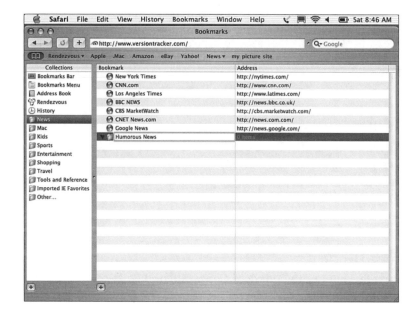

FIGURE 12.11
A new bookmarks subfolder has been named.

The Safari Menu Bar

Several features we've discussed previously in this chapter can be accessed through the Safari menu bar, but additional features are available. Let's review the menu items we've already seen and take a brief look at the others.

Safari Menu

The Safari menu contains many options typically found in an application menu. You can view information about Safari or open the Preferences window as well as access available services (mentioned during our tour of the menu bar in Chapter 1, "Introducing Mac OS X") and hide or quit the application.

From the Safari menu, you can also report bugs to Apple or easily activate and deactivate the option to block pop-up windows. To keep others from using or viewing your settings, choose Reset Safari from the Safari menu to erase your browsing history, cached files, list of downloads, Google search entries, any cookies set on your computer, and all the data saved for used by the Autofill feature. Choose Empty Cache to delete the Web pages and images saved by Safari.

Did you
Know?

Sometimes, after Web sites have been updated, Web browsers will continue to show them (or parts of them) as they used to appear because of images stored in the cache. If this happens, try choosing Empty Cache from the Safari menu and then revisit the site.

File Menu

The File menu contains the basic options to open and close new windows or tabs. As in most other applications, the Page Setup and Print features are also located here. The Open Location option simply places the mouse cursor in the Address field, ready for you to enter a Web address. Open File allows you to navigate to Web page or image files on your computer that you want to view in Safari.

Edit Menu

The Edit menu contains the standard Copy, Cut, and Paste commands as well as Select All and Delete.

Undo and Redo options are also found under the Edit menu. They pertain not to moving between pages—we have Forward and Back buttons for that—but rather to changes you make to your bookmarks. Find can be used to quickly locate a word or phrase of interest on a page. For example, in a long list of names and addresses, you can choose Find to go immediately to the entry for the person you want to contact.

Autofill, like the Autofill button mentioned earlier, helps you fill in online information.

The Spelling option won't check the spelling in Web sites so that you can recognize when they are poorly proofread. Rather, it allows you to check any text you enter in a text field on a page. For example, if you type a search term in the Search field on the Google Web page or in the Google field in the Safari Address bar, you can check its spelling before running a search. You can choose the Check Spelling as You Type option to see a wavy red line under any term your system doesn't recognize.

View Menu

You learned earlier that you can choose which interface options appear in the Safari window in the View menu. You can also control the more advanced options for text encoding and view source. You may know that Web pages are written in

HTML. View source allows you to see the HTML that the browser is using to display a given Web page.

The Text Encoding option lets you tell Safari in which format to display character sets used in Web pages. There is a default setting in the Appearance pane of the Safari preferences, but you can make temporary changes using this Text Encoding menu option.

History Menu

The History menu contains duplicates of the basic controls for moving through pages: the Back, Forward, and Home items work the same as the buttons typically found in the Address bar. Also in the History menu are the settings to mark a page for Snap Back and to snap back to the currently marked page. Finally, the History menu displays a list of addresses for pages visited in the past week and the option to clear the history.

Bookmarks Menu

The Bookmarks menu provides an alternative way to view and add bookmarks in Safari. (See the "Working with Bookmarks" section earlier in this chapter.)

Window Menu

The Window menu contains options related to viewing Safari windows—including the download manager—and tabs. It also includes the standard "minimize" and "zoom" window controls for covering or uncovering your desktop.

Help Menu

The Help menu gives you access to Apple-created instructions for using Safari and to the acknowledgements and user license agreement for the software. It also allows you to view which plug-ins recognized by Safari are installed on your system. Figure 12.12 shows an example.

Plug-ins are supplemental programs that allow you to view content from Web pages created in a format other than plain HTML. Examples include the QuickTime and Flash Players, which play movielike elements in your browser window.

By the Way

FIGURE 12.12
See what plug-ins
are available on
your computer for
Safari to use.

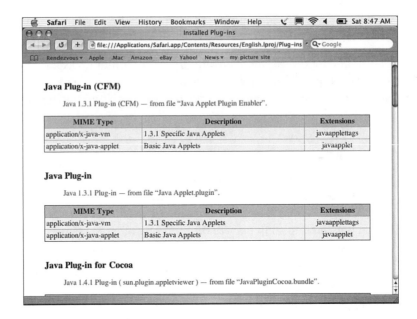

Safari Preference Options

We looked at how to change your default home page in the General section of the Safari preferences as well as how to change settings for tabs. Let's review the preferences we've already covered and look at any we've left out.

General Preferences

Options under General preferences, shown in Figure 12.13, include many common settings related to how a Safari window is launched and how pages and files are accessed.

The first option is a choice of your default Web browser, or the Web browser that launches automatically whenever you click a link received in email or through another program. The drop-down menu lists any application recognized as a Web browser by your system.

You also have the option of choosing whether new windows that open come up with a specific home page that you've chosen, as an empty page, with any page currently open, or in Bookmarks mode. (We discussed setting a default home page in a note in the "Address Bar" section earlier in this chapter.)

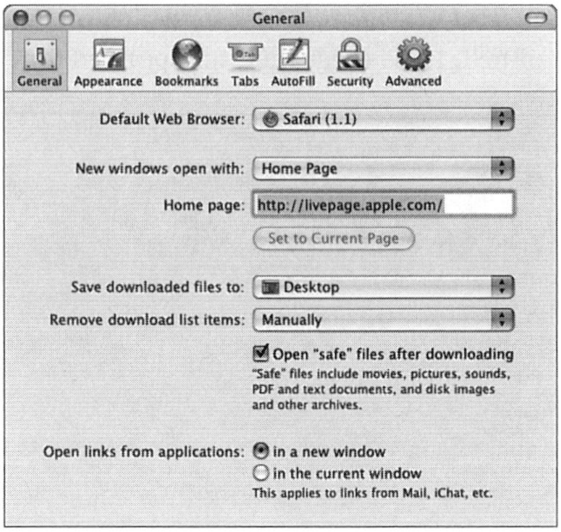

FIGURE 12.13
Choose your default Web browser and default home page in the General preferences pane.

The next three options pertain to downloading files. You have the option to save downloaded files to the Desktop or to choose another location using the standard OS X file browser. You can also decide how items will be removed from your Download list: manually, when Safari quits, or upon successful download. (Note that removing items from the list doesn't affect files that have been downloaded.) If you like to keep a record of what you've downloaded, set it to Manually; if you prefer a clean slate, choose one of the other options.

The third download-related preference is the Open "safe" Files After Downloading check box. Safe files, by Safari's definition, are files unlikely to cause harm to you system, including media files, such as images and sounds, PDF or text files, and disk images. If this option is checked, any "safe" files automatically become active when they are downloaded; otherwise, you need to double-click down-loaded files to launch or uncompress them.

The final setting relates back to how Safari reacts to links you open from other applications. You can decide whether to open links in a new window or in the current window.

Appearance

The Appearance pane, shown in Figure 12.14, contains the Web page display set-tings over which the viewer can have some input. You can choose any font on the system to be used on Web pages where another font is not specifically specified.

You can also choose a *fixed-width font*, a font for which all letters take up the same area in a line of text, to be used when the specified font needs to align in a specific way.

FIGURE 12.14
Choose fonts and character encoding preferences.

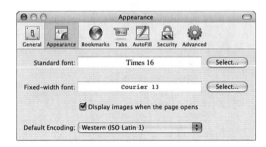

You can also decide whether to load images in a Web page, in case you'd rather not wait for them to download. Finally, you can set default character encoding, which tells your browser how to interpret characters in a Web page. For example, if you regularly read Japanese Web sites, you would only be able to see the correct characters if your character encoding and the Web page used the same setting.

Bookmarks

Choose whether to include Web pages listed in your Address Book or available on your local network in the Bookmarks bar or Bookmarks menu.

You can also choose to synchronize your bookmarks across computers using .Mac, as discussed earlier.

Tabs

As mentioned earlier, the Tabs pane, shown previously in Figure 12.5, allows you to control preferences related to tabbed browsing. You can enable tabbed browsing and choose whether the tab bar will be visible even when only one window is open. You can also set whether to open tabs as they are created, or allow them to open in the background and wait until you choose to open them.

Autofill

In the Autofill pane, shown in Figure 12.15, you can choose whether to allow Autofill access to information stored in your card in the Address Book, based on sites and passwords you've entered for it to use, or based on data from other forms you've filled in. After each option is an Edit button. Clicking the Edit button allows you view or remove any information stored for use by Autofill.

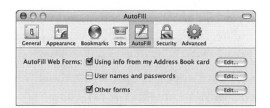

FIGURE 12.15
Set limits on where Autofill gets its information or edit what's already stored.

Security

The Security pane, shown in Figure 12.16, contains settings for how Safari should respond to different elements it encounters as you visit Web pages. The first group of options are common elements of Web pages employed mostly for benevolent uses but can be abused.

FIGURE 12.16
Security options include how your browser interacts with Web sites.

As you learned earlier, plug-ins are supplemental programs that allow you to view content from Web pages created in a format other than plain HTML. If you don't want to allow this content, you can choose to disable plug-ins. Keep in mind, however, that the elements created for use with plug-ins will not be readable.

Java is computer programming language used to write interactive Web pages or even downloadable applications that run outside a Web browser. You may choose to disable Java to prevent such applications from running on your computer.

JavaScript is a simple programming language often used to make regular Web pages show some interaction. For example, JavaScript is often used to make images change when you move your mouse cursor over them. If you find motion onscreen distracting, you can disable JavaScript. However, be aware that some pages are more difficult to understand and may even have content that is visible only to people who have JavaScript enabled for their browsers.

Another common use of JavaScript is to open new browser windows on your screen—sometime whether you want them or not. Pop-up ads are a common method of Web advertising, but Safari gives you the option to block these additional windows. Although this can be a good way to eliminate annoying ads, keep in mind that some sites open additional windows containing important content in the hopes of getting people's attention. Those who block pop-up windows may miss real content.

By the Way

You can easily activate or deactivate pop-up window blocking from the Safari menu.

Cookies are another common tool used by Web developers. Cookies are small pieces of data stored on your local computer by the computer that hosts a Web site. This is done so that the site can identify you as a unique visitor.

Mostly, cookies are used so that a Web site can provide better service. For instance, if you purchase books at Amazon.com and then return to the site, you will be welcomed by name and shown a list of books that may interest you because the site identifies your account with your computer. Use of cookies also allows a person to move freely between pages in some types of secure systems that require user login. Cookies often are required in these situations because the server hosting the Web site needs to know on every page within the secure section that you are the person who logged in, and not someone who's simply skipped over the login page without authorization. In the first example, the cookie would be stored for a long time—perhaps a year or more—so that the site would be able to welcome you. In secure sections, cookies may last only until you quit out of the Safari application.

Although many sites use cookies for benevolent visitor tracking, there is the potential for cookies to be used to track people's habits on the Web even outside the site that issues the cookie. Many people find this an invasion of privacy. For this reason, Safari give you the option to always accept cookies, never accept cookies, or to accept cookies only from sites you purposely navigate to. You can also click the Show Cookies button to view any cookies currently stored on your computer and to delete any you want to remove.

The last option on the Security pane is a check box to ask before sending a nonsecure form to a secure server. Activating this feature alerts you when you may be sending sensitive data over the Web through a server not designed to ensure privacy.

Advanced

The Advanced pane, shown in Figure 12.17, includes settings most people won't need to change.

FIGURE 12.17
The default settings of the Advanced options should probably be left intact.

The first option allows you to set your own style sheet, which is a specially formatted description of how text on a page should be displayed. For example, with a carefully written style sheet, you could have text in Web pages that is coded as a heading appear in extremely large type, or even change its color, or reset the background of a page to another color to increase or reduce contrast. (Although this feature can be useful, writing style sheets is outside the scope of this book.)

Changing settings for Proxies is another topic outside the scope of this book. Proxy servers are computers that serve as intermediaries between a user's computer, such as yours, and the computer that serves a Web page. The proxy server may be used to manage the flow of data over a network due to requests from many users. If your computer is part of a local network with a network administrator, you may want to ask about any proxy servers and settings that may be recommended.

Summary

You became acquainted with the Safari Web browser in this chapter, as well as some basics of Web browsing. You learned how to view Web pages and download files. You also learned how to create and organize bookmarks to favorite Web pages. Finally, you learned what preference options you can use to customize Safari to suit you.

CHAPTER 13

Using Sherlock for Internet Searches

As its name implies, the Sherlock application is something of a detective, tracking down information on the Internet from the clues you provide. Some people might find it difficult to get excited about a search tool, but Sherlock is far from ordinary. With specialized search categories, including yellow pages and a dictionary, Sherlock will quickly become your one-stop reference tool.

Sherlock is basically a collection of Internet search functions, each packaged in its own "channel." The default channels are listed in the Channels menu of the Channels pane, as shown in Figure 13.1. They're also listed in the toolbar at the top of the window.

By the Way

Long-time Mac users might be confused by the recent incarnation of Sherlock, which doesn't include the option to search the local machine's files. That feature is now available directly from the Finder either in the search option in the toolbar of the Finder windows or in a separate Find window opened by selecting Find from the Finder's File menu or by using the keyboard shortcut Command-F. Refer to Chapter 2, "Using the Finder," for further information.

Each channel provides a specific kind of information, gathered from another source and displayed within the Sherlock interface. Notice that at the bottom of the Channels pane is a Terms of Use link, which opens a sheet explaining that Apple doesn't produce most of the content displayed in Sherlock.

Let's take a look at each default channel's use and special features.

FIGURE 13.1
The Channels area of Sherlock displays the available search functions and brief descriptions of each.

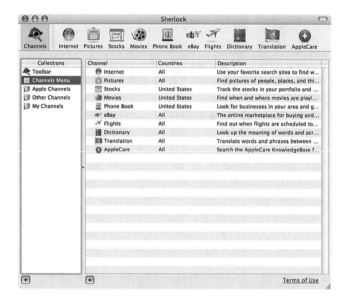

The Internet Channel

The Internet channel compiles search results from popular Internet search sites, such as Ask Jeeves and Lycos. As shown in Figure 13.2, each search result lists the title and address of a Web page, a relevance ranking, and the search site or sites that provided the entry.

To perform an Internet search, simply type your search terms into the text entry field at the top of the Internet channel pane and click the green Search button or press Return. When the results listing appears, you can select an entry with a single click to see a site description if one is available. Double-clicking launches your default Web browser and opens the page you requested.

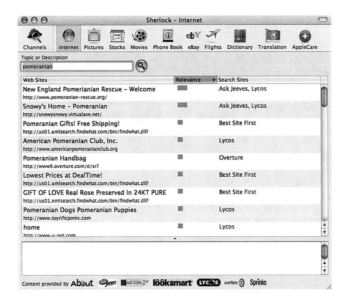

FIGURE 13.2
Searching the Internet from a variety of search engines is simplified by Sherlock.

The Pictures Channel

Similar to searches using the Internet channel, the Pictures channel queries photo databases for digital images based on your search terms. Thumbnail images of the results are displayed in the results pane, as shown in Figure 13.3. Double-click a thumbnail image in the results to open a Web page displaying the full-sized picture.

> The photos displayed in the Pictures channel searches might not be free for commercial use. Read the terms of service from the originating site if you have any questions about what's allowed.

FIGURE 13.3
Results appear as
thumbnail
images—
double-click one to
see the original.

FIGURE 13.3
Results appear as
thumbnail
images—
double-click one to
see the original.

The Stocks Channel

The Stocks channel, shown in Figure 13.4, provides details about the market performance of publicly traded companies. The information shown includes the stock price at last trade, price change, price range over the course of the day, and the volume of shares traded. You can also view charts of a company's performance over the past year or week or for the current day.

To find information about a company, enter its name or market symbol. Market symbols are unique identifiers, but many companies have similar names or several separate divisions. If you enter a name, you might see a sheet asking you to choose the company you're interested in, as shown Figure 13.5. When the correct name or symbol appears in the text entry field, click the green Search button or press Return.

Watch Out!

Market symbols and companies with similar names can make it difficult to ask for the listing you really want. If you don't enter the exact market symbol, some guesswork might be involved for Sherlock to return any results. Always check to make sure that the displayed information is for the company you thought you requested!

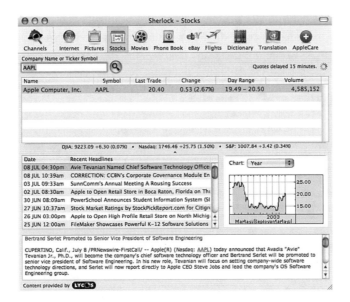

FIGURE 13.4
Enter a company's name or market symbol to see information about it, including recent news stories.

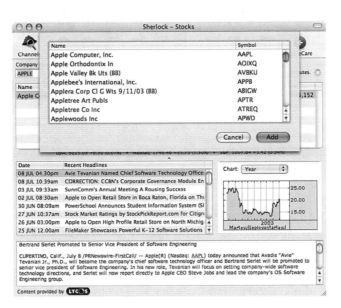

FIGURE 13.5
If you enter a string of letters that appears in more than one company name, a sheet window appears where you can choose the company you're interested in.

As you view information for different companies, they are added to the list in the middle of the Stocks pane so that you can easily return to them. If you want to remove a listing, simply select it and press the Delete key on your keyboard.

In addition to providing stock quotes, Sherlock also displays recent news articles pertaining to the selected company. To read a story, select its headline from the left of the chart, and the bottom pane displays the full text.

The Movies Channel

Sherlock's Movies channel, shown in Figure 13.6, pulls together all the information you need to choose a movie and a theater in which to view it.

FIGURE 13.6
The Movies channel displays a QuickTime preview of the selected movie as well as theater addresses.

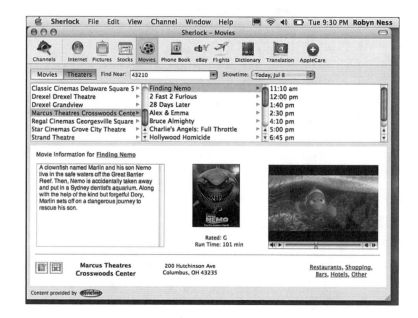

To use the Movies channel, you must enter either your city and state or your ZIP Code. Then you can choose to search either Movies or Theaters in your area. The Showtime pop-up menu enables you to choose the date of interest to you.

Choose the movie and theater listings at the top of the panel that are of interest to you, and the bottom of the window will fill with theater and movie information. In addition to a text summary of the movie, you can watch a preview for the selected option in QuickTime.

> To play the QuickTime preview, you might be prompted to set your network connection information in QuickTime Preferences if you haven't already done so. Refer to the section on QuickTime in Chapter 7, "Using QuickTime and DVD Player," for more details.

By the Way

The Phone Book Channel

The Phone Book channel has two modes: a person search and a business search.

The person search mode, shown in Figure 13.7, allows you to find a phone number and address by entering a person's name and a general location. To perform a person search, click the information button at the upper left (the one with an "i" in a white circle). Enter a last name, a first name, and either the city and state or the ZIP Code of the area to search. Then click the green Search button. In the middle pane, choose from among the list of potential matches to see detailed information, including a map.

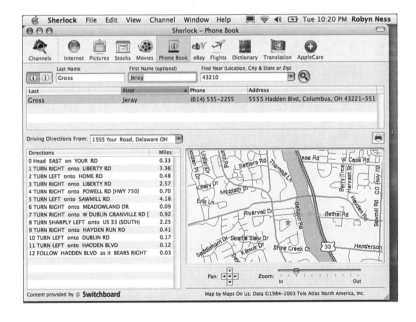

FIGURE 13.7
Locate a person by name and location.

Use the business search, shown in Figure 13.8, to obtain the phone number and address for a business and to view a map to its location. Simply click the information button on the right (the one with an "i" in a yellow circle), enter the business name and either the city and state or the ZIP Code of the area to search, and click the green Search button. In the middle pane, choose from among the list of potential matches to see detailed information.

FIGURE 13.8
Obtain contact information and personalized driving directions to businesses.

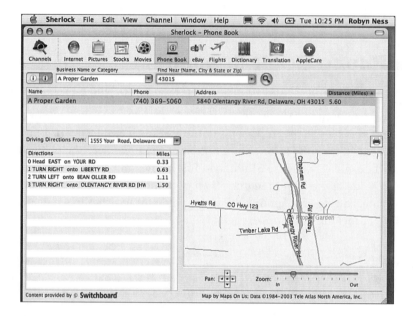

To receive driving directions to addresses turned up in either the person or business search, enter an address in the Driving Directions From text field. The Directions pane fills with step-by-step instructions.

You can then select the location you added in the Driving Directions From pop-up menu.

The eBay Channel

From the eBay channel, you can search active eBay auctions and track those of interest to you. To search, enter keywords in the Item Title text entry field and set your other parameters, such as product category, region, and price range; then click the Search button. When you choose a result from the search, its details fill the bottom panes of the screen, as shown in Figure 13.9.

To track an item, highlight it in the results listing and click the Track Auction button at lower right. Changing to Track mode using the button just below the search field reveals a list of only those items you're tracking. To remove an item, select it and press Delete on your keyboard.

FIGURE 13.9
If you enjoy online auctions, the eBay channel will delight you.

The Flights Channel

For information on current flights, go to the Flights channel. Here you can view flight status by route or by airline and flight number. Select a specific flight for details about the aircraft and flight. For some entries, you can also view a chart depicting the plane's position en route, as shown in the lower-right corner of Figure 13.10.

You can click the small switchlike button at the bottom right of the Flights pane to set preferences for the Flights channel. As shown in Figure 13.11, you can choose airlines and airports by continent on which to focus your searches.

FIGURE 13.10
View the status of
specific flights,
including a chart of
the flight path.

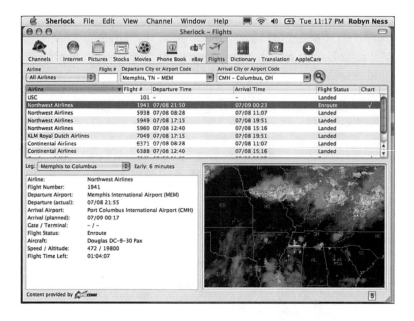

FIGURE 13.11
Choose a continent
to select all airlines
flying in a region, or
check boxes for all
continents whose
airports you want
to include in your
search.

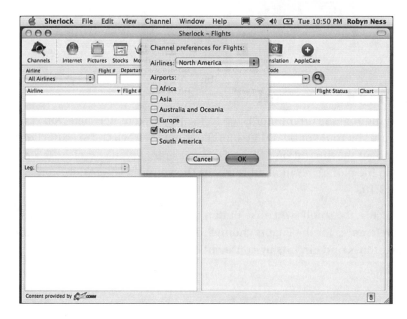

The Dictionary Channel

As you might expect, you look up word definitions in the Dictionary channel (shown in Figure 13.12). For some words, you also see a list—in the lower half of the pane—of phrases that contain that word or relate to it. (Clicking the Pronunciation Key link opens Dictionary.com's pronunciation symbol key in your default browser.)

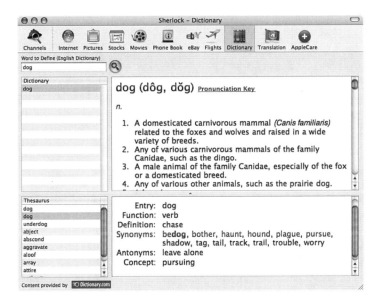

FIGURE 13.12
Expand your vocabulary with help from the Dictionary channel.

The Translation Channel

The Translation channel, shown in Figure 13.13, performs rough translations between different languages. English speakers can translate into Simplified and Traditional Chinese, Dutch, French, German, Greek, Italian, Japanese, Korean, Portuguese, Russian, and Spanish, and then back to English.

If there is a large block of text in a document or email message that you want to translate but don't want to retype, you can select the text, choose Edit, Copy from the menu, and then switch to Sherlock's Translation channel and choose Edit, Paste from the menu.

Did you Know?

FIGURE 13.13
To translate text, type the original text into the top text field, choose an option for translating the original language into another language, and click the Translate button.

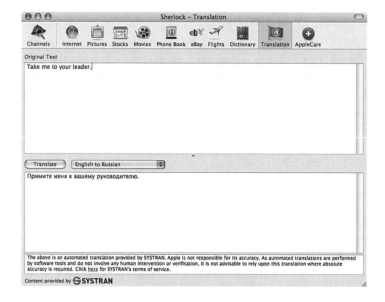

When using this service, keep in mind that computer-generated translations do not match the output of a skilled human translator.

The AppleCare Channel

If you have a specific technical question about Apple software or hardware that OS X's Help Viewer can't resolve, use the AppleCare channel, shown in Figure 13.14, to search the AppleCare Knowledge Base for reports about Apple products and issues.

Now that we have explored the default channels, let's take a quick look at some channels written outside Apple.

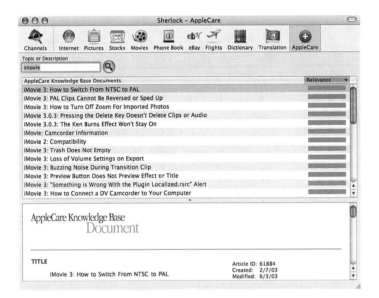

FIGURE 13.14
A quick search of
the AppleCare
Knowledge Base
can answer many
of your questions
about Apple
products.

Third-Party Channels

In addition to the Channels we've see so far in this chapter, which were created
by Apple, there are many channels written by others to view information on topics ranging from news to astrology and from song lyrics to television listings.

To access this information, click the Channels button at the upper left of the
Sherlock toolbar to open the Channels pane. Next, choose Other Channels from
the list along the left-hand side of the window. As shown in Figure 13.15, a
plethora of channels will appear in the right-hand column along with the coun-
tries to which they apply and a brief description.

To open one of these channels, simply double-click its listing. Each channel will
have its own interface to support the information it displays; you will have to follow the cues in the channel's interface to figure out what information will be provided and how to perform a search.

The quality of third-party channels varies greatly. Some are helpful; others merely
frustrate.

FIGURE 13.15
The list of channels created outside Apple.

Before we complete our tour of Sherlock, let's examine the features accessible in Sherlock's preferences.

The Sherlock Preferences

The Sherlock Preferences, as shown in Figure 13.16, are minimal. You have the option to allow Sherlock to accept cookies always or never as it searches the Internet on your behalf. *Cookies* are small files sent to your computer from some Web sites that provide specific types of services, such as personalized user accounts and online shopping.

FIGURE 13.16
Choose to accept or decline cookies, or show a list of any cookies currently stored on your computer.

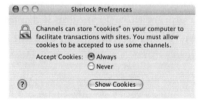

Sites use cookies to keep track of you as you interact with the site. (This is because the computer running the Web site doesn't have another way to recognize that you're the same person who looked at the preceding page.) Even though cookies are mostly harmless, some people don't like the idea of having others track their movements on the Internet, even if the information is most likely never seen by human eyes. That's why Sherlock gives you the choice of whether to accept cookies. (Note, however, that some sites require use of cookies for you to interact with them successfully.)

By the Way

If you click the Show Cookies button, you can see a list of the cookies accumulated on your computer, both by Sherlock and by any other Web browsing applications you use. If you want to remove cookies, you can select them individually and click the Remove button or choose to delete all stored cookies with a click of the Remove All button. When finished with the list of cookies, click Done.

Summary

In this chapter, you learned how to use Sherlock, your system's built-in Internet search tool. You saw the wide range of specialized search channels available from Apple, including movie listings and stock quotes, as well as a source for channels written by third parties.

CHAPTER 14

Exploring the .Mac Membership

.Mac (pronounced "dot Mac") is Apple's $100 subscription-based Mac OS X "add on." It includes a range of services built around storage space on Apple's .Mac server and is integrated with the OS X operating system and several of Apple's applications in key ways. In this chapter, we'll take a look at those services so that you can decide for yourself whether the price tag is worth the benefits.

Defining .Mac

The easiest way to define .Mac is to enumerate the features it offers:

- ▶ Network storage (iDisk)—The .Mac iDisk offers 100MB of network-accessible storage. Using your iDisk, you can access your files from other machines or even share them with friends.

- ▶ Synchronization services—.Mac, in conjunction with iSync (discussed in Chapter 8, "Working with Address Book, Keychain Access, iSync, and Ink"), provides a means for all your Macs to share the same bookmarks, Address Book information, and calendars. Instead of maintaining two sets of bookmarks on your desktop and laptop, a single global set of bookmarks can be maintained and synchronized through .Mac.

- ▶ Network-based Mac OS X information—A .Mac account can hold information that you normally access through applications on your computer and make it available to you through a network connection wherever you are. Calendars, contacts, and bookmarks are currently available with additional "access it anywhere" services in development. The .Mac screensaver (discussed shortly and in Chapter 23, "Using iPhoto") even allows you to view slideshows stored on remote users' iDisks.

- ▶ .Mac Email—Apple-hosted email services, including a nice Web interface are included as part of the subscription. An account holder receives 15MB quota of mail storage. Additional accounts with a 5MB mail quota can be added to a .Mac account for a small fee.

- ▶ Exclusive software—Although not earth-shattering, Apple is currently offering two pieces of .Mac "member's only" software: Virex (virus protection) and

Apple's own Backup (personal document backups). These pieces of software are actually a good value if you need the functionality they offer. If you were, for example, planning to buy a Virus protection package for $50 already, that's half the cost of a .Mac subscription. (See Chapter 36, "Maintaining Your System," for more about Backup and Chapter 37, "Recovering from Crashes and Other Problems," for more about Virex.)

▶ Communication-oriented Web services—The .Mac Web site makes it easy to create custom Web sites—either by using files from your iDisk or simply by exporting them from within iPhoto. Users can also send iCards created with their own or professionally photographed images.

▶ Training—Basic Macintosh tutorials and training materials are available online for common family/consumer activities such as using iTunes, creating Web pages, and so on. These features serve as nice introductions for beginners.

▶ Software Discounts—Special software discounts are offered for select packages, such as games.

Did you Know?

Apple lists iChat as one of the .Mac features. iChat, however, is available for anyone's use. A .Mac account gets you the ability to use your .Mac email address as your buddy name; *however*, even if you just sign up for a demo account, you get to keep the account name indefinitely and can use it with iChat as you like. (See Chapter 16, "Using iChat AV," for more information about iChat.)

Because describing how to use a Web site (www.mac.com) is not the purpose of this book (and the information contained on the site is variable in nature), we won't attempt to document the features that you access through your Web browser. Instead, we'll look at how .Mac's features are used in the Mac OS X desktop and then take a brief walkthrough of the Web services so that you can make the decision of whether you want to join the .Mac club.

By the Way

If you intend to rely on .Mac for mission critical (or life critical) email, check around to make sure that it offers the availability and reliability that you need. Although I personally have experienced .Mac outages rarely throughout my use (which is light), they do happen. Some users have experienced email outages that last for days. At present, Apple does not provide the support or status reporting features common to ISPs offering email and Web hosting services.

Setting up .Mac Service

To set up your .Mac services, open the System Preferences application and open the .Mac pane under the Internet & Network section. Your screen should resemble Figure 14.1.

FIGURE 14.1
Configure or create .Mac services in the .Mac preference pane.

Your choices are limited: either enter an existing .Mac member name and password, or click the Sign Up button to create a new account. If signing up for the first time, your Web browser will be launched, and you'll be taken to the www.mac.com signup page. Keep in mind that you *don't* need to commit to a full account immediately. You can apply for a 60-day free trial and try the members-only features (except for the exclusive software) before you buy.

If you already have a .Mac account, enter your information in the appropriate fields and then either close the preference window or click the iDisk button to view the status of your iDisk (this is a quick way to verify that the account information is entered correctly and everything is working as it should).

Using the iDisk

The Apple iDisk is storage space that your system automatically "knows" how to connect to without additional information.

iDisk requires a network connection and is *barely* usable on dial-in lines. Cable and DSL should be considered the minimum tolerable network requirement for making a connection.

Starting in OS X 10.3, iDisk *does* have one feature that sets it apart from a normal network share—the ability to keep a local copy of its contents that are synchronized automatically when you connect to the Internet. This means that you always have an up-to-date offline copy of the files in case your Internet connection goes down.

From the perspective of the end user, iDisk appears like any other disk whether working with the contents online or using the local copy. The synchronization occurs unobtrusively. As you make changes to the files, they are noted and automatically uploaded to the .Mac server in the background. You can also choose to manually synchronize files if you want.

iDisk Storage Space and Settings

You can customize how your iDisk works and view a quick status of how much space is available by clicking the iDisk button within the .Mac system preferences pane. The pane shown in Figure 14.2 is displayed.

FIGURE 14.2
Configure your
iDisk and view the
space available.

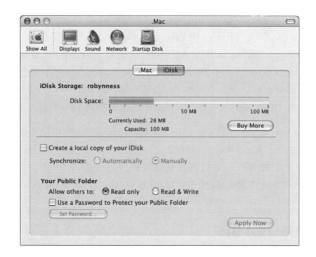

At the top of the pane is the amount of storage currently in use and the total available. You can buy additional iDisk storage space by clicking the Buy More button. Additional iDisk space is sold, like .Mac, on a subscription basis.

Here you can also choose how and whether the iDisk is synchronized—either automatically when you connect to the Internet, manually, or not at all. If you do *not* check the Create a Local Copy of Your iDisk check box, the iDisk will be accessible only over the Internet (as it was in previous versions of Mac OS X). You will not be able to work with the contents without an active network connection.

If you do choose to synchronize your iDisk, select whether it will happen automatically or manually using the radio buttons.

If you ever choose to shut off synchronization after it has been running, Mac OS X will move the disk image file it has been using as the local iDisk copy to your desktop. You can mount it to get at the contents or throw it away if you want.

By the Way

The default iDisk sync settings (keep a local copy of the iDisk and synchronize automatically) make the following two assumptions: You have a reasonably fast Internet connection, and you make small changes to the contents of your iDisk. If you find yourself replacing 100MB of files daily, synchronization is just going to eat up time and network bandwidth.

If you *always* have a fast connection and don't access your iDisk files that much anyway, not using the local iDisk option might be the most efficient option.

If synchronization takes a *long* time each time you use it (dial-in users), you might want to set it to Manually and start a synchronize only when you aren't going to be using your computer heavily.

Did you Know?

Also in the iDisk pane are controls for determining how your public folder is accessed. The iDisk public folder is a special directory on the iDisk that can be read by other Mac OS X users without needing your .Mac login information. You can use the Public folder as a place to exchange files with a few people, or perhaps to share a new piece of software you've written with the world.

To keep things under your control, Apple provides the option of choosing whether other users (that is, not you) have read-only or read-write access to your folder, and whether the folder should be password protected. If you choose to password protect the folder, you will be prompted to set a new password—*do not* use your .Mac password. This is a password that you give out to your friends so that they can connect to your Public folder.

Click Apply Now to activate your iDisk settings.

> Do *not* store copyrighted/pirated material in your public folder.
>
> Also, if you enable read/write access to your Public folder, be aware that you've turned over a portion of your iDisk storage space to the public. If your public folder is filled, it counts against your 100MB iDisk total.

Accessing and Synchronizing Your iDisk

After entering the membership information needed to connect to your iDisk, you can immediately start using the service by opening a Finder window and then clicking the iDisk icon in the sidebar or by choosing My iDisk from the iDisk sub-menu of the Finder's Go menu (Shift-Command-I). After a few seconds, the iDisk icon (a blue orb) appears on your desktop.

If this is the first time that you've used your iDisk (and you haven't configured it otherwise), Mac OS X prompts you to synchronize the entire contents of your iDisk before going any further. If you intend to keep the disk synchronized, allowing the initial synchronization is a good idea. It may take quite awhile at first, but subsequent synchronizations only need to copy the data that has changed, if any.

You can force a synchronization at any time by clicking the chasing arrow (circular arrows) icon to the right of the iDisk icon in the Finder. If you've chosen to have your Mac automatically synchronize the iDisk, you can tell when the synchronization is in progress by watching the icon to the right of the iDisk in your Finder window—it spins while synchronizing.

Open the iDisk like you would any other disk. If you clicked the iDisk icon in the Finder sidebar, the Finder window refreshes to show its contents. If you mounted it from the Go menu, you can double-click the iDisk icon on the desktop to open the window shown in Figure 14.3.

An iDisk contains nine folders, some of which are similar to the folders in a Mac OS X user account (as discussed in Chapter 2, "Using the Finder"):

- ▶ Documents—Your personal storage space for "stuff." No one has access to these files but you.

- ▶ Library—Data storage for applications such as iSync. Again, these files are maintained automatically and probably shouldn't be touched.

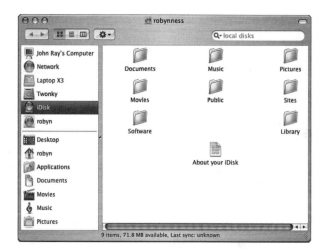

FIGURE 14.3
The folders in your
iDisk are stored on
the .Mac server.

▶ Movies—A place to store your (Webified) Movie files. Movies placed in this location are available for use within the .Mac HomePage Web site builder utility.

▶ Music—A place for you to store your Music files. With the advent of the Apple Music Store, I'd venture a guess that Apple will be adding the capability to download song purchases to this folder in the future.

▶ Pictures—Like Music and Movies, Pictures provides a content-specific place for you to drop your image files. Images placed in the Pictures folder are available within HomePage and the Apple's iCard builder.

▶ Public—Your online folder that can be opened to the public. Files stored here can be accessed (if you choose) by friends, or anyone in the world.

▶ Sites—The files for your Apple-hosted mac.com Web site are stored in the Sites folder. Files placed here are accessible via the URL `http://homepage.mac.com/<mac.com username>/<filename>`.

If you've used the Apple Backup utility, an application available to .Mac members, a folder called Backup also appears in your iDisk. This folder is created and maintained automatically, and it contains the data that has been stored.

By the Way

▶ Software—Apple's collection of freeware and demo Mac OS X software and music. If you need a quick software fix, you can find it here.

Work with iDisk as you would your hard drive or a network share, but be aware that copying files to or from the iDisk takes time. If you are configured to maintain a local copy of the iDisk, transfers will be nearly instantaneous, but the actual transfer occurring in the background may take minutes or hours, depending on the quality of your connection.

Accessing Other Users' iDisks

To access the iDisks of other users, simply choose iDisk, Other User's iDisk from the Finder's Go menu. You are prompted for the user's membership name and password, as shown in Figure 14.4.

FIGURE 14.4
Mount another user's iDisk.

To mount a user's Public folder, choose iDisk, Other User's Public Folder from the Go menu. In this case, you are prompted for the member name, but you do not need to supply a password unless one has been set by the owner of the remote iDisk account.

Did you Know?

> As in previous versions of Mac OS X, you can mount the iDisk volume with Connect To Server by supplying the URL http://idisk.apple.com/<mac.com username>.

iDisks are the cornerstone of the .Mac service and are what makes most of the other services possible. Without, for example, a central storage place to keep iSync information, there would be no means of synchronizing multiple computers on different networks.

.Mac Screensaver

The .Mac screensaver enables users to view slideshows that they (or someone else) have created and saved to their .Mac accounts using iPhoto (discussed in Chapter 23).

To use the screensaver, open the Desktop & Screen Saver option from the System Preferences pane. Choose .Mac from the list of available Screen Savers, and then click the Options button. A sheet window appears, as shown in Figure 14.5, that contains all slideshows that you've subscribed to.

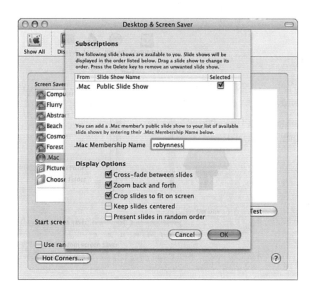

FIGURE 14.5
Create a slideshow that any Internet-connected Mac OS X user can view.

To connect to a new slideshow, enter the name of the .Mac account (such as robynness) in the .Mac Membership Name field and then click OK. Then reopen the sheet window to choose the newly added slideshow and the display options you want used during the presentation; then click OK. The next time your screensaver is activated, you'll see the selected slideshow.

If you enter "robynness" for the name of the .Mac account in the Desktop & Screen Saver preferences, you'll see a slideshow of a tulip flower and leaves that one of the authors of this book took with her digital camera.

By the Way

To remove or disable subscriptions, you must click Options again, select the slideshow, and then press the Delete key, or use the Selected check box to simply disable it.

The .Mac Web Services

The final .Mac features we'll look at in this chapter are the Web services. Accessed with a Web browser through www.mac.com, these features are aimed at families and those on-the-go types that frequently have to access the Internet or send email through computers that aren't their own.

Web Sites

The HomePage Web site builder, shown in Figure 14.6, allows anyone to create Web pages without any knowledge of HTML. Simply copy images and movies to your iDisk (in the appropriate folders, of course), choose a HomePage template, and then add your own content.

FIGURE 14.6
Use the HomePage builder to create instant Web sites.

Apple provides templates for photo albums, resumes, iMovies, and more. If you're an advanced user, you can always add your own content directly to the iDisk Sites folder and create any site you want.

By the Way

You can create simple photo album pages from within iPhoto. Find out more in Chapter 23.

iCards

The Apple iCards are a collection of elegant photographs that you can add a message to and forward to your friends, demonstrated in Figure 14.7. Images that you've placed in your iDisk Pictures folder are also available for use.

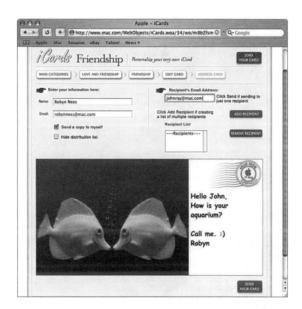

FIGURE 14.7
Create your own iCards to send to friends.

Access On the Go

Probably the most compelling Web service for advanced users is the access to traditionally "desktop" information while on the go. iSync (discussed in Chapter 8) keeps everything "connected" so that what you see on your desktop is available on other computers over the network, and vice versa. Figure 14.8, for example, shows the Bookmark browser.

Likewise, .Mac email and address book entries are also accessed through a Web interface—and carry the feel of a native Mac OS X application along with them. Figure 14.9 shows the .Mac Web-based email.

Another useful feature for users on the go is iCal, which we'll examine in Chapter 17, "Using iCal."

FIGURE 14.8
The Bookmark browser allows you to access and update bookmarks from anywhere.

FIGURE 14.9
It's like your Mac OS X email application—in a Web browser.

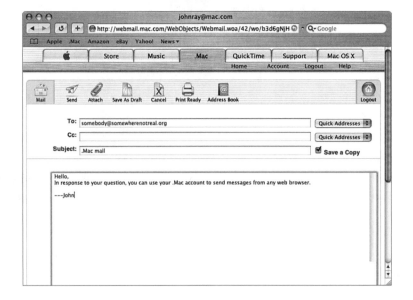

Summary

As of the time of this writing, this *is* .Mac. The direction Apple seems to be heading in is providing ways of taking your data with you. The synchronization of desktop applications with Web services is likely to be the focus of future developments. As you've seen, and will continue to see throughout the book, certain applications provide support for saving information to .Mac. As an easy-to-use method for storing and synchronizing data, you may find .Mac worth the price.

CHAPTER 15

Using Mail

The Mail application is Apple's email client that comes with OS X. Mail provides excellent support for IMAP and POP email services and includes a powerful search mechanism, junk-mail filter, and message thread display that can make managing hordes of email messages fast and painless.

If you've used other common email programs, you'll be completely comfortable in Mail. A toolbar at the top of the window gives access to commonly used functions for creating, responding to, and searching messages. (We'll go into detail a bit later, but Figure 15.1 gives a sneak peek at the main window of a loyal Mail user.)

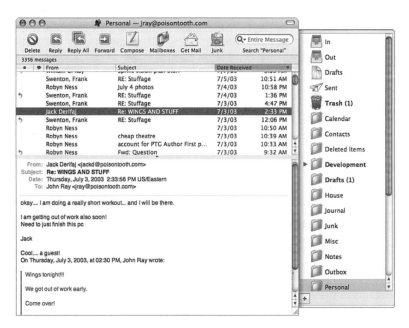

FIGURE 15.1
Mail provides a pleasant (and organized!) interface for working with email.

Setting Up Mail

During the Mac OS X setup procedure (assuming that you've installed from scratch or purchased a new machine with OS X), the installer prompts for a default email account. Although this creates a single account for a single person, additional users and multiple accounts can created within Mail itself. For many people, the first task will be setting up a new account—this provides a perfect place to start.

Using Mail for the first time on a new user account opens a setup window to configure a new email account, as shown in Figure 15.2.

FIGURE 15.2
The first time Mail is run, it forces an email account to be configured.

Seven pieces of information are required to set up an email account:

▶ Your name—That thing that people call you by.

▶ Email address—Your email address (for example, jray@mymailmachine.com).

▶ Incoming mail server—The server that stores your email. If you're using a .Mac account, use mail.mac.com.

▶ Account type—Most ISPs support the POP3 protocol for accessing email. Apple's .Mac servers include support for IMAP. Read further for more information on both POP3 and IMAP and the differences between them.

▶ User name—The username used to access an email account. This is the text that comes before the @ in your email address (that is, jray is the username for jray@mymailmachine.com).

▶ Password—The password required to retrieve mail. Leaving this field blank prompts the user to enter the password when needed.

▶ Outgoing mail server (SMTP)—The server required to send messages. Users of .Mac email accounts can use smtp.mac.com.

If you are unsure of any of these fields, contact your ISP or network administrator. Do not attempt to use the mac.com hostnames unless you are using a .Mac email address—as discussed in Chapter 14, "Exploring the .Mac Membership." These are members-only servers and will deny access to those without an account. Click OK to save your account and start using Mail.

POP3 Versus IMAP

If your email provider supports both the POP3 and IMAP protocols, you're in luck! The POP3 protocol, although extremely popular, is not practical for people with multiple computers. I access the same email account from a number of different computers—one at work, one at home, and another while on the road. Keeping all these machines in sync is virtually impossible with POP3.

POP3 (Post Office Protocol v.3) works much as it sounds: Email is "popped" from a remote server. Incoming messages are stored on the remote server, which in turn waits for a connection from a POP3 client. The client connects only long enough to download all the messages and save them to the local hard drive. Unfortunately, after a message transfers from the server, it's gone. If you go to another computer to check your mail, it won't be there.

IMAP takes a different approach. Instead of relying on the client for message storage, IMAP servers keep everything on the server. Messages and mail folders remain on the server unless explicitly deleted by the client. When new messages arrive, the IMAP client application downloads either the message body or header from the server, but the server contents remain the same. If multiple computers are configured to access the same email account, the email appears identical between the machines—the same folders, messages, and message flags are maintained. In addition, the IMAP protocol supports shared folders between different user accounts and server-based content searches.

If your ISP does not support IMAP, you can sign up for a .Mac account. Apple's POP and IMAP service provides everything you need, along with exclusive Mac OS X downloads and online services.

Importing Mailboxes

After entering your basic account information, Mail immediately starts down-loading your messages in the background and, at the same time, prompts you to import mailboxes from another email client such as Entourage or Eudora. This provides a convenient way to migrate to Mail without having to launch your old mail application to read past messages. Click Yes if you want to pull your old messages into Mail. You'll then be prompted for the mail client that you will be importing from, as shown in Figure 15.3.

FIGURE 15.3
Choose the mail application that you want to import from.

By the Way
> You can import mail you've received in other email programs at any time (not just during the initial setup) by choosing File, Import Mailboxes from the menu.

Choose your previous email application and then click the forward arrow in the bottom-right corner of the window. (If you have mail stored in the Unix mbox for-mat, use the Other selection.)

Next you are prompted for *what* you want to import. Although it appears that Apple is preparing to provide support for importing addresses along with mail, the only available option at the time of this writing is Mailboxes. Make sure that Mailboxes is checked; then click the forward arrow again.

Mail displays a message that describes where your old mail files and folders are located (read this screen carefully); then click the forward arrow.

Finally, select the location of the old files and click Choose. Mail reads your existing files and makes them available in your local Mail mailboxes.

There are two problems with importing legacy mail with Mail.app. First, not all email clients are supported. Popular emailers such as Opera and Mulberry are nowhere to be found. If you find yourself not being able to migrate to mail, Emailchemy— a universal email converter (`http://www.weirdkid.com/products/emailchemy/index.html`)—may be able to save the day.

The second problem with migrating to Mail is that your contacts (and filters) are not preserved. Unfortunately, there is no clean way to handle this issue for every email client. If you're a Eudora user, you'll be interested in Andreas Amann's Eudora Mailbox Cleaner. EMC can completely migrate your Eudora contacts, filters, and messages to Mail and Address Book in a single pass—`http://homepage.mac.com/aamann/`.

Entourage users can drag and drop vCards from Entourage to Address Book to transfer contacts—or use Paul Berkowitz's Sync Entourage-Address Book to perform the action en bulk—`http://scriptbuilders.net/category.php?search=sync+entourage`.

Adding and Modifying Accounts and Settings

Mail supports multiple email accounts for a single user. After setting up the initial account, you can add other email accounts through the Accounts pane of the Application Preferences panel. Choose Preferences from the application menu; then click the Accounts icon. Figure 15.4 shows the Accounts pane of the Mail Preferences. Existing email accounts are listed on the left.

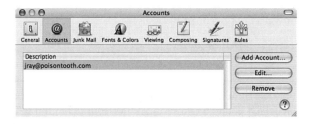

FIGURE 15.4
Multiple email accounts can be added through the Application preferences Accounts pane.

The options available in the Accounts pane of the Mail Preferences panel include

▶ Add Account—Create a new email account.

▶ Edit—Edit the selected account.

▶ Remove—Delete the selected account.

To add a new account to the list, click the Add Account button. An account information sheet appears. This information sheet is divided into three panes: Account Information, Special Mailboxes, and Advanced.

Figure 15.5 shows the general Account Information pane.

FIGURE 15.5
Enter the new email account information into this pane.

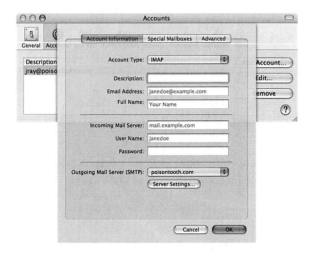

Use the Account Type pop-up menu to set the account type; then fill in the fields as you did when creating the initial account during the install process. Instead of just IMAP or POP accounts, there are three options:

▶ .Mac—Configures a mac.com IMAP account with the appropriate Apple defaults.

▶ POP—Creates a POP3 account.

▶ IMAP—Creates a IMAP account.

Did you Know?

> If you have multiple email return addresses on a single email server and you want to be able to choose which address shows up in the From field on the final message, enter multiple addresses (separated by commas) in the Email Address field on the Account Information pane. This adds a pop-up menu to the message composition window where you can choose from the listed addresses.

Near the bottom of the Account Information display are options for setting your SMTP servers. If you're using POP or IMAP, choose Add Server from the Outgoing

Mail Server pop-up menu to add a new SMTP server, or choose to use one that you've already configured. The Server Settings button edits the currently selected SMTP server.

When adding or editing an SMTP server, you are prompted for the server name, port (if different from 25), and security information. If you are accessing an SSL-protected mail server (IMAPS, POPS), click the Use Secure Sockets Layer (SSL) check box. In addition, if your server uses authenticated SMTP, choose the authentication method and provide a username and password. (You many have to ask your mail provider about these settings.)

The Special Mailboxes tab of the Mail preferences controls what Mail does with Draft, Sent, Junk, and Trash messages, including where they are stored. When configuring an IMAP account, as shown in Figure 15.6, you can choose whether these "special" types of mailboxes are stored on the server, and when mail should be deleted from the server-based boxes.

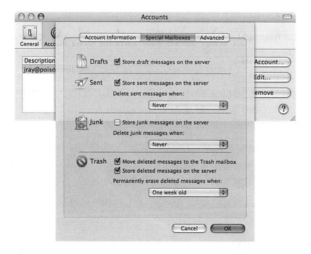

FIGURE 15.6
Special Mailboxes store Drafts, Junk, and other types of messages.

POP accounts are not given the option of storing special messages on the server. Instead, POP users will only be able to choose when messages in any of the special mailboxes are erased.

Click the Advanced tab to fine-tune your account settings. Depending on the account type that you've chosen, the available options change. Figure 15.7 displays the Advanced tab for IMAP (or Mac.com) accounts.

FIGURE 15.7
Each type of email account has different available options.

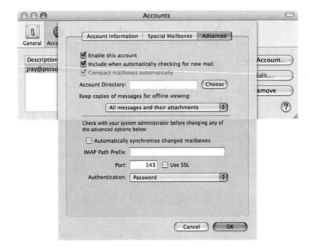

Each of the different mail account types has different available options. Choices available on the Advanced tab when using IMAP (or .Mac) include

▶ Enable This Account—Includes the account in the available account listing. If not enabled, it is ignored.

▶ Include When Automatically Checking for New Mail—If selected, the account will be polled for new messages at the interval set on the Preferences' Accounts pane. If not, the account will be polled only when the user manually checks his mail.

▶ Compact Mailboxes Automatically—Cleans up the local mailbox files when exiting Mail. The benefit of using this is slight, and it can slow down the system when dealing with large mailbox files.

▶ Account Directory—The local directory where the Mail application stores your messages.

▶ Keep Copies of Messages for Offline Viewing—After a message is received on the server, the IMAP client has the option of immediately caching the text of the message on the local machine (cache all messages locally), caching read messages (cache messages when read), or never caching messages on the local drive (don't cache any messages). If you want to be able to read

your mail while offline, you probably want the default setting of synchronizing all messages and their attachments.

▶ Automatically Synchronize Changed Mailboxes—When Mail notices a
change in a mailbox and this option is selected, it automatically downloads
the changes instead of waiting for the mailbox to be opened or manually
synchronized.

▶ IMAP Path Prefix—The IMAP prefix required to access your mailbox. This
field is normally left blank unless a value is specified by your mail server
administrator.

▶ Port—The default IMAP port is 143. If your server uses a different access
port, enter it here.

▶ Use SSL—Enable SSL encryption (IMAPS) of the email traffic. This setting
must be supported by the server in order to be used.

▶ Authentication—Choose how you will authenticate with the remote server.
Most ISPs use a plain password; special server configurations may require
Kerberos or MD5.

If you are using a POP account, you can control how messages are retrieved and
when they are deleted from your account, among other things:

▶ Enable This Account—Include the account in the available account listing.
If not enabled, it is ignored.

▶ Include This Account When Checking for New Mail—If selected, the account
will be polled for new messages at the interval set on the Mail Preferences
Accounts pane. If not, the account will be polled only when the user manually checks his mail.

▶ Remove Copy from Server After Retrieving a Message—Choose the length of
time (if any) messages should remain on the server after downloading. By
leaving the messages on the server, you can create an IMAP-like environment where multiple computers can download the same messages. This is a
"poor-man's" IMAP and does not support multiple server-based folders,
shared folders, and so on. Click Remove Now to remove downloaded messages manually.

▶ Prompt Me to Skip Messages over <#> KB—Automatically skips messages
larger than a set number of kilobytes. This setting is useful for keeping
attachments from being downloaded.

▶ Account Directory—The local directory where the Mail application stores
your messages.

▶ Port—The default POP port is 110. If your server uses a different access port, enter it here.

▶ Use SSL—Enable SSL encryption (POPS) of the email traffic. This must be supported by the server in order to be used.

▶ Authentication—Choose how you will authenticate with the remote server. Most ISPs use a plain password; special server configurations may require Kerberos or MD5.

After setting your account information, mailboxes, and options, click OK to save your account information.

The Mail Interface

Mail uses the special Mac OS X interface elements to create a unique and stream-lined user experience. Figure 15.8 shows the Mail application, ready for action. (Note the drawer is open along the right side to show various mailboxes and folders.)

FIGURE 15.8
Mail has a modern interface that takes advantage of Mac OS X's special features.

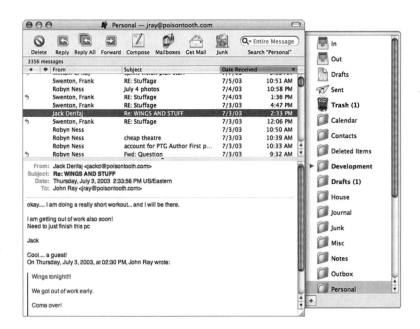

If Mail opens to a window asking for keychain access, you can decide whether to allow access once or allow access always. If you click Allow Once to continue, Mail starts but asks for the password each time it is run.

The keychain access message might appear on recently upgraded systems, or if changes are made to the Mail application. It is not an error but rather an indication that your passwords are securely stored in the Keychain Access application. (Refer to Chapter 8, "Working with Address Book, Keychain Access, iSync, and Ink," for more about Keychain Access.)

At the top of the window is a toolbar to give you quick access to common functions. In the center of the window is the message list for the selected mailbox.

To display the accounts and mail folders, click the Mailbox button in the toolbar. The mailbox drawer slides out from the side of the Mail window.

An action button at the bottom of the Mail drawer gives you easy access to functions such as adding, renaming, or deleting mailboxes and erasing deleted messages or messages filtered into your Junk mailbox. These options are also accessible from the menu bar.

Checking/Reading Mail

To check your account for messages, choose Get New Mail from the Mailbox menu. You can set up how frequently Mail checks for new messages within the General pane of the application preferences, discussed in the section "Mail Preference Options" later in the chapter. Mail downloads your messages/message headers and displays the new email in the message list.

The list columns display the default column's read/unread status, iChat status, subject, and day/time sent. Additional columns can be accessed under the Columns submenu of the View menu. As with most list views, the columns can be sorted by clicking their headings.

You might want to enable the Message Number column under the Columns selection of the View menu.

Sorting by the message number is the best way to keep track of new messages as they come in. If a client includes incorrect time or time zone information when sending a message, it will probably be sorted incorrectly when you use Date and Time as the sort field.

To read a message, highlight it in the list; the bottom of the window refreshes to contain a condensed view of the message headers along with the message content. If the message contains an attachment, an expandable list of files appears following the headers. When the list is expanded, you can drag the attachment icons to your desktop, or, alternatively, click the Save All button to save all the attachments to a given location.

You can quickly hide the message by double-clicking the divider bar between the message list and the message text. This instantly drops the bar to the bottom of the Mail window filling the window with *just* the message list. Double-clicking the bar again returns it to its original position.

Message attachments, such as word processing or text files, show up as icons within the text of the message itself. After a received attachment has downloaded, you can double-click its icon to open the file. You can also drag these icons to your desktop to save the attachments outside Mail, although you will have to wait for the attachment to be downloaded to your computer. As you drag it, a + appears if you've actually "grabbed" the attachment.

Image files and PDF documents received as attachments appear graphically in the body of the message. You can also drag these items to your desktop to store them apart from your email.

Press the Delete key, or choose Message, Delete from the menu, to remove the active message or selected group of messages from the listing. Deleted messages are not immediately removed from the system; they are transferred to a Trash mailbox. What happens from there can be configured from the Viewing pane of the Mail preferences.

Searching for Messages

To search for a piece of mail, use the Search field built into the toolbar. First access the Search drop-down menu by clicking the magnifying glass. This allows you to choose what portion of the messages are being searched—the entire message or the from, to, or subject headers—and whether to search only the active mailbox or *all* mailboxes.

Next, start typing into the Search field. As you type, the search is carried out with only the matching items displayed in the message list. The matching string is highlighted in each message as you read it.

To reset the search results and restore your full list of messages, click the "X" button at the end of the Search field.

Working with Addresses

Panther treats every email address it sees as an object rather than just an ordinary string of letters and numbers. When viewing a message, you can click on an address in the header to select it. When selected, a drop-down menu can be accessed at the right side of the contact, as shown in Figure 15.9.

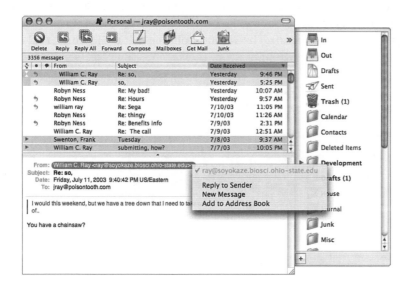

FIGURE 15.9
Addresses are recognized and can be acted on as objects.

From the menu you can add the address immediately to your Address Book, create a new message to the person, or reply to the person. After an address is added to your Address Book, the "email" portion of the address disappears from Mail and only the contact's full name is shown.

If an address has been used to send email but isn't in your Address Book, you may see the option to Remove from Address History when you activate the address object's menu. Using this option removes the email address from Mail's "short-term memory" and keeps it from being autocompleted as you type in addresses.

> If you don't like this new form of addressing, you can shut it off by selecting Show Name and Address rather than Use Smart Addresses from the Addresses submenu of the View menu.

By the Way

Threaded Browsing

In OS X 10.3 (Panther), Mail adds full threaded browsing of your email. That's nice, but what is a thread? A *thread* is a "conversation" you've had with someone over the span of several messages. Usually these are treated like separate emails (because they are) and scattered throughout your other spam...er...messages. With the Panther version of Mail, you can choose to browse your email in thread-ed mode, making it easy to follow the course of a conversation. To enable threads, choose View, Organize by Thread from the menu. Figure 15.10 demonstrates threaded mail browsing.

FIGURE 15.10
Organize your messages into threads.

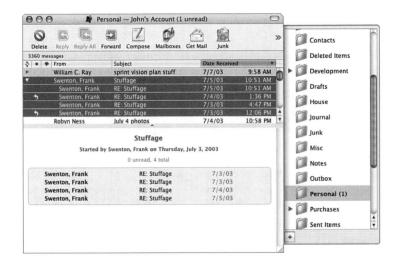

Threads are identified by a blue highlight, an arrow in front of the initial message subject that started the thread, and a number in the status field showing how many unread messages are in the thread (if any). Highlighting the initial message subject line displays information about the thread in the message content pane, such as who started the thread, when, how many messages it contains, which messages contain attachments, and how many of them are unread. Clicking a line within the content pane list jumps immediately to the chosen message.

By the Way

When Mail is in threaded mode, the threads are represented by a "virtual message" with the subject of the initial message. It isn't until you've opened the thread that you can choose and view the contents of the original message.

To browse the thread within the message list, click the arrow at the front of the thread subject line. The message thread expands to show all the available emails within the thread and immediately jumps to the first unread message. To collapse the thread, click in the first column (down and up opposing arrows) of any message within the thread or on the arrow in front of the initial thread subject line. The thread immediately collapses back to a single line.

> Threading is helpful, but it is not perfect (or psychic). Mail determines threads of related messages by subject line or other factors that show continuity. If someone replies to your content without actually using the reply option, Mail may not include that message in the thread. Also, if you have many unrelated messages with the same subject line, they may be grouped.

Watch Out!

You can use the View menu's Expand/Collapse All Threads options to quickly open and close all threads in your mailbox.

> Previous versions of Mail identified threads by highlighting all the messages in a thread in a specific color wherever they appear in the message listing. To reenable this behavior (regardless of whether your email is organized by thread), use the option When Not Grouping Messages By Thread, Highlight Thread Instead found under the Viewing application preferences pane.

Did you Know?

Dealing with Spam

Mail includes a built-in feature to help you manage the ever-increasing sea of spam that threatens to overtake your mailbox. When Mail thinks it has found a piece of spam, it highlights the item in brown in the message listing and displays a "spam" warning when you view the message, as shown (quite appropriately) in Figure 15.11.

Click the Not Junk button in the warning to tell Mail that it incorrectly labeled the message as spam. You can also use the Junk/Not Junk toolbar buttons to flag (or unflag) the currently selected messages(s) in the message listing as spam. The more you "train" Mail, the better it gets at identifying good and bad email.

> The guidelines Mail uses to decide what is spam aren't perfect. Sometimes it misses spam, and other times it labels important messages as spam. If you choose to have Mail filter messages it considers spam to a separate folder or to the Trash, you may still want to peruse these occasionally to make sure that you aren't ignoring real messages.

Watch Out!

FIGURE 15.11
Mail provides built-in spam sensing heuristics.

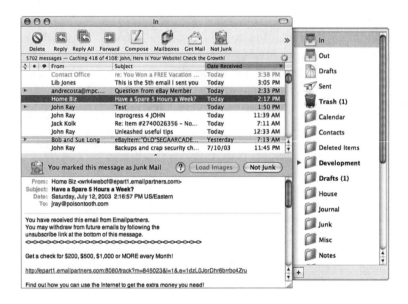

When Mail has gotten to the point where it is consistently identifying spam, you can use the Junk Mail application preferences pane to automatically move messages to a special Junk mailbox instead of leaving it in your inbox.

More Anti-Spam Features

Spammers are nasty. They use special tricks such as identifying whether your email account is active by sending HTML messages with dynamic image links to your address. If your email reader loads the images, the spammer immediately knows that the email account is active and capable of viewing HTML mail—even if you never click a link in the message! Mail understands this and provides the option of disabling the display of inline images and attachments. Under the Viewing application preferences pane you can enable or disable the option to Display Images and Embedded Objects in HTML Messages. When images are disabled, Mail automatically displays a Load Images button at the top of the message content area. Only after the button is clicked does Mail load inline content—preventing the spammers from getting any feedback from your computer.

Another method of defeating spam is to bounce mail back to them. This creates the appearance that your account doesn't exist, and, if you're lucky, results in having your name removed from their lists. To bounce a message, highlight the email in your list and then choose Message, Bounce (Shift-Command-B) from the menu. Alternatively, you can add a Bounce icon to your Mail toolbar for fast access.

iChat AV Integration

Mail integrates with iChat (discussed in Chapter 16, "Using iChat AV") such that any message from a contact who is also on your buddy list displays that person's instant message status in a column within Mail if the Buddy Availability option is selected from the Columns submenu of the View menu.

To launch an iChat AV session with an online buddy, highlight the message the buddy sent in your message list and then choose Message, Reply with iChat (Command-Option-I) from the menu.

Mailboxes/Folders

Click the Mailbox toolbar button, or choose View, Show Mailboxes (Shift-Command-M) from the menu. The mailbox drawer slides open to reveal any accounts and mailboxes that have been added to the system. You can use the disclosure arrows to collapse and expand the hierarchy of mailboxes. The number of unread messages is displayed in parentheses to the right of each mailbox.

By the Way

The default mailbox/folder icons are *huge*. If you have a few dozen like me, you'll want to choose View, Use Small Mailbox Icons from the menu.

To file a message within a mailbox, click and drag it from the list view to the mailbox or folder you want to transfer the message. If the mailbox drawer isn't open, it automatically pops open as the mouse approaches the edge of the window. Alternatively, you can use the Move To or Copy To options from the Message menu. Control-clicking or right-clicking a line in the message opens a contextual menu from which Transfer can also be accessed as well as most other options from the main Message menu.

By the Way

Apple refers to mailboxes as either *mailboxes* or *folders* apparently depending on their mood as they created the interface. You can use these terms interchangeably when working with Mail.

Certain mailboxes, such as In, Out, Drafts, and Trash, are "special" in that they contain all of a specific type of mailbox for each account and are filled automatically:

▶ In—Contains all the Inboxes for all your accounts. You can either expand the master Inbox to pick a specific account's Inbox, or use the top-level Inbox to show all incoming messages in all your accounts, be they POP3, IMAP, or .Mac accounts.

▶ Out—Messages that are *going* to be sent but have not yet left your system.

▶ Sent—Messages that have already been sent from your computer.

▶ Trash—Like the Inbox, the Trash is a collection of messages—in this case, all messages that have been marked for deletion but are not yet deleted.

▶ Drafts—Messages that you are working on but have not yet sent.

By the Way

The Mail icon displays the total number of unread messages in all the Inbox folders. Unfortunately, there is currently no way to change the mailboxes it monitors for the unread count.

Another special mailbox category is On My Mac. This category contains all the mailboxes stored locally on your computer. This is of most interest to POP3 users who cannot create mailboxes on their remote mail server.

To create new mailboxes, choose Mailbox, New from the menu, or click the "+" button at the bottom of the Mail window drawer. You are prompted for where the Mailbox will be created, and what it should be called, as demonstrated in Figure 15.12.

FIGURE 15.12
Choose where to create the new mailbox and what it should be called.

IMAP/Mac.com users can choose an email account from the Location pop-up menu. This will store the mailbox on the remote server. To create a mailbox inside another mailbox, type the full path of the mailbox you want to create. For example, if you already have a mailbox called Work and you want to make the mailbox inside it called Monkey, type **Work/Monkey** in the Name field.

As a shortcut for creating mailboxes within mailboxes, highlight the "parent" mailbox that you want to create another mailbox inside of and then click "+" or choose the New mailbox option.

Did you Know?

To delete or rename a mailbox, highlight it in the mailbox list and then choose Mailbox, Rename or Delete from the menu.

Assigning Special Mailboxes

Mail automatically creates mailboxes for storing Sent items, Trash, Drafts, and Junk mail. If you'd rather use your own mailboxes for those purposes, highlight the mailbox you want to use for a special purpose and then choose the purpose from the Use This Mailbox For option under the Mailbox menu.

Synchronizing Mailboxes for Offline Reading

If you're using IMAP or .Mac, you may want to read your mail offline. This isn't a problem if you're using POP3, but because IMAP and .Mac store messages on the server. To synchronize IMAP/.Mac messages for offline reading, highlight a mailbox in the account you want to sync and then choose Mailbox, Synchronize from the menu.

Rebuilding Mailboxes

There may be times that Mail gets "out of sync" with your IMAP/.Mac mail server. The symptoms are usually missing messages or messages with the wrong content.

From my experience, this happens most often when accessing the mail server from another client and renaming/moving mailboxes. To rebuild the contents of any mailbox, choose Mailbox, Rebuild from the menu. Mail redownloads the contents of the mailbox and (hopefully) corrects the problem. Be aware, however, that this can take a while if you have a lot of messages.

Toolbar Options

Like the Finder, the Mail application supports toolbar customization. The customization process is identical. For more information, see Chapter 2, "Using the Finder." Open the customization sheet by choosing View, Customize Toolbar from the menu. Figure 15.13 shows the available customizations.

FIGURE 15.13
Customize the mail toolbar with your favorite buttons.

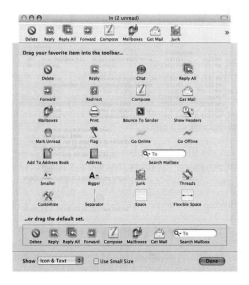

From the top left to bottom right, the available buttons are

- Delete—Delete the selected message(s).

- Reply—Reply to the author of the current message.

- Chat—Launch an iChat session with the sender of the selected message, if the sender is online. The iChat application will be discussed in Chapter 16, "Using iChat AV."

- Reply All—Reply to all recipients of the current message.

- Forward—Forward the current message (and its attachments) to additional recipients.

- Redirect—Redirect the selected message; does not quote the original message's text.

- Compose—Type a new message.

- ▶ Get Mail—Retrieve new messages from available accounts.

- ▶ Mailboxes—Open the Mailbox drawer.

- ▶ Print—Send the active message to the printer.

- ▶ Bounce to Sender—Bounce the selected message. To the original sender, it appears that the message never reached you! Useful for getting rid of spam. The original message is automatically removed after bouncing.

- ▶ Show Headers—Display all the message headers, including the relay path in the message body.

- ▶ Mark Read/Unread—Toggle the read/unread state on a message.

- ▶ Flag—Toggle the flagged/unflagged state message.

- ▶ Go Online—Take an offline email account back online.

- ▶ Go Offline—Take the active email account offline. No further attempts to connect to the server will be made while in this mode.

- ▶ Add to Address Book—Add the sender of the selected message to the Address Book application.

- ▶ Address—Open the Address Book application.

- ▶ Search Mailbox—Search the open mailbox's To, From, or Subject field by choosing it from the pop-up menu and then entering the search text in the field.

- ▶ Smaller—Shrink the font size in the open message.

- ▶ Bigger—Enlarge the text in the open message.

- ▶ Junk—Toggle a message as being junk or not junk.

- ▶ Threads—Toggle thread viewing mode.

- ▶ Customize—Customize the toolbar.

- ▶ Separator—Add a vertical separator bar to the toolbar. This is for visual purposes only.

- ▶ Space—Add an icon-sized space to the toolbar.

- ▶ Flexible Space—Add a space to the toolbar that grows and shrinks with the size of the window.

- ▶ Default Set—Reset to the default set of toolbar icons.

Click Done to save the changes to the toolbar.

When a message is opened in its own window by double-clicking in the message list, that toolbar can also be customized. The only difference is that shortcuts related to the message list and mailboxes are not included in the toolbar customization choices.

Composing Messages

To write an email, click the Compose button or choose File, New Message (Command-N) from the menu. To reply to an existing message, select that message in the list view; then click Reply to start a new message or choose Message, Reply to Sender (Command-R) from the menu. The composition window appears, as shown in Figure 15.14.

FIGURE 15.14
Mail supports styled messages and drag-and-drop attachments.

If text from the original message is selected when you choose to reply, it will be include in the new message as a quote from the original message.

Message Addressing

Three fields are provided for addressing the message. Use the To line for single or multiple addresses that serve as the primary recipients of the message. A comma should separate multiple addresses. The Cc: line adds additional recipients who are not part of the main list. The primary recipients can see these addresses. The Subject line is used to set the subject or the title of the email.

Additional fields are accessible from the Edit menu. Choose Show Bcc Header (Shift-Command-B) to add a Bcc header, or Show Reply-To Header (Option-Command-R) to add an alternative reply address. A Bcc (Blind Carbon Copy) works like a normal carbon copy except that the addresses of BCCed recipients will not be visible to the other recipients. The Reply-To header is used to provide an alternative address for replying. For example, if I'm sending email from my jray@poisontooth.com account and want replies to go to johnray@mac.com instead, I'd enter the Mac.com address in the Reply-To Header field.

To enter an address in a field, simply start typing the contact's name or email address. As you're typing into any of the available fields, Mail attempts to recognize the address either from your Address Book or from other addresses you've used recently and autocomplete the address as you type. If it gets the correct address, press Tab or click outside the area where you are typing, and the address is entered as an object. If you've entered multiple email addresses for a single contact (home and work addresses, for example), click on the object; then use the drop-down menu on the right to choose from the different addresses available for that person, as shown in Figure 15.15.

FIGURE 15.15
Choose which address you want to use for a given person.

From the same pop-up menu, you can also choose Edit Address to enter and edit the address manually, Remove Address to delete the address object from the field, iChat with Person (to start an iChat session if available), or Open in Address Book to open the Address Book application and display the appropriate record.

Address History

If Mail doesn't recognize an address or name as being in your Address Book, it might still autocomplete it if it happens to be an address stored in the Address History. The Address History is much like a browser's page history. It is a record of addresses you've used (either through direct emails or by replying to messages) that are not part of your Address Book. You can display the stored Address History by choosing Window, Address History from the menu, as shown in Figure 15.16.

FIGURE 15.16
The Address
History is a list of
addresses used
but not stored.

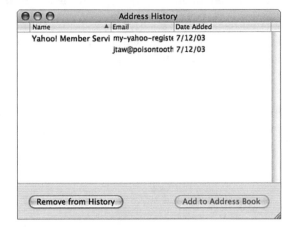

Use the buttons Remove from History to remove a selected address from the history list and Add to Address Book to move the address to your Address Book.

Address Panel

To access the Address Book, click the Address button in the toolbar or choose Window, Address Panel (Option-Command-A) from the menu, and an Address Book panel window appears. From the window, drag individual addresses, multiple addresses, or address groups, to the To/Cc/Bcc fields in the message composition window.

Protecting Against Sending Accidental Email

Its surprisingly easy to find yourself in a ton of trouble (or an embarrassing situation) by including the wrong addresses on a piece of mail, such as sending private corporate secrets to your gossipy arch enemy. To help guard against this, Mail can be configured so that mail addressed to domains outside a given "safe" domain are highlighted in red as they are entered. To activate this feature, choose Mark Addresses Not in This Domain from the Composing pane of the application preferences.

Message Composition

To create the message itself, input the text into the content area of the window. The toolbar can be used to attach files or pick fonts and colors. These options are also available from the Message and Format menus.

Be aware that to receive rich-text email, the remote user must have a modern email program such as Outlook Express (or, better yet, Mail!). To create a message that anyone can receive, compose the content in Plain Text mode, selectable from the Format menu.

To add attachments, drag images and files (and even folders!) directly into the message. Depending on the type of file, it is added to the message as an icon (application, archive, and so on) or shown within the body (picture, movie, PDF).

If you commonly use signatures with your messages, you can add signatures automatically to your message composition window through the Signatures preferences pane discussed later in the section "Mail Preference Options."

To send, click Send in the toolbar, or choose Message, Send Message (Shift-Command-D) from the menu. If you want to save the message and work on it later, choose File, Save as Draft (Command-S) from the menu. This saves the message to your Drafts mailbox where you can open it and resume work later.

When replying to a message, it is common to quote another message. You can quote a specific portion of a message by highlighting the appropriate message content before choosing Reply. Sometimes, however the "quote" level of the message isn't what you'd like. Something you want to be quoted *isn't*, whereas something you don't want quoted is. To adjust the "levels" of quoting, select the text to change and use the Increase or Decrease options under Quote Level within the Format menu to change the quoting.

Did you Know?

Toolbar Options

The message composition window can be customized just like the main mailbox view. When writing a message, choose View, Customize Toolbar from the menu. The available shortcuts are

- ▶ Send—Send the current message.

- ▶ Chat—Open an iChat session with the message addressee (if he's been added to your iChat Buddy List).

- ▶ Attach—Choose a file to attach to the current message.

- ▶ Address—Open the Address Book window.

- ▶ Print—Print the open window.

- ▶ Append—Append the messages selected in the mailbox view to the contents of the current message.

- ▶ Colors—Open the Colors panel.

- ▶ Fonts—Open the Fonts panel.

- ▶ Save as Draft—Save the message to the Drafts folder; it is *not* sent.

- ▶ Smaller—Shrink the text size in the open message.

- ▶ Bigger—Enlarge the text in the open message.

- ▶ Make Rich Text—Toggle the current message to rich text mode.

- ▶ Make Plain Text—Toggle the current message to plain text mode. Note that doing this removes all message formatting.

- ▶ Customize—Customize the toolbar.

- ▶ Separator—Add a vertical separator bar to the toolbar. This is for visual purposes only.

- ▶ Space—Add an icon-sized space to the toolbar.

- ▶ Flexible Space—Add a space to the toolbar that grows and shrinks with the size of the window.

- ▶ Default Set—Reset to the default set of toolbar icons.

When you've selected the toolbar features you want, click Done to save the changes to the toolbar.

Mail Preference Options

Mail's preferences pane contains many of the hidden features of the program—including signatures and mailbox rules (filters). Open the preferences pane by choosing Preferences from the application menu. The Accounts pane was covered earlier and will not be repeated here.

General

The General application pane contains four settings the affect your entire mail-reading experience:

▶ Default Email Reader—If multiple mail readers are installed on your computer, use this menu to choose the default email reader.

▶ Check for New Mail—Change the frequency with which *all* the email accounts will be polled.

▶ New Mail Sound—Select a sound that will be played when new messages arrive on the server. Click Add/Remove to choose a sound file stored in your ~/Library/Sounds folder from your drive, or pick one from anywhere on your drive.

▶ Play Sounds for Other Mail Actions—When checked, Mail plays a variety of sounds for different actions such as sending mail, checking an account without any messages, and so on. To silence these sounds, uncheck this box.

Junk Mail

The Junk Mail features of Mail help weed out junk mail. The Junk Mail preferences pane, shown in Figure 15.17, is your control center for managing how Mail handles messages identified as junk.

FIGURE 15.17
Control your spam from the Junk Mail application preferences pane.

Use these settings to control how Mail reacts to spam:

▶ Enable Junk Mail Filtering—Enable spam filtering.

▶ When Junk Mail Arrives—Choose to leave mail in the inbox (but highlighted as junk) or move it to the "Junk" mailbox.

▶ The Follow Types of Messages Are Exempt from Junk Filtering—To help eliminate false positives, Mail automatically exempts spam status for messages from senders in your Address Book or Address History or messages addressed using your full name. Because it's unlikely that you communicate regularly with spammers, leaving these options checked is a pretty reasonable assumption.

▶ Trust Junk Mail Headers Set By Your Internet Service Provider—Mail servers have the capability to add spam headers (X-Spam: yes) to messages that the *server* feels are spam. If checked, Mail assumes that the mail headers are correct and treats the message as spam, even if other criteria are not met.

▶ Advanced—Allows you to configure how Mail recognizes and treats Junk mail by customizing the internal "Junk" rule. This is identical to other filters (see the "Rules," section discussed shortly) but is specific to junk mail handling.

▶ Reset—Reset the junk mail database kept by Mail. If used, Mail forgets everything it has learned about what is or isn't spam on your system.

Fonts and Colors

The Fonts & Colors pane controls the default fonts used in the message list and message bodies. Figure 15.18 shows this pane.

Options in the Font & Colors pane include

▶ Message List Font—Choose the font and size used in the listing of active messages.

▶ Message Font—Choose the font and size used in the body of messages.

▶ Used Fixed-Width Font for Plain Text Messages—If this option is checked, the system uses a monospace ("typewriter") font for unstyled messages.

▶ Plain Text Font—The font to use for plain text messages.

▶ Color Quoted Text—Text included when replying to a message is automatically included and indented. If there are multiple levels of replies, each level can be set to a different color.

Using a fixed-width font is recommended for plain text messages. Many plain text messages are formatted using spaces for positioning elements—using a proportional font results in a skewed or sometimes unreadable display.

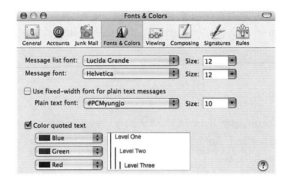

FIGURE 15.18
Choose the default message fonts and quote colors.

Viewing

The Viewing preferences control a contact's instant message status, the amount of header detail that should be displayed, and the downloading of attachments. Figure 15.19 shows the Viewing pane.

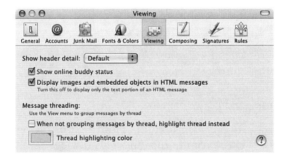

FIGURE 15.19
Control what you see when viewing messages.

Options in the Viewing pane include

- ▶ Show Header Detail—By default, only a few headers (From, Date, To, Subject) are shown. Using this pop-up menu, you can choose to hide all headers, show everything, or create a custom list of headers.

- ▶ Show Online Buddy Status—If a sender has a valid iChat buddy-list entry and this option is checked, her online status is displayed in the Buddy Availability field of the message listing.

- ▶ Display Images and Embedded Objects in HTML Messages—If this option is checked, HTML messages will download all embedded images and movies, and display them within the message body.

▶ When Not Grouping Messages By Thread, Highlight Thread Instead—Choose whether to highlight message threads within the listing and what color to use.

Composing

Choose the default message format used when creating messages. The Composing pane includes a variety of esoteric settings, displayed in Figure 15.20.

FIGURE 15.20
Choose the format
for outgoing
messages.

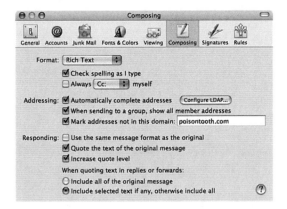

Options in the Composing pane include

▶ Format—Select between Rich Text and Plain Text as the default new message format. If you are communicating with a wide variety of people on unknown operating systems, it's best to stick to plain text.

▶ Check Spelling as I Type—When this option is checked, misspelled words are underlined in red in the message composition window. Control-click (or right-click) the word to display a list of suggestions.

▶ Always cc/Bcc Myself—If this option is checked, you receive a copy of any reply you send.

▶ Automatically Complete Addresses—If this option is checked, Mail attempts to complete email addresses as you type using the Address Book entries, Address History, and configured LDAP servers.

▶ Configure LDAP—Set up LDAP servers for address searches. Mail uses the same servers as configured in Address Book. See the Address Book section of this chapter for more information.

▶ When Sending to a Group, Show All Member Addresses—If you are including a group from the Address Book application and this option is checked, the members of the group are listed in the message header separately.

▶ Mark Addresses Not in This Domain—Set a domain name that is considered "safe." Addresses not in this domain are highlighted in red.

▶ Use the Same Message Format as the Original—When replying to messages, use the same format (rich/plain) in the reply.

▶ Quote the Text of the Original Message—Display the text from the original message as indented quoted text when replying.

▶ Increase Quote Level—When replying, increase the quote level, meaning text that has already been quoted will be quoted again and text that hasn't been quoted at all will become quoted.

▶ Include All of the Original Message—When replying, include the contents of the original message in the reply. The original message will be quoted.

▶ Include Selected Text, If Any, Otherwise Include All—When replying, include only the selected portion of the original message. If nothing is selected, the entire message is included in the reply.

To use LDAP servers for address completion, you should first obtain the appropriate LDAP server information from your network administrator and then click the Configure LDAP button. A window sheet appears listing all configured servers. Click the "+" button to add a new server, "-" to subtract an existing server, or "edit" to reconfigure the highlighted server. Figure 15.21 shows a sample (non-working) entry.

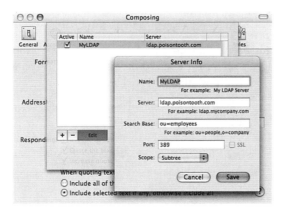

FIGURE 15.21
LDAP servers, if available, can be used to automatically complete email addresses from a centralized directory server.

Signatures

Everyone needs a signature—something to identify you as a individual or at least
to tell others who you are. The Mail application handles multiple signatures with
ease. Figure 15.22 shows the Signatures pane. The available signatures are listed
on the left side of the pane.

Options in the Signatures pane include

▶ Add Signature—Create a new signature. A text-entry pane appears in which
you type or paste a new signature. If you paste in a rich-text clipping, click
the Make Plain Text button to convert it to plain text.

▶ Edit—Edit an existing signature.

▶ Duplicate—Duplicate an existing signature.

▶ Remove—Delete a signature.

▶ Automatically Insert Signature—Choose the signature you want to use by
default, or choose to insert signatures randomly or in sequential order.

▶ Show Signature Menu on Compose Window—If this option is checked, a
Signature pop-up menu is added to the message composition window. From
this pop-up, you can add all the stored signatures.

▶ Place Signature Above Quoted Text—Position the signature in message
replies so that it falls above any quoted text.

Rules

Rules (filters) can perform actions on incoming messages, such as highlighting them in the message listing, moving them to other folders, or playing special sounds. Figure 15.23 shows the Rules pane.

FIGURE 15.23
Rules can auto-
mate the process
of going through
your messages.

Each rule in the list is evaluated once per incoming message (unless the Active box is unchecked). In fact, multiple rules can act on a single message. To change the order in which the rules are applied, drag rule entries in the list to the order you want.

> Apple includes a default rule for dealing with Apple mailings. If you aren't subscribed to any Apple lists (or if you are and don't want them to be highlighted), you can delete this rule.

There are four options for manipulating the rule list: Add Rule, Edit, Duplicate, and Remove. The function of each option is self-explanatory.

Rule creation is simple. Each rule consists of *conditions* that look at portions of the incoming message to determine what *actions* to perform. Figure 15.24 demon-strates the rule creation process.

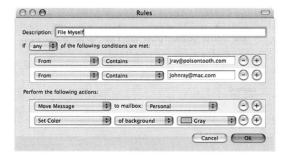

FIGURE 15.24
Unlike other email
programs, Mail's
rules are simple to
create.

When creating a new rule, first enter a description. This is used to identify the rule in the listing. Next, decide whether the rule you're creating requires *all* of a series of conditions to be met (such as "from blah@emailaddress.com *and* containing the subject 'Lottery'") or *any* of the conditions to be matched (an *or* condition such as "from blah@emailaddress.com or blah2@emailaddress.com") use the pop-up menu following If to choose Any or All condition matching.

Next, compose the conditions. The Rule starts with a single condition; additional conditions can be added by clicking the "+" button at the end of the condition line. Conditions can be deleted with the "-" button. In Figure 15.24, I'm matching any message where the "From" address contains either jray@poisontooth.com or johnray@mac.com.

Finally, choose the actions; again using the "+" and "-" buttons to add and delete as many actions as you want. In this example, I've chosen to move any messages that match my conditions to the Personal mailbox and set the message background color to gray.

The conditions and actions are flexible and allow you to match against your Address Book entries and the message content itself. Likewise, the actions give you complete control over the message:

▶ Move Message—Move the message to another mailbox.

▶ Copy Message—Copy the message to another mailbox, leaving a copy in the default mailbox.

▶ Set Color—Set the highlight color for the message.

▶ Play Sound—Play a system (or custom) beep sound.

▶ Bounce Icon in Dock—Bounce the Mail icon in the dock.

▶ Forward/Redirect/Reply To—Send the message to another email address. Click the Message button to enter text that will be included with the message being sent.

▶ Delete the Message—Delete the message. Useful for automatically getting rid of common spam messages.

▶ Mark as Read—Mark the message as read.

▶ Mark as Flagged—Flag the message.

▶ Run Applescript—Run an Applescript for advanced processing.

▶ Stop Evaluating Rules—Stop processing any further rules in the filter.

Click OK to set and activate the rule.

Mail Menus

Wrapping up our Mail application overview, we'll look at the menu options. Most of these options have already been covered somewhere in the chapter, but there are a few obscure options you might be interested in.

File

The File menu is used to create a new message, or multiple "views" into your mailboxes. It can also be used to save a message as a draft before sending:

▶ New Message (Command-N)—Create a new message.

▶ New Viewer Window (Option-Command-N)—Open another mailbox viewer. The main Mail window is called the Viewer window.

▶ Close—Close the frontmost window.

▶ Save As (Shift-Command-S)—Save the current message in an external file.

▶ Save as Draft (Command-S)—Save the current message as a draft.

▶ Attach File (Shift-Command-A)—Attach a file to the message you are composing.

▶ Save Attachments—Save the message's attachments.

▶ Import Mailboxes—Launch an assistant to import mailbox files from Outlook Express, Netscape, Emailer, or other applications.

▶ Page Setup (Shift-Command-P)—Configure the printer.

▶ Print (Command-P)—Print the frontmost document.

Edit

The Edit menu performs as you would expect. Besides the usual Paste selection, it also offers the capability to Paste as Quotation, automatically quoting the text in the Clipboard. The menu also includes spell checking and search-and-replace options.

Use these Edit menu items when composing messages:

▶ Show Bcc Header (Shift-Command-B)—Add a Blind Carbon Copy field to the composition window.

▶ Show Reply-To Header (Option-Command-R)—Add a Reply-To field to the composition window.

▶ Append Selected Messages (Shift-Command-I)—Add selected messages to the end of the message being written.

▶ Attach File (Shift-Command-A)—Attach a file to the message in the composition window.

▶ Remove Attachments—Remove any attachments in the message being composed.

▶ Attachments/Include Original Attachments—Include the attachments in a reply that were part of the original message.

▶ Attachments/Always Send Windows Friendly Attachments—Create attachments that will by "friendly" to Windows systems and not include Macintosh-specific meta-information.

View

The View menu changes the way in which messages are listed in the mail program. Users can sort, display message sizes, and display messages marked for deletion.

▶ Columns—Select the columns displayed in the message listing.

▶ Sort By—Choose the column by which the mailbox viewer window is open.

▶ Show Mailboxes (Shift-Command-M)—Show the mailbox tray.

▶ Organize By Thread—Enter threaded message browsing mode.

▶ Expand All Threads—Show the contents of all threads.

▶ Collapse All Threads—Reduce all threads to a single message listing line.

▶ Display Selected Messages Only—Hides all messages except those selected in the mailbox viewer. To restore the view of all messages, choose Show All Messages.

▶ Message—Choose to view the raw source of the message, complete headers, or the decoding type.

▶ Addresses—When Use Smart Addresses is selected in the Addresses submenu, Mail uses the "address objects" described in this chapter. To revert to the older addressing style choose Show Name and Address.

▶ Show Deleted Messages (Command-L)—Show messages that are marked as deleted. When you're not using a Trash folder, messages are hidden from view after being marked as deleted.

▶ Hide Toolbar—Hide the toolbar in the active window.

▶ Customize Toolbar—Customize the toolbar for the frontmost window type.

▶ Hide/Show Status Bar (Option-Command-S)—Toggle the message count status line on and off.

Mailbox

The Mailbox menu is used to create or modify local or IMAP-based mailboxes. Mac OS X automatically switches between local and remote mailboxes depending on your account configuration.

▶ Online Status—Log on or off all email accounts, or choose a specific account to log on or off.

▶ Get New Mail (Shift-Command-N)—Check for new mail in all accounts, or choose a specific account.

▶ Synchronize—Synchronize local mailbox with remote server for offline reading.

▶ Erase Deleted Messages—Choose to erase messages that have been moved to the Trash for all your accounts, or a specific server.

▶ Erase Junk Mail—Erase messages that have been placed in the Junk Mail folder. (This option is inactive unless you Enable Junk Mail Filtering in the Junk Mail pane of Mail's preferences.)

▶ New—Create a new mailbox. If an IMAP account is selected, the mailbox is created on the server.

▶ Rename—Rename the selected mailbox.

▶ Delete—Delete the selected mailbox.

▶ Go To—Show the contents of one of the default (In, Out, Trash, Drafts, Junk) mailboxes.

▶ Use This Mailbox For—Set the highlighted mailbox (for IMAP servers) so that it will be used to hold Drafts, Sent messages, and so on.

▶ Rebuild—Reloads the current mailbox. Occasionally, Mail gets out of sync and the message list is displayed incorrectly. Choose this option to fix the problem.

Message

Use the Message menu to operate on the message currently highlighted or being displayed. This menu can be used to clean up replies by removing attachments or appending additional messages.

▶ Send (Shift-Command-D)—Send the current message.

▶ Reply to Sender (Command-R)—Reply to the current message. If you have text selected when choosing this option, only that text will be quoted.

▶ Reply All (Shift-Command-R)—Reply to everyone who received the original message.

▶ Reply with iChat (Option-Command-I)—Open an iChat session with the highlighted message's sender, if possible.

▶ Forward (Shift-Command-F)—Forward an existing message to another address.

▶ Redirect (Shift-Command-E)—Redirect an existing message to another address. Similar to Forward Message, but does not quote the original message.

▶ Bounce (Option-Command-B)—Bounce the message to the sender and remove it from the mailbox.

▶ Mark—Toggle Read, Flagged, and Junk mail status for the message.

▶ Move To—Transfer the message to another mailbox.

▶ Copy To—Copy the message to another mailbox.

▶ Move Again (Option-Command-T)—Transfer a message to the last mailbox accessed.

▶ Apply Rules (Option-Command-L)—Apply Mail rules (filters) to the selected message or messages.

▶ Add Sender to Address Book (Command-Y)—Add the sender to the Address Book application.

▶ Remove Attachments—Remove any attachments to the message before sending. Useful for stripping replies of their attachments.

▶ Text Encoding—Choose the text encoding for the message. This is usually determined automatically by your system language settings; used for international/cross-platform communication.

Format

The Format menu is used to change to the text style within a message you are composing. The following options are available for your use:

- ▶ Show Fonts—Choose a font for message composition.

- ▶ Show Colors—Choose a color to use with your font.

- ▶ Style—Set font sizes and basic styling (bold, italic, and so on).

- ▶ Alignment—Set the text alignment (left, right, center) for the active message.

- ▶ Make Plain/Rich Text (Shift-Command-T)—Toggle between plain and rich text modes. Remember, toggling a rich text message to plain text mode removes all formatting information.

- ▶ Quote Level/Increase (Command-')—Add a level of quotes (>) to the selection.

- ▶ Quote Level/Decrease (Option-Command-')—Remove one level of quoting (>) from the selection.

Window

The Window menu operates as it does in other applications—providing quick access to open windows. In addition, it provides an Addresses selection for quick access to the Address Book window (Option-Command-A), an Address History, as well as an Activity Viewer (Option-Command-0). The Activity Viewer shows what Mail task is completing. Each account access is shown, along with a description of each action that is taking place. To cancel or stop an action, click the Stop button.

Summary

In this chapter we took an in-depth look at OS X's built-in email Application, Mail. You learned how to set up your email account, as well as how to transfer messages from your existing mail programs. You also learned how to read and send mail and work with email addresses for your contacts.

CHAPTER 16

Using iChat AV

iChat AV allows you to communicate in real-time with people who use mac.com or have an AOL Instant Messenger (AIM) account. You can use it to hold text-based conversations with friends or, with the proper equipment, even to have audio or videoconferences.

To make full use of iChat, you will need an AOL Instant Messenger (AIM) account or a .Mac username. You can sign up for a free AIM account at www.aim.com or a free .Mac username at www.mac.com, which comes with a 60-day trial of .Mac benefits. (After the .Mac trial expires, the username is still usable for iChat.) Even if you plan to use iChat AV only for its audio/videoconferencing capabilities, you'll still need one of these accounts; they are used to establish a connection.

If other users on your local network use iChat AV, you won't need to use an AIM or mac.com account to chat with them. Rendezvous-capability has been incorporated into iChat so that it can automatically generate a buddy list of users within your local network. This list appears in a Rendezvous window separate from contacts you add to your buddy list.

Setting Up iChat

The first time you start iChat AV, you are prompted for either your AIM or .Mac iChat username, as shown in Figure 16.1. To register for a free .Mac username, click the Get an iChat Account button.

Next, you are prompted for whether you want to use Rendezvous for messaging. If you have a relatively contained local network, turning on Rendezvous probably isn't an issue. If you're part of a subnet with hundreds of clients, however, your Rendezvous list may be overwhelming.

Finally, iChat provides a preview of your audio and video input. (If you want to take advantage of audio- or videoconferencing, make sure that you have a camera and/or a microphone attached to the inputs and that they are recognized by iChat

before continuing. We'll talk more about audio- and videoconferences with iChat
later in this chapter in the section "Using iChat for Audio or Video Chats.")

FIGURE 16.1
Enter your account
information.

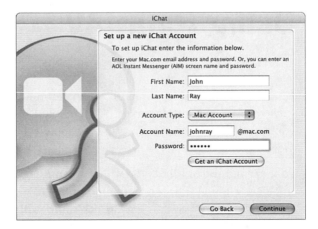

If you need to add or change settings after the first time iChat AV runs, choose
Preferences from the iChat application menu and open the Accounts pane, as
shown in Figure 16.2. Enter your AIM screen name or your full .Mac account
(including the @mac.com) in the AIM Screen Name field, and enter your password
in the Password field.

Did you
Know?

You can quickly fill in the fields in the Accounts pane with your system-stored .Mac
preferences by choosing Use my .Mac Account from the AIM Screen Name field's
pop-up menu.

FIGURE 16.2
Configure iChat for
use with your .Mac
or AIM account.

If you're using an alternative AIM server or require a proxy, click the Server
Options button to provide connection or proxy information for iChat AV. (If you
don't know what settings to change, just leave these as they are.)

Rendezvous messaging, which allows people within a local network to communicate, can be enabled or disabled by clicking the Enable Local Rendezvous Messaging check box.

After configuring iChat AV, you can log in to AIM or Rendezvous using the Log Into menu options found in the iChat AV application menu, or by setting your availability in the Buddy List window (there's a pop-up menu directly under your username). You can also log in by choosing Buddy List from the iChat AV menu extra, in the right side of the menu bar.

> The iChat AV menu extra is displayed as a "speech bubble" on the right side of your menu bar. You do *not* have to have iChat AV open to log in to or out of AIM, or to initiate a chat session. This menu is always active and can be used to set your availability or choose a buddy to start a conversation.

By the Way

The iChat AV Buddy List

When you log in to AIM through iChat, the full Buddy List window appears onscreen to show whether your friends are online (not grayed out), available to chat and what conferencing capabilities (Audio/Video) are available to them, as shown in Figure 16.3. (If your buddy list is empty right now, don't worry; we'll talk about adding buddies to your list in just a moment.)

FIGURE 16.3
You can easily see who's available to chat (and their iChat capabilities) using the Buddy List; the listings for people not connected to the AIM server are dimmed.

The video camera icon shows video availability, whereas the telephone represents an audio-chat ready contact. You can customize what details are displayed in the Buddy List and sort it by different criteria using the iChat AV View menu.

Rendezvous chatting, if active, opens a virtually identical window displaying the active iChat users on your local subnet.

Status Settings

When you are logged in to iChat AV, other members can see whether you are available for a chat. By default you can set two states for your account to use: Available and Away—accessed from either the iChat AV menu extra or the drop-down menu under your name at the top of the Buddy List window. If your computer has been idle for several minutes, it automatically kicks into an "idle" state to show that you haven't been using your computer.

To create additional states, use the two Custom options found under the Buddy List availability menu. You will be allowed to type your own custom label to be displayed in your buddies' chat clients.

By the Way

Your status, as well as the status of your buddies, is typically indicated by green (available), red (away), and orange (idle) dots next to each name (including yours) in the Buddy List window and iChat AV menu extra.

If you have trouble differentiating between the colors or just want a change of pace, the availability "dots" can be changed to shapes using the General pane within the iChat AV preferences panels.

Adding Buddies

Because your buddy list is stored on the AIM servers, you must be logged in to manage the list. To add a buddy, click the + button at the bottom of the iChat Buddy List window.

A sheet containing entries from your Address Book (covered in Chapter 8, "Working with Address Book, Keychain Access, iSync, and Ink") appears, as shown in Figure 16.4. If the person you want to add to your buddy list has an AIM or mac.com listing, highlight the person and click Select Buddy.

If the person doesn't show an instant messaging name, you are prompted for the information. If the buddy-to-be isn't currently in your Address Book at all, click the New Person button to create a new entry. Enter the person's AIM or .Mac screen name, as well as his real name and email address in the window that appears.

FIGURE 16.4
Add your AIM and
.Mac buddies to
your list.

You can drag an image file (if available) into the image well in your Address Book to set a custom buddy icon. Click the Add button to save your new buddy. (We'll talk more about buddy icons later in this chapter in the section "Setting Your iChat AV Buddy Icon.")

Did you Know?

Address Book and iChat are integrated such that adding a new buddy to iChat automatically adds a new card in Address Book. However, because your buddy list is stored on the Instant Messenger server, you can't remove a buddy simply by deleting an Address Book card. Instead, you must select the buddy in the Buddy List and choose Edit, Delete from the menu.

Also, keep in mind that deleting a buddy from the Buddy List does not remove the person's card from the Address Book.

By the Way

Editing Buddy Info

To edit any information for a buddy that is already stored, select the buddy in the list and then choose Buddies, Get Info from the menu, or Control-click on the buddy herself and select Get Info. The Info window, shown in Figure 16.5, provides quick access to your Address Book buddy information.

As with the initial setup, here you can set all the contact information for your buddy, as well as a custom buddy icon. If you *do* set a custom icon, you can choose to always use it in your buddy list. If this option is not set, your buddy icon can be overridden by any custom icon set on the remote system.

FIGURE 16.5
Edit your buddies' information and override their ugly and/or horrifying icons.

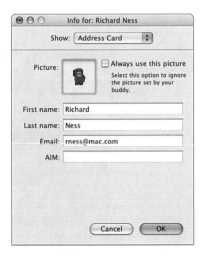

Setting Your iChat AV Buddy Icon

A unique feature of the AIM service is the ability to set custom thumbnails of all your contacts and yourself. These are known as *buddy icons* (or *buddy pictures* depending on what label Apple decided to use where). Your buddy icon is automatically transmitted to your friends so that they can see whatever you've set your icon to be. Similarly, if they've set custom icons, the icons automatically show up on your system.

By default your personal AIM buddy icon is be the image set in the Address Book application or the icon used for your account image. To replace it with one of your choosing, drag a new image into the image well beside your name at the top of the Buddy List window. An editing window appears to allow you to position and scale the image, as shown in Figure 16.6. Drag the image so that the section you want to use as an icon is centered in the bright square in the middle of the window; then use the zoom slider underneath the image to zoom in and out. The center square shows the icon that will be set, albeit larger than its final size in iChat AV. When you're satisfied with the image, click Set.

If you want to choose another image from a file, click the Choose button, and a standard file selection dialog box appears.

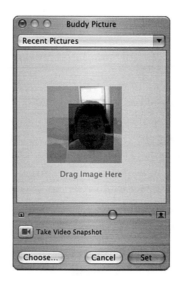

FIGURE 16.6
Position and crop
your image.

> Users with a camera attached will notice the Take Video Snapshot button at the bottom of their window. Clicking this button displays a live video preview, gives you roughly 3 seconds to primp and preen, and then automatically takes a snapshot that you can use as a buddy icon. This provides an easy way to create a new icon for your mood du jour.

In iChat AV, you can switch to any icon you've used recently by clicking your thumbnail image in the Buddy List window. A palette of frequently used icons is displayed, enabling you to quickly switch to icons to match your current mood, as shown in Figure 16.7.

FIGURE 16.7
Jump to any of your
frequently used
icons.

Use the Edit Picture selection within the pop-up palette to reposition or recrop the selected icon.

Buddy Actions

From the Get Info window, you can also access Buddy Actions by choosing Actions from the Show pop-up menu. A Buddy Action, displayed in Figure 16.8, is simply something that "happens" when one of your contacts becomes available or does something interesting.

FIGURE 16.8
Buddy actions automatically react when your contacts do something.

In this example, I've chosen to speak the text "Anne is here!" and bounce the dock item repeatedly when my buddy becomes available. Additionally, by checking the box Perform Actions Only Next Time Event Occurs the action automatically is removed after the first time it is used. I have something important to say to Anne, but usually could care less if she is online, thus the setting. (No Anne, that isn't true, I'm simply putting on airs for the reader.)

Seven possible events can be used to trigger a buddy action:

▶ Buddy Becomes Available—Your buddy has become available for IM'ing.

▶ Buddy Becomes Unavailable—Your buddy is no longer available for IM'ing.

▶ Message Received—Your buddy receives an IM that you sent.

▶ Text Invitation—Your buddy sends you a text chat invitation.

▶ Audio Invitation—Your buddy sends you an audio chat invitation.

▶ Video Invitation—Your buddy sends you a video chat invitation.

▶ Buddy Accepted A/V Invitation—Your buddy accepts an A/V chat invitation that *you* sent.

As you set actions for events, a megaphone icon appears beside the event that contains an action. This lets you keep track of what events trigger actions without having to select and inspect each one.

Buddy Groups

If you have many friends, you may quickly find youself with a long-scrolling list of buddies in your window. To better manage your buddy list, you can arrange them into groups such as People I Know, People I Like, and People I can't ignore. After creating the groups, you can choose which group (or groups) are displayed at once.

To access the groups feature of iChat AV, choose View, Show Groups from the menu. A window drawer appears, as shown in Figure 16.9. Initially, a default Buddies group contains all your buddies.

FIGURE 16.9
Arrange buddies into groups.

To add a new group, click the "+" button at the bottom of the window drawer and type a name for the group. A Group name can be edited at any time by double-clicking its name in the list. Groups (and the buddies they contain) can be removed by selecting the group name and choosing Edit, Delete from the menu (or by pressing the Delete key on your keyboard).

After adding a group, populate it with buddies by dragging their names from the Buddy List onto the group names. To remove a buddy from a group, make sure that the group name is highlighted in the drawer and then drag the buddy back into the default Buddies group.

> Make sure that you delete buddies from groups only when you no longer want them anywhere in your buddy list!

To show only the buddies within a specific group or set of groups, use the check boxes to the left of the group names to select which groups are displayed in your buddy list at a given time. The All Groups check box is a shortcut for selecting all the groups simultaneously.

To close the group drawer, click the arrow in the upper-right corner of the drawer, or choose View, Hide Groups from the menu.

> If this seems like an awkward way to display groups, I agree. Thankfully, Apple added an awkward-to-find preference that makes groups much more manageable. To add a permanent drop-down group menu to the Buddy List window, visit the General pane of the application preferences and click the Use Groups in Buddy List check box.

Instant Messaging

In iChat AV, you can choose from three types of "messaging" to communicate with your friends: text, audio, and video—represented by the "A", Phone, and Video camera icons, respectively, at the bottom of your buddy list. To start a messaging session with one of your buddies, just select the buddy's name in the list and click the appropriate icon at the bottom of the Buddy List. (Only the type of messaging your buddy can participate in will be available.)

Alternatively, you can double click the buddy's name to start a text chat, or click the telephone or video icon by the buddy's picture to start an audio or video chat. (We'll cover audio and video chats more later in the chapter in the section "Using iChat for Audio or Video Chats.")

> The iChat AV menu extra can also be used to start a chat session by choosing a buddy name from the menu. If the buddy has multiple means of communicating (besides simple text), iChat displays a window with three buttons (Text, Audio, Video) and allows you to choose your preferred chat method.

For those with who prefer to use menus, the Buddies menu also allows you to initiate a chat session, including two "special" chat types—one-way audio and one-way video. These are useful if you want to send audio or video to someone without a camera. They will be able to type their responses to you and watch/hear your audio/video stream.

Starting a text messaging session opens an empty chat window, as shown in Figure 16.10.

FIGURE 16.10
A fresh chat
window.

Type your message in the message field at the bottom of the window and press Return on your keyboard. If you're into sending "emoticons" (smiley faces), there is a convenient pull-down smiley menu on the right side of the input field. Basic formatting controls (Bold, Underline, Font, and so on) are found under the Format menu and can be used to style your text.

After you send your message, it appears in the upper portion of the window, along with whatever reply the other person sends, as shown in Figure 16.11.

FIGURE 16.11
A chat in progress.

The text of a conversation can be saved by choosing File, Save a Copy As from the menu.

If you find the conversation bubbles displayed by iChat annoying, you can use View, Show as Text in the menu to disable them (and View, Show as Balloons to turn them back on).

Further chat window View settings include the option of choosing how buddies are identified in a chat (using their pictures, names, or both), the ability to set a customized picture as the chat background, and finally to clear the background picture if you find it distracting.

If you receive a message while not already engaged in a chat session with the sender, you are alerted, and a message window appears. If you click on the window, it displays an area for you to type a response (immediately accepting the invitation). You also have the option of clicking Block to block the request and further messages from the buddy, Decline to turn down the chat with your buddy, or Accept to start chatting. Again, if you enter a response and press Return, it is assumed that you have accepted the chat.

You can add the person you're currently chatting with to your buddy list by choosing Buddies, Add Buddy from the menu.

If, during the course of a conversation, your chat buddy temporarily closes the connection or gets bumped offline, your chat window stays open. If the buddy comes back, a message to that effect appears in the already open window, and you can resume the conversation where you left off.

Private Messages

AIM messages are not (usually) a direct line of communication between people. Instead, all IM traffic is routed through instant messaging servers—in the case of AIM, AOL's servers. Although this conveniently avoids many connection problems with firewalls and inbound traffic, it also leads to privacy concerns about who could potentially be watching your chat. In addition, the extra time required to transmit through a central server can slow file transfers between individuals. To avoid this, users can activate a Direct instant messaging session where all information is passed directly between the participants' computers.

To do this, choose the buddy to send a direct IM to and choose Buddies, Send Direct Message from the menu (Command-Option-Shift-M). If both you and the recipient are connected directly to the Internet, an IM session starts, exactly as it would through the AOL servers.

Sending Hyperlinks and Files

In addition to sending ordinary text messages, iChat allows you to send files. To send a file, drag its icon from your hard drive into the message area of a chat window and press Return on your keyboard. The recipient can then drag the file onto his desktop. If you send image files, they will appear inside the chat window as part of the conversation, as shown in Figure 16.12. (For maximum compatibility with people using AIM programs other than iChat, it's recommended that you stick with JPEG and GIF image formats.)

FIGURE 16.12
Send a picture as part of your conversation.

Hyperlinks can also be sent as a special iChat object. To send a hyperlink, type a URL (including the "http://" part); drag the bookmark from your browser; or choose Edit, Attach Hyperlink to enter a clickable URL. When your buddy clicks the link, it opens her default Web browser to the page you've referenced.

Group Chat Sessions

You can participate in chats with different people simultaneously, each contained in its own separate window (the default). You can also start a chat session with multiple people where all participants can see messages and type simultaneously.

To start a group chat:

1. Highlight the buddies you want to invite to chat; then Control-click on any of the names to open a contextual menu, as shown in Figure 16.13. From the menu, choose Invite To Chat.

FIGURE 16.13
Open a group chat session.

2. Type a message inviting the participants. When the invited buddies receive the chat request (shown in Figure 16.14), they can choose to accept or decline. If they accept, they can send and receive messages as part of the group.

FIGURE 16.14
Start multiperson chats in iChat AV.

If you start a multiperson chat and want to switch to a single-user IM, you can use the Chat Options menu selection under the View menu. You are prompted for what type of IM session you want to switch to.

The chat options can also be used to view the Chat Name, which, in turn, can be used by any AIM user to join the chat, even if he is not on your buddy list. In iChat AV, choosing File, Go To Chat allows any iChat user to enter the chat name and join your chat. Other AIM clients should offer the same feature, but how it is accessed varies.

Creating or Joining a Persistent Chat Room

You can start a group chat that remains open and allows others to join whenever they wan. To do this, select File, Go To Chat (Command-G) from the menu and type a name for your chat room. The iChat AV chat window appears with *no* participants. (If you typed an existing chat room name, you will join a chat someone else has created.) Others can join your chat room using the Go To Chat feature on their copy of iChat AV.

Some chat names (including those with punctuation) are unacceptable when creating a chat room. If iChat AV does not return a chat window immediately upon using Go To Chat, the name you typed is invalid.

Using iChat for Audio or Video Chats

As you found out at the beginning of this chapter, iChat AV can be used for audio or video chats as well as instant messaging. Figure 16.15 shows an example of a video chat session in progress.

FIGURE 16.15
Videoconferencing is simple and fun with iChat AV.

With very little setup, it allows ordinary users to hold high-quality full motion videoconferences with their friends and colleagues.

iChat is not compatible with other videoconferencing applications. If you need a solution that works with people using the Windows operating system, Yahoo!'s IM client for Mac OS X supports video (and *has* supported it for some time). Download the Yahoo! client from `http://messenger.yahoo.com/messenger/download/mac.html`.

iChat works with recognized Mac OS X video sources: Firewire camcorders, Webcams, and analog A/V conversion devices. Apple's own iSight camera (`www.apple.com/isight/`) produces a high-quality image. If the $150 price tag is within range, I recommend the iSight purchase. If not, the iBot camera is available for the $50-$75 range on eBay and works fine with iChat AV.

Apple's iChat AV package includes drivers for popular cameras, including the iBot. If you've already installed third-party camera drivers, you may see the message "Your camera is in use by another application." Removing the third-party drivers and rebooting seems to solve the problem.

Of course, if you get the error message and *are* using the camera in another application, you may just need to quit the application.

If you do not have a video camera, you can use iChat AV as an audioconferencing solution with any system-recognized microphone.

System Requirements and Recommendations

It should be pointed out that iChat AV requires *at least* a 600MHz G3 for videoconferencing. If you attempt to use video on a slower machine, it reports that video is not available on your computer. Whether this is an issue with the beta remains to be seen; other video chat software provides similar functionality with much less restrictive processor requirements.

Also, no matter what high-end CPU platform or video hardware you may own, you'll need network bandwidth to accommodate audio or video streams. The low-end requirements are 56Kbps for audio, and 128Kbps for video. Realistically, 56K modem users may be able to audioconference if they have a stable and noise-free connection, but the best experience comes from a dedicated digital connection. xDSL, Cable, and LAN users should be able to carry high-quality audio/video streams easily.

Audio Chats

To initiate an audio chat, choose a buddy with audio capabilities, as represented by a phone icon next to the buddy icon and click the phone button at the bottom of the Buddy window. (Alternatively, you could double-click the phone icon, but that's just too easy!)

After an audio chat has been initiated, a small window, shown in Figure 16.16, is displayed.

FIGURE 16.16
The audio chat win-
dow displays input
level, mute, and
volume controls.

The input level meter can be used to guage whether your microphone is posi-
tioned correctly, or whether you need to adjust the input level (gain) within the Sound System Preference panel. During a chat, you can adjust the volume using the chat window's volume slider, or quickly mute the conversation by clicking the "crossed out" microphone button.

> If the volume is too high, you may experience feedback as the microphone starts to pick up the speaker sounds. You can fix this by lowering your gain, lowering the vol-
> ume, or positioning the microphone farther away from your speaker.
>
> Laptop users may notice that only a single speaker is active during A/V chats in iChat AV. This is a purposeful attempt to reduce feedback by disabling the speaker closest to the microphone.

*By the
Way*

If you are on the receiving end of an audio chat request, you are prompted with an incoming chat alert (similar to an incoming text message) and, after the alert window is clicked, given the option of accepting or declining the chat—or making a *text* reply. If you choose a text reply, you effectively open a new text chat with the remote party, and the audio chat is cancelled.

> Even if your buddy doesn't have an audio input source, you can still have a one-
> sided audio rant at them. Choose Buddies, Invite to One-Way Audio Chat from the menu to start a one-way chat.

*Did you
Know?*

Video Chats

A video chat works virtually identically to an audio chat—except that you start it by clicking the camera icon and can *see* as well as hear the remote person.

When a video chat is initiated, you see a preview of yourself until the chat is accepted. At that point, your image shrinks to the lower-right corner of the window, and your buddy's smiling face fills the rest, as shown in Figure 16.17. You can resize your mini preview by moving your cursor over it and then dragging the resize handle that appears. You can also click and drag the mini preview to any of the four corners of the window.

FIGURE 16.17
Video chats—be
seen *and* heard.

At the bottom of the video chat window is a microphone button for muting the audio portion of chat and a button with two opposing arrows for expanding the view to fill the whole screen.

When in full-screen mode, moving the mouse displays several button controls above your preview image: an "X" to close the chat, a microphone to mute, and double arrows to shrink back to a windowed view. Again, use the drag handle that appears in the upper-left corner of the preview to resize your own image onscreen or click and drag the entire mini preview window to move it to another corner.

To pause the video display at any time, choose Pause Video from the Video menu.

When recieving a video chat request, clicking the alert window gives you a preview of your own video feed so that you can make sure that you've dressed yourself properly before clicking the Accept button to start the chat. Like the audio chat, you can also decline a chat request or send a text reply rather than video.

If your friend has no video camera connected, you can still give him the pleasure of watching *you* by starting a one-way video chat using the Buddies menu.

Video Bandwidth and Settings

Depending on your and your buddies' connections, video and audio chats may be a bit choppy or sporadic. To get an idea of the throughput of your connection, choose Connection Doctor from the Video menu. Figure 16.18 shows the Connection Doctor (which doesn't really make anything better).

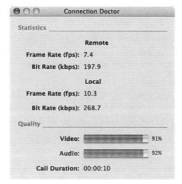

FIGURE 16.18
The Connection Doctor displays stats on your current A/V connection.

Some choppiness problems can be rectified by limiting the amount of data being streamed to your chat partner. Usually iChat AV determines the proper streaming rate automatically, but in some cases, you may want to try setting the value yourself. To do this, use the Video preferences panel within the iChat AV preferences, shown in Figure 16.19.

The bandwidth limit is initially set to *none*, meaning that iChat attempts to stream data as quickly as possible to the remote site. You can limit the bandwidth to anywhere from 100Kbps to 2Mbps. Low-end (ISDN) connections should restrict the bandwidth to 100Kbps, whereas cable and xDSL users may be able to get away with 200Kbps or possibily 500Kbps. Only local or high-bandwidth (T1/T3/ATM) connections should attempt the higher settings.

In addition to the bandwidth settings, the Video preferences panel gives you access to a preview of your video and audio input and lets you choose which of your audio input sources will be used as the microphone.

FIGURE 16.19
Adjust your iChat
AV preferences.

Users with an iSight will appreciate the option to Automatically Open iChat When Camera Is Turned On. This launches iChat when the iSight iris is opened.

Finally, there is a check box to repeatedly play a ringing sound when you're invited to an A/V chat. Why this isn't located under the Alerts preferences panel is beyond me.

Firewalls

iChat A/V's video features work extremely well as long as *one side* of a connection is not behind a firewall or connection sharing device. To use video/audioconferencing behind a firewall, speak to your system administrator. (Apple's tech notes on this topic are available at `http://docs.info.apple.com/article.html?artnum=93208`.)

Additional iChat Preferences Options and Application Settings

Although most of the iChat AV options can be controlled from the Buddy List or menu bar, a few options for fine-tuning the application must be accessed from the preferences.

General

Use the General control panel to enable or disable the iChat menu extra (Show Status in Menu Bar), switch to shape-based status, and control what happens (log in/log out) when you start and quit iChat AV.

A nice feature found in the General pane is the option to control what your computer does when you return to it after it has been set to Away status. Rather than automatically make you available, you can choose to remain away (and not be bothered by your friends), or have it prompt you to ask whether it should change your status.

Accounts

The Accounts pane is used to fill in the username and password for your .Mac or AIM account. If there are special proxy or login host requirements, the Server Options button can be used to set them.

Messages

You can make additional changes to the appearance of the chat windows under the Messages section of the iChat preferences, shown in Figure 16.20, including font color and balloon color. Because remote users have control over the fonts and colors that appear in your window, iChat AV gives you the option of reformatting incoming messages to a specific balloon and font color.

FIGURE 16.20
Change your balloon colors, fonts, and so on.

Rendezvous users can choose to show messages as they're being typed (after a short delay) by clicking the Send Text As I Type check box. You can also choose to confirm file transfers and save chat transcripts for blackmailing your friends later.

Alerts

Under the Actions preferences, choose what iChat will do when you or your buddies log in or out. Use the Event pop-up menu to choose an event to modify; then click the check boxes for the actions you want to apply, such as playing sounds, speaking text, and bouncing icons. This is similar to the individual Buddy Actions discussed earlier but applies to *everyone*, not just a specific person.

Privacy

The Privacy preferences allow you to choose who in the AIM/.Mac community can send you messages. Choose categories of users, such as those in your buddy list, or name individual users using the Edit List buttons who can or cannot contact you.

If you don't want other people to know that you're idle and that your computer is available for stealing, click the Block Others from Seeing That I Am Idle check box.

Menus

The iChat menus can be used to access a few additional features.

iChat Application Menu

The iChat application menu can be used to access the application preferences as well as log in and out of AIM and Rendezvous.

File

The File menu offers options to start chats or go to an existing chat. It also lets you save a transcript of a currently open chat session.

Edit

Under the Edit menu, you'll find the standard editing functions—such as undo/redo, cut, copy, and paste—as well as the Check Spelling option. Also in the

Edit menu are the options for inserting a Smiley, attaching a file, or adding a hyperlink.

View

The View menu can sort your buddy list based on availability or other attributes, and can even set or clear a background image used in all your chat windows.

Buddies

Under the Buddies menu, you'll find all the actions you can perform when you've selected a person on your buddy list, such as sending messages, emailing, getting info about, or even ignoring.

Video

The Video menu proves quick access to full-screen video, sound muting, video pausing, and the Connection Doctor bandwidth statistics.

Format

Use the Format menu as you would with a word processor to control the font, color, and style of outgoing text messages.

Window

Finally, the Window menu is used to open the AIM Buddy List (Command-1) or Rendezvous Buddy List (Command-2) if you've closed the windows on your computer. Address Book can also be launched by choosing it from this menu.

Summary

Apple's iChat AV can be used for instant messaging as well as for computer-to-computer video and audio chats. In this chapter, you learned how to set up iChat and add other people to your buddy list. You also learned how to initiate and join one-on-one instant messaging sessions, group chats, and chat rooms. We then looked at iChat's audio/video options, which require a microphone (or microphone-equipped computer) and a camera, respectively. Finally, we toured the preference options and menus.

CHAPTER 17

Using iCal

Apple's iCal application is a personal calendaring system that you can use to manage your schedule and even email invitations to events. It also supports network calendar publishing so that you can share your calendar, or share the calendars of other iCal users.

Depending on the version of Mac OS X you have, iCal may already be installed on your computer inside the Applications folder. If not, you can download it from www.apple.com/ical.

By the Way

The iCal Interface

On starting iCal, you'll see a three-paned window, shown in Figure 17.1, that will serve as your workspace while using the application.

The upper-left corner contains the Calendars list. Each calendar you've added or subscribed to is displayed here. By default, iCal comes with two Calendars—home and work. You can feel free to delete these or use them. New calendars are added by clicking the "+" button at the bottom left-hand side of the window, or by choosing File, New Calendar (Option-Command-N) from the menu. Calendars can be deleted by highlighting them in the list and pressing the Delete key or by choosing Edit, Delete.

Calendars with a checked check box in front of them are "active" and are displayed in the main calendar view to the right of the calendar list.

FIGURE 17.1
The iCal workspace gives you complete control over your schedule.

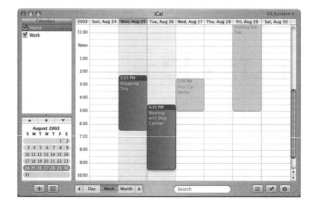

Directly beneath the calendar list is a mini-month view. Move through the months using the three icons (up arrow, diamond, and down arrow) to move back, to the current month, or to the next month, respectively. Clicking a date within one of the mini-months changes the main calendar view to that day.

By the Way

> You can collapse the mini-month view using the divider line between it and the calendar list, or by clicking the calendar icon at the bottom of the iCal window.

Along the bottom of the iCal window are several additional controls. The Day, Week, and Month buttons determine the view style of the main calendar—whether you're looking at a single Day, Week, or Month. The arrows to either side of these buttons move forward and back to the next appropriate calendar "unit" (Day, Week, or Month).

In the bottom center of the window is a single search field. Typing in this field displays (as you type) a list of events that match the string of characters you've entered. Figure 17.2 shows a calendar search in action. The search works *only* across the calendars currently checked in your calendar list.

Double-click an event that you want to jump to and it is highlighted in the main calendar view pane.

Finally, to the right of the search field are three additional buttons. The first button hides or shows the search results. The second shows or hides a new pane to the right of the main calendar view containing to-do items. The third opens a window drawer containing detailed information about the currently selected event, calendar, or To Do item.

FIGURE 17.2
Search for an event
in your calendars.

Adding and Editing Events

Adding an event is easiest within the Day or Week calendar views. Highlight the
calendar that should hold the event, navigate in the main calendar view to the
day where you want to create an event, and then click and drag from the start
time to the end time. As you drag, the event end time will be displayed near
your cursor.

A New Event box is drawn that covers the selected time and, when you release
the mouse button, the subject (title) will be highlighted. Start typing immediately
to enter a new subject (title), or double-click the event subject to edit it after it has
been deselected. Figure 17.3 shows a day view with a new event (Meeting with
Anne) added.

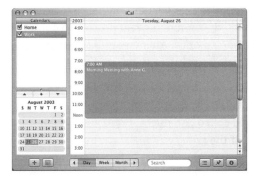

FIGURE 17.3
Add new events by
clicking and drag-
ging to cover the
desired time span.

After an event is added, it can be dragged between different time slots, or days. The event duration can be changed by putting the cursor over the bottom or top edge of the event block and dragging it to resize the box. You can also add new events using File, New Event from the menu (Command-N). This creates a new 1-hour event starting at noon on the selected day. Use the editing techniques discussed previously to position and change its duration.

Although events on the same calendar cannot be "drawn" over the same time slot, you can make two events at the same time with the same duration by creating them in separate time slots and then dragging them to the same slot.

If you prefer working within the Month view, you can add new events in this view by double-clicking on the calendar cell of a day. This creates a new event and extends the Information drawer, which provides convenient access to the time/duration values for the event.

If you'd prefer to edit the event duration by dragging, you can quickly jump to the Day view by double-clicking the date (number) in the Month view.

To set these attributes, quickly jump to the Day view by double-clicking the day's number within the Month view.

To remove any event, highlight it in any of the three calendar views; then press your Delete key, or choose Edit, Delete.

Event Invitations

Events don't usually happen in a vacuum. If you're planning a party and no one else knows they're invited, you may have a problem. iCal supports the notion of event invitations and acceptance. After creating an event, you can invite other people listed in your address book to the event, and they can then accept or decline.

To send an invitation, switch to the Day or Week calendar view so that the event you want to send invitations for is visible. Next, open the Information Drawer. You should see a field called Attendees. Here, you can simply start typing email addresses or names. If they are recognized as an Address Book entry, they will be automatically completed. Press Return between multiple addresses. After an address is added and "recognized," it becomes an object in iCal. You can use the small pull-down menu attached to each attendee to choose between multiple email addresses stored for them, or to remove them or manually edit their email addresses, as shown in Figure 17.4.

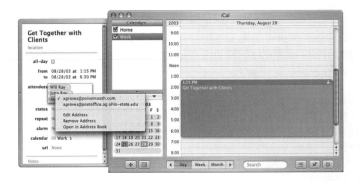

FIGURE 17.4
Enter the attendees
of your event.

Alternatively, you can invite people in your Address Book to the event by choosing Window, Show People (Option-Command-A) and dragging their individual vCard or a group vCard from the People window onto the event within the Calendar view pane. An icon of a person appears in the upper-right corner of the event in Day or Week view mode.

At this point, you've officially told iCal that you want to invite the listed people, but you haven't yet sent invitations. To do this, you must click the "attendees" label in the Information window—a drop-down menu appears with the option to send invitations. Choose Send Invitations.

When you click the Send Invitations button, iCal works with Mail to send an invitation file to the people on the list. You'll also notice that the attendees are displayed with a "?" icon in front of their names. This indicates that they are not yet confirmed as attending the event. Confirmed attendees are displayed with a check mark, whereas declined attendees show an "X."

The recipient of an invitation, assuming that they have iCal installed, can double-click the invitation icon in their email. The iCal application on their system displays the dialog shown in Figure 17.5.

FIGURE 17.5
An invitation is in
progress.

Earlier in the chapter you were told that iCal uses the iCalendar standard for storing information about events. That means that people using other iCalendar-based scheduling programs, such as Microsoft Outlook, will be able to read invitations generated by iCal.

However, sending invitations to people who don't have compatible calendaring software should be done the old-fashioned way—by sending a personally written email. (The iCal-generated messages are meant to be interpreted by computers and are not exactly friendly to human readers!)

Event Info

As you've seen, invitation management is one use of the Information drawer as it applies to events. You can also use the Information drawer to change event descriptions, durations, and schedules. Eleven fields are available when an event is selected:

▶ Event Title—The name of the event being edited.

▶ Event Location—An arbitrary value, presumably where the event is taking place.

▶ All-Day—Whether it is an all-day event (not scheduled for a specific time).

▶ From/To—The date/time/duration of the event.

▶ Attendees—Covered previously.

▶ Status—The status of the event (Tentative, Confirmed, or Cancelled).

▶ Repeat—If an event occurs over several days, weeks, months, or years, use the Repeat field to set how often it appears on your calendar. You can also choose when the recurrences will end, if ever and when the event will end, if ever.

▶ Alarm—Choose to display a message, send an email, or play a sound. After choosing an action, a second field appears allowing you to set the number of minutes, hours, or days before an event starts that the action will take place.

▶ Calendar—The calendar that the event is stored on.

▶ URL—A URL that is pertinent to the given event.

▶ Notes—General notes and other information you might want to store about an event.

If you want to store time zone information with events, you can add a Time Zone field to the Event Information display using the iCal application preferences.

To Do Lists

A To Do item differs from an event in that it doesn't take place at a certain time but often must be *completed* by a given date. iCal can track your To Do items using the To Do List. Click the pushpin icon in the lower-right corner of the iCal window to display the To Do List, shown in Figure 17.6.

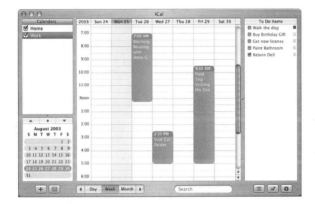

FIGURE 17.6
The To Do List contains a list of things to do.

To add a new item to the list, highlight the calendar that should contain the To Do item and then double-click within the To Do List pane, or choose File, New To Do (Command-K). A new item is added to the list. By default, new To Do items have no deadline and can be flagged as "finished" simply by clicking the check boxes in front of them.

To Do Info

To add notes about a To Do entry and set a deadline, highlight the item in the To Do list and then open the Information Window drawer.

The To Do Info window allows you to enter extended text information about the item, choose whether it has been completed, pick a due date, assign it a priority, pick the calendar that it should be a part of, and assign an appropriate URL for extended information.

Calendar Publishing and Subscribing

One of the most useful features of iCal is the ability to publish calendars to a
.Mac account (or to other computers set up to be WebDAV servers) so that the
others can subscribe to your calendar to view your schedule.

To publish an existing Calendar to the Internet, highlight the Calendar within
your calendar list and then choose Calendar, Publish from the menu. The dialog
shown in Figure 17.7 is displayed.

FIGURE 17.7
Publish your
calendar to a .Mac
account or WebDAV
share.

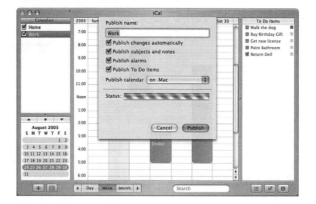

First, choose whether you're using a .Mac account or a Web server (WebDAV). If
you're using .Mac, iCal automatically uses the .Mac account information contained in the Internet System Preferences. Otherwise, it prompts (as shown previously in Figure 17.7) for the WebDAV URL, login, and password.

Next, choose the information you want to be published:

▶ Publish Name—The name that the subscribers see when viewing your
calendar.

▶ Publish Changes Automatically—Automatically update your published calendar when you make local changes in iCal.

▶ Publish Subjects and Notes—Publish the subject and note fields for events.

▶ Publish Alarms—Publish alarm information (alarm type, time, and so on)
along with your events.

▶ Publish To Do Items—Include any To Do items in the Calendar as part of
the publication.

Did you Know?

You can change any of these attributes later by selecting the calendar and opening the Information drawer.

Click the Publish button to send your calendar to the remote server. Published calendars are denoted by a "transmission" icon appearing after their name in the Calendar list.

After publishing, you are prompted with the option to Send Mail with your calendar information to those who might be interested in subscribing. You can also choose Visit Page to see a Web view of your Calendar. The Visit Page option is available only to .Mac subscribers and provides a fully interactive Web view of your calendar; non-Mac.com members can still visit the Web page to see the calendar.

You can update a published calendar with the latest changes by choosing Calendar, Refresh (Command-R) from the menu or by choosing Calendar, Refresh All (Shift+Command+R) to refresh *all* published calendars. To completely remove a Published calendar, use Calendar, Unpublish.

Subscribing to a Calendar is easier than publishing. In many cases, it's as simple as clicking a `webcal://` URL in your Web browser—this automatically creates a subscription in iCal. Apple has published a wide range of interesting online calendars in its iCal library at `www.apple.com/ical/library/`.

By the Way

Calendars available in the iCal Library cover topics ranging from official holidays to sporting event rosters, movie releases, and music tour schedules. It's definitely worth a visit!

If you want a wider variety of iCal options, check out the iCalShare Channel listed in the Other Channels pane of Sherlock (as discussed in Chapter 13, "Using Sherlock for Internet Searches").

To manually enter a subscription, choose Calendar, Subscribe (Option-Command-S). The subscription window shown in Figure 17.8 is displayed.

Enter the URL of an appropriately prepared iCal source, choose how often the calendar should automatically refresh, and whether to remove the creator's alarms and To Do items from the calendar. Click Subscribe after you've configured the subscription to suit your needs. After a few seconds, the subscribed calendar will appear in your calendar list (differentiated from local calendars by the "shortcut" arrow following its name). You can refresh a subscribed calendar by choosing Calendar, Refresh (Command-R).

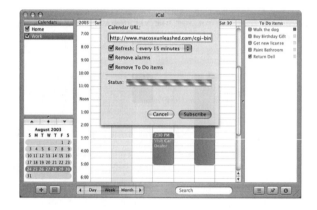

iCal Preference Options

A few final preferences can be set from the iCal application preferences, shown in
Figure 17.9.

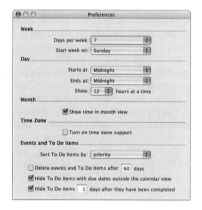

Within the Week category, choose whether iCal recognizes a work (5 day) or
normal (7 day) week, and what day of the week the calendar should use as the
start day.

Use the Day settings to define how many hours are shown in a day, and of those
hours, how many are visible onscreen simultaneously without scrolling.

To add a display of the event time within the Month view, click the Show Time in
Month View check box.

Add time zone support to the Information window using the Turn on Time Zone Support check box.

Finally, the Events and To Do Items options provide control over how To Do Items are sorted, and when To Do items and events should be deleted or hidden from the Calendar view.

iCal Menus

A few minor additional features are available from the iCal File menus that have not yet been covered in the course of this discussion.

As usual, the File menu is used to create new calendars, events, and To Do items. It can also, however, export and import calendar files.

- ▶ Import—Import calendar data from Entourage, and iCalendar or vCal format files.

- ▶ Export—Export the active calendar to an iCalendar format file.

- ▶ Print—Print a copy of the active calendar view.

Summary

iCal is a useful application for managing your schedule. With it, you can keep track of your own meetings, events, and To Do items—or even subscribe to the calendars others have set up. You can also use iCal to issue invitations to events in your calendar or share your full calendar so that family and friends will know what you're up to.

PART IV

Hardware and Related Settings

CHAPTER 18

Working with Monitors and ColorSync

Your Macintosh is a fantastic tool for communicating visually. However, there are some tricks for keeping what you create on your screen looking the same no matter where it's viewed. Images look different when viewed on different monitors or when printed. To solve the problem of "what you see isn't quite what you get," Apple created ColorSync—a means of ensuring consistent color reproduction on different output devices. This chapter introduces ColorSync and walks you through the process of calibrating your system's monitor. You learn everything you need to know about color calibration and how to work with Mac OS X's monitor settings.

Configuring Displays

To change settings for your monitor, there's only one place to do it: the Displays System Preferences pane in the Hardware category. This pane is a bit unusual in that it can change drastically depending on what type of monitor is connected to your system. Users of Apple's CRTs see geometry information for adjusting image tilt, size, and so forth. The exact display depends on the monitor type. Those who have more than one monitor can arrange the monitors' locations on the desktop and choose where the menu bar appears.

Resolution and Colors

To access your Display settings, open the Displays pane of System Preferences and make sure that the Displays button is highlighted at the top of the pane. Here you can see the basic settings for your monitor—color depth, resolution, and refresh rate—as shown in Figure 18.1. Again, what you see might vary slightly depending on the type of monitor you're using.

FIGURE 18.1
The Display section of the Displays System Preferences panel controls monitor colors and resolution.

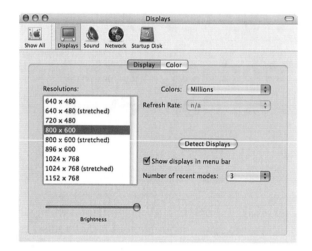

Available resolutions for your display are listed in the left column. Choosing a new resolution immediately updates your machine's display. If you plug a monitor into your computer after it has already booted (such as on a PowerBook or a PowerMac G5 with a dual-monitor video card), you can click Detect Displays to force your Macintosh to recognize the new monitor and start displaying on it.

Displays Menu Extra

If you find yourself switching colors or resolutions often, click the Show Displays in Menu Bar check box. This activates a menu extra, shown in Figure 18.2, that makes it simple to switch between different settings. The menu extra displays recent modes (resolution/refresh/color settings) that you've used—much like the Apple menu shows you recent applications and documents. To change the number of recent modes displayed, use the pop-up menu. The default is three.

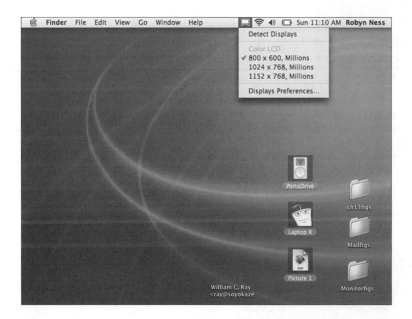

FIGURE 18.2
The Displays menu
extra provides
instant access to
color and resolution
settings.

Multiple Monitors

If you're lucky enough to have multiple monitors to connect to your system, Mac OS X enables you to use all of them simultaneously as a single large display. Note that you still need a video card for each monitor you're connecting or dual display support from a single video card. Users of iBooks and iMacs see a mirroring of their desktop on any added monitors rather than an addition of a new desktop area.

Mac OS X automatically recognizes when multiple monitors are connected to the system and adjusts the Displays Preferences panel accordingly by adding an Arrangement button at the top of the pane. For example, Figure 18.3 shows the settings for a PowerBook G4 with an external VGA monitor connected.

> There's no need to reboot to connect an external display. Just plug it in, click Detect Displays from the System Preferences pane or menu extra, and start mousing!

By the Way

By clicking the Arrangement button, you can control how the two monitors interact by dragging the corresponding rectangle. To move a monitor so that its portion of the desktop falls on the left or right of another monitor, just drag it to the left or right in the Arrangement settings section. The menu bar can also be moved by clicking its representation in the Arrangement section and dragging it to the monitor you want it displayed on. The changes you make to the arrangement take effect immediately; no need to reboot!

FIGURE 18.3
The Displays System Preferences pane changes to handle multiple monitors.

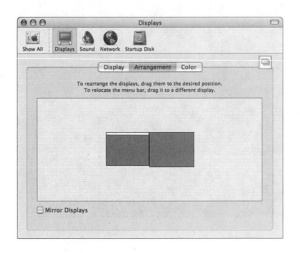

If you have multiple monitors connected, you'll also notice that each monitor has its own copy of the Displays System Preferences pane displayed in the center of the screen. By using these separate panes, you can change the color and resolution for each display independently. You should also see a small "overlapping rectangle" button (visible in Figure 18.3) displayed in the upper-right corner of the pane. Clicking this button moves the configuration pane from the other monitors directly under the pane you are working with. This cuts down on the need to mouse back and forth between monitors to make setting changes.

Did you Know?

Geometry

If you're using an Apple CRT display or a third-party CRT display that supports geometry settings through software, you might see an additional Geometry button in the Displays Preferences pane. Click this button to fine-tune the image on your display through actions such as rotating or resizing so that it has no obvious distortions. Read the operator manual that came with your monitor for more information.

Using these controls actually creates minuscule adjustments to the voltages that produce images on your screen. LCD displays generate their pictures in an entirely different manner and don't require separate geometry settings.

Color

The final button in the Displays System Preferences pane, Color, is where you can create the ColorSync profile for your monitor or choose from one of the preset profiles that come with the system. A ColorSync profile is a collection of parameters that define how your device (in this case, your monitor) outputs color. Figure 18.4 shows the available color settings.

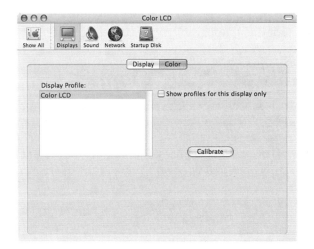

FIGURE 18.4
The Color settings are used to choose a ColorSync monitor profile or launch the calibration utility to make a new profile.

By default, Mac OS X tries to pick the profile it thinks is best for your system, but that doesn't mean it is necessarily in "sync" with your monitor. The color quality of both CRTs and flat panels varies over time, so you still might want to run a calibration even if there's already a setting for your monitor. To start the color calibration process, click the Calibrate button.

Even if you're not at all interested in graphics output and are absolutely convinced that there's no need to calibrate your system, you might still want to run the calibration utility. It gives you the ability to change how your screen looks in ways that the built-in brightness controls cannot.

For example, with a few clicks, you can create deeper, richer colors, or make whites warmer and more appealing. In short, you might have to be a graphics professional to understand the technical details of the calibration process, but the results speak for themselves.

Using the Display Calibrator Assistant

The Display Calibrator application is a simple assistant that walks you through the process of creating a profile for the monitors connected to your computer.

The steps in the calibration process differ greatly depending on the type of monitor you're using and whether you're in "expert" mode. Adjustments roughly follow these steps: set up, native gamma, target gamma, target white point, admin, name, and conclusion. For most LCD monitors, the calibration process skips several of the steps that aren't applicable.

Task: Calibrate Your Display

1. When the Display Calibrator Assistant starts, it provides a brief explanation of what it's about to do and gives you the option of turning on Expert mode, as shown in Figure 18.5. Click the Continue button at the bottom of the window to begin. You can use the Continue and Go Back buttons at any time to move forward and backward between the different steps.

FIGURE 18.5
Turning on Expert mode enables more precise adjustment; sticking with the normal mode limits your options to predefined settings.

2. The first step, Set Up: Display Adjustments, matters for CRT monitors only. It helps you adjust the brightness on your display to achieve the right black levels. To begin, turn the contrast control on your monitor up as high as it goes. Next, take a close look at the block in the middle right of the window. At first glance, the block might look completely black. In reality, the dark block is composed of two rectangles with an oval superimposed on them.

Using your monitor's brightness control, adjust the image so that the two rectangles blend together and the oval is barely visible. It's best to sit back a little, away from your screen, to gauge the effect.

3. The next step, Determine Your Display's Native Gamma, applies to both LCD/CRT monitors but usually only in Expert mode. Brightness does not increase linearly on computer displays. As the display increases a color's brightness on the screen, it isn't necessarily the same size step each time. To correct this, a gamma value is applied to linearize increases in brightness. In the second step of the calibration process, you adjust the gamma settings for the different colors your computer can display. For more information about Gamma, visit www.bberger.net/gamma.html.

On your screen you should see a block containing an Apple Logo. Using the sliders, adjust the logo's brightness and hue so that it matches the background color as closely as possible. It's impossible to get a perfect match, so don't worry if you can still see the apple. It's best just to squint your eyes until you can't make out the text on your screen, and then perform the adjustments.

4. The next step, for both CRT and LCD monitors, is Select a Target Gamma. The target gamma for your display is useful for deciding what images on your monitor look like on other displays. PCs and televisions have varying gamma settings that don't match your Macintosh defaults. This makes it difficult to create graphics on your Mac that look right on a PC monitor. Using the target gamma settings shown in Figure 18.6, you can make your Mac's display look much like that of a standard PC.

To adjust the gamma setting, select the radio button corresponding to your viewing needs. The picture in the upper-right corner of the window gives you an idea of what your choice does to your monitor's output. Choosing Use Native Gamma usually results in a very bright and washed-out image. (Those in Expert mode use a slider to set the gamma, which offers more precise control.)

Gamers might have noticed that some titles appear too dark in places. To compensate for this, just decrease your monitor's gamma settings.

Did you Know?

---

5. The final calibration step for both CRT and LCD displays is Select a Target White Point. As you know, the color white is not a color and is hardly ever truly white. When your computer displays a white image, it probably has tinges of blue, yellow, or even red. This variation is known as the *white point*. Figure 18.7 displays the white point settings.

FIGURE 18.6
Choose the gamma
setting to use on
your monitor.

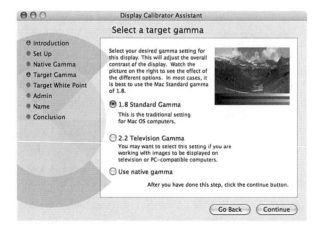

FIGURE 18.7
Choose the target
white point setting
to use on your
monitor.

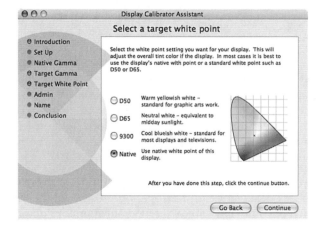

To set a white point, choose from the listed options by selecting the appropriate radio button. Once again, those in Expert mode have a slider to set a more precise level. The higher the white point value, the cooler the display; the lower it is, the warmer the display. You might need to uncheck the No White Point Correction (Native) check box before you can make any modifications (in Expert mode).

6. The Admin step, shown in Figure 18.8, and only available in Expert mode, provides a valuable feature for multiuser systems. Instead of only allowing *you* to use the profile you've created, it allows you to save it for use by any

user on the system. On a machine with a few dozen accounts at a graphic arts firm, this saves the headaches of each person needing to calibrate the monitor separately.

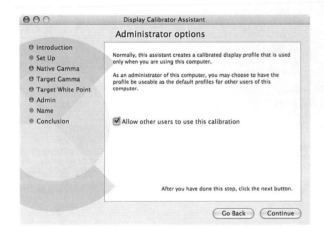

FIGURE 18.8
In Expert mode, you can choose to make the profile available to all users on the system.

7. The second to last step, Name, (see Figure 18.9), prompts you to name your profile. Entering a descriptive name for your creation makes it simple to tell them apart.

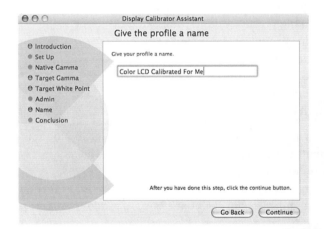

FIGURE 18.9
Enter a name for your calibrated profile.

8. Finally, the Conclusion screen displays a message signaling the successful completion of the calibration process, or, if you're in Expert mode, a summary of the profile you've created, demonstrated in Figure 18.10. Click the

Done button to save and exit. The new profile goes into effect immediately. Remember that you can switch between profiles in the Color area of the Displays System Preferences pane.

FIGURE 18.10
When finished, the
calibration profile is
immediately active.

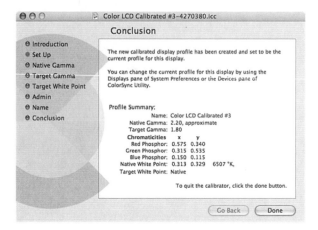

Introduction to ColorSync

As you work with color images and color output devices, you soon realize that there is no standard color monitor, printer, or scanner. A *color space* is a method for representing the possible output colors for a device by using a hypothetical one- to four-dimensional space. Each dimension in the space represents different intensities of the components that define a color. For example, a common space is RGB (red, green, blue). This three-dimensional color space is defined by using the three primary colors of light. Many other spaces exist that address other specific needs, such as printed color.

Although every monitor you buy is undoubtedly an RGB monitor, the RGB color space it supports varies depending on the quality of the monitor's components. Different phosphors produce slightly different shades of red, green, and blue. Cheap monitors might have a slight yellow or green tint to them, whereas LCD panels have vibrant hues but less consistency in gradations than professional CRT displays.

The same goes for printers and scanners. A scanner that costs more is likely to have a far broader and more consistent color space than its cheaper cousins. If you've ever seen a scan that looks dull and muddy, you're seeing a limitation of the scanner's supported color space.

ColorSync's challenge is to make sure that the colors you intend to print or display are what you end up getting. To do this, ColorSync uses a CMM, or color matching module, to translate between different color spaces. In addition, different devices (including your monitor) can have ColorSync profiles that describe the range of color they can reproduce. Using Display Calibrator Assistant, as discussed in the previous section, you can create a profile for your system's monitor. You'll find other profiles on the disks that come with your peripheral devices. You can install profiles by dragging them to the /Library/ColorSync/Profiles folder at the system level or in your home directory.

ColorSync Utility

To make it simple for graphics professionals to switch between different groups of ColorSync settings, or *workflows*, Apple included a ColorSync Utility (/Applications/Utilities/ColorSync Utility) in Mac OS X. Using this Utility, you can set up a workflow for your input devices, display, output devices, and proofing.

In addition, ColorSync Utility enables you to set default profiles for each of the ColorSync-supported color spaces (RGB, CMYK, and Gray) and choose a default color-matching technology that maps from one ColorSync profile to another. Many of these features aren't active unless you've installed additional software on your computer, however.

To switch between the utility's different functions, click the icons at the top of the window.

Preferences

Let's work through the different panes in ColorSync Utility, starting with Preferences. Figure 18.11 shows the Preferences: Default Profiles pane of the ColorSync Utility.

Use the pop-up menus to choose from the installed Input, Display, Output, and Proof profiles. This chooses the default color profile to be used with a document when a document doesn't specify a profile of its own. Don't be surprised if you don't see many options under the pop-up menus. If you completed calibration of your monitor, you should see your calibrated display under the RGB Default pop-up. You might want to check the disks that came with your digital camera or scanner to see whether they include color profiles.

FIGURE 18.11
The ColorSync
Preferences panel
enables you to set
up default collec-
tions of profiles.

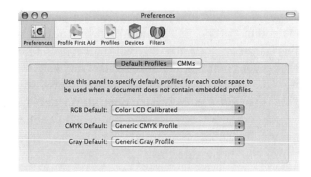

The CMMs area of the Preferences pane functions similarly. The CMMs settings offer the option of selecting alternative color matching modules. The default Mac OS X installation includes only one CMM, so there's very little to see here.

Profile First Aid

The Profile First Aid feature shown in Figure 18.12 verifies that installed color profiles conform to the ICC profile specification. If they do not, it can usually repair them. Click the Verify or Repair button to check the installed profiles on the system.

FIGURE 18.12
Verify and repair installed profiles.

Profiles

The next feature is the profile viewer, which is viewed by clicking the Profiles icon.

In this window, you can navigate through the installed ColorSync profiles on the system and display details for each one by selecting it from the list at the left of the display. Figure 18.13 shows the details for one of my profiles.

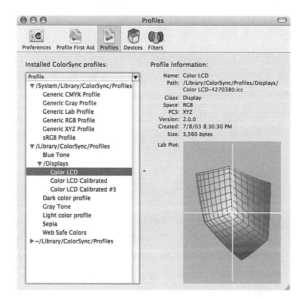

FIGURE 18.13
Easily navigate through all the installed profiles and display their details.

Devices

Click the Devices icon at the top of the window to view the information about devices and their attached profiles. Each type of device is displayed as a category at the left of the window. Expanding a category shows the supported devices in that classification. For example, the Displays category features a Color LCD devices, as shown in Figure 18.14.

When you find the device you want to configure, select it from the list. The right side of the window is updated to show information about the device, including its factory profile and any custom calibration profile you've created. Use the Current Profile pop-up menu to choose a new profile for a given device, and click the Make Default Display button to set a device as the default to be used in a given ColorSync category.

FIGURE 18.14
View the available
ColorSync devices
on your system.

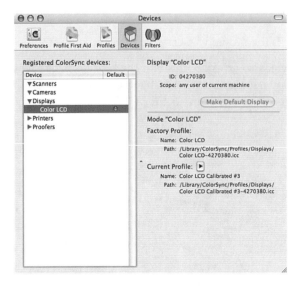

Filters

The final (and most interesting) part of the ColorSync utility are the Filters. ColorSync Filters are similar to Photoshop Filters: When applied to an image they change its appearance. Unlike Photoshop filters, however, ColorSync filters are applied to an output device (such as your printer) and modify anything you're outputting in real-time! Figure 18.15 shows the filter setup screen.

The list along the left displays configured filters, whereas the buttons on the right can be used to add, remove, export, or import filters. When adding a filter, a new untitled item is added to the ColorSync filters list. You then use the Filter details pane at the bottom of the window to adjust what transform (effect) is applied when the filter is applied, along with color settings, and many more fine-tuning options available by clicking the Color, Defaults, Images, and Domains buttons in the middle of the window.

To test a filter, click the File button on the upper-right side of the window. This allows you to choose an image file and apply the filters to see the effect, as shown in Figure 18.16.

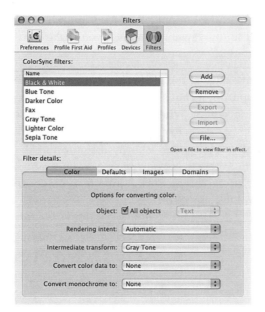

FIGURE 18.15
Create and manage
ColorSync filters.

FIGURE 18.16
Test the filters on
an image file of
your choosing.

To apply a filter, click its name in the upper left-hand list and click Apply.
Alternatively, check the Preview check box at the bottom of the window, and filters will be applied as soon as you select them.

The image you are using to test filters is *not* modified in any way by the tests.

The filter details pane at the bottom left of the window enables you to fine-tune the filter settings within the Preview. Changes you make here will carry back to your main filter settings.

Finally, after you have created the filters you want, you can use them in any ColorSync-aware application that supports filters. For ordinary users, this means the Mac OS X printing system. When printing from *any* application, you can use the print settings pop-up menu to choose ColorSync and then choose from the ColorSync filters that you've created (shown in Figure 18.17), or, alternatively, choose Add ColorSync Filters to see a preview of your document and dynamically add filters to see the effect. Finally, click Print, and your document will be output with all your chosen filters applied!

FIGURE 18.17
Apply ColorSync filters to your printed output!

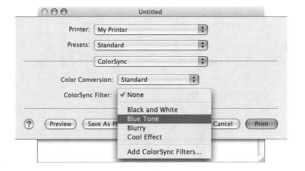

Whew! I know this all sounds complicated, and, frankly, it is! Color calibration is an important part of the Macintosh operating system and part of what makes it widely revered among graphics professionals. If you fall within that group, it's good to know that these features are available. If not, they're still fun to play with because they can breathe new life into a monitor that has a less-than-perfect picture.

Summary

Apple gives you a great deal of control over your monitor and how it displays images. In this chapter, you learned about monitor settings and calibration as well as the ColorSync system and the related System Preferences panels and utilities. Even if you don't use your Mac for precise graphic design and composition, you might find that creating custom ColorSync profiles for your system can benefit games, amateur photography, and anything else that involves the display of color on your monitor!

CHAPTER 19

Adding Peripheral Devices

Although your Mac is a marvelous tool in and of itself, you might want to supplement its capabilities with peripheral hardware, such as printers, scanners, digital cameras, and even additional hard drives. Fortunately, recent Macs come equipped with USB and FireWire ports, which make connecting to such things easy. USB and FireWire are two different standards used to convey data between computers and various devices.

If you have an older peripheral device that connects via SCSI instead of USB or FireWire, you can check with your local Apple computer vendor for a SCSI-to-USB adapter or a SCSI-to-FireWire adapter. Such adapters enable you to use older scanners, hard drives, and other devices on your computer. The only downside is with hard drives; they'll run slower on a USB port (the SCSI-to-FireWire adapter is better if your computer has FireWire).

USB Basics

Your computer comes with a type of flexible connection port called USB (short for *Universal Serial Bus*). USB enables you to attach up to 127 separate and distinct items that will expand your computer's capabilities. The USB ports on your computer will have a flat, rectangle shape and be marked with the symbol shown in Figure 19.1. USB cables also often display the symbol.

FIGURE 19.1
The USB symbol.

USB cables have two types of plugs, so that you can connect the correct end to the correct end. The part that plugs into your computer (or a hub) is small and rectangular. The side that goes into the device itself may be square. Some USB devices support a different style of connection, but it is always obvious which end goes where.

If you use a lot of peripheral devices and have filled all your computer's built-in USB or FireWire ports, you can purchase a hub to add more ports.

USB is *hot-pluggable,* which means that you can attach and detach USB-connected items without having to turn off or restart your computer.

There are times when you shouldn't unplug the device. For example, if you have a disk in a SuperDisk drive, Zip drive, or similar product, eject the disk first, before removing the drive. If you are working in a document that is using the device, make sure that you quit the program before removing the device. Otherwise, you'll risk a crash or possibly a damaged file or a damaged disk directory (the table of contents used to locate files on the disk).

FireWire Basics

Developed by Apple, FireWire is much faster than the other popular standard, USB. For that reason, FireWire is ideal for working with information-rich content, such as audio and video. In fact, it works so well that Apple won a Primetime Emmy Award in 2001 for its contributions to the television industry.

USB2 has recently become available in newer computer models. Its speed equals that of FireWire. However, FireWire 800, which works at twice the speed of USB2 and traditional FireWire, has also been introduced. As these improvements cancel each other out, it appears that USB will still be used mainly for lower performance peripherals, and FireWire will continue to be used for working with large amounts of data, as in digital video. (Also, remember that both USB and FireWire cabilities are a hardware issue—if you don't have a USB2 or FireWire 800-enabled computer, you won't experience their benefits.)

FireWire and USB are totally separate technologies. You cannot hook up a USB device to a FireWire port, or vice versa (the plug layouts don't even match).

FireWire enables you to hook up all sorts of high-speed devices to your Mac. Most digital camcorders, for example, have FireWire connections, and if you plan to use iMovie, which we introduce later in this book, you absolutely must have a computer and a camera that are FireWire-equipped.

You can also use your Mac's FireWire capability to hook up FireWire-based hard drives, removable drives, CD drives, tape backup drives, and scanners. FireWire features a plug-and-play capability similar to USB. You install the software and then plug in the device, and it's recognized, just like that.

> Not all FireWire-compatible devices refer to this technology as FireWire. Depending on the manufacturer, it might also be known as IEEE 1394 or i.LINK, but they work just the same.

By the Way

You can recognize FireWire ports and connector cables by the symbol shown in Figure 19.2.

FIGURE 19.2
The FireWire symbol.

Like USB, FireWire devices are also hot-pluggable.

Peripheral Devices

Now that you know the basics of USB and FireWire, or enough to know whether your computer is equipped with them, let's take a look at some of the peripheral devices you can connect to your computer using your computer's USB or FireWire ports:

▶ Printers—Printers come in a variety of types, ranging from basic black-and-white laser printers to photo-quality inkjet printers. When looking for a printer, do your homework to make sure that you get the features and quality you expect. (We'll talk about using printers in Chapter 20, "Printing, Faxing, and Working with Fonts.")

▶ Scanners— A basic desktop scanner is a device that looks and works something like a photocopier that reads an image one line at a time and saves the data in a form the computer can reproduce on its screen. Though scanners are most often used for documents and photographs, some scanners can be used to scan negatives and slides as well.

Many scanners also come with a simple graphics program and with Optical Character Recognition (OCR) software. OCR is an exceptionally clever and useful application that scans pages of text and identifies each character, punctuation mark, and space. After identifying them, it puts the text into an open word processing document so that you can edit and patch as needed, and then save the scanned page as a text document.

▶ Digital cameras—Digital cameras store images electronically instead of on film. You can then connect the camera to your computer to transfer them to your hard drive.

Most digital cameras contain a removable memory card, stick, or floppy disk where images are stored. Memory cards are intended to be removable and to be reused. When you fill up a card and need more memory, you can remove the full card and pop in an empty one. Then, you can put the used card back into your camera, or into a compatible card reader, to transfer the images.

▶ Digital video cameras—As their name implies, digital video cameras record video rather than still images, although some digital video cameras also have a setting for stills. Because video takes up a lot of space, digital video cameras require storage media, usually in the form of tapes. Transferring video to your computer for use in programs such as iMovie, which we'll discuss starting in Chapter 24, "Exploring the iMovie Interface." requires a FireWire connection.

▶ CD burner—If you don't have a Mac with a built-in CD burner, you can buy a standalone product with much of the functionality. External CD burners, however, might not be able to take advantage of Apple's ultra-slick, Finder-level CD writing feature.

▶ Hard drives—You can add extra hard drives to your computer for additional storage, which comes in handy especially if you plan to work with space-hogging digital media. The only consideration is that the USB port doesn't really exercise the maximum speed of a large hard drive, so you might prefer FireWire, if your computer has that feature. USB drives are fine, though, for occasional use or just to back up your precious files. You'll learn more about backup possibilities in Chapter 36, "Maintaining Your System."

▶ Input devices—You're not limited to your Mac's keyboard and mouse, although they are suitable for most folks. But it's nice to know there are alternatives. If you've migrated from the Windows platform, for example, you'll be able to take advantage of a mouse with extra buttons (the second being used for the context menus you otherwise invoke when you Option-

Click on something). In addition, you can purchase joysticks for computer games, keyboards for special needs (or just in the form of those offered on regular Macs), and even trackballs (sort of an upside-down mouse), which some prefer to a regular mouse.

▶ iPod—Apple's iPod is a portable FireWire device for listening to digital music files, but with 10 to 30 Gb of storage, it can also work as a stylish external hard drive. The iPod was built especially to synchronize with the music library on your computer via the iTunes application, which we'll discuss in Chapter 22, "Using iTunes."

Connecting FireWire and USB Device

If you've set up a desktop Macintosh, you already have some experience with peripheral devices—the standard Mac keyboard and mouse are connected via USB. Some devices, however, require an additional step or two to work.

Here's a tried-and-true FireWire and USB installation method (some changes might apply to specific products, and they'll tell you that in the documentation):

1. Unpack the device and check for an installation CD.

2. If there's an installation CD, it means that special software (a driver) is needed to make the device work. Just place the installation CD in your computer's drive. (Note, it's important to use the installation CD intended for the Mac—some products come with both Mac and PC discs.)

Mac OS X has built-in support for many of the things you connect via FireWire or USB. But some printers, scanners, and CD or DVD burners will most likely need special software. Before you try to use any of these products, check the documentation or the publisher's Web site to confirm that the product works with Mac OS X. Or visit VersionTracker.com (www.versiontracker.com) for the latest updates.

Watch Out!

---

3. Double-click the Installer icon and follow the instructions to install the new software.

Under Mac OS X, you might see a prompt where you have to authenticate yourself as administrator of your computer before a software installation can begin. Because Mac OS X is a multiple-user operating system, it wants to know that you are authorized to make serious changes of the system. Just use the same password you gave yourself when you first set up Mac OS X, and you'll be ready to go.

By the Way

4. After installation, you should be able to connect and use your device right away. In a rare situation, you might see a Restart button. If you see such a button, click it and sit back and wait for your Mac to restart itself.

5. Connect one end of the device's cable to the free plug on your iMac's connection panel or the free plug on your keyboard.

6. Connect the other end of the cable to your peripheral.

7. Turn on the device. You'll then want to check your instructions about using the device. Some products, such as scanners, require that you run special software to operate them.

> Some scanners also have special hardware locks to protect the delicate circuitry. Before you turn on a new scanner, check the documentation and see whether such a thing exists. Usually, it'll be a switch or a button with a lock icon on it. If you fail to unlock the mechanism, you might damage the unit when you try to use it.

Summary

In this chapter, we talked about USB and FireWire options for connecting additional devices to your computer. Depending on your needs, many peripherals are available for easy hookup. You'll soon be printing, shooting pictures, scanning artwork, and even, perhaps, using a designer keyboard and mouse.

CHAPTER 20

Printing, Faxing, and Working with Fonts

This chapter looks at font and printer management—two important factors in producing quality output from your system. We'll talk about setting up printers and basic print settings. We'll then look at configuring and using Mac OS X's built-in faxing capability. Finally, we'll discuss adding new fonts and using the Font Book application and system Font panel.

Using the Printer Setup Utility

In Mac OS X, the Printer Setup Utility application maintains and manages everything printer related. You can find it in the Utilities folder inside the Applications folder.

There's a pane called Print & Fax in the System Preferences. If you click the button labeled Set Up Printers, the Printer Setup Utility will be launched! (We'll talk more about the Print & Fax preferences later in the chapter.)

By the Way

When you start the Printer Setup Utility, it opens a window listing all the available printers configured on your system. For example, in Figure 20.1, one printer is configured for my computer.

FIGURE 20.1
The Printer Setup Utility shows a list of the printers configured on your system.

If a printer is set as the default printer, its name appears in bold type. You can make a different printer the default by selecting its name in the list and then choosing Printers, Make Default (Command-D) from the menu.

Setting Up Printers

Obviously, switching between printers isn't of much use until you set up a printer or two on your system. (Of course, you may first need to set up your printer and attach it to your computer, as discussed in Chapter 19, "Adding Peripheral Devices"!) To set up a printer on your system, first click the Add button at the top of the Printer List window. A printer selection sheet window appears, similar to the one in Figure 20.2.

FIGURE 20.2
Use the Add Printer sheet window to configure any connected printing devices.

At the top of the sheet window is a pop-up menu that offers several different ways in which you can find and connect to your printer:

- ▶ AppleTalk—AppleTalk is the choice to make if you're connecting to a local network Mac printer.

- ▶ Directory Services—If you're connected to a Mac OS X server computer or another directory service, there's a chance it's sharing printer information with your system. Choosing Directory Services displays the printers available to your computer through a network directory server.

- ▶ IP Printing—This option, also known as LPR, is used for many types of printers that allow access over TCP/IP. If you need to access a printer that isn't on your local network, this is probably the choice you want to make.

- ▶ USB—USB printers are the personal printers that plug in to the USB ports on your computer. Canon, Epson, and HP printers typically connect via USB.

▶ Windows Printing—If you are part of a mostly Windows network, you can use this option to choose your local network and a printer on it.

Below the four main ways of connecting are any manufacturer-specific drivers that have been installed on the system, such as Epson and Lexmark. If you're using one of these printers, select the corresponding option here.

If you choose AppleTalk or USB, Printer Setup Utility attempts to locate potential printers that your machine can access and automatically displays them. To finish adding a printer, select it from the list of detected devices. Mac OS X then attempts to automatically detect the type of printer you've chosen and select the appropriate driver. Sometimes, however, you must use the Printer Model pop-up menu at the bottom of the window to manually pick a printer type. Finally, click Add to add the selected printer to the Printer Setup Utility listing.

IP printers are configured a bit differently. If you choose IP printers in the pop-up menu, you're asked for information on where the printer is located and how to connect.

Talk to the printer's administrator to determine the IP address and queue name for the remote device. Many times you can choose to use the default queue and simply enter an IP address. Because of the nature of IP connections, you must manually choose a printer model. Click Add to finish adding the printer.

For any of the printer connection types, if Mac OS X can't automatically find your printer model, you might need to contact the manufacturer and download additional drivers for the system.

By the Way

Managing Your Printer Queue

After you start using your printers, you might occasionally want to cancel a print job that you've created or see what other print jobs are slowing down yours. You can easily do this by accessing the printer's *queue*—a list of the print jobs it is currently working on. To examine the queue, simply double-click the printer name in the Printer Setup Utility printer listing. Figure 20.3 displays a printer queue.

When viewing a printer queue, you can drag an individual print job up and down in the listing to adjust its priorities. You can also select a job and use the Delete button to remove it from the print queue entirely.

FIGURE 20.3
Double-click a printer's name to display its queue; this queue shows a stopped print job.

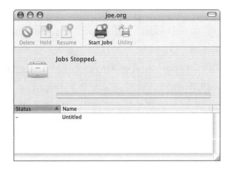

To completely stop the printer, click the Hold button. This prevents any further jobs from being processed. To resume printing, click the Resume button.

The Page Setup and Print Windows

Before anything shows up in the print queue, it must first be submitted to the printer. In most applications, you can print a document by choosing File, Print from the menu. There are also two menu commands shared by most applications that you use when printing:

▶ Print (Command-P)—Print the active document and configure settings for your chosen printer.

▶ Page Setup (Shift-Command-P)—Choose how the document is laid out when printing.

Let's start with the standard page setup sheet window, shown in Figure 20.4.

FIGURE 20.4
Choose the basic layout settings for your print job.

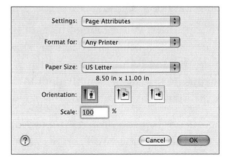

In the page setup sheet window, you can use the Settings pop-up menu to choose Page Attributes, Custom Paper Size, or Summary to see a description of how the page will be printed, including margin and size information.

The Format For pop-up menu enables you to choose for which printer the page is being laid out. Because different printers support different page sizes and margins, it's important to format a document for the appropriate printer before starting the print process. Use the Paper Size settings to select from standard paper sizes that your device supports.

Finally, you can use the Orientation buttons to choose from normal, landscape, and reverse landscape layouts and to set the Scale value to enlarge or shrink the output.

After making your Page Setup settings, it's time to use the Print sheet window shown in Figure 20.5 to finish configuring your printer and start the print job. Choose File, Print from the menu or use the keyboard shortcut Command-P to open the Print window.

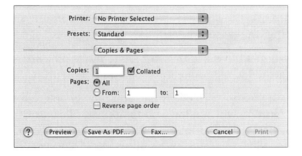

FIGURE 20.5
The print settings are used to configure the printer and start the print job.

If you've used a printer before, you probably recognize most of these settings. You can choose a printer and enter your page print range, the number of copies, and so on, and then click Print to start printing the document.

One interesting feature that relies on the Mac OS X Quartz technology is the Preview function, which displays content from another program in a PDF format. If a Mac OS X application can print, it can generate a PDF. Clicking the Save As PDF button opens a Save As dialog box from which you can save any file as a PDF.

Did you Know?

The default information displayed when you open the Print window is the Copies & Pages settings. Using the pop-up menu near the middle of the dialog box, you can select other common setting panes for your printer. These are a few that you may see:

▶ Layout—Have your printer print multiple document pages per printed page. This setting is useful if you want to print a long document for review. You can choose how to arrange the pages and whether to put borders around them.

▶ Duplex—Toggles printing to both sides of a piece of paper, if available.

▶ Output Options—If you want to output directly to a PDF file, you can set this option in the Output Options pane.

▶ Error Handling—You can choose how the system responds to errors that occur during printing. The options are No Special Reporting and Print Detailed Report.

▶ Paper Feed—Many printers have multiple paper trays. The Paper Feed settings enable you to choose which feed is active for a given print job.

▶ Printer Features—The Printer Features pane contains any special features offered by the connected printer.

▶ Scheduler—If you have a large print job to make on a shared printer, you can use Schedule to set a time for your print job to print.

▶ ColorSync—If you use a color printer, you may be interested in the ColorSync settings, which allow you to apply a filter—such as Black & White or Sepia—to your print job without the need for a graphics program. (See Chapter 18, "Working with Monitors and ColorSync," for more discussion of ColorSync filters.)

▶ Summary—The Summary settings display the status of all the preceding settings in one convenient location.

If you change several settings and want to save them for use from time to time, choose Save As under the Presets pop-up menu. Your custom settings will show up under Presets at the top of the Print sheet window for any later work.

By the Way

A nifty extra of the Mac OS X printing system is the Printer Setup Utility icon. When printing, it displays an animation of pages going through your printer and a count of the remaining pages to print. If there is an error, it displays a red page containing an exclamation mark to get your attention.

At the bottom of the Print window are buttons to Preview, Save as PDF, Fax, Cancel, or Print. If you choose to preview your document, it literally opens in the Preview application (discussed in Chapter 6, "Using Calculator, Stickies, Preview, and TextEdit") to show you what the pages will look like as, well, pages. Save as PDF opens a save window where you can choose a name and location for the PDF file that's created. Cancel exits the Print window, and Print does as it says.

Now, let's discuss faxing from your computer.

Faxing from the Print Window

Essentially, faxing is printing over the phone. With OS X, you can fax a document from the standard Print window (refer to Figure 20.5).

> We'll talk about receiving faxes through your email account in the section "Print and Fax Preference Options" later in the chapter.

By the Way

When you click the Fax button, the sheet window shown in Figure 20.6 appears. In it, you enter the following information:

- ▶ To—Enter the name of the recipient, or click the button on the right to choose a contact from the Address Book. (Note that you can only select contacts for whom fax numbers are listed.)

- ▶ Subject—Enter a subject for your fax.

- ▶ Dialing Prefix—If you need to dial long distance or enter a prefix to dial outside your organization, enter those digits here.

- ▶ Modem—Choose the "fax" machine that will send your document. Modem is the default—and likely only—choice.

- ▶ Presets—Presets allows you to save a configuration for reuse or choose one you've saved, just as in printing.

The section in the middle of the window also echoes the printing window, with options such as Copies & Pages, Layout, and Error Handling. Also available is the Cover Page option, which lets you choose to include a cover page.

> To use the cover page, select it in the pop-up menu; then be sure to click the Cover Page check box that appears.

By the Way

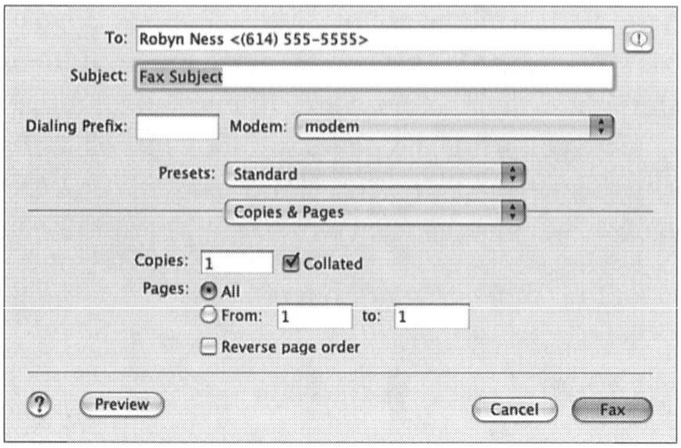

FIGURE 20.6
Prepare to send
your fax.

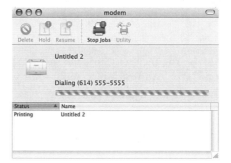

When you've entered all the appropriate information, you can click the Fax button. The icon for an application called Modem appears in the Dock. If you double-click it, the modem window appears, as shown in Figure 20.7.

FIGURE 20.7
Check the status of
your fax.

The modem status window is similar to the print queue listing for Printer Setup
Utility. You can choose Delete, Hold or Resume, or Stop/Start Jobs. (Note, however,
that the name applied to the fax job is the title of the document, not the name
you entered in the Fax sheet window.)

Print and Fax Preference Options

Figure 20.8 shows the Printing pane. The Set Up Printers button provides another way to access the Printer Setup Utility. You can also choose which printer will appear as the selected printer in the Print sheet window—the last printer used or a specific printer you have set up. You can also choose a default paper size to appear in the Print sheet window. The option Share My Printers with Other Computers allows people on your local network to access USB and FireWire Printers connected directly to your computer.

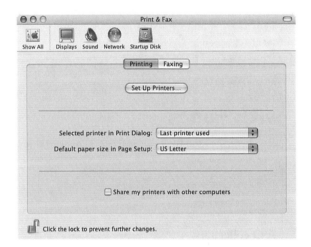

FIGURE 20.8
Check the box to share your printer on your local network.

The Faxing pane, shown in Figure 20.9 allows you to set up your computer to receive faxes. (As you learned previously, faxing from your computer is as easy as printing.) After connecting your computer to a phone line, you can check the Receive Faxes on This Computer box and enter the number for the phone line. You can choose how many rings before incoming faxes are accepted as well as where to store them and a default printer to print them. If you entered an email address in the system, it appears by default as the address to email faxes to. At the bottom of the pane is the option for you to allow others to send faxes through your computer.

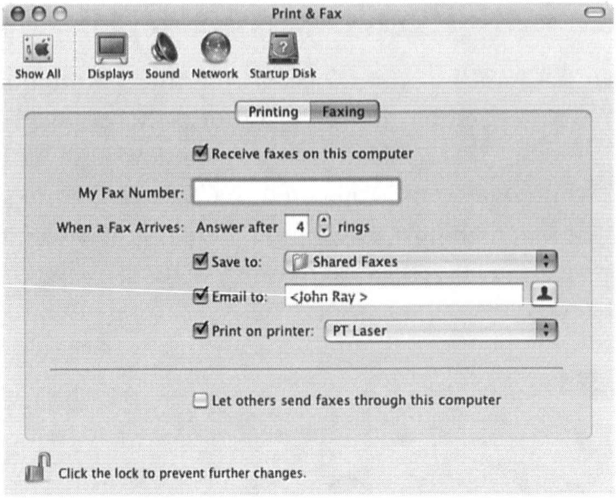

FIGURE 20.9
Turn your computer into your fax machine.

Working with Fonts

Mac OS X comes with a large collection of fonts and supports many common font formats, including

- ▶ .dfont suitcases
- ▶ .ttf TrueType fonts
- ▶ .ttc TrueType font collections
- ▶ .otf OpenType fonts
- ▶ PostScript Type 1 fonts
- ▶ All previous Macintosh font suitcases

In short, if you have a font, chances are that you can install it on Mac OS X, and it will work.

Font files are stored in the system /Library/Fonts folder or in the Library/Fonts folder inside your home directory. If you have a font you want to install, just copy it to one of these locations, and it becomes available immediately. You must restart any running applications that need access to the fonts, but you don't need to restart your computer.

Organizing Fonts with Font Book

To add a new font, you can simply place new fonts in the Fonts folder inside either the system or user-level Library folder. However, the Font Book application exists to help you view and manage a large font collection effectively. You can launch Font Book from the Applications menu.

The Font Book window, as shown in Figure 20.10, has three columns. The one on the left contains collections, or categories, of fonts. The first item in the list displays all fonts available to the current user. Several categories, such as Classic and Fixed Width, are listed by default. To add your own collections, maybe for a specific project or of a certain look, click the + button below the column.

FIGURE 20.10
Font Book helps you categorize (and even hide) your many fonts.

The middle column displays any fonts included in the selected collection. (Expanding the list by clicking the disclosure triangles shows the related fonts.) Clicking the + button at the bottom of the window allows you to navigate to fonts stored on, or connected to, your system.

The Disable button allows you to remove an option temporarily from a collection. For instance, if you feel you're in a rut and want to disallow the use of Arial in all your documents, choose it from the All Fonts list and click Disable. After you confirm that you really do mean it, Arial and its related fonts will be grayed out in the Font Book window, but in the system as a whole, they won't even appear! (To bring Arial back when you realize how much you've missed it, select it in the All Fonts list of Font Book and click the Enable button.)

The right column shows an A-to-Z and numeric sample of the selected font. Drag the size slider to view the font at different sizes, or leave the Fit default. Click and drag at the bottom of the column, near the dot, to view information such as copyright and font type.

Although it's fun to try uncommon fonts, it doesn't work to share them via outgoing email messages. If your recipients haven't installed the font you chose, the message will appear in one of the default fonts on their systems rather than with the look you wanted.

Using the Mac OS X Font Window

Applications that enable you to choose fonts often use the built-in font picker shown in Figure 20.11. This element of the Macintosh operating system is designed to make finding fonts easier and more accessible among different pieces of software. To see the Font window for yourself, open the TextEdit application in the Applications folder, and then choose Format, Font, Show Fonts from the menu.

FIGURE 20.11
The Font window is a systemwide object for choosing fonts.

In its default form (as shown in Figure 20.11), the Font window lists four columns: Collections, Family, Typeface, and Size. Use these columns much as you use the Column view of the Finder—working from left to right. Click a collection name (or All Fonts to see everything), and then click the font family, typeface, and, finally, the size.

To view settings before applying them, open the preview space by clicking just under the Font title bar and dragging.

The Font window is quite a chameleon. In addition to the two views already mentioned, there's a more simplified view as well. If you want to save space, use the window resize control in the lower-right corner of the panel to shrink the Font window to a few simple pop-up menus. (The pop-up menus also appear if you expand the preview space to its full size.)

Did you Know?

At the top of the Font window are a line of four buttons, that, from right to left control underlining, strikethru, font color, and background color. To the right of these buttons are another set of controls for adding a drop shadow to the font and controlling its placement.

Along the bottom of the Font window are several additional controls. The + and – buttons allow you to add and remove collections in the Collections list. The search field allows you to locate a font by name or character string instead of endless scrolling.

The Action pop-up menu (the little "gear" icon) gives you access to several special features of the font system:

▶ Add to Favorites—Add the current font choice to the Favorites font collection.

▶ Show Preview—Shows or hides the preview space at the top of the window.

▶ Hide/Show Effects - Hide or Show the font effects toolbar are the top of the Font window.

▶ Color—Pick a color for the font.

▶ Characters—Shows the Character Palette, shown in Figure 20.12, displaying each of the characters for a selected font.

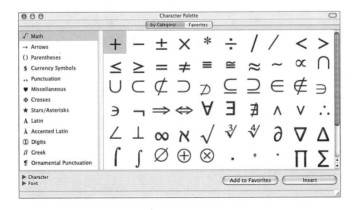

FIGURE 20.12
The Character Palette gives easy access to characters and symbols, including those for math or simply decoration.

By the
Way

Instant access to the Character Palette from any application can be added in the Input Menu tab of the International System Preferences panel. Simply check the box in front of Character Palette, and a menu extra appears. To remove the icon, simply return to the Input Menu tab and uncheck the box. In many applications, the Character Palette can be accessed directly from the Edit menu by choosing Special Characters.

▶ Typography—Opens the Typography window where you can make adjustments to the spacing of letters and lines.

▶ Edit Sizes—Opens a sheet window where you can customize the font sizes or the range of font sizes available in the Font window. You can also pick whether to use a list of fixed sizes, a slider, or both for choosing font sizes in the default Font window.

▶ Manage Fonts—Launches Font Book, where you can create and edit new collections of fonts.

One final note about fonts: Not all applications use the system Font window. When it's not supported, as with applications such as Microsoft Word, you're likely to see pull-down menus listing every installed font.

Summary

The focus during this chapter has been printing and faxing. In Mac OS X, printers are managed entirely through Printer Setup Utility and share a common look and feel throughout each of the settings panels. Also, faxing is built right into the standard print window so that you no longer have to print out things to fax them.

The font system is equally easy to use. The addition of Font Book and availability of a systemwide Font window make it simple to build font collections and find your way through hundreds of available typefaces.

PART V

Apple's iLife Applications

CHAPTER 21

Introducing iLife

The CEO of Apple, Steve Jobs, has spent a lot of time in the past few years talking publicly about making the Mac the center of your digital life-style. The introduction of iLife carries this vision forward by bringing together updated versions of the four easy-to-use digital media applications already available from Apple—iTunes, iPhoto, iMovie, and iDVD.

The updates made to these applications include added features that allow you to conveniently cross over from one to another. For instance, you can build a slideshow of your digital photographs in iPhoto with accompanying music from your iTunes music library and then, with the click of a button, transfer that slideshow to iDVD for finishing touches and writing to disc.

Avid Mac fans know that Steve Jobs makes several public addresses each year to announce new products and computer advancements available from Apple. These events are known as *keynotes*, and you can often watch them as they happen on the Apple Web site via a streaming QuickTime video feed.

By the Way

Now let's take a brief look at the four applications that make up iLife.

iTunes

If you like music, iTunes (shown in Figure 21.1) was made for you. iTunes allows you to encode music from CDs in MP3 and other common digital formats for storage on your computer—a great option for easy access and organization. You can also use iTunes to design and burn your own custom mix CDs. If you want to expand your music collection, you can use iTunes to access Apple's iTunes Music Store where you can purchase songs or albums for download in digital format.

MP3 is a compression system that reduces the size of a music file by a factor of 10 to 15, or more. How's this magic accomplished? By removing data that the human ear either cannot hear or doesn't hear as well. Audio quality can be almost indistinguishable from a CD, or, if you opt for more compression, audibly different.

FIGURE 21.1
Here's a glimpse of
iTunes.

As you will learn in the next chapter, ripping and burning are creative, not destructive, acts when it comes to digital music. *Ripping* is basically encoding a song for storage on your computer, and *burning* is writing information, including music, to a CD!

iTunes is also perfectly suited for handling streaming MP3s. If you've never listened to Internet radio before, you'll appreciate how quickly and easily iTunes enables you to find the type of music you want to hear and start listening.

iTunes also interacts with the Internet to look up information about your CDs, such as the artist and song title, based on album.

You'll learn how to use iTunes in Chapter 22, "Using iTunes."

Apple recently released iTunes 4, which added the iTunes Music Store, which allows you to purchase and download song files from participating recording companies, to iTunes' previously existing features.

iPhoto

Have a digital camera? If so, you may have struggled to keep track of image files with difficult to remember names such as 200214057. With Apple's iPhoto, there's an easy way to store, organize, edit, and share your photographs. iPhoto even connects directly to many digital cameras, so you can skip loading special software.

Some people feel that film cameras might be replaced by digital cameras altogether. As these clever devices become more inexpensive, and both image and home-printing quality goes up, it becomes more difficult to justify the trip to the super-market to get that roll developed.

By the Way

Perhaps iPhoto's greatest strength is that it allows you to visually search your entire photo collection without opening and closing folders so that you don't have to remember film rolls or dates while looking for the ones you want. Viewing tiny thumbnail images of hundreds of your pictures at a time, demonstrated in Figure 21.2, allows you to scan for the one you want. (If you need to see each image in greater detail, you can also increase the size of this preview.)

FIGURE 21.2
iPhoto makes it easy to manage a lot of images.

We'll cover iPhoto in detail in Chapter 23.

iMovie

At one time, editing a home video was a chore. You had to sit and copy each section separately from your camcorder to your VCR in the order it was to be viewed. Pros call this *linear* editing because everything is put in place in the exact sequence.

iMovie, an easy-to-use digital video editor, makes all that unnecessary. Being able to edit a digital video using a computer is a revelation because you can copy the clips or segments in any order you want. Then, during the editing process, you put things in order. This process is called *nonlinear*, and it's much more flexible.

> iMovie is a ground-breaking application. Traditionally, nonlinear digital video editing was available only to professionals willing to spend thousands of dollars. iMovie brings these capabilities to hobbyists.

Although iMovie, shown in Figure 21.3, is astoundingly simple to learn, it includes advanced features that you can use to make the most of your video footage. You can combine separate video clips using transitions, add sound effects and voiceovers, create title text, and export your final work into formats others can view.

FIGURE 21.3
iMovie makes video editing a joy.

> A large part of what makes iMovie work so well is FireWire, the connection standard discussed in Chapter 19, "Adding Peripheral Devices." In fact, to work with digital video from your camcorder using iMovie, you must have a computer and a camera with FireWire ports. That's because digital video files can be very large, and getting them onto your computer would be impossibly slow without FireWire.

How can you tell whether your Mac came with FireWire ports? Check the connection panel and see whether you have any FireWire connectors. You can identify them by their peculiar shape. Thin, oval at one end, squared off at the other.

Digital video cameras usually have a slightly different style Firewire connector (small, like a slightly misshapen rectangle) that may be labeled IEEE 1394 or iLink in the camera documentation.

If you don't have a FireWire connection, you can still use iMovie for making slideshows from still photos.

Chapters 24 through 29 cover most of the things you can do with iMovie, including adding effects and exporting.

iDVD

Are you still buying movies on videotape? Well, that's a technology that might eventually go the way of the 8-track tape. The fastest growing consumer electronics product is the DVD player. A DVD puts the contents of an entire movie on a disc the same size as a CD.

Using Apple's iDVD, you can now create your own DVDs, complete with navigation menus and motion (moving) menus.

iDVD, shown in Figure 21.4, allows you to share your home movies and still images, and integrates with both iPhoto and iMovie.

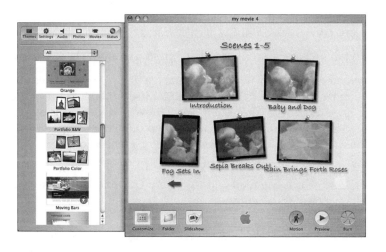

FIGURE 21.4
iDVD lets you share your digital video and digital images using professional-quality features.

To run iDVD, your computer must be equipped with a special optical drive that Apple dubs the SuperDrive. This drive, manufactured by Pioneer or Sony, the large Japanese consumer electronics companies, can play CDs and DVDs, and burn both.

By the Way

To burn your own DVDs, you will need DVD-R discs. Although they may look like CDs, their capacity is much greater—4.7GB, which is large enough to hold at least an hour of average video and many image files.

The DVDs you write will play on most DVD players and the DVD drives on a personal computer. However, some of the oldest DVD players, made during the first year the format was introduced, cannot play them. Check Apple's Web site, at www.apple.com/dvd/compatibility/, to see a list of the players that have been tested and found compatible. Newer players, even if not listed at the site, will likely work without any problem.

Like the other applications included in iLife, iDVD was designed to offer a wide range of features that are easy to use. We'll talk more about iDVD's features in Chapters 30 through 32.

Necessary Tools

Before we go any further, we need to make sure that you have the right tools to meet the expectations you have of the applications included in iLife:

▶ For making your own CDs (containing data, music, photographs, and so on), your computer must have a drive capable of writing CDs. Alternatively, you could use an external CD burner that is compatible with Mac OS X.

▶ To get full mileage from iPhoto, you'll need a compatible digital camera.

▶ If you want to use iMovie, you must have a digital video camera that uses FireWire technology (also known as IEEE 1394 or i.Link), and your computer must have a FireWire connection port. (FireWire allows large digital video files to be transferred between your camera and your computer. Without it, there is no feasible way to work with video on your computer.)

▶ To create DVDs with iDVD, your computer must be equipped with Apple's SuperDrive, which can read and write both CDs and DVDs. (Note, that although external DVD burners are sold, they will not work with iDVD.)

When you know what your computer needs to do its job, you're ready to move forward.

Installing the iLife Applications

Now that you've heard about the delights that await you when you use iTunes, iPhoto, iMovie, and iDVD and learned about any additional requirements of those applications, how do you get them? Several options are available.

First, check your Applications folder to see whether they are already installed. If you find them, you'll want to check their version numbers to make sure that you have the latest software. You should have version 4 of iTunes, version 3 of iMovie and iDVD, and version 2 of iPhoto.

> Apple often makes minor updates to its applications that make them run better, so even if you have the versions mentioned previously, you'll want to visit the Apple Web site to see whether there are newer versions, or version updates, listed for download. For instance, there was an update for iMovie listed at the time of this writing.

Did you Know?

If you don't find these applications on your hard drive, you have two options. The first, if you want iTunes, iPhoto, and iMovie, is to download them from Apple's Web site.

If you have a slower Internet connection, or if you want to use iDVD, you'll need to purchase the iLife software package. (This package includes all four applications, even though the other three are free in download.)

> iTunes, iPhoto, and iMovie are available for free via download—why isn't iDVD? The answer lies in the size of the iDVD application and files. Basically, it's huge, and trying to download it would tie up a lot of your computer's resources for a long time. Trust me, if you want iDVD, it's worth the money to pay for the installation discs.

By the Way

To install, double-click the installer icon or disc icon that appears on your desktop and follow the prompts. You will be asked to authenticate yourself first, which means that you enter the password for the administrator (or owner) of the computer. When you do that, just click OK for the license agreement and click the various Continue and Install buttons. The software will be set up on your computer in short order.

If you purchase iLife, you'll actually receive two installation discs. One is a CD containing iTunes, iPhoto, and iMovie; the other is a DVD containing all four applications. (I said previously that iDVD is huge—in fact, it's so large that it has to be offered on a DVD rather than a CD.) Having two separate discs helps ensure that those without the Apple SuperDrive can still reap the benefits of iLife without having to spend hours downloading the components. Make sure that you use the right disc for your system.

Summary

This chapter introduced you to iLife and the applications it encompasses. iTunes can be used to turn your Macintosh into the centerpiece of your entertainment system. iTunes gives you access to audio media in a straightforward and entertaining manner, and its special features make organization a snap. The recent addition of the online Music Store provides a convenient source for high-quality versions of recent releases. iPhoto helps you manage and share your digital photographs. With features for editing and sharing your work, you can easily spend hours perfecting your images and preparing them for display. iMovie, a digital video editing application, allows you to turn your home movies into finished products with titles, music, and transitions. It also lets you share your movies in several popular formats. Finally, iDVD lets you share your video or still photos in the popular DVD format, with features that rival those of professionally made DVDs. If you're a music enthusiast, digital photographer, or budding filmmaker, iLife is for you.

CHAPTER 22

Using iTunes

The newer versions of iTunes, version 4 and higher, also connect to Apple's iTunes
Music Store where you can purchase high-quality song tracks, or entire albums,
online. We'll talk about how it works later in the chapter.

Setting Up iTunes

The first time you launch iTunes, it runs through a setup assistant to locate MP3s
and configure Internet playback. At any time during the setup procedure, click Next
to go to the next step, or click Previous to return to the preceding step. Clicking
Cancel exits the setup utility and starts iTunes.

The first step of the setup process, displayed in Figure 22.1, enables you to set
Internet access options.

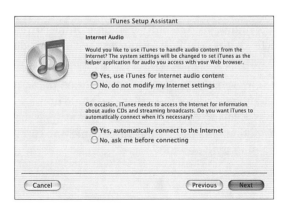

FIGURE 22.1
Choose how
iTunes works with
your Internet
applications.

iTunes is perfectly suited for handling streaming MP3s. If you've never listened to Internet radio before, you'll appreciate how quickly and easily iTunes enables you to find the type of music you want to hear and start listening. If you already have a streaming music player, tell iTunes not to modify your Internet settings.

iTunes also interacts with the Internet to look up information about your CDs, such as the artist and song title. The Yes, Automatically Connect to the Internet radio button, selected by default, enables this feature. To force iTunes to prompt you before connecting to the Internet, click No, Ask Me Before Connecting. Click Next when you're satisfied with your responses.

During the next step of the configuration, you're prompted to decide how iTunes will find MP3s and AAC files. By default, iTunes locates all the music files of these types on your drive. To disable this feature, click No, I'll Add Them Myself Later. The process of searching the drive for MP3 files can take a while, so you may prefer to add MP3s when you want to.

The final step of setup asks whether you want to go to the iTunes Music Store or go to your own iTunes Library on completing the setup. (If you choose not to explore the music store immediately, you can still reach it through the iTunes interface; we'll take a closer look at the music store later in this chapter.)

Click Done to begin using iTunes.

The iTunes Interface

Everything you need to do anything in iTunes is found in the main window, shown in Figure 22.2.

The main control areas are listed here:

- ▶ Player controls—The player controls move between different songs, play, pause, and adjust the output volume of the currently playing track. Clicking directly on the sound slider moves the volume adjustment immediately to that level.

- ▶ Status information—Displays information about the currently playing song. The top line displays the artist, the name of the song, and the name of the album. Clicking each of the status lines toggles between different types of information. Likewise, the Elapsed Time line can be toggled to display remaining time and total time.

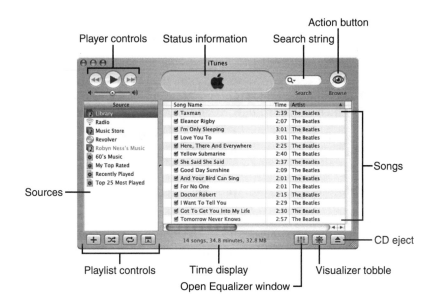

The progress bar shows how far the playback of the current song has progressed. Dragging the progress bar handle moves the playback back or forward in the audio track.

Finally, a stereo frequency monitor can be displayed by clicking the arrow on the right of the status display.

▶ Search string—Typing a few letters into the iTunes Search field immediately displays all audio tracks in the current playlist or library that match the string in any way (artist, song, album).

▶ Action button—The action button performs a different function depending on what source is currently being viewed. As you work in different areas of the program, this button changes to an appropriate action for that area:

  ▶ Library—When viewing the main song library, the action button toggles between two different browse modes. The first mode, shown in Figure 22.2, is similar to the Finder's List view. Each audio track is listed on its own line. The second mode uses a layout similar to the Column Finder view: The first column lists the artist, and the second column shows the albums for that artist. Finally, a lower pane shows a list of the song tracks for that artist and album.

  ▶ Radio Tuner—The Radio Tuner's action button is Refresh, which reloads all available stations from the iTunes Internet radio station browser.

- ▶ Music Store—With Music Store selected, the action button toggles between two different browse modes as it does in the main song library.

- ▶ Playlist—A *playlist* is your own personal list of music that you've compiled from the main library. Playlists are the starting point for creating a CD. When viewing a playlist, the action button is Burn CD.

- ▶ CD—When a CD is inserted, iTunes prepares to import the tracks to MP3 files. The action button is Import when a CD is selected as the source.

- ▶ Visual Effects—No matter what source is selected, iTunes can always be toggled to Visualizer mode to display dazzling onscreen graphics. When the visual effects are active, the action button becomes Options for controlling the visual effects.

▶ Source—The Source pane lists the available MP3 sources. Attached MP3 players, CDs, playlists, the central music library, and Radio Tuner make up the available sources.

Did you Know?

Double-clicking a source icon opens a new window with only the contents of that source. This is a nice way to create a cleaner view of your audio files.

▶ Songs—A list of the songs in the currently selected source. When in the main Library view, you can click the action button to toggle between a simple list and a column-based browser. Double-clicking a song in the list starts playback of the selected list beginning at that song. To change the visible fields in the list, choose Edit, View Options from the menu. Among the available pieces of information for each song are Name, Time, Artist, Album, Genre, Play Count, and the time it was Last Played.

▶ Playlist controls—Four playlist controls are available: Create Playlist, Shuffle Order, Loop, and Show/Hide Song Artwork. As their names suggest, these buttons can be used to create new playlists, control the order in which the audio tracks are played back, and show/hide song artwork.

By the Way

Most music you purchase from the iTunes Music Store comes with artwork, but you can add artwork to other song files. To add artwork, click the Show or Hide Song Artwork button and choose the song you want to be associated with the artwork. Then, drag any image file in .JPG, .PNG, .GIF, or .TIFF to the space at the lower left of the iTunes window.

▶ Time display—At the bottom of the iTunes window is information about the contents, playing time, and total file size of the currently selected source. The default mode displays approximate time—clicking the text toggles to precise playing time.

▶ Open Equalizer window—The Equalizer, shown in Figure 22.3, enables you to choose preset frequency levels by musical genre or to set them manually by dragging the sliders. The mode defaults to Flat, which means that all the controls are set in the middle of their range.

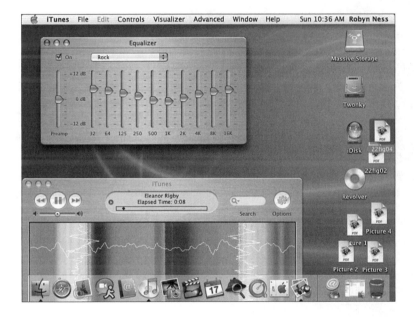

FIGURE 22.3
Choose how iTunes plays your music using iTunes' built-in equalizer.

▶ Visualizer toggle—Turns the visualization effects ("music for the eyes") on and off.

▶ CD eject—Ejects the currently inserted CD.

Audio Control Keyboard Controls

The iTunes player controls work on whatever source you currently have selected. After a song plays, iTunes moves to the next song. You can also control the playing via keyboard or from the Controls menu:

- ▶ Play/Stop—Spacebar

- ▶ Next Song—Command-right-arrow key

- ▶ Previous Song—Command-left-arrow key

- ▶ Volume Up—Command-up-arrow key

- ▶ Volume Down—Command-down-arrow key

- ▶ Mute—Option-Command-down-arrow key

Did you Know?

Some of these functions are also available from the iTunes Dock icon. Click and hold the Dock icon to display a pop-up menu for moving between the tracks in the current audio source.

To randomize the play order for the selected source, click the Shuffle button (second from the left) in the lower left of the iTunes window. If you want to repeat the tracks, use the Loop button (third from the left) in the lower-left corner to toggle between Repeat Off, Repeat Once, and Repeat All.

Did you Know?

The iTunes window is a bit large to conveniently leave onscreen during playback. Luckily, two other window modes take up far less space. Quite illogically, you access these smaller modes by clicking the window's Maximize button.

After clicking Maximize, the window is reduced to the player controls and status window. Even this window is a bit large for some monitors, though. To collapse it even more, use the resize handle in the lower-right corner of the window.

To restore iTunes to its original state, click the Maximize button again.

Visualizer

The iTunes Visualizer creates a graphical visualization of your music as it plays. While playing a song, click the Visualizer button (second from the right) in the lower-right corner of the iTunes window, or select Visuals, Turn Visualizer On (Command-T) from the menu to activate the display. Figure 22.4 shows the Visualizer in action.

The Visuals menu can control the size of the generated graphics as well as toggle between full-screen (Command-F) and window modes. To exit full-screen mode, press Esc or click the mouse button.

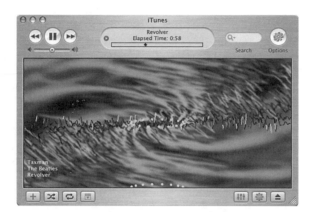

FIGURE 22.4
The Visualizer displays images to match your music.

While the windowed Visualizer display is active, the Options action button in the upper-right corner of the window is active. Click this button to fine-tune your Visualizer settings.

Adding Song Files

Encoding, or *ripping*, CDs enables you to take the tracks from a CD and save them in the MP3 (MPEG Layer 3), AAC, AIFF, or WAV format.

Import Options

You can choose these options in the Import pane of the iTunes preferences, as shown in Figure 22.5.

Here are the basic distinctions between these formats:

- ▶ MP3 files offer the option of compact file sizes and broad compatibility with MP3 players, but sound quality varies widely depending on the data rate.

- ▶ AAC files give you better quality than MP3s in a smaller file size, but may not be supported by all MP3 players.

- ▶ AIFF files are CD-quality, but much larger than both MP3 and AAC files.

- ▶ WAV files are large like AIFF files, but work better for those using Windows computers.

The Settings pop-up menu enables you to choose a data rate in kilobits per second. The higher the data rate, the better the quality of the encoded music. For

FIGURE 22.5
Pick an encoding
type here.

MP3s, anything lower than 128Kbps is different from (and inferior to) the quality of a regular audio CD. The iTunes Music Store sells 128Kbps AAC files, which are much better quality than 128Kbps MP3s. Remember also that the higher the data rate, the more disk space a music file occupies on your hard drive.

In the Import pane, you can also choose whether to play songs while importing them and whether to keep the track numbers with the filenames so that the album order can be maintained later.

Importing Song Files

iTunes makes it easy to import song files in common digital audio formats. In this section, we show you how to create MP3s from your CDs. (See the discussion on burning preferences in the section "The iTunes Preference Options" later in the chapter to learn about the options for burning in formats other than MP3.)

To import song files from a CD and encode them in digital format, find the CD you want to use and then follow these steps:

1. Insert the CD into your Macintosh's optical drive.

2. iTunes queries an Internet CD database to get the names of all the tracks on your disk. If you chose not to have this happen automatically during iTunes

setup, select Advanced, Get CD Track Names from the menu and click the Stop button.

3. Click the CD name in the Source pane to display all the available tracks.

4. Select the tracks you want to encode by checking and unchecking the boxes in front of each song title. If no tracks are selected, the entire CD is imported.

5. Click the Import action button at the upper right of the iTunes window, as shown in Figure 22.6, to encode the selected tracks. As the tracks are importing, a small graphic appears to show whether it has been imported or is currently being imported.

FIGURE 22.6
Importing a track from a CD.

The CDDB Internet database contains information on hundreds of thousands of CDs. In the unlikely event that your CD isn't located, it is listed as Untitled.

If iTunes couldn't find your song information, or you aren't connected to the Internet, you can edit each song file's stored artist/title information by hand by selecting the file and choosing File, Get Info (Command-I) from the menu.

You can even submit your updated information back to the Internet CD database by choosing Advanced, Submit CD Track Names from the menu.

After you add songs to your music library, iTunes enables you to easily assign ratings to them. Simply locate the My Rating column in the song listings and click on the placeholder dots to add from one to five stars for each song. To sort by rating, simply click the My Rating header.

By default, the encoded files are stored in Music/iTunes/iTunes Music found in your home directory. An entire CD can take from 5–74 minutes to process, depending on the speed of your CD-ROM drive. To pass the time, you can continue to use iTunes while the tracks are imported. When the import finishes, your computer chimes, and the music files are available under the Library source listing.

If you're working with an existing library of song files rather than a CD, you can easily add them to your library. Choose File, Add To Library from the menu to choose a folder that contains the files. Alternatively, you can simply drag a folder of files from the Finder into the Library song list.

The process of importing music files takes time. Each file is examined for ID3 tags (which identify information such as artist and title of a song) and is cataloged in the iTunes database.

Task: Creating and Working with Playlists

The key to many of the remaining iTunes features lies in creating a playlist. As mentioned earlier, a playlist is nothing more than a list of songs from your library. To create a new playlist, follow these steps:

1. Click the Create Playlist button in the lower-left corner of the iTunes window, or choose File, New Playlist (Command-N) from the menu.

2. The new playlist ("untitled playlist") is added to the end of the list in the Source pane. Select the playlist and rename it. Now you're ready to add songs to the playlist.

3. Select Library in the Source pane.

4. Verify that the song you want is in the main library. If it isn't, you must first add the song to the library.

5. Select one or more songs in the Songs pane.

6. Drag your selection to the playlist in the Source pane.

Using the Smart Playlist option, you can automatically create playlists based on criteria such as genre or your personal song ratings. Simply choose File, New Smart Playlist from the menu; set your criteria; and name your playlist. As an added bonus, Smart Playlists can also be set to update themselves with the Live Updating option as new material is added to your music library.

The selected songs are added to your playlist. Click the playlist to display the songs. You can drag the tracks within the song pane to choose their order.

Sharing Music on Your Local Network

After you've added music and created playlists, you may want to share your music with others on your local network. You can share your entire library or selected playlists. You also can share but require a password to limit listeners to those you invite. The settings for these options are located under the Sharing pane of the iTunes preferences (shown in Figure 22.7), which you can access under the iTunes application menu.

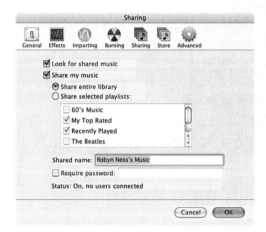

FIGURE 22.7
The Sharing preferences allow you to let others listen to your music library.

The first of the Sharing options is a check box for your computer to look for music shared by other iTunes 4 users on your local network. If checked, any libraries or playlists located will appear in blue in the left-hand side of the iTunes window, as shown previously in Figure 22.2.

If you want to share your music, you can choose to share the entire library or specific playlists. You can also give your collection a catchy name or leave it as the default, as shown earlier in Figure 22.7.

If you want to share with only those you invite, check the Require Password box, type the word or phrase you want to require, and click OK at the bottom of the preference window to activate. Now, those who try to access your music will see a pop-up window, as shown in Figure 22.8, that asks for the password.

Finally, you can see at the bottom of the Sharing preferences pane how many users are currently listening to your shared music.

FIGURE 22.8
Prospective listeners must know the password to share your music.

The iTunes Music Store

One feature of iTunes that is getting a lot of attention is the iTunes Music Store, which allows you to browse available songs and albums, listen to short samples, and then purchase song files online. To access this feature, click the icon labeled Music Store located just above your playlists on the left side of the iTunes window. While in the music store, the area that typically displays your local music files is replaced by a list that you can navigate as you would a Web page, as shown in Figure 22.9.

By the Way

The songs purchased from the iTunes Music Store are in AAC format.

In the music store, you can view lists of today's top songs and albums; look through new releases; browse by genre; or perform searches by song, artist, album, or composer name. When you find something that interests you, you can listen to a short clip of the song to see whether you want to purchase the full version. At the time of the this writing, individual songs cost 99 cents, and full albums were around $10.

FIGURE 22.9
The "home page" of iTunes Music Store.

As you click links to move around in the store, buttons at the top of the Music Store portion of the window, as shown in Figure 22.10, tell you where you are and allow you to move back and forward and to return to the home page.

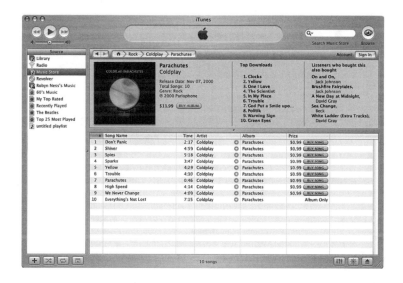

FIGURE 22.10
As you browse, the buttons above the main content area keep track of where you are.

Power Search, Browse, and Requests

Although some people may enjoy browsing the iTunes Music Store in the Web browserlike interface, others may find other options easier to use. At the top of the left-hand column are options for Power Search, Browse, and Requests & Feedback (refer to Figure 22.9), which provide more structured interfaces for targeted searches.

Power Search, as shown in Figure 22.11, provides fields for Song, Artist, Album, Genre, and Composer. This allows people who know precisely what they're looking for to locate it efficiently. However, be a bit cautious about using this search if you aren't sure how to spell the name of something—the Power Search doesn't show close matches.

FIGURE 22.11
Enter any information you are sure of to see whether the Power Search can help you find it.

The results for the power search can be sorted by song name, time (or length of track), artist, album, or relevance. (You can also sort by price, but at this time all prices for individual songs are the same!)

The Browse option, as shown in Figure 22.12, is like a more straightforward version of the main music store interface. When you choose a genre in the left-hand column, artists for that genre appear in the middle column. Choosing an artist displays albums in the right-hand column. Selecting an album displays the song tracks in the album in the bottom pane, where you can listen to a sample or make a purchase.

FIGURE 22.12
Browsing is a powerful way to search for specific songs, or to locate unfamiliar artists in a favorite genre.

If you don't know which album contains the song you're looking for, select All from the Album column to see a sortable list of all songs by your chosen artist that are available in the iTunes Music Store.

Did you Know?

Although the Power Search and Browse options are effective ways to locate songs you want, there will probably be times when a song you desperately want to buy isn't available from the music store. If that happens, you can select the option Requests & Feedback from the main iTunes Music Store pane. In the window that appears, type a short message about what you're looking for so that Apple will know what artists and/or songs it should try to include. You can also use this section to send feedback about errors you come across, such as misspellings or miscategorizations.

Making a Purchase

Now that you know how to find a song, let's see how to buy! The first step is to create an account, which you initiate by clicking the Sign In button at the upper left of the Music Store pane. This opens the window shown in Figure 22.13, where you can create an account from scratch or simply use your .Mac account (if you set one up).

FIGURE 22.13
Create an account
for the iTunes
Music Store, or use
your .Mac account.

To create an account, you will need to fill out a form with your email address, a password you want to use, and your credit card information. When you are finished creating your account, you can sign in to make your purchase.

By the Way

> Apple has made a strong attempt to keep your iTunes Music Store account, which is tied to your credit card, safe from others who use your computer. When you finish using your account, you can click the Sign Out button. To reactivate your purchasing privileges, you will have to sign in again with the email address you signed up with and your password. If you or (someone else) should happen to mistype your password three times in a row, your account will have to be reset before login can continue.
>
> To reset your account, you need to go to iForgot Web site at `https://iforgot.apple.com/` and enter your Apple ID. You have the option to have the password sent to the email address you provided when you created your account or to answer a security question to reset your password. Then, you need to change your password to continue your login to the iTunes Music Store.

When you are logged in to the music store, you can locate a song you want to purchase and click the Buy Song button at the end of the row. To make sure that you haven't accidentally clicked the buy button for the wrong song, you will see a message asking you to confirm that you want to buy and download the selected song, as shown in Figure 22.14. (You have to option to check a box not to be warned about buying songs in the future, but, remember, if you accidentally choose the wrong item, this message is your chance to correct your mistake.

When you confirm your purchase, the file will begin to download, and its status will appear in the Status Information area at the top of the iTunes window. After you've downloaded your first song, another playlist appears in the Source pane. Called Purchased Music, this playlist is just like any other playlist: songs purchased from the music store appear in it, but you can delete them from the playlist, and they will still remain in your library.

Interacting with Purchased Music

Song files from the iTunes Music Store respond a bit differently than other song files in iTunes. Songs purchased by each iTunes Music Store account can be played only on three computers, and the first time you try to play a purchased music file you will have to authorize the current computer as one of those three. (This is a measure taken to make sure that the files are not traded widely among users, which would deprive artists and record companies of revenue from the works they release.) The Authorize Computer window, shown in Figure 22.15, requires you to enter the password of the iTunes Music Store account set up on that computer.

> Songs purchased from the music store cannot be shared to other users on your local network through the Sharing options discussed earlier.

By the Way

When burning music to CD, as we'll discuss in the next section, you can burn only 10 CDs of a single playlist composed of purchased songs.

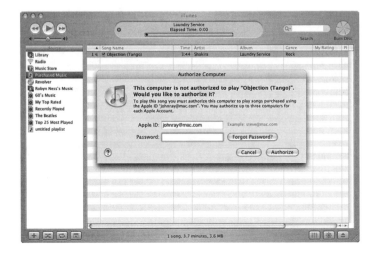

Burning CDs and Exporting to MP3 Players

After a playlist has been built, you can drag its name from the Source pane to any listed MP3 player source. The files are automatically copied to the connected player. If the player does not have enough available space, you must remove files from your playlist or select the external player and remove tracks from its memory. (We'll give special attention to using iTunes with Apple's iPod MP3 player at the end of this chapter.)

Watch Out!

Not all Macs have a built-in CD burner. If yours doesn't, you can add an external CD-burning drive. iTunes works with a number of makes and models from such companies as LaCie, Plextor, Que, Sony, VST, and other popular brands. You'll want to check with your dealer or Apple's iTunes Web site (www.apple.com/itunes) for the list of supported devices. Even if you can't burn a CD, you can still rip tracks from an audio CD using your computer's CD drive.

If you have a Mac with a supported CD burner, you can use a playlist to burn an audio CD laid out exactly like the playlist.

By the Way

When burning CDs, you have a choice between a couple types of CD media. The first type, CD-R, is a write-once CD. That means you can write your files to it just once, and that's it. If you make a mistake, you have to throw the failed CD away and use another. The CD-RW media can be erased and used over and over again, up to 1,000 times. In that way, it's like a regular drive except that CD drives run slower.

If you plan on using the files only temporarily and replacing them over and over again, the extra cost of the CD-RW is worth it. Otherwise, stick with the CD-R.

Regarding the price of blank CDs, well, the best thing to do is try a brand and see whether it works. If you get a lot of disk errors, try a different brand. The big names, such as Fuji, Imation, Maxtor, and Verbatum, should work with any CD burner. Try a few of the private store labels before buying a large bundle.

To make a CD, just insert a blank CD into your computer's CD drive (if it came with a CD burner) or into a connected CD burner. Your MP3 music player's instructions will tell you how to copy music to one of these devices.

If you have an older CD player, CDs you create yourself might not work. Unless you've spent a bundle on that CD player, it might be worth purchasing a new CD player to have the flexibility of making your own CDs.

By the Way

With the CD in place, double-check your playlist and then click Burn CD to make your custom disc. Depending on the speed of your CD burner, making a CD can take up to half an hour. When you're finished, you can eject the CD (click the Eject button at the lower right of the iTunes window). Repeat the previous steps to make more playlists and more CDs.

Listening to Internet Radio

Depending on your connection speed, Internet radio could be your ticket to high-quality commercial-free music. Unfortunately, most dial-in modems have poor sound quality, but DSL and cable modem users can listen to much higher quality streams. To see what's available and start listening requires only a few clicks:

1. To display a list of available streaming stations, click Radio in the Source pane. After a few seconds of querying a station server, a list of available music genres is displayed.

2. Each genre can be expanded to show the stations in that group by clicking its disclosure triangle. Stations are listed with a Stream (station) name, Bit Rate, and Comment (description). The bit rate determines the quality of the streamed audio—the higher the bit rate, the higher the quality—and the higher the bandwidth requirements.

3. Double-click a station to begin playing, or select the station and then click the Play button. iTunes buffers a few seconds of audio and then starts playing the streaming audio. If iTunes stutters while playing, look for a similar station that uses a lower bit rate.

Did you Know?

Conversely to what seems logical, you can drag stations from the Radio Tuner source and play them in a playlist. The playlist plays as it normally would, but starts playing streaming audio when it gets to the added Internet radio station.

You cannot burn a radio station to a CD or store it on an external MP3 device.

The iTunes Preference Options

As you can see, building playlists in iTunes and making CD copies can be done in just a few minutes. Easy as pie! If you want to look at the power of the program, however, there are some useful options to get you better quality CDs and fine-tune the program.

You'll find them under Preferences in the iTunes application menu (it's in the Edit menu with the Mac OS 9.x version).

Here's a brief look at the three preference dialog boxes available with iTunes:

▶ General—When you click the General icon (see Figure 22.16), you can set three categories of preferences. In the first section, you can pick a text size from the two pop-up menus and whether the musical genre (such as Country or Rock) should be displayed in your play list.

The option On CD Insert lets you indicate with the pop-up menu what to do when you insert a music CD. The default is Show Songs, but you can also decide to both play and import the contents of a CD automatically.

The Internet option simply enables you to select the same choices you made when the original iTunes Setup Assistant appeared.

▶ Effects—The Effects preferences, shown in Figure 22.17, allow you to enable and set the number of seconds for Crossfade Playback, an effect that overlaps the end of one track with the beginning of the next to decrease dead air time. You can also choose to enable Sound Enhancer and choose an amount of enhancement from low to high. The final option is a check box to automatically adjust the volume level to be more even between different songs.

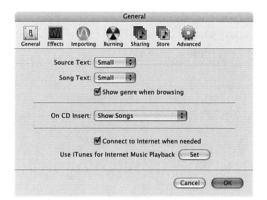

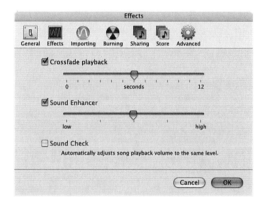

▶ Importing—You learned about the Importing preferences earlier in the section "Import Options." These settings pertain to format of music imported
from CD and how iTunes behaves during import.

▶ Burning—The Burning preferences (shown in Figure 22.18) are specific to
the kind of CD burner you are using and how you want the gap between
musical tracks handled.

▶ Sharing—The Sharing options were discussed earlier, in the section "Sharing
Music on Your Local Network." These setting allow you to look for music
shared by others on your network and to choose what of your own music
to share.

▶ Store—The Store settings, shown in Figure 22.19, allow you to choose
whether to purchase one song at a time (1-Click) or many songs all at once

(shopping cart). You can also choose whether to play songs you've purchased immediately after they download and whether to load entire song previews before listening.

FIGURE 22.18
The settings for your CD burner are shown here.

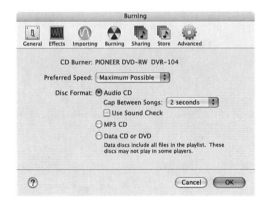

FIGURE 22.19
Customize your settings for the iTunes Music Store.

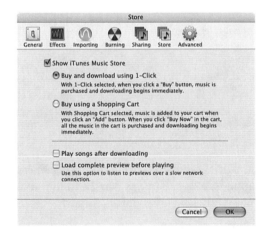

▶ Advanced—The Advanced options, shown in Figure 22.20, include where on your system to store your music, whether to keep the folder organized, and whether to copy files to the folder when you add them to the library.

You can also choose how to shuffle your music—by individual song or by album.

There is a setting for what degree—low, medium, or high—you want streaming media to be buffered. (That basically means "how much of a file playing over the Internet do you want to have waiting in reserve before it will begin to play on your local machine?" Because network connections aren't always consistently fast, setting buffering to low can result in stop-and-start audio that makes listening difficult.)

FIGURE 22.20
Change the location of your music library folder in the Advanced section of the iTunes preferences.

Using Your iPod with iTunes

Apple's tiny digital music player, the iPod (see Figure 22.21) can serve double-duty. You can use it as an extra FireWire hard drive for your computer as mentioned in Chapter 19, "Adding Peripheral Devices," or you can just stick with its core function, which is a handheld (or pocket-held) music device.

FIGURE 22.21
The iPod delivers digital music with style.

Making your iPod work with your Mac is an almost automatic process, so I'll be brief about it (aren't you glad?).

Updating Your iPod's Music Library

1. To dock your iPod to your Mac, first make sure that your Mac is running.

2. Take the FireWire cable that comes with your iPod (or any regular FireWire cable for that matter) and plug it into your iPod and your computer's FireWire port. When connected, you'll see a FireWire icon on your iPod's display. When set up, iTunes will open automatically, and your iPod will automatically synchronize its music library with the one on your computer.

> Some FireWire cables, especially those designed for DV camcorders, have a 4-pin cable at one end. These won't work with your iPod, which requires a 6-pin cable to enable it to draw current from your computer, used for recharging its battery.

3. If you prefer to transfer music manually, connect your iPod as described previously and allow iTunes to launch.

4. Select your iPod in the iTunes source list (the list of music libraries), and click the iPod icon at the bottom right of the iTunes window, which opens the program's preferences box.

5. With preferences displayed on your computer's screen, check the item labeled Manually Manage Songs and Play Lists.

> You won't be able to use your iPod with other computers without it replacing your music library if you use the standard option to automatically update your playlist when your iPod is attached to your computer. That's because it'll base its playlist strictly on the Mac to which it's connected. If you want to use the iPod on different Macs, use the manual song management option described previously.

Summary

In iTunes, Apple has latched on to a craze. The iTunes software can quickly convert your CDs into a library of digitized music or vice versa, and give you access to thousands of radio stations that play the kind of music you want to hear and to many new releases, 24 hours a day. It'll even sync with your iPod to make your music portable. If you're a music enthusiast, Mac OS X is the operating system for you.

CHAPTER 23

Using iPhoto

Apple's iPhoto brings all the functions you need for working with digital photographs together in one interface, shown in Figure 23.1, with different panes for Import, Organize, Edit, and Book views. You move between modes by clicking the row of buttons under the viewing area.

By the Way

Many recent digital cameras with USB connections are compatible with iPhoto. You can find out whether yours is one of them at www.apple.com/iphoto/compatibility/.

If your digital camera isn't compatible with iPhoto, Apple recommends using a peripheral device to read the camera's memory card directly. The type of storage media used by your camera dictates whether you need a PCMCIA Flash Card reader or some other kind.

Did you Know?

Those without digital cameras can still use iPhoto to organize digital images sent from other people and to store scanned images. We talk more about importing files into iPhoto from your hard drive later in this chapter in the section "Importing Image Files."

The iPhoto Interface

The iPhoto interface contains several distinct areas, some of which change depending on the current mode. The bottom pane contains view-specific functions, and the upper-right viewing area takes on different appearances to support the mode you're in. You can resize the contents of the viewing area using the slider to the right of the mode buttons.

Did you Know?

To jump between the smallest and the largest possible display sizes, click on the small and large image icons at either end of the resize slider.

FIGURE 23.1
The iPhoto window contains all the settings you need to import, organize, edit, and "book" your photos.

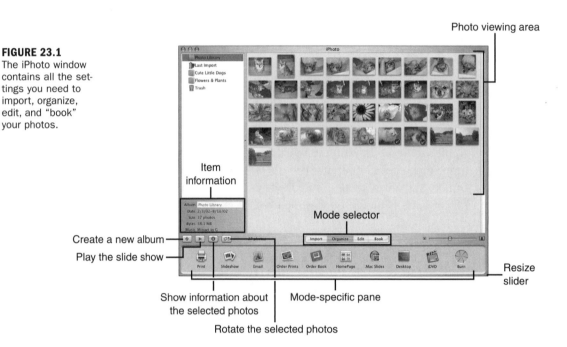

Photo viewing area

Item information

Mode selector

Create a new album

Play the slide show

Resize slider

Show information about the selected photos

Mode-specific pane

Rotate the selected photos

The elements along the left side are available regardless of iPhoto's mode. Let's take a look at them now.

The Photo Library contains all the images imported by iPhoto. Last Import is a special unit containing the most recent pictures. Below Last Import are albums, the special sets of pictures you put together, if you've created any. Selecting one of these items fills the viewing area with thumbnail images of its contents.

Below the Photo Library and albums is a section containing information about the selected item. For example, in Figure 23.1, Photo Library is selected, so the information section displays the name of the selection, the range of dates for the images it contains, the number of images it contains, and the total file size of its contents. It also displays the music currently selected to accompany slideshows, which we will discuss shortly. If a specific thumbnail image were selected, the given information would be the image title, date imported, size of image in pixels, file size, and current slideshow music. You can change the title or the date by typing in those fields.

> Additional details about a selected image can be accessed by choosing File, Show Photo Info from the menu. This opens a window containing information about the image, file, and originating camera. If your camera supports it, the window also contains technical details such as shutter speed, aperture, and use of a flash for the photograph.

By the Way

There are also four buttons just above the view-specific pane:

- ▶ Create a new album—Enables you to create a special group of chosen photos that you can arrange in any way or export as a unit. We'll talk more about albums later.

- ▶ Play the slideshow—Plays a full-screen slideshow, complete with music, of all the photos currently displayed in the viewing area. You can alter the slideshow settings under the Slideshow option of the Organize view, including the length of time each slide plays and the song to accompany the slideshow—you can even choose a song from your iTunes folder.

- ▶ Show information about the selected photos—Toggles the information area through its different configurations, including one containing a field to add comments about the selected photo. (In another configuration, the info section is hidden entirely.) You can also edit the titles by typing in the title field. We'll talk about how you can perform searches on this Comments field in a little while.

- ▶ Rotate the selected photos—Rotates the selected items. You can set the rotation direction to clockwise or counterclockwise in the iPhoto application preference dialog.

Importing Image Files

The first time you connect a supported camera to your computer and set the camera to its playback or transfer mode, iPhoto opens automatically. If it doesn't, you can manually launch iPhoto either from the Dock or the Applications folder. The iPhoto window will be in Import view.

> Mac OS X includes in its Application folder the Image Capture program that downloads images and media files from supported cameras and card readers. It also works with TWAIN-compliant flatbed scanners (given an appropriate driver) to scan images.

By the Way

The Import view, shown in Figure 23.2, displays the camera status, Import button, and an option to delete images from the camera after they're stored in iPhoto.

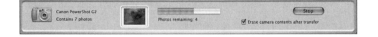

To import the photos on your camera, click the Import button in the lower-right corner of the window. If the box for Erase Camera Contents After Transfer is checked, the Confirm Move sheet, shown in Figure 23.3, appears and asks you to approve deletion of the original photo files from the camera. Thumbnails of the transferring images appear in the image well of the Import view along with the number of photos remaining to be transferred. When the import is complete, the new images will appear in the photo viewing area along with any other images you've imported.

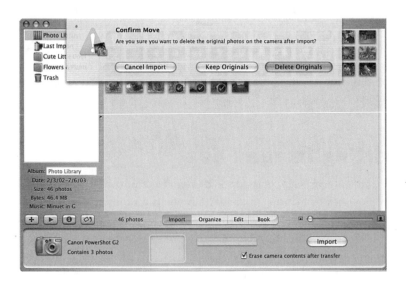

By default, new *rolls* (groups of pictures imported at one time) are added to the bottom of the viewing area, but you can change that to order with the most recent at the top inside the application preference panel.

Did you Know?

After your photos have been imported and deleted from your camera's memory, don't forget to shut off your camera!

To import images already stored on your hard drive or other media, simply select them and drag them onto the Photo Library icon at the upper left. Thumbnails appear as if the images were another "roll" of film.

Organizing Images

After you've imported some image files into iPhoto, switch to the Organize view to work with your images. The iPhoto window in Organize view, shown in Figure 23.4, looks similar to the Import view except for the controls in the bottom pane. Here, you can choose ways to share your images, which we'll talk about in the section "Sharing Your Photos" later in this chapter.

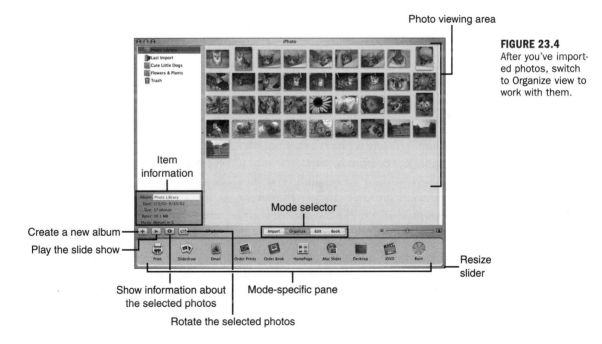

FIGURE 23.4
After you've imported photos, switch to Organize view to work with them.

While in Organize view, you can choose whether to display the images in your viewing area with additional information, including their titles, keywords, and film rolls, by selecting those options from the View menu.

Selecting Titles displays the title of each image beneath its thumbnail in the viewing area. The default titles of images imported by iPhoto aren't very helpful. You can give them more meaningful titles by clicking on the information button until the title field is visible and then typing your new text in it.

The View, Keywords option shows any keywords you've attached to an image file to the right of its thumbnail image. We'll look further at applying keywords in a moment.

Displaying by Film Rolls divides the photos in the viewing area into sections labeled with roll number, date of import, and number of photos imported.

You can choose to view your images with any, all, or none of those pieces of information.

You can tell iPhoto to order the images in your Photo Library by film roll, date, or title by selecting the appropriate option in the Arrange Photos submenu of the View menu.

You can select an image in the viewing area by single-clicking it. You can select a group of consecutive pictures by clicking just outside the edge of the first photo and dragging to create a box connecting all the photos that you want to select, or select a group of nonconsecutive pictures by holding down the Command key as you click the desired images.

If you want to delete a photo or several photos that are visible in the viewing area, highlight the photos you don't want to keep and then press the Delete key on your keyboard. In the original version of iPhoto, when you deleted a photo it was truly gone forever. In more recent versions, deleted photos are stored in a special Trash area, much like the one for your entire system.

You can view the contents of the Trash by selecting its icon on the left side of the iPhoto window. If you decide to save a photo that you sent to the Trash, you can drag it back to your Photo Library. When you are sure that you don't want to see any of the items in the Trash again, choose File, Empty Trash from the menu.

You can also drag selected photos to your desktop, which will make additional copies of them, or into a new album, which we'll discuss later in this chapter.

Applying Keywords

A good way to organize your photo collection is with keywords. When applied, keywords appear next to the image thumbnails in the viewing area whenever you check the box for Keywords.

To open the Keywords/Search window, sh̶͟ ͟ ͟ ͟ ͟ ͟ ͟3.5, choose Edit, Keyw̶ ͟ ͟ ͟ ͟ ͟ ͟ ͟ ͟ ͟ ͟ ͟ ͟ ͟ ͟ ͟ ͟ ͟Command-K.

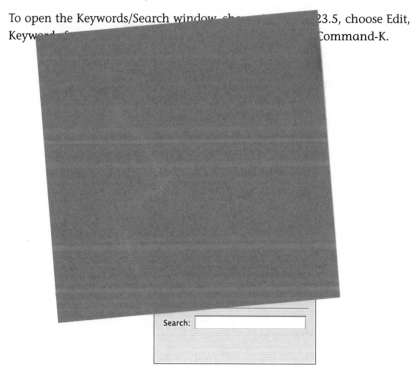

Search:

FIGURE 23.5
The Keywords/
Search window
allows you to
assign and search
by keywords.

You can use iPhoto's default keywords or create your own custom keywords. To write your own, choose New from the Keywords pop-up menu at the top of the Keywords/Search window. Then, in the line that appears, type your new keyword.

To change an existing keyword, choose Rename from the Keywords pop-up menu at the top of the Keywords window. Keep in mind that the change is passed along to any photos assigned the previous keyword.

To delete a keyword, click to highlight it in the keyword list, and choose Delete from the Keywords pop-up menu.

To apply keywords to a photo, select the image thumbnail in the viewing area and highlight the keyword you want to apply by clicking it. Then, click the

Assign button below the keyword list. To remove a keyword, select the image and click back into the Keywords/Search window. All the keywords you've added to the selected photo will be highlighted in the list so that you can remove them all, or click on only the one you want to remove.

> Included in the keyword list is a check mark symbol, which acts somewhat differently than the other keywords. Whereas other keywords are visible only when you've chosen to display them in the View menu, the check mark is always visible in the lower-right corner of the thumbnails it has been applied to. Also, the check box cannot be renamed or deleted as the other keywords can.

After you've applied keywords (including the check mark), you can search your image collection for photos labeled with a given keyword or combination of keywords. Simply open the Keywords/Search window, select the keyword you want to target, and click the Search button near the middle of the window. Only those pictures that match your search appear in the viewing area. Click the Show All button to return to the full photo listing.

In addition to searching by assigned keywords, you can also search for words in your image titles or comments. Just type the word in the Search field at the bottom of the Keywords/Search window. You don't need to click the search button, or even finish typing the word, before iPhoto attempts to match your search criteria. Delete the search term or click Show All to return to the full photo listing.

Task: Creating an Album

You can't arrange the individual images in your Photo Library just any old way. To choose the sequence of a set of images, you must create an album and add the photos you want to work with. (Keep in mind, that every photo imported into iPhoto will appear in your Photo Library; adding photos to albums doesn't move them out of the Photo Library.)

> You can choose whether to arrange the photos in an album by film roll, date, or title using the View, Arrange Photos option in the menu, just as you can for your Photo Library. However, for albums there's a fourth option that lets you arrange your images manually, which gives you the power to arrange them in any order you see fit.

Albums are a useful way to organize your photographs into collections, especially if you have many photos. Albums are also a basic unit in iPhoto that can be used when creating books, slideshows, and Web pages, which we'll discuss later.

The option to make a new album is available from any view in iPhoto. To create a new album, perform the following steps:

1. Click the button showing a + sign near the left edge of the iPhoto window, or choose File, New Album from the menu.

2. A dialog box (shown in Figure 23.6) appears, into which you can type a name for your album. (If you change your mind later, you can double-click the name of the album in the album list to change it.)

FIGURE 23.6
Enter a name for your album.

3. When you've named your album, click OK.

The album you created appears at the bottom of the album list at the upper left of the iPhoto interface. If you want to change the order of your albums, select the one you want to move and drag it to a new position. A black bar indicates where the album will be inserted, as shown in Figure 23.7. If you want to remove an album, select it and press the Delete key on your keyboard. Unless the album is empty, you will see an alert asking you to confirm deletion.

To add images to your album, make sure that you're in Organize view and select the images you want from the viewing area. You can select them one at a time or in groups. Drag your selection to your album name until a black border appears around it. As you drag, a faded version of one of the selected images appears behind your cursor, along with a red seal showing how many items you're dragging, as shown in Figure 23.8.

The images within albums are something like aliases on your desktop—you can delete a photo from an album without affecting the original file. However, when you delete an image from the Photo Library, it also disappears from any albums to which it has been added.

By the Way

FIGURE 23.7
Reorder your albums by dragging them around in the list.

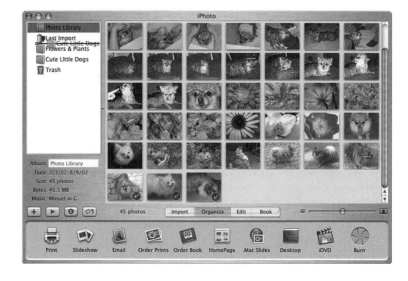

FIGURE 23.8
Drag one or more photos into your album.

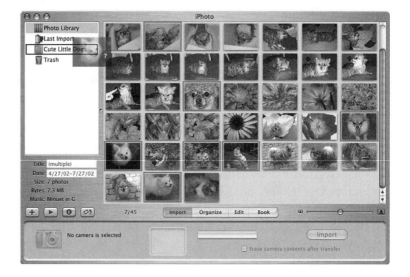

After you've created an album and added images, you can open the album and drag the contents into any order you want. You can also remove images from the album by selecting them and pressing the Delete key on your keyboard. Because the photos in your albums are always a part of the Photo Library, only the album copy will be removed. (If you want to delete a photo altogether, you'll need to delete it from the Photo Library as you learned earlier.)

Editing Photos

iPhoto's Edit view enables you to improve your existing photos by cropping them, adjusting their coloration, and performing simple retouching. To edit a photo, select it in Organize view and click the Edit button, or double-click a thumbnail image. You'll see a screen similar to that shown in Figure 23.9, with a large view of the photos and a number of editing tools in the bottom page. While in Edit view, you can use the Previous and Next buttons at bottom right to move through a group of images without going back into Organize view.

When editing a photo that's been added to an album, bear in mind that any changes appear in both the Photo Library and the album.

By the Way

FIGURE 23.9
In Edit view, you can crop your images or change their color properties.

A major function available in Edit view is *cropping* or trimming away the unimportant edges around a subject. iPhoto enables you to constrain the size of your cropped images to fit the common photos sizes 4×6, 5×7, and 8×10, as well as ratios such as square, 4×3, and a size to fit the resolution of your monitor.

Depending on the resolution of the images produced by your digital camera, you might not be able to crop to a small section of a photo without the resulting image becoming grainy or fuzzy. This is especially a problem if you plan to order prints from

Watch Out!

your photos because the images might look okay onscreen but could be unsuitable for printing. When ordering prints or books, watch out for the low-resolution warning symbol, which looks like a yellow traffic sign. It appears when creating a book or ordering prints if iPhoto determines that an image's resolution is not sufficient for the requested size of the finished image.

To crop an image, open it in Edit view and follow these steps:

1. Set a Constrain option if you want to maintain a specific width-to-height ratio.

2. In the viewing area, place your mouse pointer at one corner of the object or scene you want to select. Click and drag to form a selection box around it, as shown in Figure 23.10. To reposition the selection box, move your mouse pointer to the center of the selected area until it changes to a hand and then drag the box where you want it.

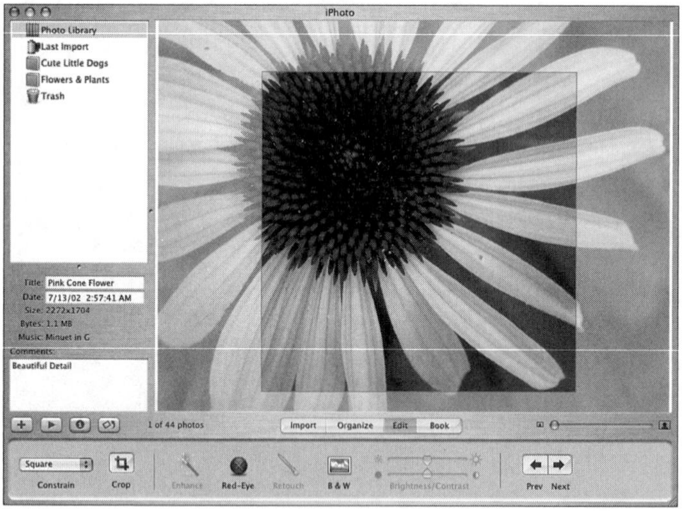

FIGURE 23.10
Drag your cursor to create a box containing the part of the photo you want to keep.

3. Click the Crop button to apply your change and see the result in the viewing area.

If you don't like the look of the cropped image as well as you liked the original, you can undo your most recent edit by choosing Edit, Undo from the menu.

After you make changes to images in iPhoto, you can always revert to the image as it was first imported by choosing File, Revert to Original from the menu. This enables you to make changes freely without fear of losing your original. However, if you achieve an effect you like, you might want to duplicate the photo in that state before trying additional edits. To do so, select the desired photo and choose File, Duplicate from the menu. That way, choosing Revert to Original after further editing returns you to that state rather than the original form of the image.

Did you Know?

In addition to cropping, you can edit your images with the Brightness and Contrast sliders. Brightness makes a photo either lighter or darker overall—it can fix minor problems from under- or overexposure. Contrast increases the difference between light and dark elements by making lighter areas lighter and darker areas darker. Contrast also increases the saturation of colors. Although these settings are good for small corrections, keep in mind that they can't save a photograph shot in really poor light conditions.

The Red-Eye and Black & White features enable you to change the coloration of entire photos or the area within a selection box. The Red-Eye option is most useful for reducing red tint from the eyes of people and pets, but it also removes the red tones from any selected area. To correct red eye, mark a crop selection box as tightly around the red eyes as possible and then click the Red-Eye button. Use the Black & White option to convert an entire image to black-and-white or create interesting effects by selecting portions to convert.

iPhoto's Red-Eye tool leaves a lot to be desired. For one thing, most red-eye regions are round, but iPhoto's cropping tool can only make rectangular selections. If you happen to select a portion of anything with red tones in it that lies outside the red-eye region you want to correct, you will also remove the red for that area. One solution is to use other photo editing software that allows oval-shaped selections.

By the Way

The Enhance feature also changes the coloration of the selected image. Specifically, it adjusts the colors in the photo for maximum contrast. To use it, simply click the Enhance button. If you don't like the results, you can always choose Edit, Undo from the menu.

The Retouch option allows you to blend specks and imperfections in your photos into the areas surrounding them. This tool is different from the options we've already discussed, all of which either work on the entire image or a preselected area. When using Enhance, your mouse cursor appears as a set of crosshairs, as it does when you are cropping a photo. You use these crosshairs to target image flaws. It may help to use the size slider to magnify the image so that you can see the area you want to retouch, as shown in Figure 23.11. When you have this cursor positioned near a discolored spot, click your mouse button and watch the color in the region around your cursor even out.

FIGURE 23.11
An enlarged view of the problem area makes retouching more precise.

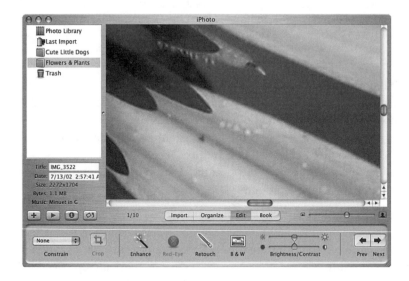

Did you Know?

When using the Retouch tool, be patient. It takes some intense processing effort from your computer to make the adjustments, so you may have to wait for it to complete the task.

Using Other Photo-Editing Software with iPhoto

Although iPhoto is a fantastic tool for organizing photos and performing simple cropping, you may want to perform your serious editing in a separate image editing program.

To open an iPhoto image file in another image editing program, click and drag an image thumbnail from the Organize view onto the icon for the photo-editing program. If you plan to edit with an outside program frequently, you can go into the iPhoto Preferences and set images to open automatically in the outside program when double-clicked.

If you do choose to edit your photos in a program other than iPhoto, keep in mind that changes saved to an original image from an outside program replace the original file in iPhoto's folders, so you cannot revert to the original image as you normally would. It might be best to make a duplicate before you begin editing.

If you choose to further edit an image that has already been altered from within iPhoto, the image is already a copy, so you will be able to revert to the original version. To check whether a file is an original or a copy before you begin editing, look at the File menu to see whether Revert to Original is an available option or is grayed out. If it is grayed out, the photo you're working with is the original.

Designing a Photo Book

Book view, shown in Figure 23.12, is a specialized option used to arrange an album's photos into a book format, including any supporting text. You can then order copies of your book in the Organize view, as we'll discuss in the section "Sharing Printed Photos" later in the chapter.

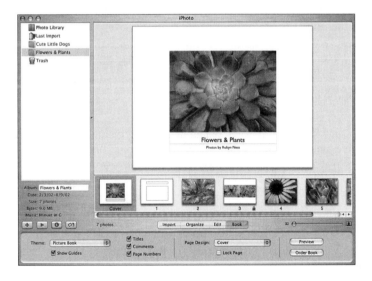

FIGURE 23.12
Book view enables you to lay out the photos in an album as a book.

In the Book options view, the Theme pop-up menu enables you to choose a basic style, including Story Book, Picture Book, and Catalog. The options differ in their picture layouts and built-in text areas, and how the photos are arranged on the page. When you choose a theme, the photos in the selected album are placed in a basic template in the order they appear in the album. The individual pages appear in a row at the bottom of the photo viewing area.

It's best to choose the look you want for your book carefully before you start customizing it. If you change from one theme to another, you lose any text (except photo titles and comments) or special page formatting you've made.

Check boxes in the Book options view also enable you to choose whether to show image Titles, Comments, and book Page Numbers on the pages, if the theme you've chosen includes space for them.

You can also choose whether to show guides for the text boxes. Check the Show Guides box if you want to edit the text. To edit text within a text area, select a page and type inside the space. If you want to check your spelling for a given page, you can do so by choosing Check Spelling from the Spelling submenu of the Edit menu. You can also change the font of an entire book in the Font submenu of the Edit menu.

When you choose a theme, an album's photos are inserted into the page template in the order in which they appear in your album. For example, the first image in the album is the default cover shot. The Page Design pop-up menu enables you to adjust the templates to show more or fewer images on a selected page. If you like the composition of some of the pages and don't want them to be shifted when you apply new templates or move other pages around, you must select the pages and check the Lock Page box. You can alter the layout of any page except the cover.

You can change the order of whole pages by dragging them to a new position. However, to change the cover photo, you must go into Organize view and rearrange the images in your album to place another photo first. Any changes made to page order in your book are reflected in the order of images in the album.

To get a better feel for the chosen layout, use the Preview button to page through your book in a separate window, as shown in Figure 23.13. When you are satisfied with your book, click the Order Book button to open a window with purchasing details.

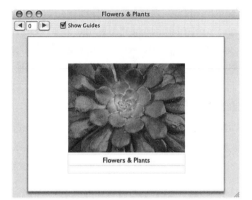

FIGURE 23.13
View your book in a separate window using the Preview button.

Sharing Your Photos

iPhoto offers a variety of ways for you to share your photos with others, both in print and onscreen. They are located along the bottom of the iPhoto window when it is in Organize view.

Sharing Printed Photos

For those who want to share their photos the traditional way, on some sort of paper, iPhoto offers three button choices at the bottom of the window: Print, Order Prints, or Order Book.

Clicking the Print button enables you make print settings for the selected item, including page size, margin width, and number of copies. If you select the Photo Library but not a specific photo, you can print the entire group. Many additional print settings, including special instructions for paper type, are revealed by clicking the advanced button at the bottom of the print window.

> As with other programs on your Mac, you can also choose to save your images in PDF format from the Print window. PDF documents can be opened by Adobe Acrobat, which is widely available and free, by people who don't have other types of image-viewing software.

By the Way

The Order Prints and Order Book buttons connect you to remote Web sites where you can choose what to order and supply your billing information. You can order prints of your pictures just as you would with pictures captured on film, or you can order a bound book of an album as you designed it using the Book view. If you order a book, keep in mind that the base size is 10 pages. If your book has fewer than 10 pages, several pages at the end are left blank. Also, additional charges are made on a page-by-page basis for books more than 10 pages.

Sharing Photos Digitally

To share your photos digitally with others, you can use the Email option. The Email option enables you to easily email a photo stored in iPhoto. Clicking the Email button brings up a dialog box in which you can choose the size of the image and whether to include the image title and comments. Click the Compose button to open a mail window containing the selected photograph and then add the email address of the recipient.

If you are a .Mac member, as discussed in Chapter 14, "Exploring .Mac Benefits," you can also use the HomePage and .Mac Slides options. Clicking the HomePage button enables you to select up to 48 images from your Photo Library or a specific album to insert into a basic Web page layout that will be stored in your .Mac account. You can view a sample page in my .Mac account at `homepage.mac.com/robynness/PhotoAlbum11.html`.

Choosing the .Mac Slides options lets you upload a set of images to your .Mac server space, or iDisk, that can be used as a screensaver by anyone running version 10.1.5 or later of Mac OS X. You can only offer one slideshow at a time, but this is a fun way to share pictures with friends and family. When you update the slides, their screensavers will also be updated the next time they are connected to the Internet.

By the Way

After you upload a .Mac slideshow, how can you share it with your family and friends? Tell them to go to the Desktop & Screen Saver pane of System Preferences and choose .Mac from the list in the Screen Saver pane. Then, they need to click the Configure button and, in the Subscription window that opens, type your .Mac membership name and click OK. It will take a few moments for the images to be downloaded from the Internet to their computers.

If you want to test drive a .Mac slideshow, you're welcome to subscribe to mine, which features my own photographs of flowers and leaves. Simply enter **robynness** as the .Mac membership name in the Subscribe window.

If your Mac has a CD burner or a DVD burner, you have two additional options for sharing your images digitally. The Burn option allows you to burn an album, or your entire library, to a CD or DVD. Simply click the Burn button and insert a blank disc when prompted. Then, click the Burn button again to write to the disc.

The iDVD option, available to those with computers equipped with Apple's SuperDrive and with iDVD installed, magically exports your iPhoto slideshows—including music choice and slide timing—into iDVD. All that's left for you to do is choose a background image for the main title page, using iDVD, and burn your DVD. (We'll talk more about iDVD beginning in Chapter 30, "Exploring the iDVD Interface."

Viewing Your Own Digital Photos

In addition to sharing your photos with others, you can also enjoy them at your own computer with the iPhoto Slideshow and the Desktop options.

The Slideshow option brings up a dialog box, shown in Figure 23.14, in which you can set the duration each image stays onscreen, whether the slides are displayed randomly and whether they repeat, and which music accompanies the show. When you've made your settings, click OK to start the iPhoto slideshow.

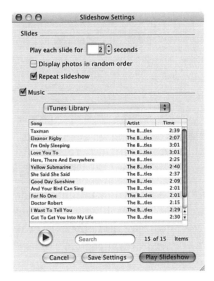

FIGURE 23.14
Customize your onscreen slideshows by choosing music and setting slide duration.

The Desktop option enables you to choose a single photo from your collection for use as a desktop background. To set a desktop, simply select the image you want and click Desktop. Your desktop background is immediately replaced with the selected image. To change your background back to a non-iPhoto background, open the Desktop & Screen Saver pane of System Preferences and choose a different image.

The iPhoto Preference Options

The iPhoto preferences, shown in Figure 23.15, allows you to customize several functions of the program.

FIGURE 23.15
Customize the appearance of the iPhoto viewing area, the action associated with double-clicking a photo, the direction of image rotation, and your default email program.

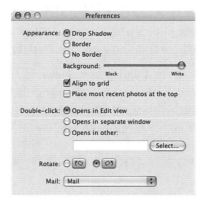

Appearance

The first grouping of preference options is for appearance of the iPhoto viewing area. Here, you can choose whether a drop shadow, a border, or no adornment appears around thumbnails and full images. You can also choose a background shade for the viewing area; your options are white, back, and shades of gray.

The check box for Align to Grid alters how thumbnails are positioned. It doesn't make much difference if all the images in your library have the same dimensions. However, if some are horizontal and others vertical, alignment will keep the same number of pictures per row rather than squeeze in however many will fit.

The option Place Most Recent Photos at the Top does exactly what it says; if left unchecked, the most recent photos are added to the end (or bottom) in the rows making up your Photo Library.

Double-Click and Rotate

Double-click refers to the action that occurs when you double-click on a thumbnail image in your Photo Library or an album. The default setting is to open in iPhoto's Edit view, but those who want to edit with an external program may want to select the radio button for Opens in Other and then select an application on their hard drive.

The Rotate options simply let you choose whether to rotate images clockwise or counterclockwise. You may find that you tend to turn your camera consistently to one side to capture vertical shots. Setting the rotate option to your liking can save you from having to rotate 270 degree (three clicks of the rotate button) to get to the point of view you want!

Mail

Mail allows you to choose which installed email program is used when you select Email from the Organize view. By default, it is set to Mail, which was installed with OS X. If you've installed another Email program, you will have the option to select it.

Summary

This chapter covered the different views of iPhoto: Import, Organize, Edit, and Book. You learned how to make albums, edit and crop your photos, and lay out your own photo book. You also looked at the various ways in which iPhoto helps you share your images both in print and onscreen.

CHAPTER 24

Exploring the iMovie Interface

iMovie lets you take video that you've recorded with a camcorder and make your own movies. It gives you the power to be your own movie director. When you go out with your digital camcorder, you might find that you quickly fill up an entire tape shooting scenes of events or people. Similarly, in Hollywood, when filmmakers shoot a movie, they take cameras and shoot a considerable amount of footage.

This is where iMovie comes in: the point at which you have your footage and want to do something with it. In Hollywood, the process of deciding which parts of the footage end up in the final product is called *editing*. If you pay attention to the credits at the end of a movie, you'll see the names of the editors. Movie editors craft the various scenes to fit together—in essence, they're making the same kind of decisions that you'll make for your iMovie.

Basic Stages—Shoot, Edit, Enhance, Share

Apple explains the process of making iMovies in four general stages, which roughly follow the general process that professional movie makers follow: shoot, edit, enhance, and share.

Shoot (and Capture)

Shooting video is simply the process of using your digital camcorder to record scenes or events for your iMovie. Most people find themselves recording sound with their video using the built-in microphone on their camcorder, but you don't necessarily need to do this. With the right equipment, you can record sound separately and then import it into your iMovie. For example, you might shoot some footage of an event and want to record yourself separately, making narrative commentary about the footage.

There are really no limits to what you can do when shooting video—you're limited only by how many blank tapes you have and how well charged your batteries are. (Hint: Extra batteries are definitely a wise investment, and you'll almost surely find yourself in situations in which they come in handy.) Keep in mind, though, that you can work only with a limited amount of the footage you have shot because iMovie temporarily stores your production on your computer's hard drive. That means that the available free space on your hard drive has a direct relationship to the amount of video you can edit at one time. For example, you can shoot as much video as you want, but you might not be able to edit all 10 tapes worth of footage at one time.

The way that you get video into the computer so that you can use it in iMovie is called *capturing* video. Apple makes it so simple to capture video, you don't really need to think of it as a separate stage in the process of making an iMovie. You simply shoot your video, connect your camcorder to your Mac with a FireWire cable, and click a button. iMovie captures the video for you and automatically processes the incoming video into separate clips.

Edit

Some people find that editing video is their favorite part of working with iMovies. This is where you get to make the creative decisions that cause the final product to take form. The most common adjustments that iMovie enables you to make when editing video are the *start* and *end* of an individual video clip. For example, let's say that you bring a new video clip into iMovie. It's a scene of a friend standing in front of a building, talking about an event, and the total length of the clip is about 2 minutes long.

But when you look at the clip in iMovie, you notice that at the beginning of the clip there's a little boy sticking his tongue out at the camera while walking by in the background. One option is to leave this type of accidental action in a clip, but ultimately you'll probably find yourself wanting to remove or add things to your iMovie—thus you'll want to learn how to edit.

If you want to edit the boy out of the scene in this example, iMovie gives you the ability to pick a new start for the clip. For example, you could start the clip 2 seconds later.

You'll learn the details of capturing video and editing scenes in Chapter 25, "Working with Video and Clips in iMovie."

Enhance (Effects)

iMovie gives you a number of tools and special effects that you can use to spice up your iMovie. In the context of video production, the word *enhance* has no special meaning, but Apple's use of the term to describe this stage of working with an iMovie is an apt description. In traditional video or film production, the same stage is referred to as *post-production*, when a movie or television show is tweaked and developed, special effects are added, and final decisions are made about how the production will turn out.

iMovie is simple to use, but powerful, and one of the places it shines is in the category of effects. iMovie comes with many built-in effects, including Brightness/Contrast and Adjust Colors.

Share

Sharing is my favorite stage of making an iMovie, and iMovie offers several options for sharing your movies: from exporting them back to videotape through your camera to exporting for use with iDVD. We'll cover the options in-depth in Chapter 29, "Exporting iMovies."

The iMovie Interface

iMovie is a simple yet powerful video editor that enables you to develop your video project with three main tools: the Monitor, where you look at the video clip; a *shelf*, which gives you the ability to look at all the clips you have to work with at a glance; and a special area at the bottom of the screen known as the Timeline Viewer, where you can put together your clips and make decisions about when you want them to start and end.

iMovie Monitor

You'll find that the iMovie workspace is easy and fun to work with, like a well-planned playroom (see Figure 24.1), and the iMovie Monitor will end up being the center of activity. After you've created a new project, the action happens in the Monitor window, which is used both to capture and preview video in iMovie. The deceptively simple Monitor window is a powerful tool that enables you to switch between looking at video that's coming from your camcorder and the clips that you already have on your Mac by toggling the import/edit control, labeled with camera and scissors icons, below the window.

FIGURE 24.1
The overall iMovie
workspace: The
Video Monitor,
shelf, and Timeline
Viewer.

The controls for the Monitor window are much like what you use on a DVD player and VCR, enabling you to quickly move through your video or jump to a specific location.

Shelf

The value of the shelf, visible to the right of the Monitor window in Figure 24.1, quickly becomes apparent when you connect your camcorder to the Mac for the first time and start capturing clips. It almost seems like alien technology at work as you watch the video clips from your tape start to appear in the shelf. The shelf is like a pantry for video—when you capture video, you load up the shelf with clips, and you can take a quick glance to see what you have to work with.

As you'll see in later chapters, the shelf gives you several additional tools to enhance your video productions, including transitions, titles, and effects, as well as a place to put audio if you've recorded it separately from your video.

Clip Viewer

The Clip Viewer (see Figure 24.2) represents one way of looking at video clips that you've added to your movie.

The alternative to the Clip Viewer is the Timeline Viewer, which is discussed in the following section. You switch between the two viewer options using the buttons below the monitor that show the icon of a film frame (for Clip Viewer) or clock face (for Timeline Viewer). The Timeline Viewer provides more editing options, so we'll spend most of our time working with the Timeline Viewer.

In the Clip Viewer, video clips are treated more like icons. You can easily click and drag an individual clip to position it differently and thus have a different order for your video production. We'll take a closer look at the clip viewer in Chapter 27, "Working with iMovie's Clip Viewer."

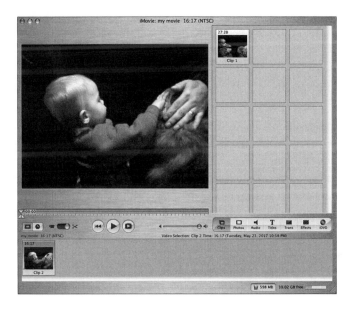

FIGURE 24.2
The Clip Viewer offers an alternative way to look at your clips.

If you're new to digital video, try imagining iMovie as your "word processor for video." You can rearrange, delete, and add material, but instead of working with paragraphs, you're working with video clips!

Did you Know?

Timeline Viewer

The Timeline Viewer, visible along the bottom of the iMovie interface in Figure 24.1, enables you to make adjustments to your video clips, such as adjusting the start and end times of each clip, as well as adjusting effects and other things that you might add to a clip.

The Timeline Viewer also enables you to see things (clips, transitions, sound effects) as they progress over time.

The Timeline Viewer makes it easy to make more specific adjustments to your project, such as in situations in which you might want to go to a specific location in a clip. It also enables you to work with multiple audio clips, so if you want to add different sounds that you've recorded, it's as easy as clicking and dragging.

Other Important Controls for the Timeline

At the very bottom of the iMovie window in Timeline view is a row of controls (refer to Figure 24.1).

The first control is a slider labeled Zoom that allows you to zoom in on the Timeline to see more detail. As you add more and more scenes to the Timeline, the proportion of the whole that each takes up shrinks—and so do the rectangles representing those clips. Use the Zoom slider to focus in one part of the Timeline by selecting a clip and dragging the Zoom controller to the right.

Next is the Speed slider, labeled with icons of a rabbit (or hare) and a turtle (or tortoise), which may call to mind Aesop's fable about the fast hare and the slow tortoise. (To refresh your memory, the slow-but-steady tortoise wins the race.) This slider controls the speed of the selected clip. If you want a clip (or other element in the Timeline) to be sped up or slowed down, drag the slider toward the appropriate side.

By the Way

> If a slider control button moves sluggishly when you try to drag it, you could instead click on the spot along the slider path where you want to set it. The button will jump precisely to that spot with ease.

Near the middle of the bottom row are controls for audio. Checking the box for Edit Volume produces a volume level in each of the elements in your Timeline. You can then adjust the volume of each clip or sound file so that there aren't unpleasant volume changes. The slider next to the check box controls the overall volume of the movie. There are some additional features of the Edit Volume check box, which we will discuss in Chapter 28, "Working with Still Photos and Sound in iMovie."

Trash and Free Space

The bottom controls row also includes a couple of helpful things to manage your iMovie project: the free space indicator and a miniature trash can so that you can easily get rid of video clips that you don't need any more.

iMovie Preferences

Before you begin any projects, let's take a brief look at the options in the iMovie Preferences panel, which can be opened from the iMovie application menu. The Preferences panel, shown in Figure 24.3, contains a relatively small number of options and is categorized into general, import-related, and advanced items.

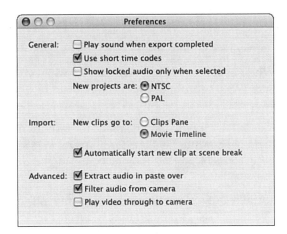

FIGURE 24.3
There are only a few iMovie preferences for you to configure.

General Preferences

Among the General preferences, most notable is the setting for New Projects are NTCS/PAL. This refers to the format for which the video in your project is prepared. In North America or Japan, televisions use a system called NTSC (National Television Standards Committee). When you design video on your computer for NTSC televisions, the screen is 720 pixels wide by 480 pixels high when it's displayed at full size.

What's a *pixel*, you wonder? Your Mac divides the screen up into a grid of individual pieces called pixels, which are essentially individual dots that make up a picture.

Did you Know?

If you live in Europe, you probably use the PAL system for working with video, which has a screen size of 768×576. The PAL system also uses a different frame rate. (See the following note for more information.)

Before starting your project, make sure that this preference is set to the correct format for your region.

By the Way

The *frame rate* of digital video is the number of images displayed in a second as they flash by, like frames in a traditional movie. In traditional movies, the individual images and frames are contained in large reels, and they go by at a rate of 24 frames per second. The frames per second measurement has been adopted by digital video, but the measurement depends on a variety of factors, including the country you live in and the way you want to deliver your digital video. For example, if you use the NTSC digital video system, the measurement is most often 29.97 frames per second (fps).

The other General preference options are

▶ Play Sound When Export Completed—Alerts you when your movie is finished exporting. (We'll talk about exporting iMovies in Chapter 29, "Exporting iMovies.")

▶ Use Short Time Codes—Shows only the digits for seconds and frames, such as 46:19, instead of showing the digits for hours as well, such as 00:46:19. Use of short time codes in projects may be confusing because the minutes digits will simply be left off.

▶ Show Locked Audio Only When Selected—Hides the indicators for locked audio unless you have selected a clip that is affected by locked audio. Checking this option removes some of the clutter from a complex movie project with added sound effects. (You'll learn about working with audio, including locking audio to clips, in Chapter 27.)

Import Preferences

The options for Import are simple. The first is a pair of radio buttons where you can choose whether clips imported from the camera are placed in the Clip pane or placed directly in the Timeline. If you are making an iMovie and want to be sure to keep all the scenes in order, choose to have the clips go directly into the Timeline; otherwise, storing them in the Clip pane while you decide what clips to add makes good sense.

You can also choose whether iMovie imports your video as clips, based on when you stopped and restarted filming. If you want to import your video as a continuous clip, be aware that iMovie limits a single clip to less than 2GB.

You'll learn how to import clips in the Chapter 25.

Advanced Preferences

Checking the box for Extract Audio in Paste Over means that if you paste one clip on top of another, the original audio track appears as a separate audio track instead of having the new audio track layer over it. (See Chapter 28 for more about working with audio in iMovie.)

Apple recommends that you keep the option to filter audio from the camera checked. If you hear clicks or popping in imported clips, double-check that filter audio is enabled.

Play Video Through to Camera allows you to watch recording on the camera and your Mac simultaneously while you import your clips.

Starting a New Project

Now that you've seen the iMovie interface and a few examples of what iMovie can do, let's see how to start a new project.

> When iMovie creates a project, it puts all your video material in one location on the hard drive, sort of like a suitcase, making it easy to store everything for your iMovie in one place. When you capture video, all the clips end up in the project; and even though there are separate files, everything stays together.

By the Way

Task: Create a New Project

Before you can begin working on making iMovies, you must know how to create a new project. iMovie makes this easy by bringing up a special screen (shown in Figure 24.4) if you don't already have a project started. (If you have already created a project, or even several projects, iMovie tries to open the one last opened on your computer.)

FIGURE 24.4
A startup screen appears if you haven't already started a project.

To create a new project:

1. Start iMovie. If you get the window shown in Figure 24.4, click the Create Project button.

If you don't get this window when you start iMovie, you can choose File, New Project from the menu bar to get the same thing.

2. When you create a new project, iMovie brings up the Create New Project sheet window to ask where you want to put the project on your hard drive (see Figure 24.5). Type in a name for your movie and click Save if you want iMovie to simply save the file directly to the hard drive.

FIGURE 24.5
The Create New Project sheet window.

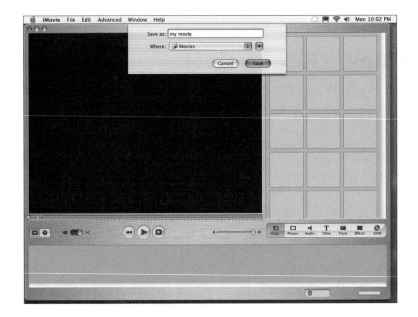

3. You might want to switch to a more convenient location than the one iMovie suggests (such as the desktop), by clicking the pop-up menu at the top of the Create New Project dialog sheet. This opens a view of your hard drive so that you can choose where to save the project.

In Chapter 25, you'll learn how to import video from your digital video camera, but before you move ahead take a few moments to look around the iMovie interface.

Summary

In this chapter, you were introduced to the basics of the iMovie interface. You took a closer look at the shelf (where video clips are stored), the Monitor (which lets you see the clips), and the Timeline Viewer (which gives you another way to interact with clips) as well as iMovie's menus and preference settings. You also learned a little bit about iMovie's capabilities and how to start a new project.

CHAPTER 25

Working with Video and Clips in iMovie

This chapter focuses on working with video, from importing video clips to moving them around within iMovie. You'll learn the way that a camcorder can be connected to your Mac and the process of capturing video through that connection. (Capturing video, simply put, is the process of importing digital video footage from a camcorder into a computer.) You'll also learn some basics of video editing and working with film clips.

Importing Video from a File

Later in the chapter, we'll get into the process of actually capturing video from your camcorder into your Mac using iMovie. But for now, let's import a file that has already been captured into iMovie. To do so, follow these steps:

1. Open iMovie and choose File, Import from the menu bar. The Import File sheet window appears from the top of the iMovie window.

2. Click the pop-up menu at the top of the sheet window and navigate to a movie file.

3. Select the movie file and click Open (see Figure 25.1). iMovie opens the clip, and when it is finished, you'll see it in both the Monitor and the shelf, as shown in Figure 25.2.

---

iMovie is designed primarily to work with video captured directly from a camcorder on a Mac, but it is possible to take video from a PC and use it in iMovie. One way to do this is simply to ask whoever is giving you the video from a PC to save it in DV format (NTSC, PAL, or SECAM, depending on what country you live in) to a portable FireWire hard drive, and to import it from there.

Did you Know?

FIGURE 25.1
The Import File
sheet window.

FIGURE 25.2
A clip selected in
the shelf, pre-
viewed in the
Monitor.

Connecting Camcorders

Today, virtually every video camera that you can purchase in a store includes a
FireWire connection, which you may remember from Chapter 19, "Adding
Peripheral Devices." FireWire is the magic behind being able to make your own
digital movie and DVD projects.

Understanding the FireWire Cable

When you want to connect your digital camcorder to your Mac, you must use a FireWire cable. A camcorder often comes with such a cable, but you can also purchase it separately.

The cable that you need to use has two different kinds of connectors: a smaller end that's known as a 4-pin connector and a larger one on the other side that's known as a 6-pin connector. The smaller, 4-pin connector is the kind most often found on camcorders, and the larger 6-pin connector is most often found on computers.

After you connect the FireWire cable to your computer, you can connect the other, smaller end into the camcorder. The location of the FireWire port on a camcorder varies, but it's usually behind some kind of protective cover. Figure 25.3 shows the smaller 4-pin end of a FireWire cable and the corresponding port on a digital camcorder.

FIGURE 25.3
Getting ready to plug the smaller end of the FireWire cable into a camcorder.

Task: Connecting Your Camcorder

This section takes you through the process of setting up iMovie and connecting a camcorder so that you can capture video.

1. Turn on the camera, and insert the smaller (4-pin) end into the FireWire connector on the camcorder. (Insert a tape that you've recorded video on into the camcorder if you haven't already.)

2. Insert the larger (6-pin) end into the FireWire connection on your Mac.

3. Open iMovie and choose File, New Project to create a new project.

4. Click the Camera/Edit Mode switch in iMovie to switch to the camera (DV) mode (see Figure 25.4).

By the Way

When you plug in most cameras on your Mac, iMovie automatically switches to Camera mode, but you can always use the switch mentioned previously if it doesn't happen.

FIGURE 25.4
Switching to Camera (DV) mode.

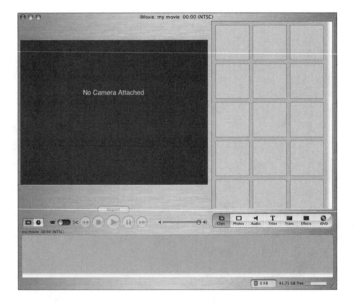

After you've connected your camera, iMovie displays a message confirming that your camera is connected, as shown in Figure 25.5.

FIGURE 25.5
iMovie confirms
when a camcorder
is turned on and
plugged in.

It's easy to record video to a tape and then forget to rewind it—so you might put the tape in your camcorder and press Play to preview it, but not see anything or see a blank blue screen! The material is still there, earlier on your videotape; you just have to rewind to get to it. The only ways you can actually erase video from a digital videotape are to record over it or subject the tape to strong magnetic fields. For the latter, consult "Task: Subjecting Your Tape to Strong Magnetic Fields." Just kidding.

By the Way

Working with Video

If you're new to working with digital video on your Mac, all you really need to keep in mind is that you're using your camera and your computer as if they were a TV and a VCR.

In essence, iMovie becomes your computer VCR but instead of recording a program from the television, iMovie records video from your camcorder. That's what capturing video is all about.

Understanding Cueing: Play, Stop, Fast Forward, Rewind

When working with video on your Mac, you use familiar controls to capture and access your video, such as play, stop, fast forward, and rewind.

When you want to capture video, you need to find a spot in your video where you want to start capturing, and that's where cueing comes into play. Depending on where you left off in the tape, when you use your camcorder to record your video, you might need to play, rewind, and so on to position and review your footage.

This positioning can be done with the camera itself, by looking at its miniature screen. But one of the most enjoyable things about working with digital video through FireWire is that you can control your camera using buttons in the iMovie screen. So, when you connect your camera, you don't necessarily have to use the buttons on the camera itself. When connected through FireWire, iMovie can actually control the camera, so you can use the Play/Fast Forward/Rewind buttons (see Figure 25.6) right in iMovie to go through your tape.

FIGURE 25.6
The play controls in iMovie.

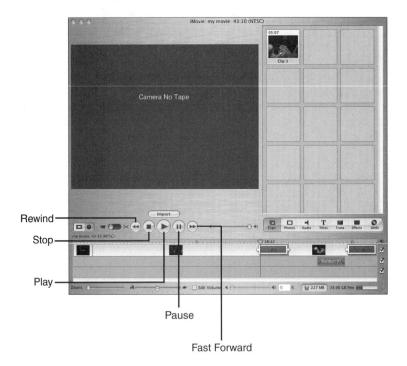

Rewind

Stop

Play

Pause

Fast Forward

Task: Finding a Spot on Your Videotape Using iMovie

Assuming that you performed the task "Connecting Your Camcorder" earlier in the chapter, follow these steps:

1. Click the Rewind button to rewind the tape (see Figure 25.7).

FIGURE 25.7
The Rewind button.

2. Click the Play button (see Figure 25.8) to begin playing your video.

FIGURE 25.8
The Play button.

Watch Out!

You might need to adjust the sound on your computer.

3. While the video is playing, try clicking the Fast Forward button (see Figure 25.9) to fast forward through the video while you're watching it. Click again to stop the tape.

FIGURE 25.9
The Fast Forward button.

4. If your video is still playing, click the Stop button (see Figure 25.10), and then click either the Fast Forward or Rewind button. This method of moving through a tape is faster, but you can't see the video moving by.

FIGURE 25.10
The Stop button.

5. Using the play controls, find a spot in your videotape where you want to start capturing.

There's no official term for fast-forwarding or rewinding from a complete stop. But if you're new to video, you could think of it as *step starting*, where the tape isn't moving and you have to take a step in a particular direction (backward or forward) to get things going. Step starting is the fastest way to get to a certain point on your tape. In contrast, watching footage going by when you're fast-forwarding or rewinding could be thought of as *play previewing*. In other words, you press the Play button and then press Fast Forward or Rewind. The disadvantage is that things go slower, but you can see exactly what's going on.

It can sometimes be helpful to start just a little before where you want to start capturing video so that you can make a fine adjustment to the starting point of your video clip in iMovie. For example, if you have footage of a short clip and you want to capture the entire thing, you can start a little bit before the action in your short scene begins. Perhaps the footage includes someone jumping off a diving board— you could position the tape a second or two before the jump so that when you capture the video, you can fine-tune exactly when the clip starts so that you don't miss anything.

Capturing Video

When you capture video, one nice thing that iMovie can do is separate your clips for you. After you shoot video with your camcorder, wherever you pressed Stop and then started shooting a new clip, iMovie separates the clips automatically.

Task: Capturing Video from Your Camcorder

After you've completed the two previous tasks (connecting your camcorder and finding a spot in your tape to start recording), follow these steps:

1. Open iMovie and start a new project.

2. Switch the Camera/Edit Mode switch to the Camera position (DV) (see Figure 25.11).

FIGURE 25.11
Switching to Camera mode to connect with the camera.

3. Click the Import button to start importing footage (refer to Figure 25.5).

4. When you've captured your video, click the Stop button.

5. Now click the Camera/Edit Mode switch (see Figure 25.12) and drag it to the right to switch back to Movie mode so that you can begin to work with your clips.

FIGURE 25.12
The Camera/Edit mode button back in Edit Mode position.

> When capturing video, keep in mind that you must keep an eye on the amount of space available on your hard drive. A common technique is to capture more footage than you think you'll use and then as you're editing your iMovies, you can delete clips you don't need, which frees up space. Another thing to consider if you're planning to export your iMovies to use in an iDVD project (see Chapter 29, "Exporting iMovies") is that when you export the file, you need just as much space as your project is taking up—in other words, when you export for iDVD, you need more space.
>
> So, when you get hooked on iMovie (not *if*, but *when*—it's inevitable), you'll probably need to start thinking about ways of backing up your projects or expanding the amount of hard drive space you have available. One option is to obtain an external FireWire hard drive. Another option is to store projects on individual DVD discs as data. In other words, instead of burning an iDVD project, you burn all your files to a blank DVD disc so that you can free up hard drive space.

By the Way

Moving Around in a Clip

One of the most enjoyable parts about playing with footage in iMovie is the way that you can easily move around in a clip in the same way that you might use the remote control on your VCR or DVD player to find a spot in a movie. In iMovie, as you're editing your creation, you'll often want to move through various parts of individual clips or the overall movie as it takes shape. Instead of playing through the entire movie, you can quickly get to the spot that you want, with a control called the *playhead*, which is located at the bottom of the Monitor window (see Figure 25.13).

FIGURE 25.13
A close-up view of the playhead along with the time stamp for that spot in your video clip.

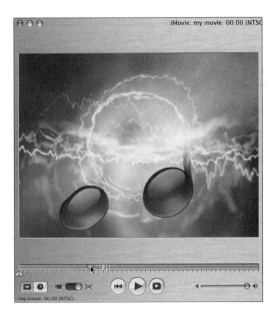

Task: Go to a Specific Spot in a Clip

To prepare for this task, if you don't already have the clip from the previous task open, open it so that you can have something to work with.

To go to a specific spot in a clip:

1. Click on the playhead, and hold down the mouse button.

2. Drag the playhead horizontally to the left or right to find the spot that you want. Notice how the number of minutes and seconds are displayed next to the playhead as you drag it, indicating how far into the clip you are. Try dragging the playhead to a precise time, such as 5:00 (5 seconds).

Task: Adjusting a Clip in the Shelf

After you've captured video, the first thing that you must do is to acquaint yourself with the clips you've captured to get an idea of what you have to work with. Playing with clips in the Shelf is a good way to accomplish this.

1. Select a clip in the Shelf by clicking it; the selected clip turns blue.

2. Move the mouse over the text in the clip and click. The area behind the text turns white, and you can type a new name in for the clip (see Figure 25.14).

Another way to see the clip name is to double-click a clip in the Shelf, which brings up the Clip Info dialog box.

FIGURE 25.14
Renaming a clip:
1) select a clip;
2) click on its
name; 3) replace
the sample text
with new text.

Making Basic Edits

To get a better taste of how the iMovie interface gives you the power of video editing, we'll take a look at how to make a basic edit using a combination of the shelf, the Monitor, and the Timeline Viewer.

Preparing a Clip

This section goes through the process of making an adjustment to a clip, but first we need to drag the clip into the Timeline Viewer. To prepare the clip, click on it in the shelf and drag it down and to the uppermost row of Timeline Viewer, which is where you put video clips. When your mouse cursor—which is normally an arrow—changes to an arrow with a "+" next to it, release your mouse button (see Figure 25.15).

After you drag the clip, the Video Monitor looks the same, but the clip now appears on the Timeline Viewer rather than the Shelf, as illustrated in Figure 25.16.

Task: Deleting Extra Footage

Now that we have a clip ready to go, we can make an adjustment to it. In our scenario, the adjustment we want to make is to delete some extra footage at the end of the clip.

To delete extra footage:

1. Drag the playhead in the Monitor to somewhere close to the end of the clip—to the point just before the clip switches to another scene.

FIGURE 25.15
Before: Dragging a
clip into the
Timeline Viewer.

FIGURE 25.16
After: The clip as it
appears in the
Timeline Viewer.

2. Choose Edit, Split Video Clip at Playhead to mark the spot so that iMovie
   knows where one clip ends and the next begins. In essence, you've just created two separate clips from one original clip (see Figure 25.17).

FIGURE 25.17
The newly split clip.

3. In the Timeline Viewer, click the unwanted clip and choose Edit, Clear from the menu. The extra footage is removed, and the desired footage remains, as in Figure 25.18.

You don't have to move clips to the Timeline to split them. You can choose a clip in the Shelf and preview it in the Monitor window; then place the playhead and split the clip as described in step 3.

FIGURE 25.18
The remaining clip now expands to fill the entire width of the Timeline.

Task: Deleting a Clip from the Shelf

One of the more common tasks in basic video editing is deleting unwanted video footage. Doing so is easy in iMovie:

1. Click on a clip in the Shelf to select it.

2. Either drag the clip into the Trash until the Trash well darkens or select Edit, Clear from the menu.

   You'll probably want to get into the habit of emptying the Trash after you've deleted a clip, or at regular intervals, so that you can keep the maximum amount of hard drive space available to work on your movie.

3. Choose File, Empty Trash to empty the Trash.

4. Click OK in the Confirm dialog box that comes up. Then see how much space you have freed up by checking the free space indicator at bottom-right of the iMovie window.

Task: Restoring Clip Media

No video editor is perfect, and sooner or later you'll decide that you want to start over again when adjusting clips. One way to back up is to go through a repeated series of undo steps by pressing Ctrl-Z on your keyboard or choosing Edit, Undo.

Another way is to use the Restore Clip option, which enables you to start over again by bringing clips back to their original state.

> If you edit clips, you can only restore clips to the condition they were in up until the last time you emptied the trash, so be careful to clean up only after you're happy with your edits.

For example, you might have recorded a friend talking at great length about an important topic, and toward the end of her monologue, she realizes that another friend has been standing behind her doing a strikingly realistic impression. So, you capture the video clip and make a few adjustments, but accidentally trim the clip too close to the humorous scene at the end. You want to start over again, but aren't sure how. iMovie to the rescue!

1. Click one of the clips in the Timeline that you made by splitting the original clip.

2. Choose Advanced, Restore Clip as shown in Figure 25.19.

3. Click OK in the dialog box that appears to restore the original clip (see Figure 25.20).

FIGURE 25.19
A clip in the
Timeline view.

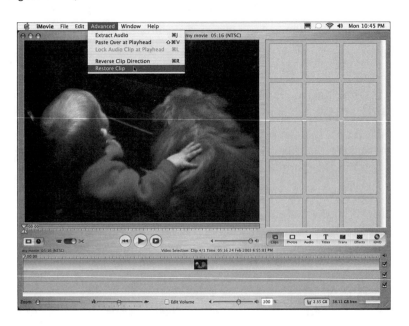

FIGURE 25.20
iMovie asks
whether you want
to restore the
modified clip to its
original state.

Restoring a clip doesn't merge pieces of the original clip back together. If you split a clip and then restore one of the pieces, the restored clip will contain some of the same footage as the unrestored clip.

By the Way

Task: Checking the Size of an iMovie Project

Just about the time you start getting hooked on iMovie, you might realize that your Mac doesn't have an endless amount of storage space on the hard drive, and you need to think a bit more about how much space your projects are taking up.

Chances are that you'll have enough space on your hard drive to work on a few projects at the same time, unless you're working on full-length movies from day one. When you're finished and have exported your iMovies to tape or iDVD, you can burn the raw files in your iDVD project folder to CD or DVD or move them to an external hard drive.

Whichever way you go, it can be helpful to know how much space your project is taking up. It's good to keep an eye on things so that you can decide when you have to delete your collection of accumulated media files.

1. Double-click the icon on your hard drive to launch a Finder window.

2. Locate the folder with your iMovies—when you created a new iMovie project, you named it something.

3. Select the folder and choose Get Info from the Action pop-up menu. An Info window appears, as shown in Figure 25.21.

In Mac OS X this folder is probably in the Movies folder within your home folder.

Did you Know?

FIGURE 25.21
Showing informa-
tion about the size
of your movie
project.

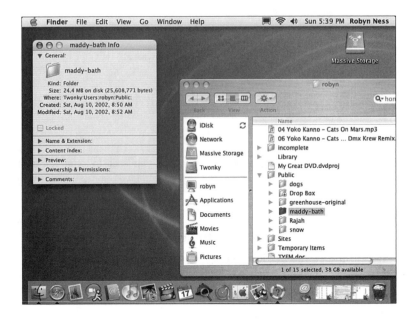

The Get Info window gives you a variety of information, including the size of your folder.

Summary

In this chapter, you learned how to get video into your Mac through the process of capturing it using the FireWire interface. You also learned about some introductory, basic video editing tasks, such as adding clips to the Timeline, making adjustments, and deciding to do it all over again to make it perfect.

CHAPTER 26

Adding Titles, Transitions, and Effects in iMovie

In this chapter, we'll look at some enhancements you can make to your movies and clips. First, we'll look at titles, which allow you to add text portions to your movies (or even write a text-only movie). Then, we consider transitions, which enable you to enhance your iMovies with between-clip features, such as fade in, fade out, cross dissolve, and others. Finally, we'll talk about visual effects that can be applied to the clips themselves to change color or add special effects, such as lighting effects, sparkles, or fog.

Titles

When you're ready to try adding a title to your iMovie, you'll be working in a new area of iMovie: the Titles palette. Until now, you probably spent most of your time simply capturing video and working with clips in the Shelf, the Monitor, and the Timeline. But now you'll start switching back and forth between various windows in the Shelf. You get to the Titles palette, if you're looking at clips in the Shelf, by clicking the Titles button.

When the Titles palette comes up, you'll see a number of options, including ways to adjust the size and color of the letters in your title, as well as a list from which you can select different titles (see Figure 26.1).

But if you're new to digital video, don't worry about all the options. You can add a title to your iMovie simply by choosing one (such as Bounce In To Center) from the list, clicking on it, and dragging it into the Timeline.

Sooner or later, you'll want to take advantage of all the things you can do to spruce up and modify titles to give your productions a customized touch. To get your feet wet, let's take a look at a couple of the basic titles included with iMovie. Later, we'll dive into adjusting and customizing titles.

FIGURE 26.1
The Titles palette.

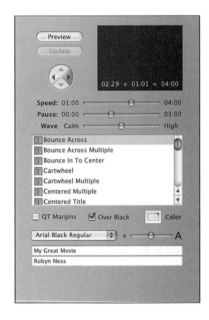

Sample Title—Bounce In To Center

Near the top of iMovie's title list is Bounce In To Center, and it's a great starting place to play around with titles. In Figure 26.2, you can get a sense of how the text moves in from the top and bottom of the screen.

FIGURE 26.2
A sample title.

Sample Title—Centered Multiple

At first glance, Centered Multiple might sound like an abstract algebraic principle, but after you start playing with it, its value becomes apparent.

Centered Multiple is an example of a title to which you can add multiple lines of text. In essence, iMovie makes it easy to create multiple "screens" by enabling you to add additional lines of text to some titles.

On the left in Figure 26.3, you see the first screen (imagine the text fading in, pausing, and then fading out), and on the right, you see the next screen, where the same thing happens again.

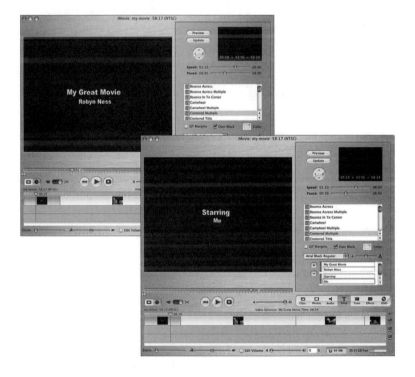

FIGURE 26.3
A fade from left to right.

If you're having difficulty picturing what's going on, don't be concerned. When you start playing in the program, it'll become clear, and you'll see the nice effect that this kind of title has.

iMovie makes it easy to enter text in titles like this one. As with the previous title we examined, the text you enter in the bottom of the Titles palette appears in the title (see Figure 26.4).

FIGURE 26.4
The text input area
in the Titles
palette.

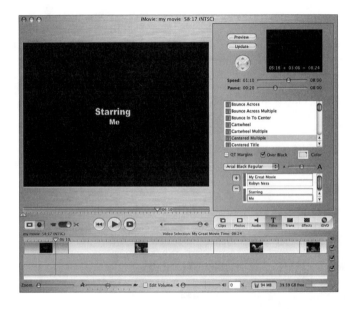

With a multiple line title, you can click and drag the blue scrollbar down (the blue scrollbar to the right of the text) to reveal more lines of text.

If you haven't tried them (although we aren't officially in the middle of a task), the + and - buttons to the right of the title text enable you to add and remove lines of text, which generates more screens. This particular title is a nice way to have introductory screens fade in and out before a movie starts.

Now that you've gotten a taste of two basic titles, take a moment to consider all the titles you have available (see Table 26.1).

TABLE 26.1   Titles in iMovie

Title Type	Description
Bounce Across	Two lines of text appear from either the left or right and move like a wiggling worm toward the center of the screen.
Bounce Across Multiple	Like Bounce Across, but with multiple screens of text.
Bounce In To Center	Two lines of text appear and move toward the center of thescreen.
Cartwheel	Two lines of text, each letter rotating, move diagonally toward the center of the screen.

TABLE 26.1   Continued

Title Type	Description
Cartwheel Multiple	Like Cartwheel, but with multiple screens of text.
Centered Multiple	Multiple titles fade in and out in sequence, one after another. It's a nice movie-style effect.
Centered Title	A single title fades in and out.
Converge	Two lines of text with broadly spaced letters gradually move to the left to form words.
Converge Multiple	Like Converge, but with multiple screens of text.
Converge to Center	Two lines of text with broadly spaced letters gradually move to the center to form words.
Converge to Center Multiple	Like Converge to Center, but with multiple screens of text.
Cross Through Center	Two lines of text start out with letters and lines reversed and rotate until correctly positioned.
Cross Through Center Multiple	Like Cross Through Center but with multiple screens of text.
Drifting	Multiple lines fade in from different directions.
Flying Letters	Letters of title fade into the screen to form words of title.
Flying Words	Entire lines of title fly in at one time. Nice effect.
Gravity	Two lines of text fall into place from one edge of the screen.
Gravity Multiple	Like Gravity, but with multiple screens of text.
Music Video	Enables you to put a music video–style paragraph of text that can appear in the corner of the screen. Useful.
Rolling Centered Credits	Enter multiple lines of text to get the effect you see at the end of movies. Very nice.
Rolling Credits	Similar to centered credits; different formatting.
Scroll with Pause	Titles roll on to screen, pause, roll off; helps with being able to read individual credits.
Scrolling Block	Will scroll an entire paragraph of text by; something like the original Star Wars credits.
Spread from Center	Two lines of text appear from a pile of letters at the center of the screen.
Spread from Center Multiple	Like Spread from Center, but with multiple screens of text.

TABLE 26.1   Continued

Title Type	Description
Stripe Subtitle	A nice title to put in the corner of a screen to introduce a new section of a video.
Subtitle	Gives you the ability to add text to the screen to simulate the subtitle effect of a DVD.
Subtitle Multiple	Multiple subtitles.
Twirl	Two lines of text appear at the center of the screen with each letter rotating.
Typewriter	Creates the effect of words being typed on the screen.
Unscramble	A jumble of letters separates into two lines of text.
Unscramble Multiple	Like Unscramble, but with multiple screens of text.
Zoom	Creates a zoom effect, moving close in on video.
Zoom Multiple	Multiple zooms.

Using Titles over Black

One simple way to have titles appear is against a black background so that your attention is focused on the title itself. To accomplish this, you simply click on the Over Black option in the Titles palette (refer to Figure 26.4).

Overlay (over Video) Titles

Another method you might want to try is to uncheck the Over Black option so that your title appears over a video clip, as shown in Figure 26.5. The only requirement is that you have a video clip in the project!

Task: Selecting a Title

To begin working with titles, you need to know how to find a particular title listed previously in Table 26.1.

1. Click on the Titles button in the main iMovie window to display the Titles palette.

2. Click the blue scrollbar for the list of titles, and drag it down so that the title you're looking for is revealed.

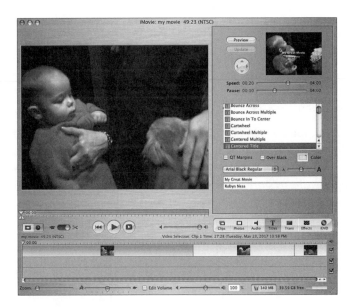

FIGURE 26.5
Clicking on a title
with Over Black
unchecked to see a
mini-preview with
the title displayed
over a video clip.

3. When you find the title you want to try, click to select it, as I've done with the Typewriter title near the end of the list (see Figure 26.6).

FIGURE 26.6
The selected title
will be previewed in
the mini-preview
window in the Titles
palette.

Adding Titles

The ultimate goal of making titles is to introduce or otherwise enhance your movie. You could have a title at the beginning, a rolling credit at the end, and any number of titles in between to introduce different scenes (reminiscent of silent movies?) or sections (such as a training video).

Earlier in this chapter, we talked about the two different ways that titles can work: either displayed against a black screen (Over Black), or as an overlay displaying directly over video. Either approach can be fun and work in different situations, but you might want to start out with a standard Over Black title (by clicking the Over Black check box).

Task: Adding a Title to a Movie

Adding a title to a movie is as easy as adding a clip to a movie; it's a similar, almost identical process. In fact...it is identical. As Austin Powers might say, drag and drop, baby!

1. Open an iMovie project and drag a clip into the Timeline. If the Clip Viewer tab is visible, just click the Clock icon in the lower-left corner of the screen to display the Timeline tab.

2. Click on a title of choice in the Titles palette, and drag it down into the Timeline until your video clip moves aside to make room for the title (see Figure 26.7). Drop the title into the open space.

3. Notice in Figure 26.8 how the small red bar travels from left to right underneath your title to indicate that the title is being processed.

4. Now that your title is in the Timeline, try clicking on the playhead and dragging it through your title to get a quick glance at how the title animates (see Figure 26.9).

Did you Know?

To experiment with a title that you have created, try changing a setting in the Titles palette and then clicking the Update button in the Titles palette.

When you've dragged a title into the Timeline, you can click in the Timeline to select it (it'll change to blue) and make adjustments to it. Then you need to click Update for iMovie to process it and give you a preview.

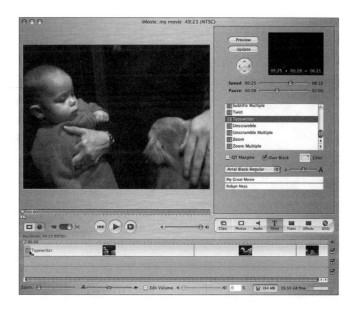

FIGURE 26.7
Dragging a title from the Titles palette down to the Timeline in front of the video clip.

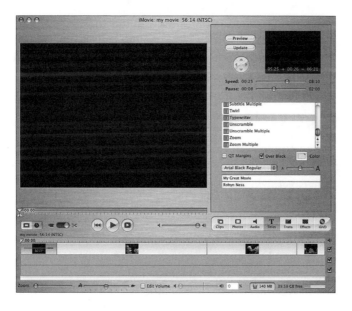

FIGURE 26.8
A little red bar going to the right underneath the title in the Timeline indicates that your Mac is processing your title.

> You can actually layer different titles in iMovie. For instance, you can add one long-duration title that is set over black and have other titles that aren't set over black cross over top of it.

By the Way

FIGURE 26.9
Dragging the play-
head to check out
the title, just as
you would check
out a video clip. In
essence, iMovie
uses the settings
in the Titles palette
to generate video
clips for you.

iMovie can quickly build a miniature preview in the Titles palette when you make changes. But digital video takes a lot of processing power. So, for it to catch up with changes when you place it in the Timeline, it has to be processed before you can get the final preview of how it'll look on a television.

Adjusting Titles

As soon as you start trying out the different titles, you'll want to know how you can adjust them, and Apple has done an excellent job again of making things easy and intuitive, yet flexible. Essentially, you can do no tweaking at all or as much as you want.

Task: Adjusting a Title

In this task, we look at how to make adjustments to a title. iMovie makes it easy to try things out with titles and then go back and expand or change them, all without having to type in the text over again.

1. Follow the steps in the previous task to select a title. In this example, we're using Drifting.

2. Try clicking the Text Size slider, marked with a small and a large capital A, and dragging it to the left or right to change the size of your title text.

3. To choose a different color for the text, click once on the Color button. A pop-up menu of colors appears (see Figure 26.10).

4. Click on a color that you want to use for your text, and then click somewhere outside the pop-up menu to deselect it.

FIGURE 26.10
Use the color picker to choose a color for your text.

5. Try clicking and dragging the blue Speed slider to the left or to the right to see how it affects the behavior of the title text.

6. To see the miniature preview of a title again, just click on the title, and it appears again in the preview area.

Task: Typing In a New Title

It's simple to change the text for a title; just click and type away.

1. Locate the text input field for the title you're using.

2. Move the mouse arrow and click once on the line you want to change.

   After you single-click it (as opposed to a double-click), a blue outline appears around the line of text to indicate that it's selected. You'll also see a flashing text insertion cursor, just as you have in a word processing program.

3. With the text selected, you can just type in new text to replace the old.

4. Repeat steps 2 and 3 to change an additional line of text.

5. Click the Apply button when you are finished.

Transitions

Transitions could be thought of as the bread and butter of video editing. Or, perhaps, as the peanut butter that makes scenes stick together.

When you deal with clips, if you choose wisely, one clip can in many cases cut to another without anything between the clips. To get a better understanding of the concept of a *cut*, try watching a few minutes of television or a movie and looking for the spots where the camera switches from one view to another—this usually happens most rapidly in music videos. Some people prefer cutting from one scene to another without any blending.

But there are times when you want to find a way for one clip to lead smoothly to another, and a transition is a perfect way to accomplish this. The following is a list of iMovie's transitions:

- ▶ Circle Closing—The first clip appears in a gradually shrinking circle, behind which the next clip is revealed.

- ▶ Circle Opening—The first clip disappears behind a gradually increasing circle containing the next clip.

- ▶ Cross Dissolve—Blends one video clip into another.

- ▶ Fade In—Brings the desired video clip slowly into view from nothing.

- ▶ Fade Out—Fades the video clip slowly out of view to nothing.

- ▶ Overlap—One clip slides over the other until it completely replaces it onscreen.

- ▶ Push—One clip "pushes" another off the screen in the direction chosen, (left/right/up/down).

- ▶ Radial—One clip "sweeps" another away in a motion like the second hand on a clock.

- ▶ Scale Down—Reduces the size of the first clip, while revealing the next clip.

- ▶ Warp Out—The first clip is split at the center by the next clip in a gradually increasing circle.

▶ Wash In—Brings the desired video clip slowly into view from bright white.

▶ Wash Out—Lightens the video clip slowly out of view to bright white.

Figure 26.11 shows the Transitions palette in iMovie, which can be easily accessed simply by clicking the Trans button. The Transitions palette enables you to choose a transition to use in your iMovie, as well as make some simple adjustments to the way the transition appears.

FIGURE 26.11
The Transitions palette.

Sample Transition—Cross Dissolve

To get a better understanding of transitions, let's take a look at the Cross Dissolve transition. Simply put, a cross dissolve is a standard tool used all the time in television and films to blend one scene into another. You probably see hundreds of cross dissolves every week without even realizing it.

We'll start with a movie containing two clips. If we watched the movie as is, when one video clip ends, it would simply cut from one video clip to another. But a cross dissolve could help the scenes blend.

iMovie gives you the ability to drag and drop a transition between the two clips, and Figure 26.12 shows the transition. The transition appears between the clips.

Essentially, over the course of a cross dissolve transition you see less of the first clip and more of the second. Figure 26.13 represents the blending of two video clips.

FIGURE 26.12
Two clips "sandwich" the Cross Dissolve transition.

FIGURE 26.13
Cross Dissolve—At the beginning, you see the first clip. Toward the middle, you still see the original clip, but you also see a fair amount of the second clip, "merged in" with the original clip. At this stage, both clips are semitransparent. At the end, you see the second clip.

Working with Transitions

Transitions are easy to work with. Just as with other enhancements that you can add to an iMovie, a transition takes a few moments to process, and if you add many transitions to your iMovie, you might have to wait a few minutes. But when the processing is done, you have a nice way to spice up your iMovie. It's worth experimenting to find and develop your own style.

In general, there are three ways of working with transitions: adding, adjusting, and removing.

Task: Adding a Fade In

Adding a transition is as simple as clicking to select it, dragging it into the Timeline, waiting for a moment while it processes, and then watching it to see how you like it.

Keep in mind that to try a transition, you must have at least one video clip in the Timeline. Some transitions are better suited to be before or after a clip (rather than in between), such as the fade in transition, which is a good way to start off your iMovie.

1. Open an iMovie project and drag a video clip from the Shelf into the Timeline.

2. Click the Trans button in the main iMovie window to access the Transitions palette.

3. Click the Fade In transition. After a transition is selected, a mini-preview of it plays in the window at the upper right.

4. If you are satisfied with the selected transition, drag it to a point in the Timeline window to the left of the current clip's centered icon. When you are in the right region, the current clip moves aside to make room for the transition, indicating that you can let go of the mouse button to drop the transition in place.

Which side of a clip you drag a transition to depends on the transition being added. Fade In must come before a clip, so you drag it to the left side of the affected clip. Fade Out must follow the clip, so you would drag it to the right side. If you try to place a transition on the wrong side of a clip, an error message tells you whether the transition you have chosen must be placed before or after a clip.

By the Way

Transitions that require two clips to work—such as Cross Dissolve, Overlap, and Push—give you an error if they aren't sandwiched between two clips. (Somewhat confusingly, this error message is the same one that appears when you place a transition on the wrong side of a single clip—the one that tells you to place the transition on the opposite side of where you've placed it. If you follow that advice with only one clip in the Timeline, another error tells you to place the transition on the opposite side.)

5. The red processing indicator shows you how long it will be before your transition is processed and you can see the preview of your movie. You can click on the Zoom slider at the bottom of your iMovie window to switch to a larger view of the transition so that you can see the thin red indicator line travel to the right underneath the transition until it's finished (see Figure 26.14).

FIGURE 26.14
After a transition is dragged into place, your Mac must think about it for a few moments to make sense of it and deliver the video you're asking for.

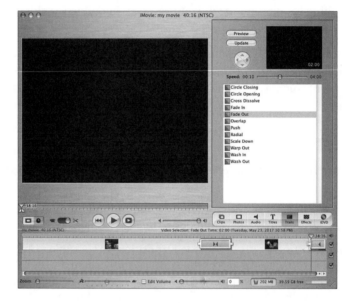

6. When the processing is finished, try dragging the playhead through the transition to see how your iMovie now starts black, and the video clip slowly fades in (see Figure 26.15).

A fade out is like a fade in but is used mostly at the end of an iMovie or at the end of a clip. You add it in a similar way, except that you place it at the end of the clip you want to fade away to black.

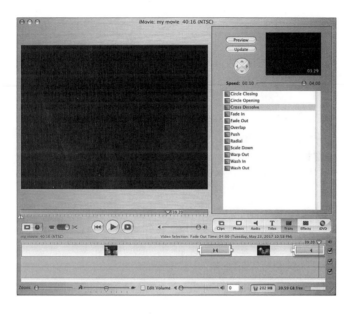

FIGURE 26.15
After the processing is finished, you can drag the playhead back and forth to get a quick preview of the transition.

Task: Changing and Replacing a Transition

At some point, you might want to change a transition that's already been added, and doing so is easy:

1. Open your iMovie project in which you have a clip (and a transition) that you want to replace. In Figure 26.16, you see our trusty sample project. In this scenario, we've decided that we want the fade out to be longer; that is, we want the fade to start earlier in the clip.

2. Click on the transition to select it; a translucent box appears around it.

3. Click on the blue Speed slider in the Transition window to adjust the Speed setting and change it to 4 seconds (4:00).

> The higher the Speed setting, the more seconds of space the transition will take up. So, if you want a longer transition, you want a higher Speed setting—toward 04:00. For a shorter transition, you want a lower setting—toward 00:10.

4. Click the Update button in the Transition window. When the processing is finished, drag the playhead back and forth on the Timeline to see the effect of the adjusted transition, or position the playhead to the left of the transition and click the Play button below the Monitor window.

FIGURE 26.16
Selecting the
transition.

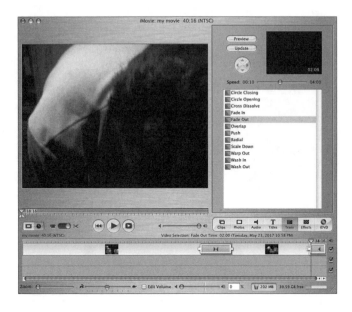

Compare the relative lengths of the transition and video clip in Figures 26.16 and 26.17. Notice how the transition in Figure 26.17, which has been adjusted to 4:00, is longer and therefore takes up more space in the Timeline than the original transition shown in Figure 26.16. The transition starts earlier in the video clip.

FIGURE 26.17
Viewing the results
of the adjusted
transition, which
has to process
first.

Replacing a transition works the same way, except that you can choose a different transition than the one originally in place. The old one is removed to make room for your new choice.

Task: Removing a Transition

Removing a transition is simple:

1. Open your iMovie project in which you have a clip (and a transition) that you want to remove.

2. Click on the transition to select it; a translucent box appears around it.

3. Choose Edit, Clear, and the transition is removed.

Effects

Effects represent another way that you can enhance your iMovies by adding something to them. You take plain video and make it stand out or spice it up to create your own movie-making style.

For example, if you want to give a historic feel to a portion of your iMovie, you could use an effect to make the movie either black-and-white or a sepia tone to give it the feel of an early moving picture.

Sometimes the video you use might give you ideas. For example, there might be a scene in a movie that's supposed to represent a person's dreams, and you could use the Fog effect to give that scene a surreal feeling. Maybe you could even combine it with another effect to change the colors around, and when the person in your iMovie wakes up, everything returns to normal, and you don't see the effects anymore.

In essence, to add an effect, you simply choose a clip in the Timeline and then choose and apply an effect—you can make adjustments anytime you want. If you want to add an effect to only a portion of your iMovie, use the Split Video Clip at Playhead command (for a refresher, see the section "Deleting Extra Footage" in Chapter 25, "Working with Video and Clips in iMovie") to separate a portion of your video and then apply the effect to it.

Effects are similar to transitions and titles in that the magic happens in the relevant palette in iMovie (see Figure 26.18); the Effects palette gives you a convenient place to try out different things.

FIGURE 26.18
The Effects palette
in iMovie.

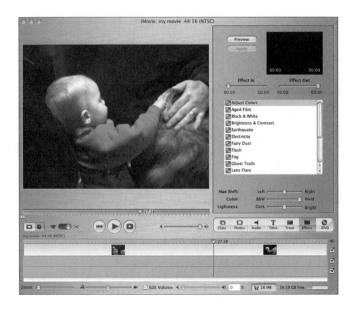

If you like to keep things as simple as possible, you can simply choose an effect; but iMovie also enables you to completely customize each effect if you choose to. You might find that you start by simply adding effects with their default settings and then end up coming back to the Effects palette to try different options when you get ideas for how some adjustment could work better for a particular clip. Table 26.2 lists the effects available in iMovie.

TABLE 26.2   List of Effects in iMovie

Effect Name	Description
Adjust Colors	Enables you to adjust various aspects of color, as if you were shining different colored light on your video
Aged Film	Adds dust and scratches to a clip, as if it were from an old news reel
Black and White	Enables you to take a step backward in time before color television or movies
Brightness & Contrast	Helpful for adjusting video when you want to make it look better, such as video that was shot in low light situations
Earthquake	Makes the image shake and blur is if the video were shot during an earthquake

TABLE 26.2   Continued

Effect Name	Description
Electricity	Adds a blue zap of electricity, which you can rotate for better placement
Fairy Dust	Adds a trail of sparkles to the clip
Flash	Adds an instant of bright white to the clip
Fog	Adds an overlay of moving fog to the clip
Ghost Trails	Faint impressions of the clip echo the motion in the real clip
Lens Flare	Gives the feel of an old photograph
Letterbox	Display the clip in letter-box format, with black space in the open area at the top and bottom of the screen
Mirror	Mirrors half of the clip on the other side of the screen
N-Square	Splits the screen in N equal squares containing the selected clip
Rain	Adds an overlay of moving rain to the clip
Sepia Tone	Gives the feel of an old photograph
Sharpen	Can enhance video that's slightly out of focus
Soft Focus	Adds a soft feel to video

Sample Effect—Brightness/Contrast

When you use an effect in iMovie, you choose a clip, such as the one in Figure 26.19, and decide you want to do something to it. In this case, we have a video clip in which the picture came out a bit dark.

But with a bit of tweaking, using the Brightness/Contrast controls, we can improve the clip so that you can see the subject a bit better (see Figure 26.20).

Because effects are simple to add, it can be easy to overdo effects, making things so "affected" that they look worse than when you began. So, if you want to preserve the quality of the video, you have to keep things somewhat balanced by not going overboard and using the most extreme settings in each effect.

FIGURE 26.19
A dark clip before
the Brightness/
Contrast effect is
applied.

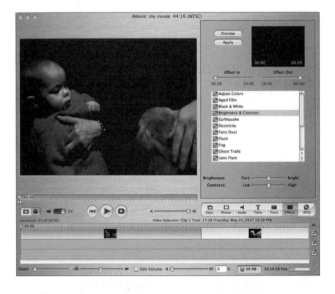

FIGURE 26.20
The clip after the
Brightness/Contrast
effect is applied.

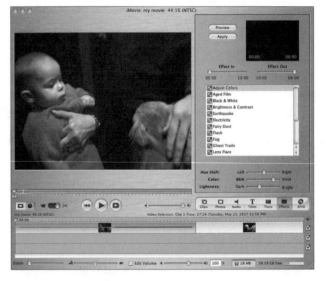

Working with Effects

When you try out effects, you can experiment without waiting for iMovie to process, or render, an effect, which can take several minutes. Then when you've made a decision, you can apply the effect and allow iMovie to render it, and you can continue to add other effects to that clip if you want.

In general, the options when working with effects are Preview, Apply, and Restore Clip.

Previewing

The Preview button enables you to see an effect on the main Monitor area in iMovie. It becomes active when you select an effect in the Effects palette.

When you first click on an effect in the Effects palette in iMovie, a small preview window appears that contains a miniature version of your iMovie, and it's helpful to get a general sense of what the effect does. But ultimately it's nicer to see how the effect looks at normal size, in the main iMovie Monitor area, as shown in Figure 26.20.

> In some versions of iMovie, the Preview function does not work. To see an approximation of the chosen effect with the changes you've made to settings, watch the mini-preview space at the upper right closely as you click on the control settings.

By the Way

Applying

Applying an effect is simply the process of going beyond the preview stage and actually having iMovie change your video clip by employing the effect on the clip you have currently selected. At this point, iMovie processes (or *renders*) the effect, which may take several minutes. The status of the processing appears as a red bar at the top of the affected clip in the Timeline (see Figure 26.21).

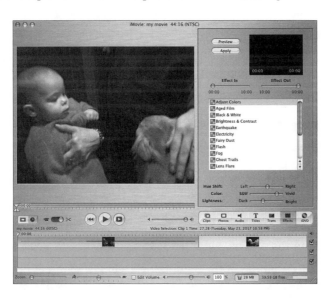

FIGURE 26.21
If you're happy with the preview, you can click Apply.

Restoring Clips

After you apply an effect, if you want to go back to how the clip originally was, choose Advanced, Restore Clip from the menu (see Figure 26.22).

FIGURE 26.22
An effect has been applied, and now the same clip can be restored to its original state.

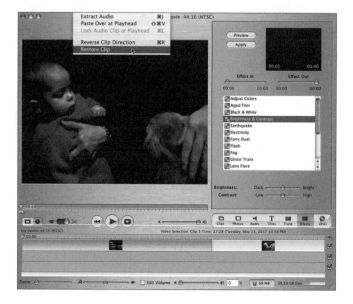

Undo/Redo

The Undo/Redo option in iMovie is a handy thing to keep in mind when working with effects. The top portion of the Edit menu changes to display the standard editing functions currently available.

Task: Enhancing a Clip with Brightness/Contrast

In this example, we take a video clip that came out dark and use the Brightness/Contrast effect to tweak the video so that we can see the people in the video better.

1. Open an iMovie project, and if you haven't already done so, drag a clip into the Timeline.

2. Click once on the clip you want to use in the Timeline to select it.

3. Click the Effects button in the main iMovie window to display the Effects palette. Then click the Brightness/Contrast effect as shown in Figure 26.23.

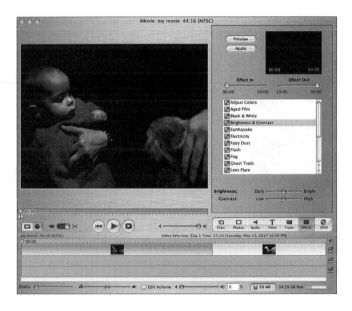

FIGURE 26.23
The Brightness/
Contrast effect with
the Brightness set-
ting adjusted to be
midway between
Dark and Bright,
and the Contrast
setting adjusted to
midway between
Low and High.

4. Start adjusting the clip through increasing the contrast by clicking the blue slider button, holding down the mouse button, and dragging a small bit to the right to bring out the brighter colors and distinguish the darker colors from them (see Figure 26.24).

5. Click the Brightness slider button and slowly drag it to the right, keeping an eye on the video clip (see Figure 26.25). At any time, you can click the Preview button in the Effects palette to see how things look in iMovie's Monitor area, or watch the mini-preview window as you adjust the settings.

6. When you like how the previews look, click Apply, and iMovie begins to process the video (see Figure 26.26).

When iMovie is finished processing your clip, you can play the movie to see how the effect looks.

Sometimes, after you apply an effect and iMovie begins to render it, you change your mind. What do you do to stop iMovie from rendering the rest of the clip? If you press the Command key and the period on your keyboard at the same time while iMovie is rendering any element, that process will be cancelled, and the clip will remain as it was before you started.

By the Way

FIGURE 26.24
Moving the
Contrast slider
toward the higher
setting helps to
give you a brighter
clip.

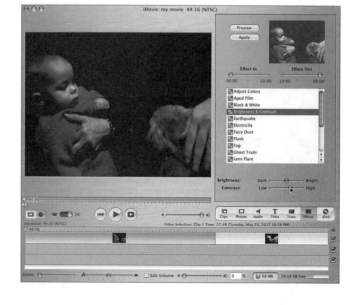

FIGURE 26.25
Moving the
Brightness slider
from Dark to Bright
also enhances the
brightness of the
clip.

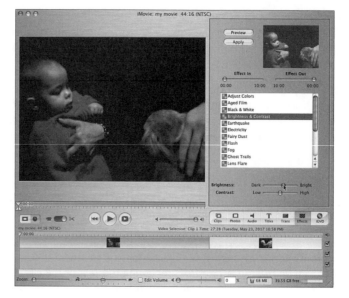

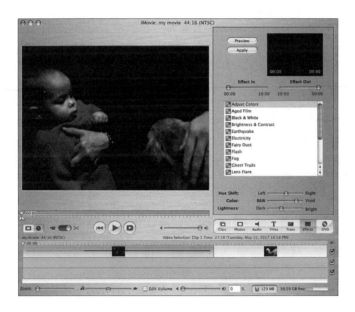

FIGURE 26.26
The clip with the
Brightness/Contrast
effect renders in the
Timeline.

Task: Enhancing a Clip with Adjust Colors

The Adjust Colors effect can come in handy when you want to make certain colors stand out, or want to give the clip a distinct imaginary feel of some kind. It gives you three subsettings that you can play with: Hue Shift, Color, and Lightness.

▶ Hue Shift—Shifts the entire video clip to a different color

▶ Color—Changes the amount and vividness of color, from no color (black-and-white) to Vivid (as much color as possible, which is how the effect starts out with no changes made)

▶ Lightness—Similar to the Brightness/Contrast effect

In this example, we want to give the video a washed-out feeling by taking out the color (also known as *desaturating*) and increasing the brightness/lightness.

1. Open an iMovie project, and with a clip selected in the Timeline, choose the Adjust Colors effect in the Effects palette (refer back to Figure 26.18).

2. Click the Color slider and drag it to the left to make the video black and white (B&W).

3. Click the Lightness slider and drag it to the right to make the video brighter.

4. Click the Apply button in the iMovie window to set iMovie going on processing your video.

The Hue Shift option changes the overall tone of the clip. Dragging the slider from one end to the other should give you nearly the full range of the spectrum, from warm reds to cool blues.

By the Way

> Keep in mind that the colors available in the Hue Shift option depend somewhat on the colors, brightness, and other features of your original video.

Making Changes to Effects

After you've tried effects by simply applying them to successive clips, you'll probably discover that you want to make things more interesting or customized.

By the Way

> You can drag and drop transitions, but the drag-and-drop feature doesn't work with effects.

Because you've already applied an effect to a clip, you will need to reapply the changed effect. To do this, select the clip you want to change the effect for, choose the effect you want to change, make the changes, and then click Apply. A sheet window appears in some cases to let you know that the new effect invalidates the previous one. You must choose OK for your new effect to be processed.

Task: Changing and Updating an Effect

This example picks up where we left off with the last task. We want to try the mysterious Effect In and Effect Out features in the Effects palette. We want to slowly increase the impression that the effect has on our clip over the space of a few seconds by bringing in the effect to give the clip a unique feel and then fading out the effect.

1. Select a clip in the Timeline that has an effect applied to it.

2. Click the blue slider in the Effect In area of the Effects palette, and drag it a bit to the right to choose the length of time that it takes for the effect to develop to full strength.

3. Now click the Effect Out slider and drag it to the left to choose how long it takes for the video to return to normal.

4. Click the Apply button to reapply the effect with these new settings.

When you click the Apply button, iMovie starts to process the video. In a short while, you can preview want to slowly increase the impression that the effect has on it to see the final version of the video. Of course, if the effect doesn't measure up to your expectations, you can repeat steps 1–4, trying out different adjustments until you're happy with the effect.

Summary

In this chapter, you found out how you can bring your iMovies one step closer to their Hollywood (or living room) debut by learning about titles, transitions, and effects. You learned how easy it is to make and adjust titles in iMovie. You also learned how iMovie enables you to add professional-looking transitions to a project, which can help digital video to look and feel more like a real movie. Finally, you saw how, in certain situations, an effect such as Brightness/Contrast can actually help you to see your video better if it was shot in a setting where there wasn't much light, also known as a *low-light situation*.

CHAPTER 27

Working with iMovie's Clip Viewer

As you learned in Chapter 24, "Exploring the iMovie Interface," the Clip Viewer is an alternative to the Timeline and might be preferable for some as a way to work with clips. In some ways, the Clip Viewer is the "lite" version of iMovie.

Although the Timeline view provides an excellent way to work with clips and is easy to use, the Clip Viewer is even easier to use, and it might be a good starting place for some people. If you want to have a simplified introduction to working with iMovies, you might want to work in the Clip Viewer. Also, children might find it easier to play with iMovie in the Clip Viewer because there are fewer skills to master—just clicking, dragging, and dropping.

Adding and Rearranging Clips

In the Clip Viewer, you can do just about everything you can in the Timeline, including adding transitions, effects, and titles. One of the only major differences is that you can't work with audio in the Clip Viewer. When you try to drag a sound effect into the Clip Viewer, it switches you back to the Timeline.

Figure 27.1 shows the Timeline with three successive video clips arranged from left to right. The leftmost part of the Timeline represents the beginning of the movie, and the rightmost part of the Timeline represents the end of the movie.

FIGURE 27.1
Three clips in the Timeline view.

Now take a look at the Clip Viewer in Figure 27.2, which is accessed simply by clicking on the film frame symbol at the left corner of the screen.

FIGURE 27.2
The same three clips in the Clip Viewer.

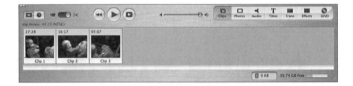

The video clips represented in Figure 27.2 are the same video clips that you saw in Figure 27.1. If you have iMovie open, take a moment to click back and forth between the Timeline and the Clip Viewer to investigate the differences.

Some people might prefer to think of the Clip Viewer as being like a *slide sorter* (a device that enables you to easily sort slides that have been developed from a traditional camera). If you've ever seen slides developed from traditional film, you'll notice that the icons that represent the Clip Viewer and clip shelf look a lot like slides.

Task: Adding Clips

Adding clips is simple in the Clip Viewer. You can basically handle things the same way that you will learn to do in the Timeline: by dragging clips into the Clip Viewer from the shelf.

1. Open an iMovie project that has several clips in it.

2. To access the Clip Viewer if it's not already open, click the film frame icon in the lower-left corner of the screen.

3. Choose a clip for your iMovie by single-clicking one of the clips in the shelf, holding down the mouse button, and dragging it down toward the Clip Viewer area as shown in Figure 27.3. When you have the mouse arrow over the Clip Viewer area, you can let go of the mouse button and drop the clip there.

4. To add another clip, repeat steps 2 and 3 to drag the next clip down and drop it to the right of the first clip.

When you've finished dragging clips into the Clip Viewer, they'll be lined up in a row. If one of the clips is a blue color, that simply means it's selected. If you want to deselect it, you can click somewhere other than on the clips in the Clip Viewer.

Task: Rearranging Clips

The Clip Viewer comes in particularly handy for rearranging clips if you want to reposition one clip after another or easily try different combinations of scenes. Open an iMovie project with a few clips in it, and before looking at the Clip Viewer, try the Timeline view (click the clock icon). Notice how things look. For comparison, you might want to try clicking on a clip to try moving it around, as shown in Figure 27.4.

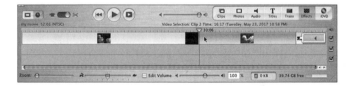

Now you're ready to reposition:

1. Open an iMovie project with at least three clips in it, and click on the film frame icon at the lower left to see the Clip Viewer.

2. Click the first clip, and holding down the mouse button, drag the clip to the right, until a space opens up between the second and third clips (see Figure 27.5).

FIGURE 27.5
The Clip Viewer is a bit more convenient; rearranging is as easy as dragging back and forth.

3. Let go of the mouse button to drop the clip in place.

Besides repositioning clips, the Clip Viewer is also good for putting clips back on the shelf if you've decided not to use them for the time being. Simply click on the clip to select it, and drag it back into an empty square in the shelf.

Previewing Clips

When you want to watch one of the clips you're using in your iMovie, simply select it by clicking the clip and then click the Play button. And when you want to preview the entire movie, you click the Play button without any clip selected, and iMovie plays all the clips in succession.

Task: Previewing a Single Clip

It's easy to look at a single clip in iMovie when you want to see what it contains.

1. Open an iMovie project with clips that have been dragged into either the Timeline view or the Clip Viewer.

2. Click the film frame icon to display the Clip Viewer.

3. Click once on a video clip to select it in the Clip Viewer.

4. Click the Play button under the Monitor to watch the clip, or click the playhead and drag it to the left and right to rapidly review what's going on in the clip (see Figure 27.6).

Notice how, in Figure 27.6, iMovie displays how much time each video clip takes up at the upper-left corner of each clip icon. By the time you reach the end of the clip, the playhead is to the far right of the blue bar, telling you how many seconds have elapsed. In video, there are 30 frames per second, so the farthest number on the right reflects the frame, and the number to the left of the colon represents the number of seconds.

FIGURE 27.6
The playhead is at
the end of the clip
after it plays.

Task: Previewing an Entire Movie

Previewing an entire movie is as simple as previewing a single clip; you just have to remember not to have any one clip selected when you click the Play button.

1. Open an iMovie project with clips that have been dragged into either the Timeline or the Clip Viewer.

2. Click the film frame icon to select the Clip Viewer.

3. Click somewhere other than on a clip to make sure that you don't have any clip selected—they should all be a white color.

4. Click the Play button below the iMovie Monitor, and iMovie plays through all the clips, giving you a preview of your entire iMovie.

Notice how, in Figure 27.7, iMovie draws a small red marker that moves slowly to the right in the Clip Viewer area as you watch your movie. The position of the red marker corresponds to where the playhead is positioned in the Monitor window as well. Both the playhead and the red marker are essentially ways of keeping track of where you are in your movie project.

The folks at Apple, in their typical subtle elegance and imaginativeness, have built a helpful way of seeing where one clip starts and one clip ends directly into the Monitor window. Small vertical lines in the scrubber bar below the Monitor correspond to where one clip ends and another begins. This feature is sort of like having a timeline even when you're in the Clip Viewer.

FIGURE 27.7
The Clip Viewer has a red marker (visible here as a thin white line in Clip 1) that goes through the clips when previewing, to indicate where you are in the iMovie.

Enhancing Clips

Adding transitions, effects, and titles in the Clip Viewer is as simple as it is in the Timeline. In many cases, you simply click a button to display the palette you need to work in, drag your enhancement where you want it in the Clip Viewer, and you're there!

Task: Adding a Transition

It's easy to add a transition in the Clip Viewer:

1. Open an iMovie project with clips that have been dragged into either the Timeline or the Clip Viewer.

2. Click the film frame icon to select the Clip Viewer.

3. Click the Trans button in the main iMovie window to display the Transitions palette.

4. Click a transition and drag it to a spot in the Clip Viewer. (Try clicking Fade Out and dragging it into position after the last clip in your iMovie.)

After you drag the transition into place, iMovie attaches a small indicator to show you how the processing is going, with a small red line that moves to the right (see Figure 27.8). When it gets all the way to the right, the transition is officially processed, and you can preview the clip.

Task: Adding an Effect

You learned about video effects in Chapter 26, "Adding Titles, Transitions, and Effects in iMovie." Adding them to a clip is as easy as any other enhancement.

FIGURE 27.8
The new Fade Out transition is processing, making a preview of what the fade out will look like.

Let's say that we shoot some video in a dimly lit location and then decide that we want to brighten things up a bit. No problem!

1. Open an iMovie project and click the film frame icon to look at the Clip Viewer.

2. Click the Effects button to display the Effects palette.

3. Choose a clip and click it to select it.

4. With the clip selected, go into the Effects palette and click the Brightness & Contrast Effect to select it.

5. Drag the Brightness slider, shown in Figure 27.9, a bit to the right. Then play with the Contrast setting until the subject is easier to see.

6. You see the changes, a little bit rough, in the preview window at the top of the Effects palette. (You could also click the Preview button in the Effects palette to view your settings in the Monitor window before applying them, but in some versions of iMovie this feature is disabled.)

7. If you liked what you saw in the preview window, click the Apply button in the Effects palette to tell iMovie that you've decided you want to use this effect. (iMovie then processes the effect and marks the clip with a checkerboard icon to show that an effect has been applied.)

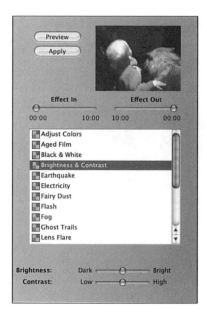

If you don't like your settings, you can choose Edit, Undo (or hold down the Command key on your keyboard and then press the Z key—another handy way to undo).

Adding a Title

In addition to adding transitions and effects, you can also create title segments while in Clip Viewer. Simply open the Titles pane, choose an option and customize the text, and then drag it into the Clip Viewer to the place where you want it to appear.

Summary

In this chapter, you were introduced to shelf the Clip Viewer, which can be considered the "lite" version of iMovie. Clip Viewer can be used as an alternative to the Timeline when working with video clips and is a good starting place for people who want to jump right in to digital video editing. Although you cannot work with audio, which will be discussed in the next chapters, you can use the Clip Viewer to add and arrange clips and apply transitions, video effects, and titles to your project.

CHAPTER 28

Working with Still Photos and Sound in iMovie

iMovie isn't useful only for people with video cameras. Still images with accompanying sound can be used to create high-impact presentations or documentaries and can be used to spice up live-action films with professional title and credit backgrounds. Even if you're a digital photographer who is completely satisfied with iPhoto, you'll find that iMovie can create new and exciting ways to display your masterpieces.

If you've added view clips to your project from your camera or from other sources, they've almost certainly had sound accompanying them. What if you decide that you don't like the sound that goes along with your movie clip? Do you have to reshoot the video just for a new audio track? No, not at all. iMovie provides you the ability to use dozens of canned sound effects, record audio from your computer's microphone (if available), use music from your iTunes library, or even take the sound from other video clips and use them with different video sequences.

Photos and iMovie

iMovie is known for the ease with which it allows you to import and manipulate digital video with special effects and transitions. iMovie 3 integrates completely with iPhoto 2, providing instant access to your photograph library.

Photographs can be worked with much like video clips. You can apply the same effects and transitions, as well as use a special effect designed specifically for digital photographs—an effect dubbed the "Ken Burns Effect." This effect, which we'll discuss later in this chapter, can add motion and depth to otherwise still images. Figure 28.1 shows a still image within the Timeline—it appears identical to a video clip.

iMovie supports a number of native image formats through QuickTime's media framework. TIFFs, JPEGS, and even PDF files can be dragged into an iMovie project as a source of still images.

FIGURE 28.1
Still images work virtually identically to video clips within iMovie.

Importing into iPhoto

The best and cleanest way to handle importing images into iMovie is to first import them into iPhoto. iMovie automatically connects to your Photo Library and provides access to all your digital images the same way it does with digital music and iTunes. The drawback to this is that even if you only want to insert an image or two into iMovie, it's best if they are added to your Photo Library. Let's review some of the basics of working with iPhoto that were first explained in Chapter 23, "Using iPhoto."

By the Way

> You should start iPhoto at least once before using iMovie; otherwise, the iPhoto/iMovie integration will not be complete, and iMovie may behave strangely when attempting to access photo features.

There are two straightforward methods for getting images into iPhoto. The first is to connect a supported camera to your computer and then follow your camera's instructions to place it in playback or transfer mode. Your computer will sense the connected camera, launch iPhoto, and present you with the Import pane, shown in Figure 28.2.

FIGURE 28.2
Images in iPhoto are imported directly from the digital camera.

Clicking the Import button transfers files from your camera. Thumbnails of the transferring images appear in the image well of the Import pane along with the number of photos remaining to be transferred. When the import is complete, the new images appear in the photo viewing area along with any other images you've imported. If the box for Erase Camera Contents After Transfer is checked, you are asked to approve deletion of the original photo files from the camera.

Imported images are stored in groupings called *rolls* in the Photo Library. Any image, in any roll, can be added to an arbitrary *album* by first creating the album (choose File, New Album from the menu) and then dragging from the Photo

Library into the Album name displayed along the left side of the iPhoto window. This helps you keep track of your images and provides a convenient means of accessing them in iMovie.

The second method of importing images assumes that you already have a group of image files on your computer but not in iPhoto. In this case, you can select them in the Finder and drag them into the Photo Library. This, once again, creates a new roll in the Photo Library and gives you access to the pictures from within iMovie—no camera required.

Adding Photos to iMovie

As mentioned previously, there are two ways to add photos to iMovie, either from files on your desktop, or via iPhoto integration. Because iPhoto is the preferred method, we'll start there.

iPhoto Integration

To add a photograph that you've previously stored within your Photo Library, click the Photos button in the icon bar in the lower-right portion of the iMovie window. The Photo pane appears, as shown in Figure 28.3.

At the top of the pane are the controls for the Ken Burns effect, followed by the library of available iPhoto images. The pop-up menu at the top of the image catalog can be used to limit the images being displayed to any of the iPhoto albums you've created, or two special categories:

- ▶ Photo Library—All images imported into iPhoto that haven't been deleted.

- ▶ Last Import—The last group of images you imported into iPhoto.

Choose the album or category that contains the image you want to use and then scroll through the image catalog to find the exact picture you want to add.

Finally, drag the image to the Timeline or Clip Viewer at the bottom of the iMovie window. iMovie behaves exactly as if you are adding a video clip with a specific duration. (You can change the duration by dragging the slider in the Photos pane that is labeled with a rabbit (for quicker) and a turtle (for longer-lasting). Figure 28.4 shows a collection of three images that have been added to the Clip Viewer in iMovie.

FIGURE 28.3
The Photo pane provides direct access to iPhoto images.

FIGURE 28.4
Just think of still images as video clips without much video.

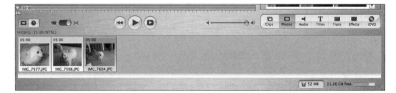

Unfortunately, this is the point where some of Apple's user friendliness gets in the way. The software immediately tries to render the Ken Burns effect within your image. Because you don't even know what the Ken Burns effect is yet, you probably aren't that anxious to use it! To cancel the rendering, simply add the image to the Timeline, select it within either the Timeline or the Clip view, and press the escape (Esc) key. iMovie stops trying to add the special effect, and we'll get exactly what we want—a 5-second still clip of the photograph.

By the Way

If you're an adventurous sort and want to disable the automatic application of the Ken Burns effect completely, open the file ~/Library/Preferences/com.apple. iMovie3.plist in a text editor such as TextEditor (discussed in Chapter 6, "Using Calculator, Stickies, and TextEdit") and then look for the line that contains the text autoApplyPanZoomToImportedStills. Shortly after that line you'll see the word "true". Change the word "true" to "false", leaving everything else the same. Restart iMovie, and suddenly the program imports "still" stills without any extra effort on your part!

The Ken Burns Effect

So, what is the Ken Burns effect that Apple so desperately seems to want us to use? It is a method of bringing life to still images that was pioneered by the film-maker Ken Burns, who has created many award-winning documentaries, and whose work has even been nominated for an Academy Award.

For a complete background on Ken Burns and his work, visit http://www.pbs.org/ kenburns/.

By the Way

The effect is really simple. Instead of just putting a photograph onscreen while someone narrates, a virtual "camera" pans over the image, zooming in or out as it goes. A photograph of a bouquet of flowers, for example, could start zoomed in on one particular flower and then zoom out, centering the bouquet on the screen as it goes. When the effect is used properly, the end result is stunning and can make the viewer forget that he is not watching live video.

To use the Ken Burns effect in iMovie, first make sure that you are in the Photos pane. Then select the image that you want to apply the effect to. At the top of the Photos pane are the controls that you will use to determine the path that the virtual camera will take, how long the resulting video clip will be, and how far in or out the virtual camera is zoomed.

For example, I've chosen a picture of an orchid that I want to apply the effect to. I've decided that I want to start out zoomed in on one of the flowers and then zoom out to show several. To do this, I click the Start button and then click and drag the image within the Ken Burns effect image well. This allows me to center where the camera will be starting when the effect is applied. Next, I adjust the Zoom level either using the slider control or by directly typing in the Zoom field. Figure 28.5 shows the start settings of my Ken Burns effect.

To complete the effect, I need to repeat the same process for the Finish point of the effect. This time, I click the Finish button, click and drag the image so that it appears as I want it in the image well, and then adjust the zoom so that I can see several of the orchid's flowers, as shown in Figure 28.6.

FIGURE 28.5
Choose the starting location and zoom for the image.

FIGURE 28.6
Set the finish point and zoom level to complete the transition.

To preview the Ken Burns effect before you actually apply it to an image, click the Preview button. To reverse the path that the virtual camera takes (effectively switching the Start and Finish points), click the Reverse button. If you want the total time the transition takes to last longer (or shorter) than 5 seconds, adjust the duration slider, or type directly into the Duration time field. Finally, to add the image with the Ken Burns effect to the Timeline or Clip View, click the Apply button. The effect may take several minutes to apply (watch the little progress bar that appears above the image in the Clip Viewer or Timeline).

> The settings you choose when adding the Ken Burns effect to a photograph are used as the default for subsequent images you add. Because iMovie attempts to apply the Ken Burns effect to everything, make sure that what it's doing is really what you want.

By the Way

Adding Photos Directly

You can easily add photos directly to iMovie by dragging the image files from your desktop into either the Clip shelf, the Clip Viewer, or the Timeline Viewer. In all these cases, iMovie adds the image, just like a video clip, but, again, automatically tries to apply the Ken Burns effect using the current settings within the Photos pane unless you uncheck the box labeled Ken Burns Effect. (As mentioned previously, you can cancel the Ken Burns effect and just use the image as a still by pressing Escape (Esc) or Command-.(period) immediately after adding it to iMovie.)

> Using Command-. to cancel rendering of the Ken Burns effect also cancels all active rendering, so be careful not to use it before your titles, transitions, or effects are processed.

By the Way

So, what if you want to add photos directly and use the Ken Burns effect? If the settings for the Ken Burns effect are already configured the way you want before you add your picture, you literally don't have to do anything. Just add your image and allow the Ken Burns effect to be applied automatically. If, however, you want to customize the effect for the image you're adding, you must follow these steps:

1. Add the image by dragging it into iMovie.

2. Cancel the automatic application of the Ken Burns effect by pressing Escape (Esc) or Command-.

3. Click on the image in the Clip Viewer or the Timeline to select it.

4. Switch to the Photos pane by clicking the Photos icon in the icon bar in the lower-right portion of the iMovie window.

5. The selected image appears in the Ken Burns Effect pane.

6. Choose the effect settings you want; then click Apply.

7. The Ken Burns effect with your custom settings is applied to the image you've added to iMovie directly.

As you can see, working with the iPhoto integration is a much more straightforward means to managing images and applying the Ken Burns effect.

Still Images from Video

One final source for still images is a video clip itself. iMovie makes it easy to create a still image from any frame in a video file. To do this, switch to the Timeline Viewer and drag the playhead until the image that you want to use as a still appears within the main viewer. Next, choose Edit, Create Still Frame from the menu. iMovie adds a still image with a 5-second duration to the available iMovie clips.

By the Way

Surprisingly, when you create a still image from a video clip, iMovie does *not* attempt to apply the Ken Burns effect!

Still Images and Duration

A point of confusion when working with still images is the duration, and how duration can be changed. A still image that does not have the Ken Burns effect applied is, by default, treated as a 5-second video clip. To change the length of time that it is displayed onscreen, simply double-click it within the Timeline or Clip Viewer. A window, as shown in Figure 28.7 appears, where you can manually enter how long the clip should last.

The same, however, cannot be said for an image that has had the Ken Burns effect applied. Double-clicking a Ken Burns image shows a noneditable duration, as shown in Figure 28.8.

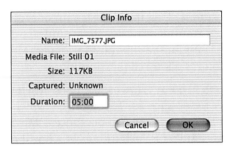

FIGURE 28.7
Change how long a still image is displayed.

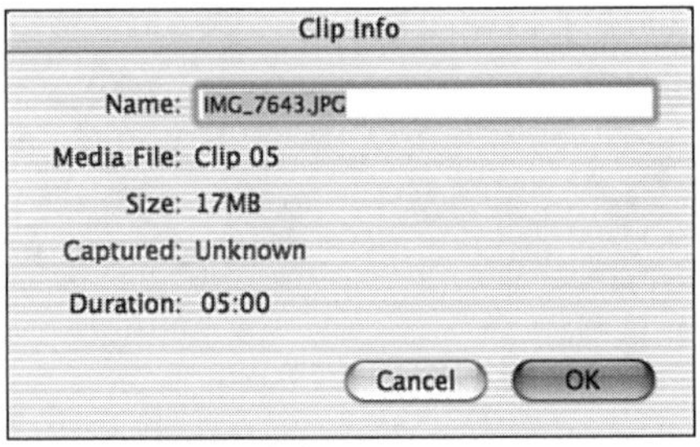

FIGURE 28.8
You cannot alter the duration of a Ken Burns effect image without reapplying the effect.

The reason for this difference is because an image that has had the Ken Burns effect applied to it is effectively a piece of video. It has different frames that iMovie calculated based on the settings you gave it. A "real" still image is just a single frame that iMovie understands should display for a set length of time.

To change the duration of a Ken Burns effect image, select the image within the Timeline or Clip Viewer; then click the Photos button to switch to the Photos pane. The selected image is shown in the Ken Burns preview, and the settings used to create the image are loaded. Adjust the duration using the duration slider; then click the Apply button to re-render the effect with the new duration.

Still Images, Effects, and Transitions

iMovie makes it simple to apply effects and transitions to images that you've added to your project. In fact, there is virtually no difference between working with still or Ken Burns effect image clips and video clips. There are two specific situations, however, when you may be prompted to do something that isn't quite clear:

▶ Increase Clip Duration—Sometimes the length of a still image clip isn't long enough for a given transition (a wipe, fade, and so on) to be applied. In this case, iMovie tells you that the clip must be longer. All you need to do is adjust the duration (as discussed previously).

▶ Convert Still Clip to Regular Clips—Sometimes, when you apply an effect that changes over time—such as "Earthquake," which makes each frame shift slightly to create a "shaking" appearance—iMovie states "This effect generates different results for each frame, which will not show up on Still Clips," as shown in Figure 28.9.

FIGURE 28.9
Some effects require that still clips be converted into regular clips.

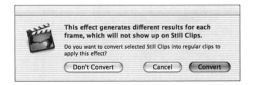

To apply the effect, iMovie must effectively change the still image into a video clip. Click the Convert button when prompted, and iMovie renders the effect. The only drawback to this is that, like an image with the Ken Burns effect added, you won't be able to change the duration as you would with a normal still image. To revert to a normal still clip, you'll need to delete the converted clip and re-add the original image.

Sound in iMovie

In an iMovie project, sound often plays almost as important a part as video. Sound and music can set the stage for a romance, suspense, comedy, or thriller. It can help create pacing for the movie and smooth through otherwise troublesome video transitions. If you've been using iMovie to import and arrange movies from your camera, you've already got audio in your projects. Movie clips themselves can contain embedded sounds, and these are usually transferred and saved along with the movie files. Although this is convenient if you only want to use the sounds you've recorded with your camera, it doesn't give you the flexibility to mix sounds or add additional sounds to your movie.

Audio Tracks

To accommodate additional sound effects, iMovie includes two sound tracks that can hold any sound, music, or audio that you want. Figure 28.10 shows the three available iMovie tracks: Video/Audio, Audio Track 1, and Audio Track 2.

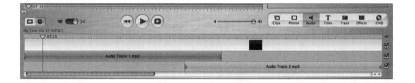

FIGURE 28.10
Audio can be part of a video track, or can be added to either of the two audio tracks.

There is no difference in functionality between the audio 1 and 2 tracks. You can use one track to hold sound effects, the other for background music, or mix and match them as you choose. In addition, each track can overlap audio clips, allowing you almost limitless layers of audio. You could, for example, have a base piece of background music in Audio Track 1, then perhaps an environment sound track layered on top of it, and, finally, sound effects layered on top of that in Audio Track 2. Figure 28.11 shows a layering possibility much like this scenario.

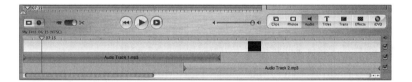

FIGURE 28.11
Audio can be layered via the different audio tracks, or within a single audio track.

> You've probably figured this out, but you must be in the Timeline view rather than the Clip view to see the available audio tracks.

By the Way

Sounds added to either of the audio tracks can be moved to the other track by clicking and dragging between the tracks in the Timeline. No matter what type of sound you're adding, it is referred to within iMovie as an *audio clip*.

Audio Playback

However you've decided to layer your audio, iMovie automatically composites it correctly when you play back your movie project. If you've included audio clips in all the tracks, they'll automatically all play back when you play the movie.

Sometimes this can get to be a bit of a pain as you try to fine-tune your special effect sounds and don't want to hear the dialog from your video tracks, or the background music you've added. To enable you to focus on a single set of audio, Apple has provided the ability to control audio playback using the three check boxes to the right of the video and audio tracks, shown in Figure 28.12.

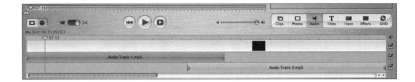

You can also control the overall volume of the movie using the volume control slider to the right of the main playback controls.

Working with Audio

There are a number of different ways to add audio to a project, so we'll start with one of the most common (and useful) Then we'll discuss how to work with audio clips that have been added to a Timeline, and, finally, examine other means of importing audio.

Accessing the iTunes Music Library

Adding audio to an iMovie project takes place through the Audio pane, accessed by clicking the Audio button in the icon bar on the lower right half of the screen. Figure 28.13 shows the iMovie window with the Audio pane active.

Your iTunes library is the default source for audio that is added to the project. You can use the pull-down menu at the top of the iTunes listing to choose between your iTunes playlists or type a few characters into the search field at the bottom of the song list to filter the songs that are shown.

When using the search field to find your iTunes music, you'll notice that an "X" appears at the end of the field after you've typed in a few characters. Clicking the "X" clears out the search results and returns to the full list.

If you have a library of thousands of songs and can't remember which one you're looking for, you can choose a song from the list and then click the Play button underneath the list to listen to the song.

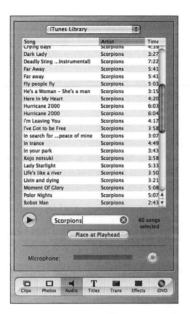

You must remember that using copyrighted material is against the law. Be sure that any songs you're using on a movie are public domain or properly licensed. If you're making the movie just for yourself, you can use music you own, but if the final product may be seen by others, you cannot distribute the copyrighted material.

Watch
Out!

Adding iTunes Audio to the Project

After you've located the song file that you want to add to the iMovie project, position the playhead where you want the sound to be inserted, click within the audio track that should receive the sound file, and then click the Place at Playhead button in the Audio pane. iMovie takes a few seconds (or minutes, depending on the length of the file), and then the corresponding audio clip appears in the selected audio track as a colored bar labeled with the name of the audio file, as shown in Figure 28.14.

In the current version of iMovie, there is no obvious means of telling which audio track is currently selected. The last track you clicked on is the one used for inserting audio.

If you happen to end up with audio inserted in the wrong track, simply click and drag the audio from one track to another.

Another, perhaps more elegant, way to add audio clips to the project is to drag a name from the list in the Audio pane to the audio track where it should be inserted. As you drag the name into the Timeline, a yellow "insert" bar appears to show you where the audio will be inserted when you stop dragging.

You can even extend this technique to the Finder by dragging audio files directly from your desktop into the Timeline.

Manipulating Audio Within the iMovie

After a piece of audio has been added to an audio track, it can easily be manipulated to match up with your video tracks, or the volume can be changed to better mix with the video or other audio files.

Repositioning Audio

Sometimes you place a sound in a movie, and it "just doesn't fit," or doesn't sync up with the video. To move an audio clip, click and drag it horizontally within the Timeline. The audio segment moves to any position you want within the project. While you are dragging, the playhead automatically tracks the start position of the audio, enabling you to position it perfectly within the project, as shown in Figure 28.15.

For extremely fine control of audio positioning, click to select the audio clip in the Timeline (it will darken in color to show that it is selected); then use the left and right arrow keys to move it frame by frame along the Timeline. Holding down the Shift key increases the movement to 10 frames at a time.

If you decide that you want to remove an audio clip from the project, simply click on it; then press Delete or choose Edit, Clear from the menu.

Locking Audio to a Video Clip

Often the act of moving audio around is an attempt to synchronize it with a piece of video. iMovie's capability to position on a frame-by-frame basis makes this simple, but what if you decide later that you want to reposition the video clip? If you drag the video, all your hard work synchronizing the audio will be lost.

FIGURE 28.15
Drag the audio clip to reposition it.

To "lock" a piece of audio to the video track, select the audio that you've positioned where you want it; then choose Advanced, Lock Audio Clip at Playhead from the menu. The audio track will then be "attached" to the video that occurs at the same place as the audio. Moving the video track within the timeline moves the audio as well, keeping your synchronization intact. You can tell a lock is in place by graphical "pushpins" that appear on the audio and video tracks, as shown in Figure 28.16.

FIGURE 28.16
Pushpins denote an audio track that is locked to a video track.

To unlock an audio clip, select it within the audio track; then choose Advanced, Unlock Audio Clip from the menu.

Locking audio to a video clip works one way. It does not lock the video to audio. If you drag the video clip, the audio moves with it, but not vice versa. Dragging the audio simply repositions the lock to the video, potentially losing any synchronizing work you've done.

By default, all locked audio clips are displayed with the pushpins all the time. To change the display so that the pushpins are shown only when the audio clip is selected, be sure to check the Show Locked Audio Only When Selected option within the iMovie preferences.

Using Crop Markers

Like video, audio clips also have crop markers that can be used to choose how much, or how little of a clip is played. These two arrows appear at the ends of an audio clip and can be dragged with the mouse to limit audio playback to a certain part of a sound, as demonstrated in Figure 28.17.

FIGURE 28.17
Drag the crop markers to limit what parts of the song are played.

To completely crop (remove) the portions of the audio clip that aren't being played, mark off the appropriate portions with the crop markers; then choose Edit, Crop from the menu.

Adjusting Volume

Suppose that you want soft background music in one portion of your movie, but want it to slowly build to a blaring orchestra in another? Before iMovie 3, the only way to do this was to edit the sound files in another audio program. Now, adjusting the volume is as simple as clicking and dragging.

To edit the volume editing mode, click the Edit Volume check box at the bottom of the iMovie window. Within a few seconds, all the audio clips (and the video clips that contain audio) display little lines through them. These lines represent the volume level of the clips.

To change the volume level of a clip, highlight the clip within any of the tracks (remember, even the video track's audio can be adjusted here); then click and drag the volume adjustment at the bottom of the iTunes window, or type a new volume level (100% being the "default" volume) into the field beside the volume slider. As you change the volume level, the line raises or lowers within the clip. Multiple clips can even be selected at once (Shift-click) and simultaneously be adjusted with this control.

You're thinking, "Okay, that's nice," but it still doesn't get me the fine-tuned control I need to really mix different audio clips together. Don't worry, volume adjustment can be as simple (as you've seen) or as complex (as you're about to see) as you want.

To alter the volume level within a specific part of an audio or video clip, click and drag the volume line within the clip. As you drag, an adjustment *handle* (a big yellow dot) appears. Dragging this dot up or down raises or lowers the volume at that point. To carry the volume change through to a different part of the clip, simply click wherever you want another volume adjustment handle to be added, and the level changes are carried through to that point.

Each handle that is added also carries with it a transition point that determines how the audio clip transitions to the new volume level (will it happen abruptly? smoothly?). The transition point is displayed as a small red/orange square to the right of the adjustment handle. The point can be dragged so that it is right above or below an adjustment handle, making for an immediate transition in volume, as shown in Figure 28.18.

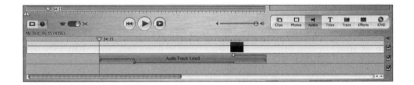

FIGURE 28.18
Moving the transition point directly above or below the adjustment handle causes an immediate volume transition.

To smooth things out a bit, the transition point can be dragged all the way along the volume line up to another adjustment point. The transition then occurs all the way between these two points. For example, Figure 28.19 shows the same volume adjustment being made as in Figure 28.18, but the transition takes place over a much larger span of the audio clip.

Volume adjustment can be used to ramp down an audio clip while ramping up another (similar to video transitions that blend the end of one clip with the beginning of another; this is called a cross-fade), or to create any number of other effects within your project.

FIGURE 28.19
The transition point
can be used to
spread the volume
transition out over
a long span of the
audio clip.

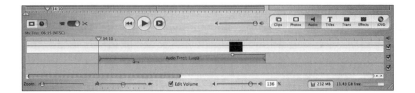

Splitting Audio

If you have a sound or song that you want to play part of at one time, and
another part at another time, you have two choices: You can import the audio
clip twice, or you can simply "split" the existing clip into different pieces and use
them wherever you want. To split an audio clip, position the playhead where you
want the clip to break; then choose Edit, Split Audio Clip at Playhead from the
menu.

New crop marks appear at the location of the split within the audio clip. You can
use these markers to fine-tune the split location, as shown in Figure 28.20.

FIGURE 28.20
Using the split fea-
ture adds crop
markers at the
location of the
playhead.

To "finish" the split, you must choose Edit, Crop from the menu; otherwise, the
split audio segments will still be attached to one another and won't be able to be
moved separately.

Other iMovie Audio Sources

Now that you've learned how to work with audio clips in iMovie, let's take a
quick look at the other sources of audio available for adding audio clips to your
project. At the top of the Audio pane is a pop-up menu with additional choices
for importing audio clips. As you've already seen, the iTunes Library and playlists
are available.

iMovie Sound Effects

A great source for canned sound effects is the included iMovie sound effects library, accessed by choosing iMovie Sound Effects from the top of the Audio pane in iMovie. The iMovie sound effects, shown in Figure 28.21, encompass a wide range of environmental and special effect sounds. The "Skywalker Sound Effects" (from George Lucas's Skywalker ranch) are extremely high-quality effects that can be used to create an impressive sound track.

FIGURE 28.21
Choose from dozens of built-in sound effects.

Unlike iMovie music, you cannot click the Place at Playhead button to insert a selected sound effect (I can't imagine why not, but it doesn't work!). Instead, you must click and drag the name of an effect into your audio track. After it is added, it behaves like any other audio clip.

Audio CDs

To add a sound track from an audio CD, put the CD in your computer's CD-ROM drive and then wait a few seconds. iMovie automatically switches to Audio CD mode, queries the Internet CD database to get a list of track names, and then displays the contents of the CD in the Audio pane, as shown in Figure 28.22.

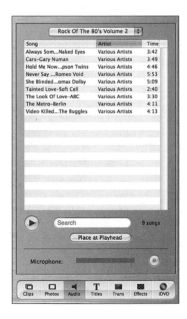

Choose the song you want to add to one of your iMovie audio tracks; then either use the Place at Playhead button or drag the song to the Timeline to add it to the project.

Recording a Voice Track

If you want to narrate a portion of the video, position the playhead where you want to start recording from your computer's microphone; then click in the audio track that should receive the audio. Finally click the red Record button to the right of the Microphone label at the bottom of the Audio pane. A graph of the level of sound input is shown beside the label as it records. To stop recording live audio, click the Record button again.

The new audio clips are added to your project with the sequential labels "Voice 1," "Voice 2,", and so on.

Extracting Audio from Video Clips

As we've already mentioned, the video track often also contains audio that accompanies a video clip. When adjusting volume, you can adjust the volume of a video clip just as you would an audio clip in an audio track.

Having video so closely tied to audio, however, has a disadvantage: You cannot manipulate the audio and video independently of one another. Thankfully, iMovie allows you to "decouple" the audio and video from one another. To do this, select a video clip with audio; then choose Advanced, Extract Audio from the menu. After a few seconds, the audio from the video clip appears in the audio track below the video clip. Figure 28.23 shows a video clip in the Timeline before audio extraction, and Figure 28.24 shows the same clip after extraction.

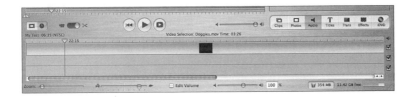

FIGURE 28.23
Normally, audio is embedded in the video clip...

FIGURE 28.24
...but it can easily be extracted.

After audio is extracted from a video file, it can be manipulated like any other audio clip.

In some cases, audio extraction happens automatically. If, for example, you cut and paste a video clip using the Paste Over at Playhead option of the Advanced menu, iMovie automatically extracts the audio of the original clip and moves it to an audio track so that it is not replaced by the paste over. The video clip that is pasted over will be lost, but the audio will remain.

This feature can be disabled by deselecting Extract Audio in Paste Over within the iMovie preferences.

iMovie has the capability to speed up or slow down video clips, as well as reverse their playback. These features do not work on audio clips. You can, however, apply the transformations to a video clip and then extract the audio, and the changes will carry with it.

Did you Know?

Summary

In this chapter you learned how to use photographs and audio in iMovie. You learned how still images can be added to iMovie presentations and how they can be made "dynamic" through the use of the Ken Burns effect. In iMovie, a still image behaves almost exactly like a standard video clip and can have all the same transitions and effects applied. Although simple to use, iMovie's audio features can allow novice editors to create layered audio tracks with ease. You learned how to work with a variety of audio sources available for adding sound to your video project.

CHAPTER 29

Exporting iMovies

In this chapter, you take a look at what you can do with your movies after you complete them—prepare them for email, Web, and disc delivery. You look behind the scenes at how you can export in different directions, and take a brief look at how an iMovie can be delivered with programs such as Mail (for emailing), Roxio's Toast (for CD-ROM and Video CD), and PlayStream's Content Manager (for putting iMovies on the Web). You'll also learn how to export your iMovies to iDVD for delivery via DVD.

When your iMovie is edited and ready to share, you can deliver it in two ways. Each method can be easily accessed from iMovie. You can deliver your iMovie using either tape (using a camera) or a file (when you'll be delivering by email, the Web, or disc such as CD or DVD).

When you're going back out to tape, some of the main considerations are how much time you have left on the tape and how long your iMovie is. But you'll generally want to put your iMovie at the beginning of the videotape so that it's easy to get to.

When you want to share an iMovie as a file, the file size could be more of a consideration. When you share an iMovie through email, the Web, or on disc (CD/DVD), each method of delivery results in a file that has a particular amount of compression. To get an appropriate file size that fits the delivery method, iMovie has to squeeze the file. So, you might notice a considerable difference in the image quality between what you see in iMovie and what you see when you send the file.

As with some other aspects of iMovie, you can take its advice, and when you choose a way to share your iMovie, you can accept the suggested compression settings that Apple engineers have calculated as the appropriate settings for typical situations. Doing so makes it easy to take your iMovie in a number of different directions. (You can also use the Expert settings mentioned in Chapter 24, "Exploring the iMovie Interface," to accomplish advanced adjustment of your iMovie.)

Choosing a Way to Share Your iMovie

When you're ready to export your iMovie, simply choose File, Export from iMovie's menu bar. Then choose one of three options in the Export Movie dialog box: To Camera, To QuickTime, or To iDVD.

Exporting to Camera

When you export to camera, you're connecting the same camcorder that you used to capture your video and sending the finished iMovie back out to Mini-DV or Digital-8 tape. From there, you can watch the finished product by connecting the camera to the television, recording from the camera to your VCR, or sending the tape off to have a number of copies duplicated.

Exporting to QuickTime

When you export to QuickTime, the method you choose to share your iMovie results in a particular kind of file, based on the settings that are chosen. For example, when you export an iMovie that you want to email to someone, it creates a relatively small file because it has to travel over the Internet, and you don't want the person on the other end to have to wait too long to download the attachment. Or, when you want to burn a CD with iMovie, the CD can hold a much larger file than an email could handle, so the movie quality is much better, but still not as good as the original iMovie.

Exporting to iDVD

When you export to iDVD, the option is basically a preset that generates a high-quality video file that iDVD then converts for use on a DVD disc. It takes up the largest amount of hard-drive space of any of the export options.

Besides exporting to iDVD from the Export dialog box, an iDVD palette lets you add "chapters" to your movie in iMovie and then launch it as an iDVD project. We'll talk about how later in the chapter in the section "Exporting iMovies to iDVD."

Making Videotapes from iMovie

To view an iMovie on television from a tape, the first step is to export the movie to your camcorder. Then you can either connect your camcorder to your television, or make a VHS tape from your digital tape (Mini-DV or Digital-8).

Task: Exporting to Camera

When you've finished your iMovie and are ready to take it to the next level, exporting to a camcorder allows you to display it on the television. With a few simple steps, you can make the video ready to share in a one-time event, where you play the video only from the camera. Or, after you have exported the video from iMovie to your camcorder, you can then go on to make a tape from there.

1. Load a blank tape into your camcorder and turn it on. (Make sure that you aren't about to record over something you want. Keep a pen around just for labeling tapes—and label those tapes!)

2. Connect your digital camcorder to your computer with a FireWire cable.

3. In iMovie, choose File, Export Movie, and choose Export to Camera from the Export pop-up menu (see Figure 29.1).

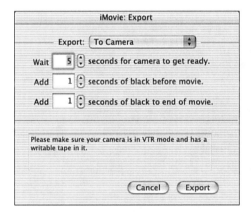

FIGURE 29.1
Exporting an iMovie to a camera.

4. Click Export.

If you want to make VHS copies of the digital tape that you just made, you can connect your camcorder to your VCR using standard RCA cabling, where you connect a series of cables to the Video Out and Audio Out jacks of your camera. The video connector is usually indicated by a yellow color. Two cables carry the audio, where each cable carries half a stereo signal (the left audio channel is the white connector; the right audio channel is the red connector) (see Figure 29.2).

Then you connect the cables to the Video In and Audio In jacks of your VCR (see Figure 29.3).

FIGURE 29.2
The Video/Audio
Out connectors
on a typical
camcorder.

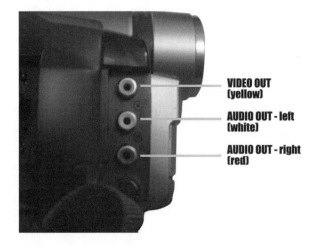

VIDEO OUT
(yellow)

AUDIO OUT - left
(white)

AUDIO OUT - right
(red)

FIGURE 29.3
The Video/Audio In
connectors on the
back of a typical
VCR.

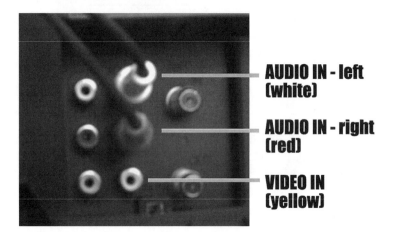

AUDIO IN - left
(white)

AUDIO IN - right
(red)

VIDEO IN
(yellow)

Emailing iMovies

When you want to email an iMovie, you export it from iMovie and save it to your hard drive. Then you connect to the Internet and use your email program to attach the iMovie file to an email. If you've never emailed an attachment before, keep in mind that it can take a few minutes for the attachment to upload, depending on whether you are using a 56K modem or a higher-speed DSL or cable modem connection.

Also keep in mind that it will probably help you to choose a special name for the email version of your iMovie, such as my movie-email. Save it in a place that you can easily find on your hard drive so that when it comes time to send it via email, you know which file to send and right where it is. (What you don't want to do is try to send your original iMovie via email. It'll be several hundred megabytes large and would probably take a few weeks to send via modem.)

Task: Exporting to Email

You don't have to do any special preparation of your iMovie to send it via email—that's what the Export function is for: to save it in a format that can be emailed.

1. Choose File, Export, and then choose To QuickTime from the Export pop-up menu.

2. Choose Email in the Formats pop-up menu (see Figure 29.4).

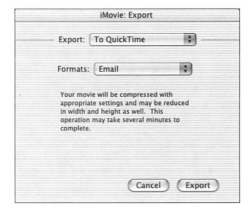

FIGURE 29.4
Exporting an iMovie for email.

3. Click Export and save your iMovie to a spot on your hard drive.

4. Open the program that you use to send email (such as Mail, which we talked about in Chapter 15, "Using Mail").

5. Compose a new email and click the appropriate button to add an attachment to the email. (In Mail for OS X, you choose Edit, Add Attachment from the menu—or simply drag the file into the compose window and skip the next step.)

6. Locate the iMovie that you want to send by email and attach it to your email. Figure 29.5 shows the iMovie attached to the email.

FIGURE 29.5
Looking at an email that has an iMovie attached.

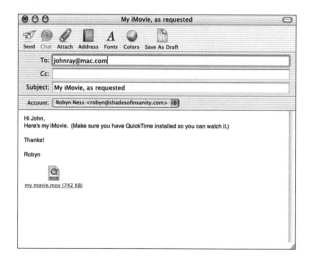

7. Connect to the Internet and send the email (see Figure 29.5). You don't necessarily have to connect to the Internet before you attach the email. You can compose an email and attach a file before connecting with many email clients, and then you send the email when you do connect.

Some email providers have file size limitations. For example, at the time of writing, you probably can't send a file larger than 10 megabytes through AOL. (And it would take a long time to upload or download that large a file anyway if you're using a 56K modem.)

Putting iMovies on the Web

Putting iMovies on the Web is a bit more involved than putting them on tape or sending them via email, but taking the time to figure out how to do it can make for an ideal way of sharing your iMovies with people who are far away.

There are two ways that iMovie can save your movie for delivery on the Web: as a Web movie or a streaming Web movie. A Web movie is uploaded to a standard Web server, and a streaming Web movie is uploaded to a streaming Web server.

Here are some terms and concepts that are helpful to consider; entire books and series of books have been written about each item, but just taking a look at each can be helpful later when you start to put more things of your own up on the Internet.

- ▶ Server—A *server* is the name for the computer used as the central storage location for Web pages. When you create a Web page on your computer, you have to upload the files to a server. Then, when people view your Web page, the Internet basically functions as a network connection to the server computer. When people hit your Web page, all they're really doing is downloading a series of files (text, graphics, HTML, and so on) from this Web server (the same place that you uploaded the files) to their computer.

- ▶ Standard server (for Web movies)—This is the most common type of server. When you put your Web page file on the server and a person clicks on the file, it's downloaded like any other file; then the person double-clicks the file to view it. A standard server is basically any server that doesn't have QuickTime streaming capability. So, if you're not sure what kind of server you have and you don't know that it's specifically capable of streaming QuickTime, chances are it's a standard server.

- ▶ Streaming server (for streaming Web movies)—True streaming video is when you can watch a video without downloading the entire file. Streaming video enables you to watch video in *real-time*, meaning that you establish a connection with a streaming server and watch the video as if it were a miniature television show. True streaming video basically means that you have a smoother, higher-quality experience. Streaming video is usually more expensive and more complicated to set up, but many companies and individuals find that the effort and expense are worth it. In addition to QuickTime, other forms of streaming video that you might recognize include RealMedia and Windows Media. All forms of streaming video require some kind of player application, such as QuickTime, to be present on a person's computer.

Keep in mind that even true streaming video is still dependent on how fast your connection is—video can be streamed on typical 56K modems for example, and the streaming version is smoother than a non-streaming version, but the quality is not as good as you would have on a higher-speed connection such as DSL.

By the Way

Task: Exporting a Web Movie for Use on a Standard Web Server

You'll probably want to save your iMovies using the Web Movie option, unless you specifically know you'll be using the file on an official QuickTime streaming server. In the next section, we'll take a look at the streaming server as well as investigate an easy-to-use method of streaming video provided by PlayStream.

1. Choose File, Export; then choose To QuickTime from the Export pop-up menu.

2. Choose the Web option in the Formats pop-up menu (see Figure 29.6).

FIGURE 29.6
Exporting an iMovie as a Web movie, for a standard Web server.

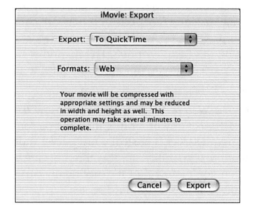

3. Click Export and save your iMovie to a location on your hard drive from which you can then upload it to a Web server.

4. Using an FTP application or a Web page creation program such as Dreamweaver, upload your file to your Web site.

5. Using a Web page creation tool, make a link to your iMovie, as shown in Figure 29.7. Here's some sample HTML link code:

```
Click<A HREF=http://www.psrecords.net/stdwebmovies/fantasia.mov>here</a>
to see Fantasia,<p>a cat who thinks she's a kitten
```

Figure 29.8 shows the Web page with a linked iMovie playing on top.

Even though this isn't a true streaming server, QuickTime has the capability to play as much of the movie as you've downloaded. If you have a fast connection, it can be almost as if it were a streaming clip. (Note, however, that the viewer may have to adjust the QuickTime preferences to play movies automatically to get this effect.)

FIGURE 29.7
A sample Web page with simple links to the iMovies that we uploaded.

FIGURE 29.8
The iMovie plays when you click on the link.

When you are sharing your iMovies with people on a Web site, you might want to include instructions for people visiting your Web page to describe how they can actually download the file to their hard drive instead of watching it on the Web page. Instruct Mac users to hold down the Ctrl key on their keyboard, click the movie link, and choose Save Link As or Download Link to Disk option (see Figure 29.9).

FIGURE 29.9
Holding down the Ctrl key on a Mac while clicking on a link for an iMovie in Internet Explorer.

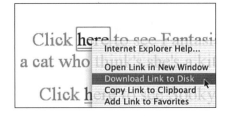

Instruct Windows users to right-click the link and choose the Save Target As option to save the file to disk.

You might also want to instruct people that, to view your iMovie, they might need to download and install the latest version of QuickTime, which is a free download available from www.apple.com/quicktime/download.

Task: Exporting for Streaming Server

Exporting your iMovie as a streaming Web movie for use on a streaming server is similar to exporting your iMovie as a Web movie for use on a standard server.

1. Choose File, Export; then choose To QuickTime from the Export pop-up menu.

2. Choose the Web Streaming option in the Formats pop-up menu (see Figure 29.10).

3. Click the Export button and save your file on your hard drive in a location you can find later to upload to the streaming server. You might want to name the file so that you can easily distinguish it later as a streaming file, something like my movie-streaming.mov.

4. Use your FTP program or Web page creation and upload tool to upload the iMovie to the streaming server.

FIGURE 29.10
Exporting an iMovie
for use on the Web
on a streaming
server.

As mentioned earlier, setting up a QuickTime file for a streaming server can be more complex and might require some experimentation and research. At the minimum, you must set up a Web page account and address (www.websitename.com) with a host company capable of QuickTime streaming (for example, www.metric-hosting.com).

You might also want to investigate a company such as PlayStream, whose mission is to make the process of streaming video as easy as possible. PlayStream has special accounts that exist only to host streaming video. So, if you already have a Web page, you can put your video on a PlayStream account and link to it from your current Web page. Or you may simply want the increased quality of streaming video without the typical hassles, so a service like PlayStream might be a worthy option.

PlayStream is nice because it offers a free 15-day trial, and its accounts enable you to host the major three forms of streaming video—QuickTime video, Real Media, and Windows Media—so that you can reach the maximum audience. Preparing your video for the different formats can require downloading or purchasing additional software, but it might be worth it because most people usually either have the ability to view video encoded for the Real Player or Windows Media Player.

For some people, it might actually be easier to try a service such as PlayStream and use full streaming video instead of getting Web creation software. PlayStream enables you to simply use your browser to upload files, and you don't even need your own Web page—when you upload files, you're given a link that you can email to people to get them directly to your video.

Task: Uploading a Streaming Web iMovie for PlayStream

If you want to try the PlayStream option, you can sign up for a free 15-day trial at www.playstream.com.

It's a way of getting right into putting your iMovie on the Web without spending any money.

1. Go to www.playstream.com and log in; then click the Content Manager link.

2. Click the Browse button (as shown in Figure 29.11) to locate the streaming Web movie file you saved earlier to your hard drive.

FIGURE 29.11
Using the Browse button right in the Web page to upload your video file—no special software required.

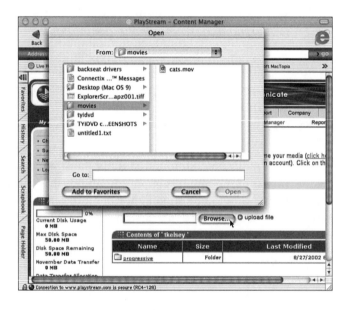

3. Click the Upload File button in the Content Manager on the PlayStream Web page to upload the file to your space on PlayStream. A window pops up (see Figure 29.12) that gives you a progress indicator of the upload.

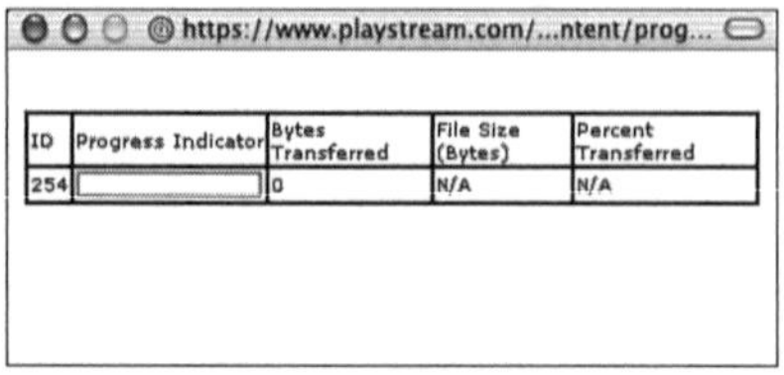

FIGURE 29.12
The Progress Indicator window showing the file being uploaded.

4. After the file is uploaded, select the text in the Stream Link field (see Figure 29.13) and copy the link into memory by choosing Edit, Copy from the menu at the top of the screen.

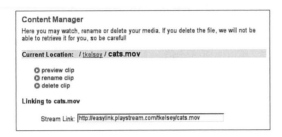

FIGURE 29.13
An automatic link is generated that you can either email to someone, put in a Web page to link to your streaming Web movie, or simply save for later use and paste directly into a Web browser window to see the movie play.

5. Paste the link text somewhere you can get it later, such as in an email to yourself or in a text document.

6. To allow access to the movie, insert the Stream Link text in an email, use it as a link on a Web page, or just paste it right in your Web browser.

You might want to include in your instructions that to see your iMovie, some people might have to download and install the free QuickTime software from www.apple.com/quicktime/download. Doing so installs a special plug-in file for the person's Web browser (Internet Explorer/Netscape/AOL) that enables him to view the streaming video file.

By the Way

Burning iMovies to CD

If you have a CD burner and want to share your iMovies via CD, you can simply save as a CD-ROM movie, which generates a QuickTime movie file that you can then burn to CD. If a person is on a Mac, she can see the movie without installing special software. Many Windows PCs have QuickTime software installed, but if it's not on your recipient's computer, she can download it free from www.apple.com/quicktime/download.

Another fun option for burning iMovies to CD is called Video CD, where you can actually put the resulting disc in most DVD players. The quality is only a little better than VHS, but you can fit about an hour's worth of video on the disc, and it's cheaper than burning DVDs.

Task: Exporting iMovie for CD-ROM

If you want to share the CD-ROM iMovie, you must investigate how to burn a CD that's compatible with the computer owned by the person you're sharing the iMovie with. If you burn your CD on a Mac, it's compatible with other Macs. But if you want to share it with someone on a Windows PC, you must learn how to burn a PC-compatible CD-ROM or a hybrid CD-ROM that works on both Macs and PCs. We'll take a look at burning with Roxio's Toast (www.roxio.com), a popular program that enables you to burn in just about any format you want.

To export an iMovie for CD-ROM:

1. Choose File, Export; then choose To QuickTime from the Export pop-up menu.

2. Choose the CD-ROM option in the Formats pop-up menu (see Figure 29.14).

FIGURE 29.14
Exporting an iMovie for delivery on CD-ROM.

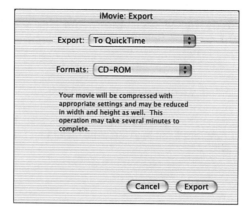

3. Click Export and save your file in a location on your hard drive where you can find it later.

4. Using your CD-burning software (such as Toast), drag your CD-ROM movie file into the program and burn a data CD (as opposed to an audio/music CD). Choose a format that's compatible with the computer of the person you're burning it for, such as the Mac OS/PC Hybrid CD option in Toast, which makes the CD-ROM compatible with either Mac or PC.

Exporting iMovies to iDVD

Distributing your iMovies on DVD is the ultimate in digital video. You start by recording your footage digitally, editing in iMovie, and retaining the digital quality by going directly to DVD. iMovie makes creating DVDs simple by linking up with iDVD.

> Be aware that you can't use iDVD unless you have a Mac with Apple's SuperDrive, which can read and write both CDs and DVDs.

Task: Exporting to iDVD

Although there is an Export To iDVD option in the Export dialog box, the message, shown in Figure 29.15, tells you that it is no longer necessary to export to iDVD because iMovie prepares projects for iDVD every time they are saved. You can still choose to "export" your project this way.

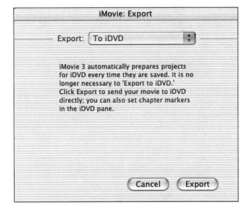

FIGURE 29.15
Exporting an iMovie for iDVD.

Alternatively, you could open the iDVD palette on the right side of the iMovie interface and click the button for Create iDVD Project. It takes a moment for your movie to open in iDVD where you can customize the menus and add movies.

Task: Adding Chapters to Your Movie

Besides maintaining video quality, DVDs offer another benefit to your iMovies: chapters. Adding chapters allows you to segment your video project so that people viewing the completed DVD can skip straight to the part they want to see, just like on a commercial DVD.

Follow these steps to add chapters to an existing iMovie:

1. Open a finished iMovie project and make sure that you are in Timeline view.

2. Click the iDVD button in the main iMovie window to display the iDVD palette.

3. In the Timeline Viewer, move the playhead to the point in your movie at which you want to start a new chapter.

4. In the iDVD palette, click the Add Chapter button.

5. A row for the newly created chapter appears in the iDVD palette, where you can type in a Chapter Title, as shown in Figure 29.16.

6. A small yellow diamond appears in the Timeline Viewer to mark the location of chapters, as shown in Figure 29.17.

FIGURE 29.16
Type a descriptive title for your chapter.

FIGURE 29.17
Chapter markers appear as yellow diamonds at the top of the Timeline.

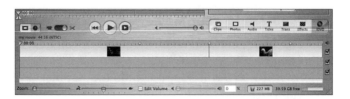

7. You can repeat steps 4 through 6 until you've added up to 36 chapters to your iMovie.

8. When you are finished adding chapters, click the Create iDVD Project button to open your iMovie in iDVD, as shown in Figure 29.18, where you can choose themes to customize the menu that displays your chapters. Before iDVD can be launched, you will be asked to save your project.

By default, iDVD saves your project in the Documents folder of your user account with the file extension .dvdproj. (We talk about customizing your presentation in iDVD in Chapters 30 through 32.)

FIGURE 29.18
This is an iMovie with chapters after export to iDVD.

Summary

In this chapter, you learned how to take your iMovies and share them in a number of different ways. Some methods, such as streaming Web video, might require more effort than others, but learning how to put an iMovie on the Web can open up new audiences for your creative works. You literally gain the ability to go worldwide with your iMovies!

CHAPTER 30

Exploring the iDVD Interface

It used to be that putting together a DVD project was complex, requiring the DVD author to perform many steps and have a significant amount of knowledge about the underlying technology. iDVD simplifies the process of DVD authoring—it's as easy as dragging and dropping files into the iDVD window, and iDVD handles encoding the files.

In this chapter, we begin with a look at DVD basics by investigating the way that DVD video works. We then take a look at iDVD, Apple's revolutionary, easy-to-use DVD-authoring software.

The DVD Creation Revolution

iDVD marks an historic moment in personal computing because, before Apple introduced it in early 2001, the only tools available for people who wanted to make their own DVDs were prohibitively expensive. Not only was the software complex and pricey, but the DVD burners themselves cost more than many computer systems. For example, before iDVD came out, the only available DVD burner, the Pioneer DVR-S201, shown in Figure 30.1, cost about 4,000 U.S. dollars.

FIGURE 30.1
Pioneer DVR-S201 DVD burner.

By cooperating with a few different companies including Pioneer, Apple was able to introduce a desktop G4 Power Mac model that included a DVD burner, as well as iDVD software, for the same price that just a DVD burner alone cost at the time. This DVD burner, known as the SuperDrive, brought the power of DVD authoring to the masses, giving them the ability to take digital video and make it into DVD video (see Figure 30.2).

FIGURE 30.2
The revolutionary SuperDrive, on countless desktops around the world, with a blank DVD disc.

By the Way

Apple issued an important update for some SuperDrive-equipped computers. This update prevents permanent drive damage when some models of SuperDrive manufactured by Pioneer are used with newer high-speed media. To see whether you need to install this update, follow these steps:

1. Open the Apple System Profiler application, which can be found in the Utilities folder in the Applications folder.

2. Open the Devices and Volumes tab.

3. Expand the CD-RW/DVD-R item by clicking the disclosure triangle.

4. Examine the information given. If Pioneer is the vendor, you may need the update. To find out for sure, look at the Product Identification code. For drives with the Product Identification DVR-104, no update is required if the Device Revision number is A227 or higher. For drives with the Product Identification DVR-103, no update is required if the Device Revision number is 1.90 or higher.

If your drive comes from Pioneer and doesn't have the upgrade in place, go to the Apple Web site (www.apple.com), search for "SuperDrive update," and then download and install it before attempting to write a DVD.

How DVD Video Works

DVD video is a form of *digital* video, and much like the way digital video is stored on a computer hard drive, digital video is stored as data files on the DVD disc. When you insert a DVD disc in a player connected to a television, a small computer in the DVD player looks for the DVD video files and displays them on the TV screen.

A DVD *menu* is simply a screen that gives you several choices, with selectable buttons of some kind that lead directly to video or to other menus.

When you watch or make a DVD, there are two types of video that you can experience: regular video such as a movie (as seen in Figure 30.3) and video contained in a motion menu.

FIGURE 30.3
Watching regular video in a DVD.

A *motion menu* is simply any screen on a DVD from which you're making menu choices and something is moving in the background behind the DVD menu. iDVD refers to the video used in motion menus as *background video* (see Figure 30.4).

One advantage of iDVD is that it enables you to incorporate motion menus in your DVDs by allowing you to choose from various customizable motion menu backgrounds. The creation of motion menus normally can be complex, but iDVD gives you the advantage of motion menus without all the hassle.

Task: Examining a DVD

To get a better sense of what's going on under the hood of a DVD, try taking a closer look at a DVD movie that you own or have rented using your Mac as a "DVD microscope."

FIGURE 30.4
A DVD motion
menu with back-
ground video of
clouds slowly pass-
ing by, which adds
an interesting
touch to an other-
wise motionless
DVD menu.

FIGURE 30.4
A DVD motion
menu with back-
ground video of
clouds slowly pass-
ing by, which adds
an interesting
touch to an other-
wise motionless
DVD menu.

By the Way

If you recall from Chapter 7, "Using QuickTime and DVD Player," DVD Player is a program that plays DVDs on your computer desktop.

1. Insert the DVD in the DVD drive on your Mac.

2. Wait a few moments. If your Mac automatically launches the DVD player software, either quit out of the software entirely by pressing Command-Q or choose Quit from the DVD Player menu. If the DVD takes up the entire screen, you can move the mouse up to the top of the screen to reveal the menu.

By the Way

The first time you insert a DVD into your drive, you will be asked to set a drive region. When set, your DVD drive will automatically read disks encoded for that region. If you should need to play a disc from another region, insert it, and DVD Player will ask whether it should change your region code. Keep in mind, however, that your drive region can only be changed five times following the initial setting. After that, it will keep whichever region settings were made last.

3. Look on your desktop for the icon that represents the DVD, and double-click to open it (see Figure 30.5).

4. When the window that represents the DVD opens up, you'll see a VIDEO_TS folder. This same folder is on every DVD that you can watch in a DVD player. If the VIDEO_TS folder isn't there, the DVD player won't understand the disc. Double-click the VIDEO_TS folder (see Figure 30.6) to open it.

FIGURE 30.6
The infamous VIDEO_TS folder is present on every DVD.

5. When the VIDEO_TS folder opens, you might want to choose View, As List to see the files better (see Figure 30.7).

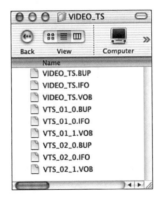

FIGURE 30.7
The files within the VIDEO_TS folder, which contain everything a DVD player needs to create the interactive experience.

It isn't particularly important to understand what the individual files in a VIDEO_TS folder do, but it can be interesting to look at things from the perspective of what a DVD player does. At this point, the digital video files within a VIDEO_TS folder have been encoded into MPEG-2 and multiplexed into their final DVD-ready form.

The following list explains what the file extensions (the last three letters of the file) mean for files on a DVD:

▶ IFO (stands for *information*)—These files contain the information about the DVD menu screens that a DVD player uses to construct the interactive experience.

▶ BUP (stands for *backup*)—These files are simply copies of the IFO files.

▶ VOB (stands for *video objects*)—These files are the actual video on the DVD.

The iDVD Interface

The iDVD interface, shown in Figure 30.8, has two distinct parts: the viewing area and the Customize tray. The viewing area is where you can see how your project looks at a given time, but it also acts as work space for arranging items menus and for creating slideshows of still images.

FIGURE 30.8
The iDVD interface.

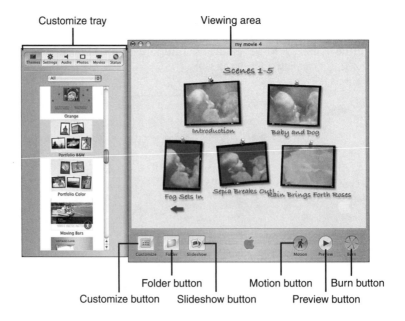

Below the viewing area are six buttons: Customize, Folder, Slideshow, Motion, Preview, and Burn. Let's examine what they do.

Motion Button

You might discover that sometimes when you're working on a DVD project, you want to turn off the motion. (Recall that you can add motion menus with iDVD, and this movement can be distracting while you are trying to design your DVD.) You can turn off motion in menus simply by clicking the Motion button.

Preview and Burn Buttons

As you work on your DVD project, you can test it by clicking the Preview button. This plays the current version of your project as it would appear on a finished DVD, including menus and video clips.

When you are satisfied with your project, you're ready to burn a DVD disc. You simply click the Burn button to activate it (see Figure 30.9) and then click it again.

Before

After

FIGURE 30.9
Clicking the Burn button.

When you click the Burn button a second time, the SuperDrive opens so that you can insert your DVD disc (see Figure 30.10).

FIGURE 30.10
Insert a blank DVD.

Slideshow Button

The Slideshow button allows you to add a series of still photos to a DVD and to choose background music. DVD slideshows are a nice way to share digital pictures, so that people who watch your DVD can see the pictures on their televisions. Just as when you're working with video clips in iDVD, a slideshow is as easy as dragging and dropping digital pictures into the iDVD window (see Figure 30.11).

FIGURE 30.11
Slideshow editing window with individual images.

When you drag digital pictures into the editing window, you can easily rearrange them and preview the show, just as you might have done with a traditional slide projector and the infamous slide sorter.

By the Way

> You may recall from Chapter 23, "Using iPhoto," that you can easily export a slideshow created in iPhoto to iDVD.

There's also an option for iDVD to draw arrows on the screen so that when a person views your DVD, there's a visual reminder to press the arrow keys on the remote to select which slide he wants to see. See Figure 30.12 for an example.

Folder Button

Although you can add individual items (such as movie clips and slideshows) to your DVD menus, you can also create folders in the menu to add a secondary menu in which to add even more movie clips and slideshows. Simply click the Folder button at the bottom of the iDVD window. Double-clicking a folder in the viewing area will open this "submenu" so that you can work with it as you would the top-level menu.

FIGURE 30.12
Slideshow preview showing arrows that indicate there are additional slides to view.

> You'll know you are in a submenu rather than the main menu if a button marked by an arrow appears in the menu. (Refer to Figure 30.8 for an example.)

Did you Know?

Customize Button

When you click the Customize button, the Customize tray opens along the left side of the iDVD window, as you saw earlier in Figure 30.8. The Customize tray consists of several different panes with controls for different tasks. Let's take a brief look at what you can do in each pane.

Themes Pane

The defining characteristic of a DVD is that it gives you the ability to watch digital video interactively on your television. It's possible to make a DVD disc that goes directly to the video when you put it into a DVD player, but most DVDs have some kind of menu.

Apple, with its consistently good taste, has put together a number of customizable templates, called *themes*, which give you the ability to make professional-looking menus for your DVD projects. You can choose a theme from the list in the Themes pane of the Customize window, shown in Figure 30.8.

By default, the Apple logo is shown in the lower right-hand corner of all the themes. To remove it, open the iDVD preferences and uncheck the box for Show Apple Logo Watermark.

Some available themes have video clips as backgrounds, and some also include sound. These themes enable you to include what's known as a *motion menu* on your DVD. You can even set your own motion backgrounds in some themes by dragging a movie into a customization area known as a *drop zone*.

Settings Pane

After you've chosen a theme, you may want to go beyond the default colors chosen for text. To customize a theme, open the Settings pane to select colors and text (see Figure 30.13).

FIGURE 30.13
iDVD gives you the ability to choose your own color and font for text.

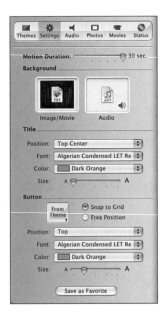

Another great feature of iDVD is that it enables you to choose different styles of button shapes for your DVD screens. (These options are also available from the Settings pane.) You can also change, or remove entirely, any background music for the menus.

When you choose to customize your DVD, and if you like what you've done, you can save the settings for later use in a Favorites list. A customized theme can be saved so that you can access it later for other projects.

The Audio, Photos, and Movies Panes

You can insert a variety of DVD content, including music, still photos, and movies. The Audio pane, shown in Figure 30.14, integrates with your iTunes library to allow you to add background music to your chosen DVD theme.

Besides integrating with your iTunes library, iDVD connects directly to your iPhoto library. From the Photos pane, shown in Figure 30.15, you can drag and drop photos to create slideshows, which we'll look at shortly, or to customize themes that contain special drop zones where you can put in one of your own images or video clips.

Make sure that you've upgraded your version of iPhoto to at least version 2 and launched iPhoto at least once (so that it can perform file system changes) before trying to integrate with iDVD.

By the Way

FIGURE 30.14
Select songs from your iTunes library.

FIGURE 30.15
Drag and drop
photos from your
iPhoto library.

The Movies pane lists all the movies stored in the current user's Movies folder, which is the default location for iMovie to store your projects.

Status Pane

When you make your own DVDs, at some point in the process the computer system has to *encode* the video into a special format (MPEG-2) so that a DVD player can play it properly.

It used to be that you had to use a separate program and adjust a variety of advanced settings to prepare video for DVD. In iDVD, you simply drag your iMovie into the program, and—if iMovie hasn't already encoded it—iDVD automatically encodes the video for you as you work on your project. And if you want to check in on how things are going, iDVD can give you an update on how the encoding is coming along, when you open the Customize tray window and click on the Status tab, as shown in Figure 30.16.

You can also use the Status pane to add DVD-ROM content to your DVD and to organize that "bonus" material into folders. DVD-ROM files can be any computer files, including photographs and documents, meant to be viewed on a computer rather than displayed by a DVD player. We'll see how to add these files to your projects in Chapter 31 "Designing DVDs in iDVD."

FIGURE 30.16
Taking a look at
how encoding is
going.

iDVD Capabilities

When you're just starting out with a few video clips and DVD screens, you might
not need to think much about exceeding iDVD's capabilities. But at some point,
you'll probably be curious about how many minutes of video you can fit on a
DVD, how many menu screens you can have, and so on.

▶ Items on a menu = 6—When you create a DVD, the buttons on the menu
screen can lead to movies, slideshows, or other menus. iDVD enables you to
have up to six buttons on each screen.

▶ Images in a slideshow = 99—You can add up to 99 digital pictures to each
slideshow that you have on your DVD.

▶ Movies/slideshows on a DVD = 99—You can add a total of 99 movies and or
slideshows to a DVD project, assuming that the total amount of video used
in the movie portion of your DVD does not exceed 90 minutes. Because digital pictures take up a relatively small amount of space, you don't have to
be concerned about how many pictures you add.

▶ Motion menus in a DVD = 30—Because motion menus use short video clips,
you're limited to using 30 of them on a DVD project, whether you are using
a motion menu from a built-in theme or importing your own.

▶ Minutes of video in a DVD = 90—The total number of minutes of video you can fit on a DVD is 90 minutes, or one and a half hours.

▶ Encoding for 60 minutes or less = high quality—If you use less than an hour of video, iDVD encodes your movies at the highest quality setting.

Technically speaking, iDVD automatically encodes your video at a particular *bit rate*, a setting that essentially determines the quality of your video.

When computers encode video, the higher the bit rate used, the higher quality video you get. And when you have a higher bit rate, the video takes up more space on the disc.

So, when you have less than one hour of video in a DVD project, iDVD encodes the video at a bit rate of 8 megabits per second (8Mbps).

▶ Encoding for 90 minutes or less = good quality—When you have between 60 and 90 minutes of video, iDVD uses a lower bit rate so that it can fit more video on the disc. In this situation, iDVD encodes video at 5 megabits per second (5Mbps).

The iDVD Preference Options

Before you move on to Chapter 31—where you'll learn how to design DVDs, customize menus, and add DVD-ROM content—we will take a brief look at the iDVD preferences, which are divided into General, Slideshow, and Movies options.

General Preferences

The General Preference settings, shown in Figure 30.17, affect entire projects. Under the Project Settings header are check boxes for the following four options:

▶ Show Drop Zones—As you learned earlier in this chapter, drop zones are areas in iDVD themes where you can insert photos or movie clips of your own. If the Show Drop Zones option is checked, these regions are emphasized by a yellow and black border so that you can recognize them more easily during the design process.

▶ Show Apple Logo Watermark—If this option is checked, an Apple logo will appear on the menu screens in your project.

▶ Enable Background Encoding—Keep this option checked to allow iDVD to encode your project's content to DVD format while you work.

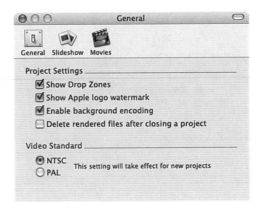

FIGURE 30.17
A typical configuration for the General preferences—if you live in North America!

▶ Delete Rendered Files After Closing a Project—Each DVD project you create consists of the raw files and the files that have been encoded for DVD. To save space on your hard drive, you can select this box to remove the encoded files each time you close a project. (Because the encoded files can be constructed from the raw files, iDVD creates them again if you open the project.)

The Video Standard options are NTSC or PAL. As discussed in Chapter 24, "Exploring the iMovie Interface," video standards differ by region. These standards specify the picture dimensions as well as a frame rate. If your intended audience lives in North American or Japan, be sure to use NTSC; if your viewers will be from Great Britain, choose PAL.

Slideshow Preferences

The Slideshow preferences, shown in Figure 30.18, affect how iDVD copes with images you add to slideshows. The first check box is Always Add Original Slideshow Photos to DVD-ROM, which includes the raw image files on the DVD along with the DVD-version of the slideshow. This gives your audience access to the original images for printing, editing, or otherwise working with on a computer.

Checking the second option, Always Scale Slides to TV Safe Area, scales each image in a slideshow to leave room around the edges of the screen. This ensures that extreme edges of your images will not be cut off when played on some older television screens. When slides are scaled to fit the TV safe area, a black border appears around each image. You'll learn how to create slideshows in Chapter 31.

FIGURE 30.18
Slideshow options
allow you to auto-
matically add
DVD-ROM content.

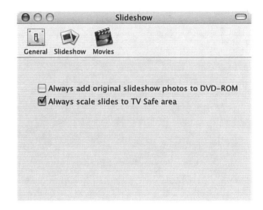

Movies Preferences

Movies preferences, shown in Figure 30.19, allow you to choose whether available chapter markers are recognized by iDVD when a movie is imported. (Recall from Chapter 29, "Exporting iMovies," that chapter markers can be added in iMovie to allow you to skip to a specific place in a movie clip or movie.) The options are to automatically create chapter markers, never create them, or to ask each time a project is opened.

FIGURE 30.19
Choose how to
cope with chapter
markers and where
to find movie files.

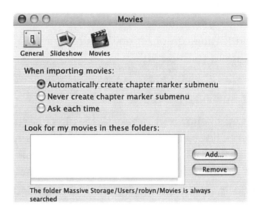

You can also choose where on your system iMovie will search for video clips to list in the Movies pane we talked about earlier in this chapter. (By default, iMovie tries to save files in an account holder's Movies folder, so that's the default place the iDVD will look. If you prefer to save your projects to the desktop, you can tell iDVD to also look on the desktop.)

Summary

In this chapter, you learned about the basic DVD features as well as some background about DVDs in general. You became acquainted with the iDVD interface and the various options it provides for making a variety of DVD projects that can include a combination of movies and digital pictures. You also saw the controls you'll use to customize your DVD menus as well as preview your project and burn it to DVD.

CHAPTER 31

Designing DVDs in iDVD

In this chapter, we'll delve into constructing a DVD—from adding content to customizing the look of the menus. You'll also learn some tips and tricks for getting started with a project. Let's start there—at the beginning!

Preparing the DVD Project

To begin, we start a new project in iDVD, adjust a few settings, and generally get things off the ground. There are no particular rules about what you have to do first, but in general it's a good idea to save your project frequently. As you work on your project, you can get in the habit of choosing File, Save at regular intervals so that you don't lose your work if lightning happens to strike or your Mac freezes up for some reason.

Task: Preparing the DVD Project

To prepare for this project, we get a few things in order to set the stage for importing video into the DVD project:

1. Launch iDVD and create a new project. You will be prompted to name and save your project automatically.

> The name you give your project is the name that will be automatically applied to the DVD disc when you burn your completed project. However, you can change the original project name to a different one by choosing Project, Project Info from the menu at the top of your screen. Then, in the window that opens, simply type a new Disc Name and click OK.

By the Way

2. Choose iDVD, Preferences to bring up the Preferences dialog box (see Figure 31.1).

3. In the Preferences dialog box, click to uncheck the Show Apple Logo Watermark option. This removes the Apple logo from the lower-right corner of the DVD production. Of course, you can leave it in if you want.

FIGURE 31.1
The iDVD
Preferences dia-
log box.

4. In the main iDVD window, click the Customize button in the lower-left corner, click the Themes tab if necessary, and click to select a theme (see Figure
31.2). (Using the pop-up menu in the Themes tab, you can choose to view
Old Themes, New Themes, or All. You can also view a subset of Themes
you've customized and saved as Favorites.)

5. To customize the title in your theme, click the text so that it's selected (as
shown in Figure 31.3), and you can start typing.

FIGURE 31.2
You can use the
iDVD Themes menu
to select a back-
ground for your
iDVD project. In our
example, we use
the Theater theme.

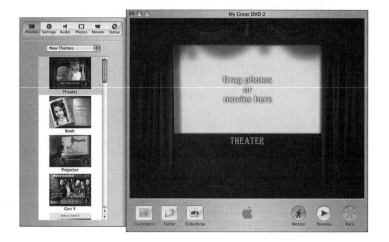

FIGURE 31.3
The placeholder text "Theater" can be replaced with your own text.

Importing Files

You learned in Chapter 29, "Exporting iMovies," that you can create an iDVD project directly from iMovie if you want. That would open your iMovie directly into iDVD, including any chapter markers you've added to make it easier for viewers to skip to specific scenes.

If you wanted to add clips rather than your entire iMovie, there are three methods for importing video:

1. Select File, Import, Video.

2. Open the Movies tab in the Customize tray window.

3. Drag the file directly into the DVD from a Finder window.

> Remember that video clips imported with iMovie have automatically been encoded in the appropriate format for them to be compatible with iDVD. iDVD supports only QuickTime movies with linear video tracks. Other formats, such as QuickTime VR, MPEG, Flash, streaming or encrypted movies, or QuickTime spanned movies, cannot be added to your iDVD project.
>
> If you try to import a file that is not compatible with iDVD, a message saying "Unsupported File Type" appears.

By the Way

Using the iMedia Browsers

The integration between the applications that make up iLife (iTunes, iPhoto, iMovie, and iDVD) is apparent in iDVD's iMedia browser tabs. *iMedia browsers* is the collective term for the Audio, Photos, and Movies tabs, which link directly to the folders on your hard drive that contain your iTunes library, your iPhoto library, and the default location for storing iMovie projects. These tabs give you direct access to these elements so that you can incorporate them into your DVD projects.

For these sections to function, however, you need to make sure that you are using compatible versions of each of the i-applications. See Chapter 21, "Introducing iLife," for more information.

To use the Audio and Photos browser tabs, you also need to have opened iTunes and iPhoto at least once after they've been updated to compatible versions so that your media libraries can be cataloged in a format that iDVD understands.

By the Way

Although iPhoto and iTunes make it more difficult to move the location of your media, iMovie lets you store your movie files anywhere you want. To solve the problem of the Movies browser not knowing where to locate your movie files, you can add paths to them in the Movies section of the iDVD preferences.

Task: Importing Video Files

When you choose a theme for your DVD in iDVD, the DVD buttons consist of either small images or text buttons that represent the video you've imported.

1. Open the folder containing your video clips and drag one directly from the Finder into the iDVD window (see Figure 31.4).

2. Continue dragging the clips into the project, until you end up with something like Figure 31.5.

3. At this point, you could click the Preview button in the main iDVD window to preview the project, which is always a good way of seeing whether things turned out the way you wanted them to.

As you add files to your project, it's wise to keep an eye on the size of your files. (DVDs hold a lot of information, but video takes up a lot of space!) You can monitor the size of your project in the Status tab, as shown in Figure 31.6.

Remember, you may need to click the Customize button to get to the Status tab.

FIGURE 31.4
You can drag QuickTime movies (at the left) directly into the iDVD window, and the filename becomes the DVD button name.

FIGURE 31.5
iDVD automatically creates titles from the filenames of the imported QuickTime movies.

FIGURE 31.6
Encoder status:
iDVD encodes your
video clips while
you work on your
project.

Customizing DVD Menus

In general, DVD menus consist of a background and a series of buttons that lead to other parts of the DVD—such as video clips, which you just learned to add. In iDVD, the first thing you do is choose your background from the list of available themes.

By the Way

As you learned earlier from importing video, every element you import appears on the menu as either a button or text label. How they appear depends on the theme you've selected.

Throughout this section, we take a look at some individual tasks that you end up doing as you work on your DVD menus.

Themes

iDVD makes it easy to choose a background theme for your DVD project. You could simply scroll through the list of options in the Themes tab.

There are three basic categories of themes:

▶ *Static background* themes display a regular, nonvideo image. An example is Chalkboard.

▶ *Motion* themes display short video repeats. An example is Global.

▶ *Drop Zone* themes include areas where you can add your own slideshows, movies, or still images. An example of a Drop Zone theme is Theater, which you saw earlier, where the stage curtain opens and closes over a space in which you can add your own scene.

Different types of themes suit different purposes, but switching between them isn't difficult. You can always click on a different theme when you're working on your project—iDVD enables you to play and experiment as much as you want. All the elements in your DVD and the titles you've given them will carry over between themes.

<table>
<tr><td>Notice that some of the themes include music. We'll talk about setting background audio later in this chapter.</td><td>**By the Way**</td></tr>
</table>

Task: Choosing a Theme

After you've started a new project:

1. Click the Customize button in the lower-left corner of the main iDVD window to display the Themes list. If the Themes list doesn't appear, you might need to click the Themes tab.

2. Click a desired theme in the Themes list, and it automatically displays a theme in the main iDVD window.

<table>
<tr><td>If you choose a theme that has background sound or motion (indicated by a small circular walking man symbol) or displays previews of the project clips as video buttons, you might want to temporarily disable the sound or motion if it becomes distracting or seems to slow your computer's reaction time.

You can do so by clicking the Motion button, displaying an icon of a walking person, at the bottom of the main iDVD window.</td><td>**By the Way**</td></tr>
</table>

Working with Drop Zones

Earlier, you learned that some themes include Drop Zones, or areas that you can customize by adding slideshows, movies, and still images. To add a movie or image to themes containing a Drop Zone, select the media file and drag it on top of the Drop Zone, as shown in Figure 31.7.

FIGURE 31.7
The borders of the Drop Zone change when you drag a file on top of it.

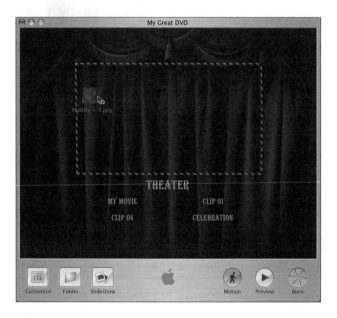

> If you are using a Drop Zone theme and you want to add a movie as content to your project, drag it to an area of the screen that is not a Drop Zone. It becomes a text button. If you want, you can change it to a picture button in the Settings pane of the Customize window. We'll talk more about customizing buttons shortly.

By the Way

When your file is added, it fits inside the Drop Zone, as shown in Figure 31.8.

The aspect ratio of the image you insert will be preserved, with the image scaled to fit against either the top and bottom or left and right edges of the region. If the best part of the image doesn't fall in the center of the space, you can reposition it to choose which portion of the image is visible in the Drop Zone.

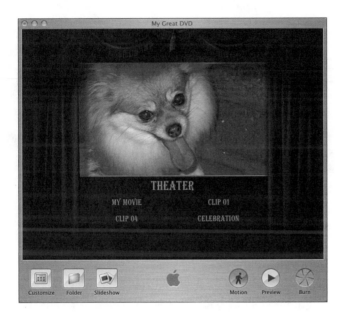

FIGURE 31.8
The Drop Zone now displays the file you added.

When you drag a movie to a Drop Zone in a DVD menu, the movie you added plays over and over again when the menu is onscreen. You can set the duration of the movies using the Motion Duration slider in the Settings pane of the Customize tray window. You can choose the number of seconds you want the movies to loop, up to 30 seconds.

By the Way

To remove files from the Drop Zone, drag the image out of the Drop Zone and out of the iDVD window. Be sure that you are dragging it outside the window, or else you will only move the image, not delete it!

Customizing Titles

The Title area of the Settings tab enables you to change various settings to customize the title text that appears on your DVD screens. iDVD automatically chooses a certain size for title text when you make your DVD, and the size is usually a good match for many DVD projects—large enough to read on the TV, but small enough so that you can type a reasonable number of letters. You'll probably want to change text at some point; the following list corresponds to the options in the Title section of the Settings Tab, shown in Figure 31.9.

FIGURE 31.9
Options for changing the Title text in iDVD.

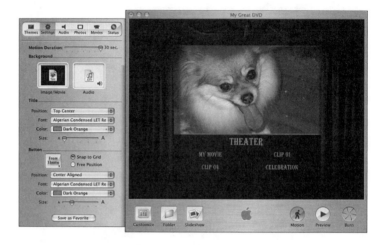

You can customize your title using the following settings:

▶ Position—Enables you to choose a preset position or Free Position

▶ Font—Enables you to choose a different style of text

▶ Color—Enables you to choose a color for your title text

▶ Size—Enables you to make the text bigger or smaller

DVD Buttons—Video and Text

In iDVD, you can have two different kinds of buttons, depending on the theme that you choose. In some themes, there are text buttons, which contain only letters (refer to Figure 31.8).

The process of making a text button is as simple as choosing a theme that supports text buttons, choosing a clip, and adding a video clip. The text button is automatically named according to the filename of the clip that's imported, but you can always click on the text in the button to change it if you want.

In other themes there are video buttons, which include letters and a preview of the video clip or slideshow you're linking to (see Figure 31.10).

Making a video button is as easy as making a text button. In fact, a video button is basically a text button that also includes video, except you must choose a theme that supports video buttons.

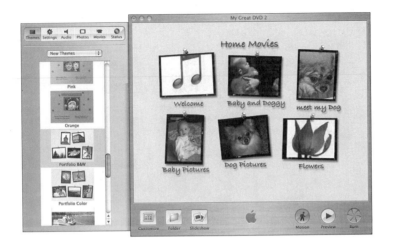

FIGURE 31.10
A video button with
a preview of the
clip.

Task: Adjusting a Video Button

iDVD gives you a number of ways to make simple adjustments to a video button right in the main iDVD window. The automatic setting is for the button to start playing the movie from the beginning, but you can change where the video displayed on the button starts or simply have a picture appear instead of the video.

1. Click a video button to get the adjustment controls, as shown in Figure 31.11.

2. Click the slider and drag it to the desired position within the mini-movie to change where the mini-movie starts.

3. If you don't want the video button to be in motion, uncheck the Movie option and use the slider to choose the nonmoving image from the mini-movie.

4. When you're finished adjusting, click on the video button again, and you'll see the customized video button.

When working with video buttons, remember that they are in motion as you're working on them only if you have motion in iDVD turned on. If the Motion button at the bottom of the main iDVD window is green, motion is activated. Similarly, unless you specifically uncheck the Movie option as described earlier, your video buttons will move.

By the Way

FIGURE 31.11
Clicking a video
button gives you
the button controls.

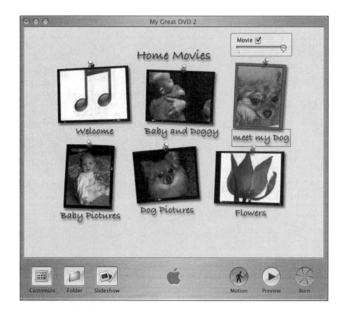

Customizing Buttons

The Button area of the Settings tab gives you the ability to choose from a variety of different options to add a nice touch to the way buttons look in your DVD project. It also enables you to adjust things if the automatic settings don't suit your taste. Refer to Figure 31.9.

The adjustments you can make include the following:

▶ From Theme—Enables you to choose a different button shape and enables you to choose between text-only and video buttons.

▶ Snap to Grid/Free Position—Determines whether buttons on the screen start out being automatically aligned to each other (Snap to Grid) or not aligned (Free Position).

By the Way

If you choose to use Free Position for your buttons, be careful not to position them in ways that your viewers will find difficult to use! You may even want to turn on the TV Safe Area feature under the Advanced menu. This puts a border around the region of your menu that is most likely to be visible across different models of televisions. (In case you are wondering, the preset button positions used with Snap to Grid already fall safely inside the TV Safe Area.)

- ▶ Position—Affects the position of the Button text in relation to the button.

- ▶ Font—Affects the style of text.

- ▶ Color—The same colors are available here that were available in the Title area mentioned previously.

- ▶ Size—Affects the size of the button text.

Adding Submenus

Earlier you learned that iDVD allows you to add up to six menu items per screen. But sooner or later, you'll probably want to add more than six items to your DVD. To do this, you'll need to add additional screens, or submenus, to your DVD project. Each submenu can contain an additional six items, up until you hit the limit of 99 movies or slideshows or 30 motion menus.

iDVD represents submenus with the metaphor of folders. Think of DVD folders just like you have folders on your hard drive. You can put multiple items in a folder, and to get to the contents, you click on the folder. Similarly, in iDVD, the folder provides the audience a way to get to another screen.

When you add a DVD folder, you always add the first folder to the main menu, and then you can add additional folders to the main menu or within other folders.

> As you learned in Chapter 29, chapter markers can be set in iMovie for export to iDVD. When you import a movie with chapter markers, iDVD creates a button with the title of the movie, so the viewer can play the entire movie, and a Scene Selection button that links to a scene submenu, so the viewer can select which scenes to watch and in what order. If you want, however, you can set your iDVD preferences so that scene submenus are never created or so that iDVD asks what you want on each imported movie.

By the Way

Task: Adding a DVD Folder

You can add a folder to a theme that includes text buttons or video buttons.

> You can change the type of buttons in any theme, so it doesn't matter whether the theme is preset to use text or video buttons.

Did you Know?

Follow these steps to get a sense of how things work:

1. Import a video clip as you learned earlier in this chapter.

2. Click the Folder button in the main iDVD window to add a folder. If you are using a theme that supports video buttons, iDVD adds a button that displays an icon that looks like a folder (see Figure 31.12). (If your theme supports text buttons, your folder is added as a button labeled "My Folder.")

FIGURE 31.12
When added, a new folder appears with a generic icon like the one at lower right.

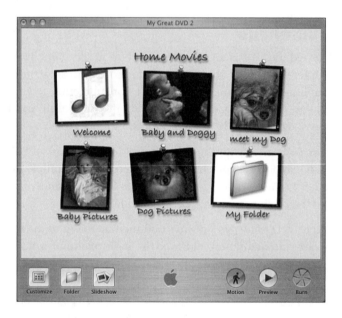

3. Double-click the new folder button in your menu to get to the new folder screen you have just added (see Figure 31.13).

By the Way

One thing that you might not realize is that if you want a different theme on different screens, you aren't limited to using one theme throughout your DVD. In other words, if you use the Portfolio B&W theme on one screen in a DVD, you could choose a different theme (such as Sky) for another screen on the DVD.

4. Drag additional files into the new screen. If you want, customize the buttons using the techniques you learned earlier. Then click on the small arrow in the lower-left corner of your folder screen, as shown in Figure 31.13, to get back to the main screen.

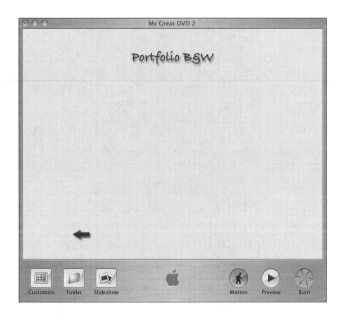

FIGURE 31.13
Double-clicking on
the newly added
button takes you to
the new folder
screen.

5. Single-click on the folder button in the main screen to activate the button
   controls.

6. Drag the slider to the far right side to have the button display the background of the main menu for the folder.

   Use the slider in the button controls to choose which button from your submenu you want to feature. (The changes that you made to the video buttons on your submenu are carried over to this preview.)

When you're finished, you will have a video button on your main menu that
leads to a submenu.

Customizing Menus

Although Drop Zones add a lot of opportunity to make a theme your own, customizing a menu by adding your own overall background or theme music is
something you might want to do.

You can drag elements into two wells in the Background section of the Settings
area in iDVD (see Figure 31.14).

FIGURE 31.14
The Image/Movie
and Audio wells in
the Background
section of iDVD's
Settings tab.

To add a new background image to a DVD project, you must have an image prepared that you want to drag in. It could be something like a digital picture you have taken, an image you have downloaded from the Web, or an image that you've prepared in a program such as Adobe Photoshop Elements (or its professional equivalent, Photoshop). Apple suggests you make sure that your image is sized to 640×480 to fit the screen exactly.

To import a new background image

1. Open a Finder window containing the file that you want to be the new background and position it next to iDVD.

2. Click and drag the file into the Image/Movie well in the Background section.

The new background file becomes the new image you see in your DVD screen (see Figure 31.15).

By the Way

If you like the changes that you've made in customizing your DVD project, you can save this customized theme in the Favorites list of iDVD. Simply click the Save as Favorites button at the bottom of the Settings tab and give your creation a name in the dialog box that appears. When you want to choose your special theme, you can access it in the same Themes list where you normally choose a built-in theme by clicking the pop-up menu and selecting Favorites. The main value of this Favorites option is that it saves you from having to manually adjust things on every screen in a custom DVD project.

FIGURE 31.15
The new background image that was dragged into iDVD.

Task: Adding a Sound to a DVD Menu

If you want to add a sound to your DVD menu, you can drag it into the Audio well in the Background area of the Settings tab.

1. Open your iDVD project. In the main iDVD window, click the Customize button to see the tray window.

2. Click the Settings tab in the drawer.

3. Drag a sound file into the Audio well in the Background section of the Settings tab (see Figure 31.16).

The icon in the Audio well changes to reflect the type of file that you're dragging in. For example, compare the new icon in Figure 31.14 with the icon of the file that's being added in Figure 31.16.

Notice the Motion Duration slider near the top of Figure 31.16. The automatic setting is for 30 seconds, which is the time that the sound/music plays before repeating. This also holds true for the video portion of a motion menu.

FIGURE 31.16
Dragging a sound
file into iDVD. You'll
know where to drop
the file because a
"+" will appear next
to your cursor.

If you decide that you no longer want the sound that you've added to a project,
drag the sound file icon from the audio well to anywhere outside the iDVD window. When no audio file is set as the menu's background, the audio well appears
as in Figure 31.17.

FIGURE 31.17
This menu is not
accompanied by
sound.

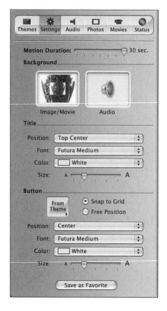

By the Way

If you want to temporarily silence a menu to keep it from playing over and over again as you work, you can click the speaker icon in the lower right of the audio well to mute it. Remember to unmute it before you burn the final version to DVD, or no sound will be heard on the DVD.

DVD Slideshows

In this section, we examine how to work with DVD slideshows in iDVD. DVD slideshows are a nice way to enhance a DVD production; they enable you to add digital pictures to a DVD project that also has video in it. Or, you could make a DVD project that's nothing more than a slideshow.

By the Way

You may recall from Chapter 23, "Using iPhoto," that you can export a slideshow created in iPhoto directly to iDVD—including the slide duration and background music. However, slideshows exported from iPhoto need to be added to the top level of the DVD project, so if you want to add a slideshow to a submenu you may have to create the slideshow in iDVD. (But don't worry—that's not difficult!)

Using iDVD to create a slideshow is as simple as using other parts of the program; it's a simple matter of dragging your files directly into the iDVD window. After adding your pictures to the slideshow in your DVD project, you can make a number of adjustments if you want.

Task: Creating a Slideshow

Before you can create a slideshow, you must open a new iDVD project or reopen a DVD project that you've been working on that you want to add a slideshow to.

1. Open your DVD project.

2. Click the Slideshow button at the bottom of the main iDVD window to create a slideshow.

By the Way

To customize the name of your slideshow, click the My Slideshow label. (We'll discuss how to customize the thumbnail image of the button and change it from the image of slides that appears a bit later.)

3. To get into the slideshow editing window, double-click on the My Slideshow button that appears on your main DVD screen.

When you double-click the My Slideshow icon, the slideshow editing window opens. From there, you can add slides and make adjustments to your slideshow (see Figure 31.18).

FIGURE 31.18
The slideshow edit-
ing window.

Task: Adding Slides

Adding slides to an iDVD slideshow is as easy as dragging and dropping the files into the iDVD window. You can drag files in from the desktop, or you can drag images from your iPhoto library from the Photos tab. (Remember, to open the Photos tab, you need to click the Customize button at the bottom of the iDVD main window.) You can also use the File, Import, Image option.

For iPhoto and iDVD to integrate, you'll need to be using iPhoto version 2 or later. Also, you must have opened that version of iPhoto at least once for your photo library to be encoded in a format that iDVD can work with.

1. Open your iDVD project and click on the Slideshow button in the main iDVD window to reveal the Slideshow editing window shown previously in Figure 31.18.

2. If you are importing photos from your iPhoto library, open the iPhoto tab. If you are importing photos from somewhere else on your hard drive, position a Finder window with the picture files you want to import to the left of the iDVD window.

3. Click on one of the desired image files and, while holding down the mouse button, drag the file into the slideshow editing window (see Figure 31.19).

You can also drag multiple files at once into the slideshow editing window. To accomplish this, place the mouse pointer near one of the file icons, click and hold down the mouse button, and drag upward and over all the icons you want to select. Then click directly on one of the selected icons, and you can drag them all over at once.

FIGURE 31.19
Importing or dragging Slideshow picture files into iDVD.

The slides appear and can be repositioned and adjusted according to your taste, as you'll see later in chapter.

Slideshow Options

The slideshow editing window has a variety of options that you can use to adjust both the order of slides and how the slides behave.

Display Arrows During Slideshow

The Display Arrows During Slideshow option causes arrows to be displayed on your slideshow screens, as shown in Figure 31.20, that are a reminder that there are previous or remaining slides.

Adding Picture Files to DVD-ROM

When you add a slideshow to your DVD project, the images are encoded as part of the DVD. If someone wanted to work with one of the images as a file to print or send in an email, she wouldn't be able to do this. However, the Add to DVD-ROM option enables you to add the individual slides to your DVD as graphics files—a nice option for enabling people to watch the slideshow on television, as well as being able to put the DVD in their computer to have the pictures files available.

When you burn your final DVD with this option checked, the slides in your slideshow are converted into a series of individual files. They're saved on the DVD disc along with the normal DVD project and are accessible by any computer with a DVD-ROM drive. We'll talk more about DVD-ROM content in Chapter 32, "Creating DVDs with iDVD."

Setting Slide Duration

The Slide Duration option enables you to set the time that a slide displays on a screen (see Figure 31.21).

The Manual setting basically means that the user presses the right or left arrow on her DVD remote control to advance to the next slide or go back to a previous slide. But if you want a slideshow to run on its own, you can adjust the duration. To adjust the duration of a slide, simply click the Slide Duration pop-up menu and choose a duration.

FIGURE 31.21
The Slide Duration pop-up menu controls how long a slide appears.

Thumbnail Size

The Thumbnail option determines the size that the mini-preview of each slide appears in the slideshow editing window in iDVD.

There are two options for thumbnail size. The Large setting works better to see a preview of the individual slides, whereas the Small setting works better when you need to see more slides in the window at a time, such as when you're adjusting the order of slides.

> The Thumbnail setting affects only the slideshow editing window that you see while you are working in iDVD. It has nothing to do with the slideshow on the finished DVD.

By the Way

Audio

The Audio option enables you to add a sound file to a slideshow. It works the same as adding audio to a menu as discussed earlier in the chapter. You simply drag a file into the well. To delete, drag the audio file from the Audio well out of the iDVD window.

> Under Slide Duration, the Fit to Audio option is available only after you've added background music to your slideshow, as we will discuss shortly. Also, after you've added an Audio file, the default setting becomes Fit to Audio, and the Manual option is no longer available.

Working with Slides

One of the most common tasks you'll undertake when working with slideshows is rearranging slides so that they appear in a different order. It's really easy to do this and can be fun to play around with as you develop your slideshow. Remember, at any time, you can click on the Preview button at the bottom of the iDVD window to preview your slideshow. Just remember that to get back out of the preview mode, you have to either close the miniature remote control by clicking Enter or click the Preview button to return to editing mode.

Task: Rearranging Slides

Rearranging slides is as simple as clicking and dragging:

1. Click on a slide, and while holding down the mouse button, begin to move the slide toward the position you want it to be in (see Figure 31.22). As you move the slide, its new position is outlined in black.

2. Put your slide into position and let go of the mouse button.

The slide snaps into position, and you can continue to make adjustments to your slideshow or add new slides.

Task: Changing the Slideshow Icon Image

One nice thing about the way that iDVD enables you to customize DVD menus is apparent when you're working with slideshows in a theme that supports video buttons. After you've added slides to your slideshow, the image on the button that leads to your slideshow can be changed to display one of the slides.

1. After adding slides to your slideshow, come back to the menu containing the button that leads to your slideshow and click it once (see Figure 31.23).

FIGURE 31.22
Moving the first slide to a new position in the slideshow editing window.

FIGURE 31.23
Clicking on the button that leads to a slideshow gives you a slider that enables you to choose pictures.

To come back to the menu that leads to your slideshow, click the button labeled Return, which displays a bent arrow, at the lower right of the slideshow editing window.

2. Move the slider to choose the picture you want to appear on the DVD button (see Figure 31.24).

FIGURE 31.24
No more boring generic icons: The DVD button for the slideshow with a new image in place. Great!

3. Click somewhere on the menu screen outside the button you have selected to deselect it.

Remember, iDVD also allows you to customize buttons representing folders, or submenus, in a similar way.

DVD-ROM Content—Including Computer Files on a DVD

DVD is a flexible medium for creating and sharing interactive presentations, but the possibilities aren't limited to what you can view on a television. Thanks to the nature of the DVD disc, you can also include files on a DVD that people can access using their computers. This feature is known as DVD-ROM.

DVD-ROM is essentially the equivalent of CD-ROM. ROM stands for *read-only memory*, which means that you can put data on the disc that can be read by a person with the appropriate drive in his computer. The most typical use for CD-ROM is the discs you use to install software on your computer. Software manufacturers haven't completely switched over to DVD-ROM discs yet, but DVD-ROM drives are becoming much more common in computers, so it's just a matter of time before DVD-ROM drives and discs become as popular as CD-ROMs.

> Software that currently comes on several CDs could fit on a single DVD. If you installed iLife to run iDVD, that software is delivered on a DVD-ROM.

By the Way

With Hollywood DVDs, the typical use of the DVD-ROM possibilities of DVD is WebDVD, which is sometimes referred to as *Web-connected DVD*. For example, you might have inserted a rented or purchased DVD in your computer and looked at special features of the DVD available only when looking at the disc through the computer. This could include things such as the opportunity to look at the screenplay of the movie, or games and other programs that aren't possible to view on a DVD player (see Figure 31.25).

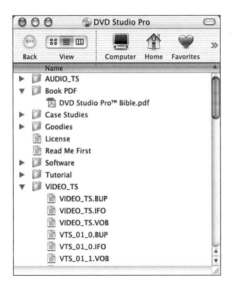

FIGURE 31.25
Example of DVD-ROM content, from the DVD that comes with the Macworld DVD Studio Pro Bible. The disc features the VIDEO_TS folder that contains the standard encoded video for a DVD player, as well as the DVD-ROM content, a series of folders including tutorial files, a PDF version of the book, and so on.

The great thing about DVD is that you can put your video on the DVD and someone can view it on his DVD player connected to a television, but you can also put data files that he can access on his computer. It could be that you want to include Web links, documentation, pictures, or any other kind of computer file.

For example, when you make your DVD, you start by creating an iMovie. Then, in iDVD, you can also use the slideshow feature to add pictures that can be viewed on the television. But let's say that you want to pass a number of digital pictures along as files so that your colleagues can use the pictures on their Web pages. You might ask yourself, "Do I have to burn them on a CD?" With the DVD-ROM feature in iDVD, you can put the pictures right on the disc.

Or, let's say that you have a number of stories or a screenplay that you've written in a word processing program such as AppleWorks or Microsoft Word. Now, if you want, you could include the files on the DVD disc. So, you could make a DVD with the video that can be watched on the television, and if the recipient wants to, she could put the DVD in her computer and look at the original screenplay by opening the file as she would with any other kind of disc she inserts in her computer.

DVD-ROM content isn't anything that you have to do—it's just a great thing to have the flexibility to add computer files to your DVD.

- ▶ Consideration Number One—Does the person have a DVD-ROM drive? Many computers these days have DVD-ROM drives, but not all of them. If the person you want to share files with doesn't have a DVD-ROM drive, you might be better off using your SuperDrive to burn that person a CD.

By the Way

The purpose of the DVD-ROM feature in iDVD is to add extra material to video DVDs. It isn't recommended as a way to back up your data files. Instead, use the Burn Disc option available in the Finder's File menu to burn a data DVD.

- ▶ Consideration Number Two—Is the person on Mac or Windows? If you're burning files to a DVD and you want a person on Windows to be able to use them, be sure to include the appropriate file extensions on your files.

Did you Know?

Microsoft Windows relies on the file extension in order to recognize which application is needed to open a file. For example, JPEG files need a .jpg at the end for a Windows machine to launch a program capable of displaying JPEGs. These days many Mac programs automatically put on a file extension, but you'll want to be sure to use them if sending your DVD to Windows users.

Task: Adding Computer Files to a DVD

You can easily add computer files to your DVD using iDVD.

1. Launch iDVD and open your project (see Figure 31.26).

2. Click the Customize button in the lower-left corner of the iDVD window.

3. Click the Status tab, which initially gives you a running report of how any background encoding is progressing. (This is the automatic encoding of video that's being done while you're working on your project—see Figure 31.27).

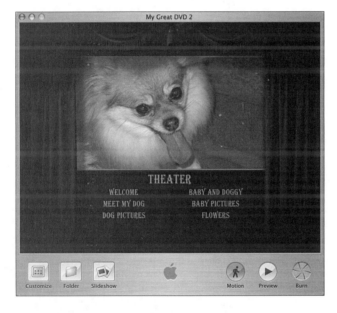

FIGURE 31.26
The main iDVD window.

4. Click the Status pop-up menu and switch from Encoder Status to DVD-ROM Contents as shown in Figure 31.28.

5. Drag files and folders into the DVD-ROM Contents area. In Figure 31.29, a number of digital pictures and a QuickTime movie have been added. iDVD also may add a file called .DS_Store, which you can ignore.

As you drag large media files in as DVD-ROM content, remember to keep an eye on the size of your project. (Conveniently, this information appears at the top of the Status tab.)

Watch Out!

FIGURE 31.27
The Status tab of
the tray in iDVD.

FIGURE 31.28
Add DVD-ROM
files—and view
what's been
added—in the
DVD-ROM Contents
window.

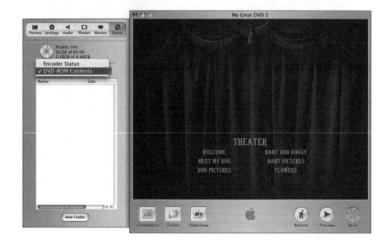

By the Way

Technically speaking, the .DS Store file is created by the Finder. Per Apple: "Each directory in the filesystem can contain a hidden object, '.DS_Store' containing data which includes a list of files stored there. This object is created when a local user views a given directory using the Finder." The .DS_Store file isn't necessary for burning.

iDVD doesn't move the files you add as DVD-ROM content, or make duplicates of them. Instead, it creates a reference to the file on your system. If you delete a file or move a file after you've added it to the DVD-ROM list, its name appears in red to tell you something's wrong. If you try to burn the disc anyway, a "File not found" error message appears.

Watch Out!

To delete a file from the DVD-ROM Contents list, select it and press Delete.

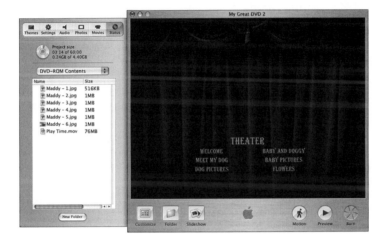

FIGURE 31.29
Dragging files from the hard drive into the DVD-ROM Contents area in iDVD adds them to the disc.

Summary

In this chapter, you learned how to design a DVD, including adding content and creating and customizing menus. We examined how DVD menus are put together, using a combination of backgrounds and buttons (and don't forget the movie clips, slideshows, and computer files!). As you've seen, your projects can look just fine without adjusting any additional settings, but if you want to, there are ways to customize the way the DVD works and looks.

CHAPTER 32

Creating DVDs with iDVD

The ultimate outcome of most iDVD projects is, obviously, a DVD that you can play on your computer or your home theater system. This chapter walks you through the final steps needed to "burn" your project onto a DVD, such as previewing the contents so that you can catch any mistakes before they are permanently written to a DVD. We'll also talk about options for having your DVDs professionally manufactured. But first, let's start by taking a closer look at DVD discs themselves and various types of DVD discs, including the kind that you use with iDVD and the built-in SuperDrive.

DVD Discs

There are many DVD formats and options out there, and the new variety of recordable disc formats could lead to some confusion when you're at a store trying to figure out which kind of blank disc to purchase. This potentially frustrating situation with DVD formats has been brought about by competition among the makers of DVD players who are pitting DVD-R against DVD+RW and so on. But a simple review of what DVD discs are, and what kinds are compatible with your Mac, will prepare you to avoid the confusion and get on with having fun.

Recordable DVDs

Recordable DVDs (DVD-R) enable you to write data a single time to a disc. They're much like the CD-R discs that are so popular these days. Much like the phenomena of dropping prices with CD burners and recordable CDs, the price of making your own DVDs will continue to drop.

The kind of recordable DVDs that you can use with the built-in SuperDrive on your Mac are known as *DVD-R media*, which technically speaking, is called DVD-R General media. In most cases, when people refer to recordable discs, they don't specify DVD-R General media—they drop the word "general" (see Figure 32.1).

DVD-R compatibility is an important factor to take into account when you're considering distribution of a DVD project on DVD-R media. Theoretically, if you make a

DVD project and burn a DVD-R disc, that DVD-R disc should play in the majority of DVD players. The newer the player is, the more likely it is to be compatible with DVD-R media. And, vice versa, the older a player is, the less likely it is to accept DVD-R media.

FIGURE 32.1
Apple's DVD-R media, blank and ready to go.

Compatibility lists are available online at a variety of sources, including www.apple.com/_dvd/compatibility/, where companies and individuals have tested DVD-R media with a wide range of players. The questions to ask are what kind of project are you going to share? and what kind of audience is it?

Rewritable DVDs

The development of the SuperDrive was a joint effort between Apple and Pioneer, and in addition to recording to CD-Rs, CD-RWs, and DVD-Rs, the mechanism used in the SuperDrive has the capability to record to DVD-RW discs (see Figure 32.2).

You can record to a DVD-R disc only once. At the time of writing, the best price you can get for DVD-R media is $3.00 (U.S.) each, so blank DVDs are still fairly pricey. So, if you're just testing your project, and essentially use the DVD-R disc only once, you're out a few bucks.

FIGURE 32.2
Pioneer's DVD-RW
discs, compatible
with the
SuperDrive.

> At the time of writing, $3.00 U.S. is a common price that can be found when doing a price search on a Web site such as cnet.com.

By the Way

This makes the idea of using a DVD-RW disc even more appealing. It's a great way to back up video files and to move DVD-related files from one place to another. DVD-RW discs are twice as expensive, but you can use them over and over again.

> Apple doesn't emphasize the fact that the SuperDrive can burn DVD-RW discs, and perhaps for good reason. DVD-RW discs are compatible with only about 70% of DVD players out there, compared with DVD-R discs, which are compatible with closer to 90%.

Watch Out!

DVD Storage Capacity

Unless you plan to include computer files on your DVD, as discussed in Chapter 31, "Designing DVDs in iDVD," the best way to think of DVD storage capacity with iDVD is in terms of how many minutes of video you can fit on the disc. The amount of video you can fit on a disc is determined by how much the video is compressed. Because iDVD does the encoding automatically, the limit is about 90 minutes of video on the disc.

If you're talking about the disc in terms of bytes and megabytes, however, you might be familiar with the often-quoted measurement of 4.7 gigabytes (GB)— that is, the claim that you can store up to 4.7 gigabytes of data on a single-layer DVD disc.

This is only partially true. If you were putting data files on a DVD and had 4.7 gigabytes' worth of files on your computer, you'd find that you can fit only about 4.37GB on the DVD—this has to do with the difference between the way data is stored on a computer hard drive and the way it's stored on a DVD. Essentially, you can store 4.7 billion bytes of data on a DVD, but only about 4.37GB.

Regardless of how you look at it, DVD is an incredible medium. The CD format typically allows only 650MB of data on a disc, whereas the DVD format enables you to put up to 4,370MB on a disc! To put this in perspective, consider that many computers you see on the shelves in stores are likely to have 3.5-inch floppy disk drives. Each of these plastic floppies holds about 1MB of data, so a DVD disc holds the equivalent of about 4,370 floppy disks see Figure 32.3).

FIGURE 32.3
The relative capacities of different storage methods.

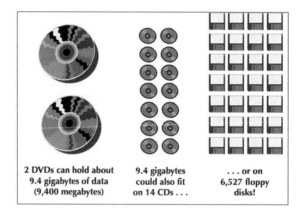

2 DVDs can hold about 9.4 gigabytes of data (9,400 megabytes)   9.4 gigabytes could also fit on 14 CDs . . .   . . . or on 6,527 floppy disks!

Purchasing the Right Blank DVD Discs

The easiest thing to do when you need to purchase blank discs is to get them directly from Apple, which ensures compatibility and has always had good pricing.

But if you want to get blank DVDS on your own, make sure that you're purchasing DVD-R General media. If the product packaging or salesperson says that the disc is DVD-R, but there's no indication of whether it's General, chances are that you're fine. You'll occasionally come across DVD-R Authoring media, which won't work in the SuperDrive.

Another thing to look out for if you're shopping for blank discs is that you're purchasing DVD-R (minus R) media and not DVD+R (plus R) or DVD+RW (plus RW) discs. The plus discs are designed for other kinds of DVD burners.

To get a better sense of things, glance through Table 32.1, which gives a good indication of the situation consumers face as a result of the Format Wars. (It's sort of like the VHS versus Betamax competition when VCRs first came out. But, in a nutshell, DVD-R is better and more compatible with DVD players, and that's what you have in the Mac, so get DVD-R media.)

TABLE 32.1 DVD Recordable Media

Format	Features	Compatibility with SuperDrive
DVD-R (General)	Can be recorded to once	Yes
DVD-R (Authoring)	Designed for older DVD burners; easy to confuse with DVD-R General media	No
DVD-RW	Can be recorded to many times (up to 1,000 times)	Yes (Note: Projects burned to DVD-RW discs are compatible with only about 70% of DVD players)
DVD+R (plus R)	Similar to DVD-R	No
DVD+RW (plus RW)	Similar to DVD-RW	No

Burning Your DVD

Burning a DVD is really as simple as clicking a button and waiting for your masterpiece to be created. There are, however, several steps you should take to be sure that the DVD really is ready to go: Previewing the contents, preparing your computer, and, finally, burning the DVD. We'll cover these steps in detail now.

Task: Previewing Your Project

Before you burn your finished DVD to disc, you should preview it to make sure that everything is exactly as you want it. Although it's tempting to skip this step when your project is so close to being completed, you will have to burn the project all over again, and end up waiting twice as long to view it, if you made any mistakes.

1. To preview your project, click the Preview button.

2. In the remote control that appears on your screen, click the arrow buttons to select a menu button, as shown in Figure 32.4. When you press Enter, the content linked to the selected button plays.

3. Repeat step 2 until you've tried all the elements in your project, even those in submenus, to make sure that you finished all the portions of your project.

FIGURE 32.4
In Preview mode,
iDVD displays a
remote control so
that you can navi-
gate through the
menus of your
project.

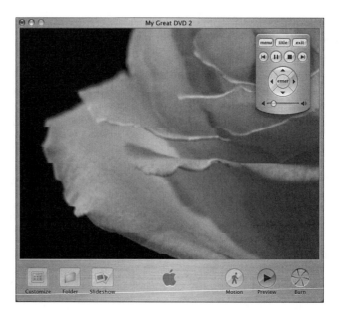

FIGURE 32.4
In Preview mode, iDVD displays a remote control so that you can navigate through the menus of your project.

4. When you have tested everything, click the Preview button or click the Exit button on the remote control to return to edit mode.

By the Way

While previewing your project, make sure that you have motion activated so that you can see any motion effects in the menus or menu buttons. You'll know motion is activated if the Motion button is green.

Preparing Your Computer

After you've tested your DVD project and are certain everything is as you want it in the final version, you're almost ready to burn your project to DVD disc. Before you do so, however, there are a couple of things you need to do to make the process go smoothly.

First, you should quit out of any other applications you have running, such as iMovie or an email program. Burning DVDs is a resource-intensive process, and it's best to let your computer focus all its processing power on iDVD.

Next, make sure that your Mac doesn't go to sleep in the middle of burning. (This doesn't seem to affect all Macs, but it's better to be safe than to waste a DVD-R.) To do this, go to the Apple menu at the upper left, and open the System

Preferences panel. Choose Energy Saver from the Hardware section, and set the slider that controls the length of inactivity before the computer sleeps to Never (see Figure 32.5).

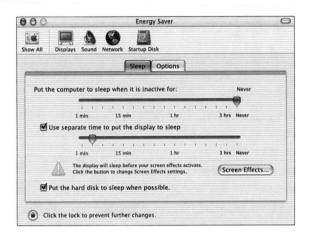

FIGURE 32.5
Open the Energy Saver pane of the System Preferences to ensure that your computer doesn't sleep during disc burning.

Task: Burning Your DVD

After you've tested your project and prepared your computer, burning the actual disc is simple. Just make sure that you don't want to add anything else to your project. Remember, after you burn a DVD-R it can't be reused.

> As you learned earlier in this chapter, there are many kinds of DVD media. Make sure that you are using 2.0 General DVD-R discs. Also, some brands of discs—even the right kind—don't seem to work in iDVD. For that reason, it's best to test a single disc before buying DVDs in bulk from one manufacturer.

By the Way

1. Click the Burn button. When clicked, the gray button retracts to reveal a pulsing button in its place.

2. Click the pulsing button to confirm that you are ready to burn your project to DVD.

> If you have forgotten to turn on motion, iDVD asks whether you want to burn a DVD without motion menus. You can click Cancel to back out of the burning process you've initiated and turn on motion, or you can click Proceed to burn your disc with motion disabled.

By the Way

3. You are prompted to insert a blank DVD-R disc into the drive, as shown in Figure 32.6.

FIGURE 32.6
iDVD prompts you to insert a blank disc.

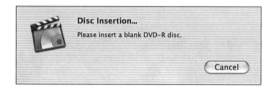

4. Insert your disc and wait for iDVD to do its thing.

Watch Out!

> Be careful not to press the Eject key while burning is in progress. This may interrupt burning and result in an unusable disc.

It takes a while for your computer to create the disc. Exactly how much time depends on your computer's processor and how much content is on the disc. Generally, it takes two to three times the length of the video on the disc for that video to be encoded and written.

Task: Testing Your DVD

After your DVD is written, there's one step yet remaining—make sure that the disc works! To find out whether the disc has been created correctly, the best option is to try it in the computer that wrote it. If the DVD works in your computer, chances are good that it will play in most newer DVD players and DVD-drive equipped computers. (See www.apple.com/dvd/compatibility/ for a list of compatible players.)

1. To test your DVD, insert it into your computer's drive.

2. The DVD Player application should open automatically with your DVD main menu visible.

3. Using the remote control that appears on your screen, click the arrows to select a button and click Enter to watch that segment of your DVD.

Manufactured DVDs

The only way to guarantee 100% compatibility with all DVD players is to manufacture a DVD. This means sending the project off to be manufactured by automated machinery. There are companies such as EMVUSA (www.emvusa.com)

that are aggressively going after the do-it-yourself DVD market by offering attractive pricing and accepting DVD-R media as a master disc. Accepting DVD-R media as a master disc is a break from the tradition of requiring a DVD project to be submitted on a special format known as *DLT*, or *digital linear tape*.

In addition to compatibility, other things you gain are the ability to have more professional packaging and a better-looking disc. When a DVD is manufactured, a design is imprinted directly on the DVD itself instead of a label being applied.

Manufacturing Discs

More and more local video production-type companies are offering the service of duplicating DVDs, which basically means that they can take your DVD and make copies of it, put labels on, and probably even have some options for packaging. This is basically another way of burning your own DVDs; it's just that someone else is burning them, onto the same discs you would, and is probably saving you a lot of time.

As there is still less than 100% compatibility for discs burned in iDVD, the only real way to ensure that your project will play in all players is to send it off to be manufactured. Fortunately, DVD manufacturers increasingly accept DVD-R discs as masters, and if you have the need, you can use a DVD you burned on your Mac and have small or large quantities reproduced.

Task: Having a DVD Commercially Manufactured

To get a DVD manufactured

1. Go online and investigate your options, see Figure 32.7. Call a manufacturer or two and ask questions. One to try is EMVUSA, online at www.emvusa.com.

   Be sure to get enough information that you understand what you need to provide to them in terms of files, and so on, and so you can get a sense of the options and prices.

2. As your project is developing, think about the art that will appear on the disc. If you are not a designer, you may want to hire someone to make a nice-looking design. Templates are usually available for download, such as the one shown in Figure 32.8, which is for a small-sized 3-inch DVD that places like EMVUSA are capable of making.

FIGURE 32.7
EMVUSA is an example of a DVD manufacturer that you can visit online and then work with to get a project done.

> **By the Way**
> Three-inch DVDs can play in anything except slot-loading drives found on some iMacs and PowerBooks, and they can hold a little more than 1GB. These small discs are great attention-getters because they aren't that well-known yet.

FIGURE 32.8
An example of a DVD template available for download.

3. After you've sent in your master disc, be patient as your DVD is being put together and prepare for the pleasure of receiving the finished product.

Summary

In this chapter you learned all about DVD discs—essential to the success of every iDVD project. You also learned the steps you should follow when burning a DVD: Previewing the contents, preparing your computer, and burning the DVD. iDVD makes it simple to burn a DVD, and it is often tempting to just click the Burn button as soon you've finished your creation. Unfortunately, this can sometimes lead to DVDs that don't burn properly or aren't exactly what you expected. Following the steps presented here will make sure that your project turns out as close to perfect as possible on the first try. Finally, you learned about having a DVD manufactured for maximum compatibility with DVD players and a more professional appearance.

PART VI

System Administration and Maintenance

CHAPTER 33

Sharing Your Computer with Multiple Users

As you know from previous chapters, Mac OS X is a true multiuser operating system because everyone who works on the computer has a separate, private area in which to store personal files. Although you don't have to use the multiuser capabilities of your Mac, they affect the system's structure, which may require special attention, in terms of both their benefits and problems.

Understanding User Accounts

In a multiuser system, everyone who works on the computer can have a separate account in which to store personal files. In practice, that means when one user saves a document to the desktop, it does not appear on the desktop that the other users see. Also, each person can set system preferences that show up only when he or she is logged in. Users can customize the Dock and the desktop appearance and expect them to remain that way.

> An interesting feature of multiuser operating systems is related to a feature called remote access. Because the operating system assigns a separate desktop to each account, multiple users can use different files on a single computer at the same time. Although this requires connecting to the machine from another computer and enabling remote login, the OS is designed to cope with different simultaneous processes so that users can work as though they were alone on the system.

By the Way

The home folders for user accounts are located in the Users folder of the Mac OS X hard drive, as shown in Figure 33.1. A house icon is used in the Finder window toolbar to represent the current user's home folder. Inside the home folder are several different folders, which were discussed briefly in Chapter 2, "Using the Finder," when we talked about file structure.

FIGURE 33.1
Every user has a home folder in which to store files.

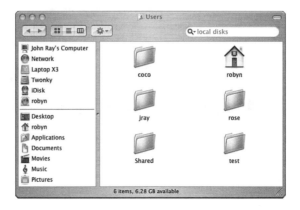

Although individual users can see the contents of most files on the hard drive, they cannot see most of each other's files. That's because users in a multiuser system can set permissions on their files that restrict access to keep their work private. They can specify whether a file can be read or altered by everyone, by a limited number of other people, or only from within the account in which the files were created.

For example, Figure 33.2 shows what the home folder of the user jray looks like to another user. Most of the folders have an icon with a red circle containing a minus sign. That means these folders are not accessible by users who do not own them.

FIGURE 33.2
By default, other users are restricted from accessing all but the Public and Sites folders.

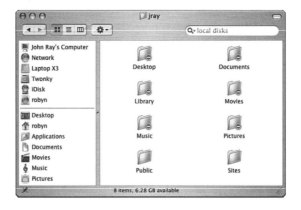

> You can change the permissions on a file or folder that you own under the Ownership & Permissions section of the Info window (Commmand-I). We discuss permissions further later in this chapter.

By the Way

Adding and Editing User Accounts

When you first installed Mac OS X, an account was created using the name you supplied. The system uses the short name you gave as your account name, but you can use either your full or short name to log in to the system at the console. Because this account can access sensitive system settings and install new software, it's referred to as an *administrator account*.

When logged in with an administrator account, you're granted the privilege of adding other users, and you can choose to give them administrative privileges as well. Remember, however, creating additional administrator accounts means that other people can add new accounts and modify the system, so you should do so judiciously. Be sure that you trust your users not to delete important files or disrupt the system in other ways before you give them administrator privileges.

New user accounts are added from the Accounts Preferences pane, shown in Figure 33.3.

FIGURE 33.3
The left side of the Accounts Preferences pane lists current users and enables you to edit them or add new ones.

To create a new user account, follow these steps:

1. Click the "+" button at the lower left of the Accounts pane.

2. Type the name of the person using the account as well as a short name to be displayed for logging in.

> Note that although you can change many things about a user account later, you can't alter the short name used to log in. Choose wisely the first time.

3. Type a password once, and then type it again to verify it. The Password Hint box is for a short description or question to remind the user of the password if it is forgotten.

> If you want separate accounts only to aid organization/file storage, you can leave the password fields blank. This allows people to log in without using any password. However, for computers connected to the network, be sure personal file sharing, windows sharing, and remote login are deactivated in the Sharing pane of the System preferences if you are going to leave your accounts un-password protected. (We'll talk more about these options and other security issues in Chapter 35, "Sharing Files to Windows and Unix Computers.")

4. Click the Picture button near the top of the Accounts pane and choose an icon to represent the new user, as shown in Figure 33.4. (This picture shows up next to the user's name in the login screen, as discussed in a moment, as well as in the user's Address Book and in iChat.)

5. If you want your new user to have administrative powers, as discussed previously, click the Security button and check the Allow User to Administer This Computer box. (We'll talk about further limitations that can be set on nonadministrative users in just a moment.)

As soon as you click out of the Password settings of the Accounts pane, your system recognizes your new user, who has a folder in the Users folder.

Through a similar process, you can edit an existing user account, including changing the name, password, and password hint. Simply select the user account to be edited from the list at the left and click the Password button. You can't change the short name after an account has been created. ' If you want to change the picture associated with a user, click the Picture button and choose a new icon.

FIGURE 33.4
Choose an icon to represent a user.

> To alter the name or password for the currently active administrative account, you must enter your current password to provide authorization. If you have forgotten your password and need to reset it, you will need to use your installation discs.

By the Way

You can also change whether a user is allowed to administer the computer under the Security settings—changes appear the next time the user logs in. (Note that this option is grayed out for the first-created account, which must be an administrator account.)

Setting Limitations

If you want to further control the access of users who aren't allowed to administer the computer, you can click the Limitations button to choose their level of access to the system.

> If you don't see Limitations as an option in the row of buttons near the top of the Accounts pane, you may have selected a user account with administrator privileges, for which you can't set limits. In place of the Limitations button, you'll see Startup Items, which we discussed in Chapter 5, "Setting System Preferences and Universal Access Options."

By the Way

The options are

▶ No Limits—Under this setting, users can interact with the system almost like an administrative user—except that they are unable to create other user accounts, change secure preferences, or install software in system-level folders.

▶ Some Limits—With the Some Limits options (shown in Figure 33.5, you can set whether users can access System Preferences, change passwords, modify the Dock, and burn CDs or DVDs. You can also control which applications are available to them.

FIGURE 33.5
Restrict access to specific system functions or applications.

▶ Simple Finder—If you want to pare down the desktop for a given user, you can enable a setting called Simple Finder, which simplifies system navigation by opening all Finder elements in a single window.

Deleting User Accounts

Now that you know how to add a user, you should learn how to remove a user. This again requires you to open the Accounts Preferences pane. To delete a user account, simply select the account to be deleted and click the "-" button at the lower left. In this way, you can delete any user account except the original administrator account. The sheet window shown in Figure 33.6 appears to confirm your choice. You have the option to Delete Immediately, which doesn't save anything in the user account, or to click OK, which stores the deleted user's files as a disk image (.dmg file) in the Deleted Users folders. (If you choose OK and find later that you don't want the contents of the deleted account, you can open that folder and delete the .dmg file.)

When an account is deleted for the first time, the Deleted Users folder is created. You may choose to retain or delete the .dmg file of the deleted user's account. If you want to remove the entire Deleted Users folder, you can drag it to the trash, but you will need to enter an administrative user's password to authorize the action.

By the Way

Logging In

Now that you know how to create additional accounts, you may be wondering how your users will access them. One aspect of maintaining a multiuser system is keeping track of who can use the computer, which files they have access to, and where their work is stored. These objectives are met by requiring people to sign in before using the machine. This process of identifying yourself to the system, which involves presenting a username and password, is known as a *login*.

If you're logged in on a Mac that's used by other people with their own accounts, it's a good habit to log off when finished. This allows the computer to return to a state that enables others to log in. If someone forgets to log off, that person's account and files could be accessed by anyone because the system does not know that the owning user is no longer at the controls. (This isn't necessarily a serious problem, but it's neater to have everyone's files in their own account.)

By default, Mac OS X sets the system to log in automatically to the account of the first-created user every time the computer starts up. In this mode, your computer won't require you to enter your username and password. If you don't see a need to force a login each time your computer turns on, you can keep this setting.

However, if other people have access to your computer, you might want to create separate accounts for them and require them to log in. Many people dislike the idea of requiring a login to use their computers, but it is a good idea to disable automatic login if your computer has more than one user. Why? Without required logins, your documents and system settings can be modified by whoever uses the machine. Besides, giving each user his own desktop can cut down on clutter, prevent accidental deletion of files, and enable everyone to customize settings.

To change your system so that it requires each user to log in, go to the System section of the System Preferences pane, and click the Accounts button. In the Accounts pane, click the Login Options item at the lower left to view the login preferences, as shown in Figure 33.7. From those options, uncheck the box in front of Automatically Log In As [Username]. We look at the options for customizing the login screen in the next section.

Customizing the Login Window

The screen in which users supply their names and passwords is referred to as the *login screen*. Figure 33.8 shows an example.

Although the login screen looks simple, several of its characteristics can be altered in the Login Options window of the Accounts Preferences pane, which appeared in Figure 33.7. You can indicate what you want the login window to look like: either a list of usernames with an associated picture, as shown in Figure 33.8, or two blank fields for username and password. When a login picture format is used, clicking on a user reveals a space to type the user's password.

You can also choose whether to allow users to access the Shut Down and Restart buttons on the login screen.

FIGURE 33.7
Login options include setting your system to automatically log in when your computer starts.

FIGURE 33.8
Mac OS X gives the option to choose an icon to represent each user.

Fast User Switching

The bottom check box under Login Options (refer to Figure 33.7) enables or disables *fast user switching*, a feature borrowed from Windows XP and useful for families of shared computers. By default, if you've added multiple user accounts to your computer, you have to close your applications and then choose Log out from the Apple menu to allow another user to access the system. In Panther, fast user switching preserves your current desktop but lets another user log in and use her account. Users whose accounts are logged in but not onscreen can then return to where they left off.

With fast user switching enabled, a menu item appears with your name in the upper-right corner of the menu bar—the switching menu. Displaying the menu reveals a list of local user accounts with login enabled along with a Login Window option. Choosing a user's name prompts for that user's login information and then switches to her desktop. Choosing the Login Window selection leaves your applications running but displays the login window—allowing other users to log in without disrupting your workspace.

Did you Know?

If you want to be able to switch to another user account without entering that user's password, the other user *must* have a blank password.

Users accounts that are "active" (have running applications) are denoted with an orange check mark in front of their name in the switching menu and the login screen, as shown in Figure 33.9. Switching to an active account is almost instantaneous.

FIGURE 33.9
Active sessions are denoted by an orange check box in the switching menu and login screen.

Users should log out (Shift-Command-Q) completely when finished using the computer. Shutting down or restarting your computer while there are active sessions could result in lost data for the users who are still logged in. If you try to shut down while other accounts are active, you will need to enter an administrator name and password to authorize it.

File Permissions

In addition to letting you decide who can log in to your computer, Mac OS X enables you to control who can interact with your files. If you create a file while you're logged in to your account, you own that file. Without your password, other users can be prevented from accessing your folders and files in any way; they can neither read nor alter your files and folders unless they are stored in your Sites or Public folders. For example, the folders in the home folder created for each user have some of these restrictions set by default.

Changing privileges in a file or folder is done though the Info panel of the Finder, as discussed in Chapter 4, "Working with Folders, Files, and Applications." These are the steps to use this panel:

1. Highlight the icon of the file or folder whose access you want to change. Users who are administrators can change the permissions on almost any file, but those who are normal users can change the permissions only on files they themselves own.

2. To open the Info panel, choose Get Info from Action pop-up menu at the top of a Finder window or from the File menu. Alternatively, you can use the key command Command-I.

3. Open the Ownership & Permissions section of the panel and click the disclosure triangle in front of Details to show levels of access, as shown in Figure 33.10. If the lock button shows a closed lock, click it to unlock the settings.

4. Access can now be set so that different users have different privileges. The main options for levels of access are Read & Write, Read Only, and No Access. For folders, there is also the Write Only option, which enables a drop-box feature so that users can copy files into the folder, but only the owner can view its contents.

FIGURE 33.10
Protect or share
your files by chang-
ing permissions in
the Info window.

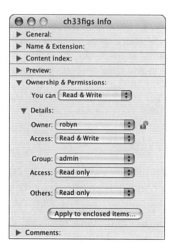

By the Way

You may have noticed that you can set permissions such that even you can't read or write to files you own. Why is that option available? If you've ever accidentally delet-ed an important file, you'll understand why. Sometimes it's best to impose a few rules on yourself to avoid bigger problems. Remember, though, that file owners can always change the permissions, even after they've turned off read or write access for themselves.

5. When you've set the permissions you need, close the pane.

By the Way

When changing access options for a folder, you also have the Apply to Enclosed Items button to apply the access rights you've selected to all files and folders within the original folder.

Understanding Groups

You might have noticed that the Ownership & Permissions section of the Info panel enables you to specify permissions for the owner of the file, the group to which that user belongs, and others. But what is a group? Let's look at that con-cept briefly now.

In Unix systems, users can be classified into many different groups so that they can access, or be excluded from accessing, certain information. In other words, some files are needed by more than one person but shouldn't be accessed by everyone. To facilitate appropriate file sharing, groups are defined to identify who can have access to which system features.

There are many possible groups to choose from in the Owner and Group pop-up menus of the Ownership & Permissions section. Among them are the names for each of the user accounts on your computer, which are used to assign a file to those users. There is also an option labeled System to which applications and other things available for use systemwide are assigned. The remaining list of groups contains specialized groups that you won't need unless you plan to treat Mac OS X as a Unix system.

Summary

Multiuser systems are new territory for most Mac users, but the basics aren't difficult to understand. This chapter introduced you to this concept as it relates to Mac OS X and explained different types of users, user groups, and file privileges and how to work with them. You also explored some of the settings you need to create, delete, and edit user accounts and to change read/write file permissions.

CHAPTER 34

Sharing Files and Running Network Services

The Macintosh has always made it simple to share files with other Macs on the same network and over the Internet. Mac OS X's strong Unix roots bring even more sharing capabilities to the Mac, including the capability to connect to Windows systems. In this chapter, you learn how to activate various sharing features.

Sharing Services

A *service* is something that your computer provides to other computers on a network, such as running a Web server or sharing files. In Mac OS X, you can enable or disable all the standard information-sharing services from the Services section of the Sharing pane in System Preferences, as shown in Figure 34.1.

> Be aware that turning on or off any service in the Sharing pane activates that service for all user accounts on a computer. If sharing is on for one user, it's on for everyone. If it's off, it's off for everyone!

Watch Out!

You can enable or disable the following services:

▶ Personal File Sharing—Share your files with other Mac users across a local network. We'll discuss activating AppleTalk, if needed, in just a moment.

▶ Windows Sharing—Share your files with Windows users on your local network.

▶ Personal Web Sharing—Serve Web pages from your own computer using Mac OS X's built-in Web server.

▶ Remote Login—Allow users to interact with your computer remotely using Secure Shell (SSH) command-line access.

▶ FTP Access—Allow access to your machine via FTP, (File Transfer Protocol).

▶ Apple Remote Desktop—Allow individuals using Apple's full version of Remote Desktop to access your computer.

FIGURE 34.1
The Services options of Sharing Preferences enable you to choose which sharing services you want running on your computer.

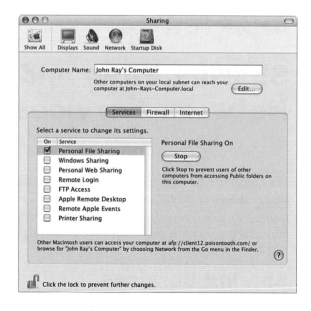

Essentially, Apple Remote Desktop allows someone to look over your shoulder (or even take the controls if needed) as you work, without being in the same room. To make this work, the remote viewer does need to purchase and install a copy of Apple's Remote Desktop, but this is a great option for people in learning labs or help-desk situations!

▶ Remote Apple Events—Allow software running on other machines to send events to applications on your computer using the AppleScript scripting language. We don't delve into this option, but AppleScript is discussed in Chapter 39, "Introducing AppleScript."

▶ Printer Sharing—Grant other computers access to the printers connected to your computer. With this service enabled, your printers appear in the Printer Setup Utility's printer list for other users on your local network. General information about connecting to printers is covered in Chapter 20, "Printing, Faxing, and Working with Fonts."

The Firewall section of the Sharing control pane contains a list of the same options as the Services section, with the exception of Apple Remote Desktop. A *firewall* sits between the outside network and network services on your computer to protect your computer from network-based attacks. The Firewall options enable you to activate Mac OS X's built-in firewall software to prevent access to your computer through those services you don't want to run. We'll discuss this further in Chapter 35, "Sharing Files to Windows and Unix Computers."

Now, let's take at look at starting and using these services.

Activating Personal File Sharing and AppleTalk

Personal File Sharing is Apple's method of sharing files with other Mac users over a network, either via TCP/IP or AppleTalk. AppleTalk is a legacy protocol for browsing and accessing remote workstations that share files or services, such as printers. Apple is transitioning to use of the TCP/IP-based Service Locator Protocol (SLP) and a local network-based services feature called Rendezvous, mentioned in Chapter 16, "Using iChat AV." However, you might still need to enable AppleTalk to access older devices or Macs running pre-OS X operating systems.

Follow these steps to share your files with another Mac user:

1. Determine whether you need to use AppleTalk to access computers and printers on your network. If all the other computers are Mac OS X machines and your printer is USB-based, you probably don't need AppleTalk support—skip ahead to step 8. If you're not sure, go to step 2.

2. Open the Network Preferences pane, found in the Internet & Network section of System Preferences.

3. Use the Show pop-up menu to choose the device you're using to access your network (such as AirPort or Ethernet).

4. Click the AppleTalk button to reveal the options shown in Figure 34.2.

5. Check the Make AppleTalk Active check box. (To make the change, you might first have to click the small lock button at the bottom of the window and type an administrator's username and password.)

If you don't recall the difference between administrative and nonadministrative users, you may want to review Chapter 33, "Sharing and Securing Your Computer and Files." For now, all you need to know is that the first-created user account is an administrative account. Other accounts may or may not be administrative, depending how they were set up.

By the
Way

FIGURE 34.2
Make sure that
AppleTalk is active
before trying to
share files on a
network containing
users of both OS X
and older Mac
OSes.

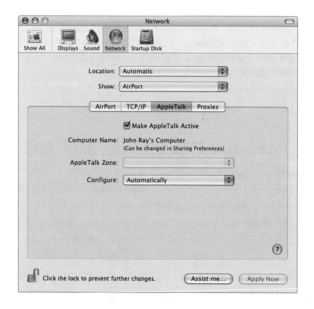

FIGURE 34.2
Make sure that AppleTalk is active before trying to share files on a network containing users of both OS X and older Mac OSes.

6. If necessary, choose an AppleTalk Zone to use. You might want to speak to your network administrator if you aren't sure what to choose.

7. Click Apply Now.

8. Open the Sharing Preferences pane, as shown previously in Figure 34.1, and check the box for Personal File Sharing, or highlight it and click the Start button.

9. Close the System Preferences window.

Your Mac OS X computer should now be able to share files with other Macs on your network. We'll talk about how to actually connect to other users' files later in this chapter in the section "Connecting to Shared Folders."

Activating Windows Sharing (Samba)

Windows computers use a different protocol than the Mac for file and print sharing. To share files with Windows computers, your Mac must employ the same protocol through a piece of software called Samba.

To turn on Windows Sharing (Samba), open the Sharing System Preferences pane to the Services section and then either click the check box in front of the Windows Sharing line, or highlight the line and click the Start button. The Sharing pane updates and shows the path that can be used to map (mount) the drive of your Mac on a Windows-based computer, as demonstrated in Figure 34.3.

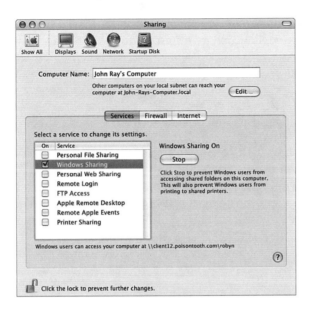

Like AppleShare file sharing in Mac OS X, the built-in Samba configuration is limited to sharing each user's home directory. By default, user accounts are enabled for login from Windows. The home directory of the user can be accessed through the path that appears in the Sharing preferences pane in the Services section when Windows Sharing is highlighted, as in Figure 34.3. (We'll talk about accessing files from a computer running Windows in the section "Connecting from a Windows Machine.")

Activating Web Sharing

Mac OS X makes it easy to run a simple Web server using a popular, and powerful, open source server called Apache. (Apache is actually the server that powers most Internet Web sites. It's built to run complex sites, including e-commerce and other interactive applications, and it's running on your desktop as a part of Mac OS X.)

Mac OS X can share a personal Web site for each user on the computer. In addition, it can run a master Web site for the whole computer entirely independent of the personal Web sites.

To turn on Web sharing, open the Sharing System Preferences pane (shown in Figures 34.4) and check the box for Personal Web Sharing, or highlight it and click the Start button. The Apache server starts running, making your Web site immediately available. Make a note of your personal Web site URL as shown at the bottom of the window and then start Safari to verify that your personal site is online.

FIGURE 34.4
Turn on Web Sharing and note the address of your Web site.

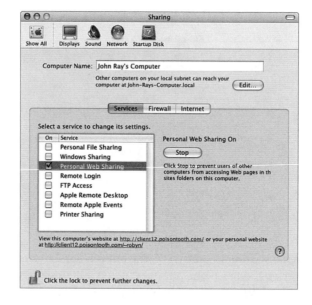

With Safari running, enter your personal Web site URL, which should be the following format:

```
http://<server ip or hostname>/~<username>
```

The tilde (~) is extremely critical. It tells the server that it should load the Web pages from the Sites folder located inside the user's home directory. Note that after you activate Web sharing for one user, it's active for all users, so make sure that all users are ready to have their Web sites shared with the rest of the world.

Assuming that you entered your URL correctly, you should see the default Mac OS X home page, as demonstrated in Figure 34.5.

FIGURE 34.5
Apple includes a default personal home page.

To edit your Web site, just look inside your Sites folder. The default page is generated from the file index.html and the Images folder.

> Under Mac OS X's user interface, it isn't possible to change the filename of your home page. When you start creating files, make sure that the first page you want to be loaded is named index.html; otherwise, your site might not behave as you want.

Watch Out!

To edit an HTML document, you can open it in a text editor, such as the TextEdit application discussed in Chapter 6, "Using Calculator, Stickies, Preview, and TextEdit." (Note that you will need to adjust the preferences to ignore rich text commands in HTML files, or you will see a Web page rather than an editable HTML page.)

> If you are interested in making your own simple Web pages, I highly recommend reading *Teach Yourself HTML and XHTML in 24 Hours* to learn the basics.

By the Way

You may have noticed that two Web site addresses are shown at the bottom of the screen when Web Sharing is activated: there's one for your own account and one without the ~<*username*> portion. The one that doesn't specify an account is the Web site for the computer rather than a specific user. If you haven't already done so, enter that address in a browser now. If no one with access to your system has created a new page for your computer, you should see something similar to the page shown in Figure 34.6.

FIGURE 34.6
The default page for your system looks different than your default personal page (shown in Figure 34.5).

This is the system Web site, and it can be used for anything you want, but you must do a bit of digging to reach the directory that holds it.

The system-level site is in the Documents folder located in a folder labeled Webserver inside the Library folder of the hard drive. (Note, there are several folders labeled Library at various levels in OS X—this one is at the same level as the Applications and System folders.) Any administrator can make changes to this directory, so make sure that the other admin users on the system understand its purpose and that they don't assume that it's related to their personal Web sites.

Viewing Web Site Statistics

For every visit made to a Web site located on your computer, the Apache Web server makes an entry in its log files. These log files can tell you who looked at your files, what they looked at, and the IP address of their computers. Keeping track of this kind of information helps you understand who the audience for your Web site is and what types of information they're seeking. (If your site has more than one page, seeing what pages people visit can show you what people like (or what they can find) and what may need more work!)

The logs for your server are located in the /var/log/httpd directory and are named access_log and error_log by default. You can open these files in a text editor, view them from the command line, or monitor them using the Console application by following these steps:

1. Open the Console application located inside the Utilities folder of the Applications folder.

2. From the File menu, select Open Quickly, select /var/log, select httpd, and, finally, select access_log.

3. A window such as the one displayed in Figure 34.7 opens with the contents of the Apache access_log file.

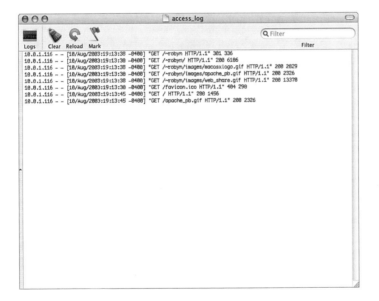

FIGURE 34.7
The Console application can be used to monitor your logs.

As you and other users access the Web sites on your computer, you can view information about each of the hits within the log window. Each row displayed is a record of what computer has visited your site, what was viewed, and when it was viewed. Take for example the following log entry:

```
10.0.1.116 - - [10/Aug/2003:19:13:38 -0400] "Get /~robyn http/1.1" 301 336
```

Essentially, this means that the computer with the IP address 10.0.1.116 visited on the 10th of August, 2003, at 7:13 PM to view the default page for the user "robyn." The extra numbers at the end of the entry are a code reporting how the Web server responded to the request and the size of the file (in bytes) served to the viewer's computer for the given item.

> Hits represent each of the page elements that are served to create a Web page. The list of hits in Figure 34.7 is from viewing the page shown in Figure 34.6 and the system-level default Web page once each. (There are so many rows of information because the Web pages and each separate image count as a hit.)

Although accurate, this information can be difficult to interpret—especially if many visitors have viewed your Web site. You can install a number of applications (both free and commercial) to help translate the raw Web logs into something a bit more meaningful. To help you get started, take a look at the following products and Web sites:

▶ Analog—`www.summary.net/soft/analog.html`

Analogy is a robust, fast, free program for analyzing Web statistics. Reports include basic bar graphs and pie charts.

▶ Summary—`www.summary.net/summary.html`

Summary produces Web statistic summaries of just about anything that can be determined from Web page requests, including search terms that lead to a page and various types of errors that occurred on a site. It is available for a free 30-day trial.

▶ Traffic Report—`www.seacloak.com/`

Traffic is another Web statistics analyzer that presents a wide variety of reports. It is available in a lite and full version, with pricing to reflect the levels of functionality. A 30-day free trial is available.

▶ Sawmill—`www.sawmill.net/`

Sawmill produces attractive, easy-to-read Web statistics reports with graphs and color-coding. It is available for a free 30-day trial.

Activating Remote Login and FTP

Two additional methods of file sharing available in Mac OS X are FTP and SSH. FTP (File Transfer Protocol) simply provides cross-platform file-transfer services. The second type of sharing, SSH (secure shell), enables a remote user to access the command prompt of a Mac OS X computer from anywhere in the world.

Both of these protocols can be turned on in the Services section of the Sharing preferences pane. SSH is turned on through the Remote Login check box you saw previously in Figure 34.4. Activate FTP by clicking the Allow FTP Access check box. Alternatively, you can highlight the option you want to activate and click the Start button.

Now that you know how to turn these services on, let's see what they can do for you!

Remote Login (SSH)

SSH, or as Apple calls it in the Sharing pane: Remote Login, is a new concept for most Mac users. If you've seen a Windows or a Linux computer before, you've probably occasionally seen someone open a command prompt and start typing text commands instead of working with an icon-filled desktop. Although SSH isn't the command line itself, it provides a secure means of accessing the command line from a remote location. In an SSH connection, the entire session is encrypted. As such, administrators can log in to their systems using SSH and edit user accounts, change passwords, and so on, without the fear of giving away potentially damaging information to those who are watching network traffic for information to exploit.

For the most part, all you need to know about SSH is that from the Terminal application located inside the Utilities folder in the Applications folder you can access your account on a remote system by typing

```
ssh <username>@<ip address or hostname>
```

(The specific information for your computer is shown at the bottom of the Sharing pane after SSH is enabled.)

After you enter this command, the remote machine prompts you for the account password and then gives you full control over your account and the resources you have access to. It's as if you launched the Terminal application directly on the affected computer. (If you're wondering what exactly you can do with SSH, don't worry! We'll talk more about using the command line from the Terminal in Chapter 38, "Using Basic Unix Commands.")'If you're not interested in the command line, don't worry—there's absolutely no reason why you have to use SSH. If you prefer a GUI solution to remote system administration, check out Apple's Remote Desktop application, mentioned in a note in the section "Sharing Services" earlier in this chapter. It allows you to do things such as use your work computer from home and vice versa.

If you're planning to serve FTP and SSH only occasionally, shut off the services in the Sharing pane until you're ready to use them. This closes some potential points of attack on your computer. You can still use the Mac OS X clients and command line to access other SSH/FTP servers, but remote users can't connect to your machine.

FTP

With FTP enabled via the Sharing preferences on your computer, a remote user can type into a Web browser a URL of the form:

```
ftp://<client number>.<ip address or hostname>
```

This tells the Web browser to contact the Mac OS X computer running the FTP server'. From there, the user is prompted to enter any valid username and password for the computer being accessed (as shown in Figure 34.8).

FIGURE 34.8
Authentication requires a valid username and password.

After a user has connected via FTP, a special icon appears on the desktop to represent the remote system that is now linked to, or *mounted on*, your desktop. When double-clicked, a Finder window containing the files on the remote system appears.

Although the built-in FTP option provides some basic FTP functions, most users prefer to use heartier third-party software. Here are some of the most popular options:

▶ Fetch—`fetchsoftworks.com/`

Fetch is a full-featured FTP client that allows you to resume file transfer if interrupted. (The cursor appears as the silhouette of a running dog to show when transfers are in progress.) A 15-day trial is available.

▶ Interarchy—www.interarchy.com/

Interarchy allows you not only to transfer files but also to diagnose connection problems.

▶ Transmit—www.panic.com/transmit/download.html

Transmit allows you to transfer files and create a list of frequently accessed servers—all in a user-friendly interface. You can download a free trial version that doesn't expire, but you will have to purchase Transmit to unlock all the features.

If you need to share files over the Internet, FTP is one of the best ways to do so. It's fast, effective, and an efficient protocol. Unfortunately, it's also not easy to work with behind firewalls, and it transmits its passwords unencrypted. If you set up a nonadmin user account, perhaps called Transfers, for the sole purpose of moving files around, the password issue shouldn't be much of a problem. Firewalls, on the other hand, are something you might need to discuss with your network administrator before you activate FTP.

You learn how to use FTP from the Finder in the next section.

Connecting to Shared Folders

Your Mac OS X computer can connect to a number of types of network resources from the Finder, specifically:

▶ Macintosh systems—Other Mac computers that are sharing files via AppleTalk or AppleShare IP.

▶ Windows/Linux computers—If Windows or Linux computers are using SMB or CIFS file sharing (the standard for most Windows networks), your Mac can access the files easily.

▶ WebDAV shares—WebDAV is a cross-platform file sharing solution that uses the standard Web protocols. The .Mac iDisk storage uses WebDAV.

▶ FTP servers—File Transfer Protocol servers are a popular means of distributing software on the Internet. Your Mac OS X machine can connect (read-only) to FTP servers.

▶ Linux/BSD NFS servers—NFS is the Unix standard for file sharing. Your Mac (being Unix!) can obviously talk to them as well.

To connect in these various ways, choose Go, Connect to Server (Command-K) from the Finder menu. This opens a new dialog box, shown in Figure 34.9, that enables you to connect to remote computers.

To make the connection to Macintosh and Windows servers, enter the address of the server you want to access and then click Connect. After a few seconds, you're prompted for a username and a password, as shown in Figure 34.10.

Click Connect. You may then see a window similar to Figure 34.11 where you can choose different accounts on the remote computer. After you choose one and click OK, the volume is mounted on your desktop. Double-click the icon to access the remote computer.

By the Way

If you're connecting to another Mac OS X computer, you can use either an account holder's full name or username to connect. You must enter a valid password for that account.

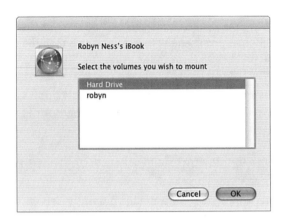

FIGURE 34.11
Select the volume
you want to mount.

Connecting to WebDAV and NFS shared volumes is similar.

Your network administrator should be able to give you the exact information you need, but for the most part, the URLs follow a format like this:

FTP shares: `ftp://<server name>/<shared volume>`

For example, I have an FTP server named Xanadu on my network (poisontooth.com) containing a folder called waternet at the root level of the server. To access it, I would type **`ftp://xanadu.poisontooth.com/waternet`** and then click Connect.

WebDAV is even simpler. WebDAV shares are actually just Web resources, so they use the same URLs that you would type into your Web browser. For example, to access the iDisk storage of your Mac.com account, you would type **`http://idisk.mac.com/<your Mac.com username>`**.

NFS follows the same pattern. If the remote server is configured to allow connections, an NFS connection URL looks like this: `nfs://<server name>/<shared volume>`.

> Windows and Macintosh shares can also be mounted via the URLs prefixed with `SMB://` and `AFP://`, respectively.

By the Way

Connecting from a Windows Machine

Earlier in this chapter, you learned how to enable Windows Sharing. Now, we'll talk about how someone on a Windows computer can connect to your computer.

The following steps are for Windows XP. Those running different versions of Windows may have to consult other documentation because some features may be labeled, or even accessed, differently.

There are essentially two options for connecting. For a Windows computer on your own network, you can browse to a shared Mac account in the following way:

1. Open the Control Panel from the Windows Start menu.

2. Choose Network and Internet Connections from the items under the header Pick a Category.

3. Choose My Network Places from the list along the left with the header See Also.

4. Under the header Network Tasks, choose View workgroup computers.

5. Under the header Other Places, choose Microsoft Windows Network.

6. Double-click the Workgroup icon to see a screen similar to Figure 34.12, in which the shared Mac appears as an option.

FIGURE 34.12
Choose a Mac that's part of the current PC's Windows Workgroup.

7. Double-click the desired Mac OS X Client to initiate contact. You then have to enter the username and password of the Mac account holder to access the account.

Keep in mind that the person logging from Windows must be identified as the same user the Mac account recognizes, meaning that it is necessary to log in to Windows using the username and password of the account on Mac OS X. Be sure to enter your username in all lowercase characters and the password just as you entered it in Mac OS X.

By the Way

After logging in, the Windows user double-clicks the account icon to view the folders in the Mac user's account, as shown in Figure 34.13.

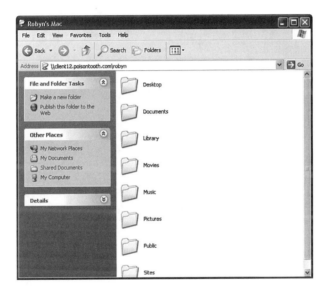

FIGURE 34.13
The familiar files of an OS X user's home folder in an unexpected interface!

For Windows XP users outside your local network, the connection process requires them to map a path to your shared account using the address displayed in the Sharing pane when you enabled it for Windows Sharing (similar to the address shown at the bottom of Figure 34.3.)

Here are the steps to map a networked drive:

1. Open the Control Panel from the Windows Start menu.

2. Choose Network and Internet Connections from the items under the header Pick a Category.

3. Choose My Network Places from the list along the left with the header See Also.

4. Choose Add a Network Place from the list along the left with the header Network Tasks.

5. A wizard appears to guide you. Click Next and select the Choose Another Network Location option.

6. Click Next to see the screen shown in Figure 34.14. There, type the path given in the Sharing pane of your Mac. (Be sure to type it exactly as shown, including the back-slash characters.) Then click Next. You may have to wait a moment as the Windows computer locates the requested account.

FIGURE 34.14
Enter the path to the shared Mac OS X account carefully.

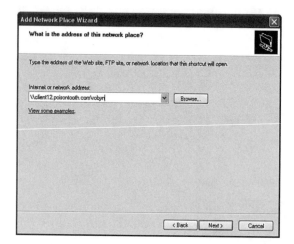

7. If all goes well, you see the screen shown in Figure 34.15, where you can give a name to the network place your computer has just identified. Click Next.

8. The final screen of the wizard requires you to click Finish to wrap things up.

To connect to a mapped network drive, open the Control Panel and choose Network and Internet Connections. Under the See Also heading on the left side of the window, choose My Network Places. You will see the place you just added under the Internet header in the middle of the screen. You can double-click it to view the folders in the Mac user's account, as shown previously in Figure 34.13.

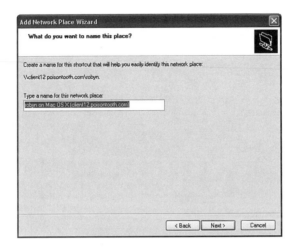

FIGURE 34.15
Give a short but descriptive name to the shared account.

Sharing Your Internet Connection

If you have multiple computers that need access to the Internet but only one Internet connection, you can set up Mac OS X to share the connection it has with other computers on your network. Here are some possible configurations:

▶ If your primary connection is via AirPort, any machines connected to it via ethernet can connect to the Internet.

▶ If your primary connection is an ethernet connection, your machine can become an AirPort base station and share its connection to others using AirPort wireless technology (assuming that the sharing computers all have AirPort cards). It can also share with other computers using ethernet.

▶ If your connection is a modem, your machine can share connections through both AirPort and ethernet.

Even though this sounds like a truly wonderful feature, it should be used with caution. Some network arrangements can be disrupted when their member computers start sharing Internet connections. Check with your network administrator, or any nearby network administrators of wireless networks, before you try this.

To share your Internet connection, open the Internet section of the Sharing System Preferences pane, shown in Figure 34.16, set the Share Your Connection From pop-up menu to the type of connection used, and check the box for the type of connection to the computers that will be connecting. After you have these settings in place, click the Start button.

FIGURE 34.16
Share your network connection with a friend.

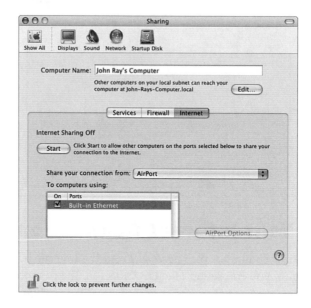

Summary

The Macintosh has always made it simple to share file information between computers. Mac OS X keeps the process simple but imposes some limitations that users might not be prepared for. At the same time, it opens up compatibility with Windows and Linux computers by adding SMB/CIFS and WebDAV support. In addition to the standard file sharing services, Mac OS X can be configured to act as an FTP or SSH server, making it possible to access information and control your computer from anywhere on the Internet.

CHAPTER 35

Securing Your Computer

Mac OS X is a powerful Unix-based operating system, and with that power comes the responsibility to minimize security risks. If your computer may be used by other people, it's wise to secure it against users who may not realize the consequences of their actions, or those who may intend to wreak havoc. If you're connecting your computer to the Internet, it's necessary to take preventive measures to guard against unwanted connections over the network.

Local Security

Mac OS X is a true multiuser operating system. In Mac OS X, you have complete control over who can do what, but you must realize that exercising that control is essential if you intend to have a shared computer that doesn't self-destruct after one or two adventurous users decide to play around.

Problems due to local users might not seem likely, but an unmanaged public computer can easily be turned into a powerful tool of attack—sometimes unintentionally. (As you learned in Chapter 34, "Sharing Files and Running Network Services," and will explore further in just a moment, even turning on network services can expose your computer to risk from malicious strangers.)

Much of local system security is common sense coupled with a reasonable amount of watchfulness. Because implementing a local security policy is easier than maintaining network security, that's where we start.

Your first decision is what type of computer you're setting up.

If the machine is destined to be in a public library and serve as both a Unix and a Macintosh workstation, your security considerations are far more complicated than if it sits at your desk and has only you as a user.

Let's take a look at a series of steps you can take to minimize the risks to your system. Some obviously don't apply to your particular circumstances, but they're worth noting regardless.

Create Only "Normal" Users

Many people aren't clear on what happens when you create a user in Mac OS X. As you learned in Chapter 33, "Sharing Your Computer with Multiple Users," two types of user accounts can be created in the Accounts pane of the System Preferences: normal users and admin users. The only difference when setting up accounts is checking the box that reads Allow User to Administer This Computer.

Many systems that I've visited have had all the users set to be administrators. When asked why, the owners replied that they wanted everyone to be able to use the computer to its fullest. An understandable sentiment, but the implications of using this setting are enormous. A user who has this check box set can

- ▶ Add or delete users and their files
- ▶ Remove software installed in the systemwide Applications folder
- ▶ Change or completely remove network settings
- ▶ Activate or disable the Web service, FTP service, or SSH (secure shell)

Removing Administrative Access from an Existing User

Although it's unlikely that users who are given administrative privileges could completely destroy the system, 'they can make life difficult for others even if they don't mean to.

To remove administrative access from an existing user, follow these steps:

1. Open the System Preferences.
2. Click the Accounts item under the System section.
3. Select the name of the user to edit in the list along the left.
4. Open the Security section and uncheck the Allow User to Administer This Computer box, as shown in Figure 35.1.

By the Way

> If you try to change the administrative access for the first-created user account, the Security options are grayed out. That account must remain an administrative account.

FIGURE 35.1
Create as few
administrative
users as possible.

If your computer has only a few accounts for people you know, this security precaution is probably the only one you need. However, if you want your system to
be a bit more impenetrable, keep reading.

Disable Usernames

It's obvious that Apple wanted to create a system that would be friendly and
accessible for any level of user. In doing so, it also set a few defaults that make it
easy for a public system to be "cracked" by a persistent attacker with direct access
to the machine. One precaution that's easy to take is not to display login names
on the Login Preferences panel. To shut off this feature, follow these steps:

1. Open System Preferences.

2. Click the Accounts button in the System section.

3. Choose the Login Options button at the bottom of the list of users.

4. Click the Display Login Window as Name and Password radio button to
   select it.

5. Close the panel to save the settings.

Now, let's take a look at 'ways to secure your system online.

Network Security

There are two steps to network security: figuring out what your machine is doing and disabling those things that you'd rather it not do. Neither of these tasks is as easy as it sounds because you must check a number of places before you can be sure that your machine is secure. The end result, however, is a Mac OS X computer that you can leave online without worrying about the consequences.

Disabling Network Services

As discussed in Chapter 34, your Mac OS X computer has several built-in methods of sharing information over the Web—through network shares, FTP, and more. Each of these features relies on a special Mac OS X background application called a *server daemon*, or simply a *service*. As its name implies, a service provides additional functionality to the system. With network services, this functionality can be accessed remotely over a network connection. Therein lies the potential for a cracker to access and modify your computer, and is the primary source of our concern.

Each network service that runs on your computer requires a *port* that can be used to accept incoming connections. Think of network ports as power receptacles with multiple outlets. Connections to your computer are "plugged" in to the outlet and then communications can begin. Mac OS X has the capability to accept many incoming connections via many different ports. You can enable many of the commonly-used ports under the Services section of the Sharing Preferences, as detailed in Chapter 34.

By the *Way*

> If you need to run services, as with some types of file sharing or instant messaging, that use some of the less common ports, you can activate them under the Firewall section of the Sharing preference pane. Click the button labeled new and choose a port name or, if none apply, choose Other. If you choose other, you will neet to set the port number or range; talk to your system administrator if you feel there are custom settings you should configure.

The biggest risk of having several network services active is that there could be a bug or backdoor associated with one of them. The Mac OS X architecture uses complex applications to provide its network services. Improperly setting up one of these services, or failing to keep your system updated, could open your account to being accessed by an unauthorized user who can tamper with your files. Even worse, it is possible for an intruder to take over your machine and use it to launch attacks on even more computers!

When your computer is connected to the Internet via a direct connection to a cable modem or DSL line, it can be a direct target for attack from outside. The more network services that are running, the greater the chance that a potential intruder can discover and compromise your system.

Disabling Network Sharing Services

Your first concern should be the network services that Apple included with your system. Although it's tempting to go through your system and activate every feature, doing so isn't always a good idea. If you turn on everything in the Sharing Preferences pane, your system would have the following services and ports active:

► FTP Access (port 20 or 21)—FTP is a quick and easy way to send and retrieve files from a computer. FTP Sharing starts an FTP server on your computer. Unfortunately, it provides no password encryption and is often targeted by attackers. If you don't have to use FTP, don't enable it.

► Remote Login—ssh (port 22)—The secure shell enables remote users to connect to your computer and control it from the command line. It's a useful tool for servers, but only presents a security risk to home users.

► Personal Web Sharing (port 80)—Your personal Web server is server called Apache. Apache is a stable program and should be considered the least of your concerns, unless you've manually customized its configuration files.

► Windows File Sharing (port 139)—Enables Windows users to access the shared folders on your computers.

► svrloc (port 427)—The Service Locator Protocol allows remote computers to detect what services are available on your computer over the Internet.

► afpovertcp (port 548)—The Apple File Protocol is used to share your disks and folders over a network. If you have Personal File Sharing turned on, be aware that potentially anyone on the Internet can connect to your computer.

► Printer Sharing (port 631)—Enables other users on the network to use printers connected to your computer.

► ppc (port 3031)—Program-to-program communication enables remote applications to connect to your computer and send it commands. It's unlikely that you would need this feature in day-to-day use. PPC is controlled by the Remote Apple Events setting in the Sharing Preferences panel.

To disable any of these built-in network services, follow these steps:

1. Open the System Preferences pane.

2. Click the Sharing item under the Internet & Network section.

3. In the Services preferences, uncheck the boxes for the listed services to toggle them on and off, as shown in Figure 35.2.

FIGURE 35.2
The Sharing Preferences pane controls the built-in network services.

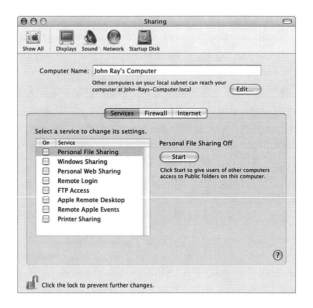

Firewalls

The "ultimate" solution to network security is the use of a *firewall*, a piece of hardware or software that sits between your computer and the Internet. As network traffic comes into the computer, the firewall looks at each piece of information, determines whether it's acceptable, and, if necessary, keeps the data from getting to your machine.

By the Way

You might be asking yourself, "If a firewall can be a piece of software that runs on my computer, how can it both look at network traffic and keep it from reaching my machine?" After all, to look at the information and determine whether it's trouble, the data obviously must have reached my computer!

That's true, but firewall software operates at a low level, intercepting network traffic before your computer has a chance to process it and make it available to components such as your Web server or FTP server.

Software Firewalls

A software firewall is the quickest way to get unwanted traffic blocked from your machine.

Mac OS X includes a built-in personal firewall, accessible from the Firewall section of the System Preferences Sharing pane shown in Figure 35.3.

To activate the firewall, click the Start button. Checked boxes appear next to those services/ports that you've turned on under the Services pane of the Sharing Preferences pane.

Because disabling a port disables its service and unenabled ports require no securing, you must go to the Services pane to change the status of the services in the Firewall pane.

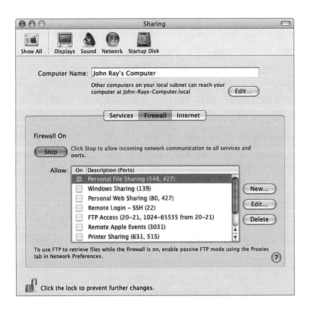

FIGURE 35.3
The Mac OS X personal firewall can be enabled to secure the services/port you don't want to operate.

In addition to starting or stopping your personal firewall, you can add and delete additional ports to be opened between your computer and the outside world. This may be necessary for some people who want to play games online, use some specific file sharing or Internet chat software, or interact in other ways via a network. Consult your system administrator or ISP if you have questions.

If you need even more flexibility, several other firewall builder packages make it easy to point-and-click your way through setting up a firewall on your computer. You may want to consult another source, such as *Maximum Mac OS X Security*, by John and William Ray (Sams Publishing, 2003), for deeper coverage of security issues.

Hardware Firewalls

A growing number of network hardware appliances can virtually eliminate the threat of attack by making your computer unreachable from the Internet. Although slightly more expensive than a software-only solution, they provide a worry-free answer to the problem of network security!

Here are a few Mac-friendly firewall solutions you might be interested in checking out:

▶ Apple AirPort—The Apple wireless network server can make an effective firewall when configured with the option to Share a Single IP Address Using DHCP (Dynamic Host Configuration Protocol) and NAT (Network Address Translation). Although more expensive than other options, it's a Mac-friendly solution and a great way to gain security and go wireless at the same time.

▶ LinkSys cable/DSL routers (www.linksys.com)—Largely responsible for creating the first mass-produced personal firewall, LinkSys has a variety of different options available for home users. LinkSys offers both traditional wired and wireless products.

▶ NetGear routers (www.netgear.com)—Much like the LinkSys routers, the NetGear offerings are available in wired and wireless configurations and feature easy Web configuration and an attractive price point.

As you shop for a hardware firewall, you might notice that many of the devices you see are advertised as routers. A *router* is simply a generic term for a network device that moves network information from one place to another. For your personal system, it routes information from your computer to the Internet and vice versa.

During the process of routing data, the device also performs its firewall activity.

The biggest drawback to using a personal hardware firewall is that if you run a Web server (or other processes that enable people to connect to your machine over the Internet), you must specially configure the firewall to let requests pass through to your computer. This isn't usually difficult, but it requires more than simply plugging it in and having it work.

Summary

Mac OS X security presents several challenges for Mac users. Its underlying Unix subsystem makes it an attractive target for network crackers as well as any unscrupulous person who might have access to the system. In this chapter, you learned several ways to help protect your system from both local and network attacks by limiting access to critical features and shutting off network services that you might not need. The topic of security is broad, so consider chapter only a start to maintaining a secure computer—not an end-all guide.

CHAPTER 36

Maintaining Your System

In this chapter, you learn some maintenance tips that will help keep your computer running smoothly and keep your files safe. Because Apple frequently releases critical security updates and patches that should be installed quickly, we'll talk first about automating system software updates. Then, we'll discuss the importance of backing up your files so that you won't lose all your hard work and important data in the event of system disruption. Finally, we'll check out a built-in tool for monitoring the effort expended by your system.

Automating Software Updates

Mac OS X allows you to receive software updates from Apple over the Internet, so you don't have to go looking for the updates to the operating system or Apple-created software. You can enable this feature in the Software Update Preferences pane of the System Preferences.

Running Software Updates Manually

Although automating software updates can take most of the burden off you, there are times when you want to force your system to search for recent updates instead of waiting for your scheduled time. (For example, when Apple releases a new version of a fun application such as iChat—see Chapter 16, "Using iChat AV"—you may be eager to get your hands on it.)

Here's how you can check for updates anytime:

1. Launch the System Preferences application from the Dock, the Apple menu, or the Applications folder. (Or choose Software Update from the Apple menu and skip to step 4.)

2. Click the Software Update pane, which opens the screen shown in Figure 36.1.

3. If you want to check for updates right now, click the Check Now button. Your computer will use the Internet connection you've configured to contact Apple's support Web site to check for possible updates.

FIGURE 36.1
Apple enables you
to download the
latest updates for
your computer auto-
matically over the
network.

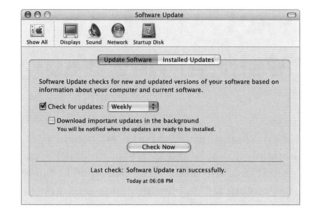

4. If updates are available for your computer, you'll see a screen listing what's available, as shown in Figure 36.2. From there you can click the check boxes for the items you want and accept the download process.

FIGURE 36.2
The Software
Update window
displays a list of
updates for your
system.

5. When the downloads are complete, the software installers will launch, and your computer will be updated with the new software. Then there usually is an "optimizing" process, which allows the update to function with full efficiency. (For some updates, you will need to click the Restart button to finish the process.)

Depending on the software package, you might see a license agreement at some point in time during the installation. Simply click OK to proceed.

Setting Up Regular Software Updates

If you want to have your computer check for Apple software updates automatically, click the Automatically check box, and then click the Check for Updates pop-up menu to set the interval. You can choose Daily, Weekly, or Monthly (Weekly is best, considering the unpredictable nature of the software update process).

After you've set the schedule, quit System Preferences. After you select Automatically, Software Update checks Apple's Web site at the specified intervals as soon as you log in to your computer and have a connection to the Internet. The window shown in Figure 36.2 appears where you can see what updates are going to be made.

It goes without saying that if your computer isn't on when the scheduled update is set to take place, it just won't happen. The check will be skipped until the next scheduled run.

Sometimes the list of updates includes features you don't need or want, such as iPod updates when you don't own an iPod. Although not checking the box for those items prevents them from being installed, they may continue to show up in your Software Updates window unless you choose Update, Ignore Update from the menu. If you ever change your mind, you can choose Software Update, Reset Ignored Updates from the menu to make the updates visiable again and allow the system to perform any you decide are needed.

Installed Files

Many users, for good reason, want to keep track of what software has been installed on their system. Opening the Software Update preference pane and clicking the Installed Updates button displays a log of installed updates. This listing is shown in Figure 36.3.

FIGURE 36.3
The Installed Updates pane displays a list of installed update packages.

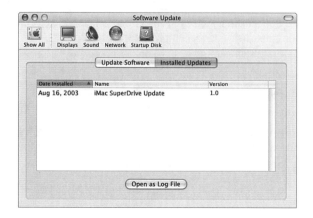

Backing Up Your Data

Although keeping a secure and updated operating system is important, that's not as important as maintaining an archive of your important data.

When a program or computer crashes, it's possible that one or more files on your computer's drive can be affected (especially if you're working on a file when the computer locks up). Even though Mac OS X offers strong resistance to system failure, the world is unpredictable, and the potential for events ranging from simple human error to theft, make backups an important consideration.

Backup Strategies

You can follow different types of backup techniques, depending on the kind of documents you're creating and how many of them there are. Here's a brief look at the sort of things you can do without having to buy extra software:

▶ Select backups—You already have copies of your programs on a CD, or can obtain them if you really need them. A complete packet of CDs came with your computer, containing all the software Apple installed on your computer. In addition, most new software you buy will also come on an installation disk of some sort. So the fastest backup method is just to concentrate on the documents you make with those programs.

Watch Out!

If you purchase software that must be downloaded, it's wise to create backup copies in case of system failure. Or, if you can download the software freely but need a code to unlock it, you may simply want to store your codes in a safe place so that you can recover use of applications for which you've paid.

▶ Full backups—Even though you already have a separate copy of the software, it can be time-consuming to restore all your software and redo special program settings. If you back up everything, however, it's easier to restore a program with your settings intact without fuss or bother. In addition, having a complete backup of your computer's drive is extra protection in case something happens to both the computer and software disks. The downside, however, is that making a full backup can be time-consuming and requires a large amount of storage space.

▶ Incremental backups—This technique requires special software (such as Retrospect, which is described later), but it is designed to make a backup strictly of the files that have changed since your last backup. A thorough backup plan might include a full backup at regular intervals, say once a week, and then a daily incremental backup. This method also takes a lot less time, and you won't need as much disk space to store it all.

Data Storage Options

Another part of your backup plan is deciding where and how to store the data you will be copying from your hard drive. The best method is to get a separate drive with media (disks) that you can remove. That way you can store the backups in a separate location for the ultimate in safekeeping. That's the method the big companies use.

Here are some storage options you should consider:

Watch Out!

It's just not a good idea to back up your files to the same drive they were made on (such as your Mac's hard drive). If something should happen to that drive, or the entire computer, your backup would be gone.

▶ Data CDs—Many Macs come equipped with an optical drive that can make CDs. You can use this drive to copy your files to a CD/R or CD/RW disc (the latter is the one that's rewritable). This is a convenient and inexpensive way to copy your valuable data on a medium that will last for years. If you don't have a built-in CD burner on your Mac, no problem. There are plenty of low-cost external drives that can work from your computer's FireWire or USB ports (but of course the first will run much faster).

By the Way

Does your Mac have Apple's SuperDrive? If so, you can also burn data DVDs in the same way you make a CD. The advantage is that you can store much more data on the DVD—4.7GB compared to 650MB or 700MB for a CD. Though DVDs are more expensive than CDs, if you have a well-populated hard drive this might be a good option.

▶ External backup drive—Iomega Jaz, Peerless, or Zip drives are convenient, and the drives and disks aren't too expensive (well, the Jaz and Peerless media aren't exactly cheap). There are also several varieties of tape drives that work with backup software as a fairly stable backup medium.

▶ Networked disks—If your computer is on a network, a drive on another Mac (or actually even a Windows-based PC set up to handle Mac files) can be used for your regular backups. Before you set up a networked drive for this purpose, you'll want to set up a strategy with those who run the network. Some companies plan on having all files backed up to one drive or drives, and then they do their own special backup routine on those files.

By the Way

Notice that I'm not saying anything about floppy disks here. Unless you only make a few small files, floppy disks aren't practical. You'd need dozens of them at the minimum, and they just aren't as robust as the larger disk techniques.

▶ Internet backups—If you have a good Internet connection and you don't want to back up a large number of files, you can use backup via the Internet. An easy way to get storage space is to sign up with Apple's .Mac program, as discussed in Chapter 13, "Using Sherlock for Internet Searches." As part of the package, you get 100MB of iDisk storage space at Apple's Web servers, and you can buy extra space if you need it. Visit www.mac.com to sign up. However, unless you have really fast Internet access, the process of copying files to your iDisk can be slow.

By the Way

After you've set up a .Mac account, you can access your iDisk. Simply click the iDisk icon on the Finder's toolbar to connect to your disk. If you aren't connected to the Internet, the service will be dialed up first.

Here are some additional considerations related to storing backups of your data:

▶ Careful labeling—Make sure that your backup disks are carefully labeled according to date and content. If the label isn't large enough, you might want to prepare a short listing of contents in your word processor and then pack it with the disk. Often something such as "Backup for February 28, 2002" is sufficient.

> CDs and DVD media are write-once media, which means that when you burn one of these discs that's it, unless, of course, you opt for CD/RW media, where you can rewrite data up to 1,000 times.

By the Way

▶ Reuse of media—If you need to keep an older version of a file, you'll want to keep the backup in a safe place. However, if you are using reusable media and you no longer need a file from a particular time range, there's no problem in putting that storage media back into service for newer backups.

▶ Making multiple backups—If your files contain important data on them (financial or otherwise), make a second backup and store it in a secure location (such as a bank vault). In the unlikely event something happens to your home or office, you'll be protected.

There's one more important element in a backup plan—setting a consistent schedule. It's a good idea to set aside a time to do your backup at regular intervals—perhaps at the end of your work day before leaving your office (or before shutting down your computer for the day if you're at home). Remember, it does no good to intend to backup your files if you never actually do it, so try to work out a system and a schedule that you can maintain over time.

Making Backup CDs

Mac OS X Finder makes writing a CD similar to moving files to any other storage device. To make the process as simple as possible, Mac OS X stores applications, files, and folders in a special folder until you tell the system to burn the CD. Files are actually transferred to the CD media only after the burn starts.

> To burn a CD using an external burner, you must have your CD writer connected and powered on. Check Apple's Web site for supported writers.

By the Way

Of all the methods mentioned previously for storing backup copies of your data, the simplest is burning a data CD. Here's how:

> To choose File, Burn Disc from the menu, the active Finder window must be the CD's window. If the CD is not the active window, the menu item will be disabled.

1. Insert a blank CD into the CD writer. The Mac OS X Finder prompts you to prepare the CD. This doesn't actually write anything to the CD yet, but it tells the computer what your intentions are for the disc to ensure that you use the appropriate kind of CD.

2. Choose the Open Finder option from the Action pop-up menu. (We talked about burning from iTunes in Chapter 22, "Using iTunes," and we will look at burning CDs from an application called Disk Utility later in this chapter in the section "Creating Disk Images with Disk Utility.")

3. Enter a name for the CD you're writing. The disc appears with this name on the desktop.

4. Click OK to start using the CD on your system. An icon representing the CD appears on your desktop. At this point, you can interact with this virtual volume as you would any other under Mac OS X. You can copy files to it, delete those files, and so on.

5. When you create the CD layout you like, you can start the burn process by choosing File, Burn Disc from the menu. In addition, dragging the CD to the Trash also prompts burning to begin. This process takes a few minutes and is tracked by the Finder much like a normal Copy operation.

> If you decide against writing the CD, you can click the Eject button in the CD burning dialog box to remove the media and erase the CD layout you created. If you want to insert a CD in the drive but don't want to prepare it (for use in another CD-burning application), click Ignore rather than OK in the window that appears when you first insert a CD.

When the disc is done, eject it from the drive and put it a safe place. It's not a good idea to subject backup media to hot sunlight, high humidity, moisture, or extreme cold. If you live or work in a climate with temperature extremes, try to locate a cool, dark place (such as a metal closet) to put the backup disks.

Copying Your Hard Drive

In addition to the methods previously mentioned for storing your data, your Mac comes equipped with a piece of software that turns files into *disk images* that are read by computers as if they were CDs. This software, called Disk Utility, is located in the Utilities folder within the Applications folder of your hard drive. Disk Utility is mainly used to fix file permission discrepancies and hard drive errors, but it also includes a slick tool that is useful for creating an exact duplicate of your hard drive. Disk Utility even has built-in CD-burning capabilities to make turning a disk image into a real CD a matter of a few clicks.

Creating Disk Images with Disk Utility

There are two ways to generate an image in Disk Utility: by copying an existing item, or by creating an empty image file, mounting it, and then copying files to it.

To create an empty image file:

1. Open Disk Utility, and don't select any drives.

2. From the Images menu, choose New, Blank Image. The dialog box shown in Figure 36.4 appears.

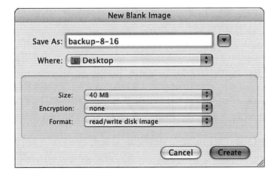

FIGURE 36.4
Make a new image and then copy files to it.

3. Fill in the Save As field to give a name to the image file.

4. Choose a size for the image from the Size pop-up menu. There are a variety of preset sizes for common media, such as Zip disks, CDs, DVDs, and a Custom setting for arbitrary sizes.

For each image you create, you must have enough free space on your hard drive. For example, to create a CD image, you need approximately 650MB free. Currently shipping Apple computers come with at least 10GB drives, so this really shouldn't be an issue.

5. If you want to encrypt the disk image, choose AES-128 in the Encryption pop-up menu.

6. Choose a format in the Format pop-up menu. The options are read/write disk image, which takes up a set amount of space, or sparse disk image, which fills only the space needed for the files it holds. (Sparse disk images are used for the distribution of software over the Internet—why require customers to download more than they need to?)

7. Click Create.

After the blank image is created, it will appear in the sidebar in the Disk Utility window. To add files to it, select the each file and drag it to the newly created disk image.

To create a disk image from an existing folder drive, open the Images menu and choose an available folder or drive from the New submenu. In the window that appears, similar to the one shown in Figure 36.4, give your disk image a name, choose a location to save it, and pick an image format and whether to encrypt. Finally, click the Save button.

A Progress window appears to show how much of the image has been created. Depending on the size of the folder or drive being duplicated, it may take a while.

After you have a disk image of your data, you can move it over the Internet or network to a safe storage place or burn an actual CD of it.

To burn a CD from Disk Utility, follow these steps:

To burn a CD from within Disk Utility with an external burner, you must have your CD writer connected and powered on. Check Apple's Web site for supported writers.

1. Open Disk Utility.

2. Locate the disk image you want to burn in the sidebar of the Disk Utility window.

3. Select the image in the sidebar, and click the Burn button in the toolbar.

4. Place a blank CD-R or CD-RW in your CD writer.

5. Click OK in the confirmation window to begin burning.

Using Backup Software

If you have many files, or if your files need to be backed up from more than one Mac OS computer on a network, you'll do better with some backup software.

Such software can

▶ Perform scheduled backups—You can set the software to perform the back-ups at a regular time (daily, every other day, weekly, whatever). At the appointed time, you only need to have the backup media in place and the computers turned on for the process to go.

Although automatic backups are great, a backup can stop dead in its tracks if the media runs out of space, the media isn't ready, or the computer is shut down by mistake. If you have many files, make sure that your disks have enough space, or be prepared to check the backup process every so often in case of trouble.

Watch Out!

▶ Perform networked backups—With the right software, backups can be done from all computers on a network to one or more backup drives.

▶ Back up the entire drive or selected files or folders—When you set up your backup, you can instruct the software to limit the backup to the items you want. By default, they do the entire drive and then incremental backups for each disk, unless you pick a full backup.

Choosing Backup Software

When you've decided on the backup software route, you'll want to know what to choose. Fortunately, several good Mac OS software packages will give you great automatic backups. They vary in features, and you'll want to pick one based on what you need.

Regardless of the software you choose, make sure that it is compatible with Mac OS X. The file structures of Mac OS X files are often different from the ones used in the Classic Mac OS. This means that non-native applications won't recognize those

Watch Out!

files, hence your backup won't be complete. If you only intend to back up document files, of course, this doesn't matter, but if you want to back up your applications and operating systems (or the whole drive), it's very important.

Here's a brief description of backup programs:

▶ Backup—For home users who just want to make sure that their critical data is backed up to CD, DVD, or iDisk, Apple's aptly named Backup may be the right answer. Shown in Figure 36.5, Backup is a simple piece of software capable of selecting common file types (such as Word documents), System information (such as Safari preferences), or arbitrary files and folders and backing them up to your Mac's optical drive or .Mac iDisk. It does not currently offer incremental backups, nor a way of performing unattended backups.

Backup is a .Mac membership exclusive application. This means that to download and use the tool, you'll need to pay the $100 entrance fee (www.mac.com/). See Chapter 14, "Exploring .Mac Benefits," for more information about the benefits of .Mac.

FIGURE 36.5
Apple's Backup is a simple tool for backing up data files.

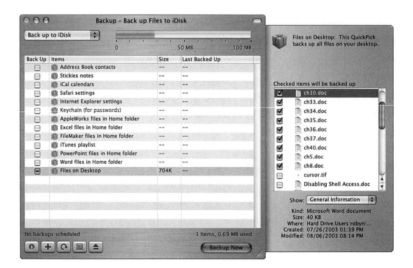

▶ Data Backup from ProSoft Engineering (www.prosoftengineering.com/products/data_backup.php) is a complete personal backup system that

picks up where Apple's tool leaves off. It offers advanced features such as scheduling, compression, mirroring, synchronization, incremental backups, and an "evolutive" mode that preserves different versions of files as they change across backups. For personal workstations, Data Backup X is difficult to beat. If you can afford the $50 expense, Data Backup X is the most feature-filled personal backup software currently available.

> On a positive note, .Mac membership also buys you a copy of Virex virus scanning software, along with the mac.com email, iDisk, and iSync capabilities. For Mac users who aren't running servers or using Unix tools, this might be a wise investment. For others, however, the money might be better spent on a third-party backup solution.

By the Way

▶ Retrospect—From Dantz (www.dantz.com), this is a heavy-duty backup program that does just about everything you can imagine in backup planning with little fuss or bother. You can use its EasyScript feature to create a complete backup plan simply by answering some basic questions. Backups are compressed (to save space) and saved in a special format for efficient retrieval. Unlike other backup programs, Retrospect can work with tape drives, which can store many megabytes of files on little cartridges. Retrospect can also work with Internet-based backup services. For large networks, there's the Retrospect Network Backup Kit and even a Windows version with similar features.

▶ Retrospect Desktop—This program distills the most important features of Retrospect and puts them in a smaller, less-expensive package.

Activity Monitor

After looking at software updates and backing up data, we'll round out our system management discussion with a look at system resources. With the multitasking capabilities of Mac OS X, you may find it interesting to check what your system resources are being used for.

Activity Monitor, found in the Utilities folder of the Application folder on your hard drive, can illustrate system activity with simple graphs for CPU, System Memory, Disk Activity, Disk Usage, and Network activity. Figure 36.6 shows Activity Monitor at work.

FIGURE 36.6
The Activity Monitor
shows how active
your computer is on
a number of differ-
ent measures.

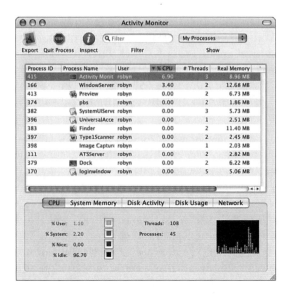

At the top of the window is a live list of active processes. You can also choose whether to view only your own processes, all processes, or other subgroups of processes from the pop-up menu at the upper right. The data displayed about each process includes the percentage of CPU time, the amount of memory it consumes, and the user running it.

Summary

Mac OS X gives you a great deal of flexibility, but it also requires more responsibility to run. To successfully keep your computer running smoothly and safely, you must stay current with system patches and create backups. If system performance problems arise, it may be beneficial to understand the effort your computer is expending to do the tasks you ask of it. We began the chapter with a look at Apple's automated software updates. Next, we looked at several options for backing up your data, including burning data CDs and creating disk images to transfer over the Internet or network to a safe storage place. To finish up, you learned about the Activity Monitor Utility, which allows you to observe the processor function of your computer.

CHAPTER 37

Recovering from Crashes and Other Problems

In this chapter, you'll learn ways to react to application and system crashes and ways to be proactive about virus protection. You'll also learn to use your OS X install CD to reset your password and, in times of widespread system failure, to reinstall your operating system.

Application Unexpectedly Quits

One of the more common problems you'll face is an application quitting. Suddenly, without warning, the document window disappears from the screen, and you'll see a message similar to the one shown in Figure 37.1.

FIGURE 37.1
This unfriendly message might sometimes appear when you're working on a document.

> Unfortunately, when a program quits while you're working on a document all the work you've done since the last time it was saved will be gone—unless the application has a recovery feature that autosaves, such as Microsoft Word. For that reason, save your documents often so that you won't lose much if something goes wrong.

By the Way

Mac OS X is designed to be stable despite localized problems with applications because of its protected memory feature. So if an application unexpectedly quits, you can continue to compute in safety without needing to restart.

Restarting Classic

When there's a rule, there's always an exception: If the application happens to be running in the Classic environment (see the section on running Classic applications in Chapter 4, "Working with Folders, Files, and Applications"), the net effect is that Classic itself becomes unstable, so it's time to take the safe way out and follow these steps:

1. Quit all your open Classic programs if you can.

2. Launch the System Preferences application from the Dock, the Apple menu, or the Applications folder.

Watch Out!

> Even if Classic seems to run satisfactorily after a program quits, don't just sit there and continue working (and definitely don't consider trying to launch the program that quit again). It's the nature of the Classic Mac Operating System to be unstable after a crash, even though it won't affect your regular Mac OS X system. To avoid an even worse crash (and possibly lose information in your files), you should restart Classic immediately.

3. Click the Classic icon to open the Classic Preferences pane (see Figure 37.2).

4. Click the Restart button. If it fails to work, click Force Quit (see the following section "Other System Crashes") and OK the choice; then try Restart again.

FIGURE 37.2
You can restart or configure Classic from this preferences pane.

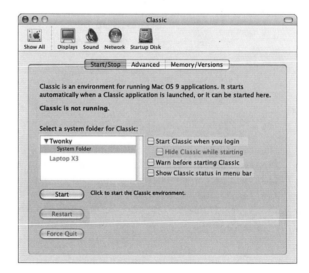

If you don't plan on using a Classic application after using the Force Quit function, you don't have to restart that environment. Whenever you do launch a Classic application, Classic is restarted as part of the package.

Other System Crashes

Not all crashes cause an application to quit. Sometimes the application just stops running. The mouse might freeze, or it might move around but won't do anything.

If this happens, follow these steps:

Using Force Quit

1. Force quit the program. Hold down the Cmd-Option-Esc keys, or click on the Finder icon in the Dock; then choose Force Quit from the Apple menu. You see a Force Quit Applications window as shown in Figure 37.3.

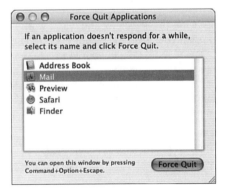

FIGURE 37.3
Choose the application to Force Quit from this window.

2. Normally, the application you were just running is selected. If not, select the application.

3. Click Force Quit. Over the next few seconds, Mac OS X should make the program quit. If it fails to occur, try again. Sometimes it takes two tries for the system to get the message.

4. If the program really doesn't quit, go to the Apple menu and choose Restart. At this point, there might be systemwide instability, and it doesn't hurt to start from scratch.

An occasional Mac OS X system error is called a *kernel panic*. The symptoms are instructions in several languages to restart your computer. The instructions tell you to hold down the power button for several seconds. If holding down the power button does not restart your computer, use the following instructions to force a restart.

Forcing a Restart

If your computer refuses to shut down or restart in the normal fashion, you'll have to force the process by using the reset function. Resetting is done in different ways on different models of Macs. On flat-panel iMacs and other newer models, you must press and hold down the power button for 5 seconds. After the computer shuts down, turn your computer on as you normally would.

On older Macs, you may have to search for a tiny button labeled with a triangle-shaped icon and then press it. (On some models you may need to use the point of a pencil or a straightened paperclip to press the button.) As soon as you press and release the reset button, your Mac should restart normally.

Consider this action only if the previous process won't work because it's much more drastic. If attempting to reset your Mac fails, your only remaining option is to pull the plug, literally. Now wait 30 seconds, plug in your Mac again and turn it on. At this point, you should be able to start normally, except that you might find the startup process pauses for some extra seconds at the Checking Disks prompt on the Mac OS X startup screen. This is because a forced shutdown could cause minor disk directory damage, which is fixed during the startup process. This should not be any cause for concern.

Don't push the start button or reset button too hard.

Causes of Crashes

A rare system crash, maybe once every few days or so, is normal behavior for a Mac OS computer or even one of those computers from the *other* side. Don't get me wrong—Mac OS X is a resilient system; you could go for days or weeks before a crash occurs, but it can still happen. It's just the nature of the beast. If you encounter crashes several times a day, however, something is definitely wrong. You might be seeing a conflict with some new software or hardware you've installed.

Fortunately, there are ways to check for the cause of such problems. Consider the following:

▶ Recent software installations—What did you do just before your computer began to crash? If you just installed some new software that runs only in the Classic environment and puts files in the Classic System Folder, maybe one of those files is causing a conflict. You'll want to check the program's documentation (or Read Me, if there is one) to see whether the publisher is aware of any problems. As a test, with a Classic application open, you can open Extensions Manager (from the Control Panels folder) and disable any system programs used with the new software, by running a Mac OS 9.x Base set (or the set that applies to the system you have). This restricts it to the bare bones stuff you need to boot your computer. Then restart and see whether the problems continue. Of course, you might be disabling something needed to make the program run, but at least you'll be able to see what might have caused your problem. If the problem goes away, go back to Extensions Manager and restore the other extensions a few at a time. After a few restarts, you're apt to come to a probable solution.

▶ Recent hardware upgrades—If you just installed a RAM upgrade on your computer and it is now crashing, maybe the RAM module you installed is defective. It's always possible and not easy to test for. You might want to consider removing the RAM upgrade, strictly as a test. Then work with your Mac to see whether the crashes go away. If they do, contact the dealer for a replacement module. If you've installed an extra drive, scanner, or other device, disconnect it (and turn off its software) and see whether the problem disappears.

▶ Hardware defects—As with any electronic product, there's always the slight chance one or more of the components in your computer might fail. In the vast majority of cases, however, a software conflict (or defective RAM) causes constant crashes. If you've tested everything and your Mac still won't work reliably, don't hesitate to contact Apple Computer or your dealer and arrange for service.

Resetting PRAM

PRAM (pronounced P-RAM) is a battery-powered portion of your computer's memory where default settings for basic functions (including video display and what's connected to certain types of ports) and some system preferences (including the startup disk) are stored. If, on starting your computer, the picture doesn't display properly or other basic functions (such as the time) don't reflect the preferences you've set, you may need to reset the PRAM.

> If you frequently have to reset your PRAM, it may be time to replace your computer's internal battery.

To reset, or "zap," the PRAM, restart your computer while holding down the keys Command-Option-P-R. Wait for your computer to chime twice before releasing the keys. (The screen also flashes when the PRAM has been reset.)

> Although resetting the PRAM is sometimes necessary, remember that doing so resets many of your Mac's essential preferences and may result in loss of some settings. The bottom line is that you may not want to do this without reason.

Viruses

Without getting overly technical, a computer virus is simply a chunk of code that attaches itself to a document or program. After the program is run, the virus begins to do its thing. Some viruses are destructive and will destroy your files and possibly damage your hard drive.

Few, if any, viruses affect Mac OS X. Unfortunately, this doesn't mean that viruses that affect it can't, or won't, be created—it's better to be safe than sorry.

A Look at Virus Protection Software

As with any software product, a specific set of features might be more appealing to you, but any of the programs I'm describing will do the job.

▶ Norton AntiVirus—This program, published by Symantec, at www.symantec.com is designed to check for viruses every time you insert a disk into a drive, mount a networked disk on your computer's desktop, or download a file from the Internet; the latter courtesy of its Safe Zone feature. So-called suspicious activities are also monitored. You can perform scheduled scans, where the program launches automatically at a predetermined hour and scans your drives. One intriguing feature is called Live Update, where the program logs on to the publisher's site every month and checks for updates to protect against newly discovered viruses.

Such features as Live Update, which retrieve minor program updates and new virus definitions, don't mean that you'll never have to pay for a new version of the software. From time to time, usually every year or two, a publisher will release an upgrade that you actually have to purchase. That's how they stay in business.

▶ Virex—This is published by Network Associates, at www.nai.com (see Figure 37.4). Many of the features offered by Norton AntiVirus are also available with Virex. The program scans files from a networked drive or the ones you download, and it performs scheduled scans. A special technology called heuristics is designed to check for viruslike activity to help protect you against unknown viruses. Updates to the program are usually offered on a monthly basis and are available via its Auto Update feature.

Virex is part of the package available to those who subscribe to .Mac. If you're in the market for virus software, check out Chapter 14, "Exploring .Mac Benefits," to see whether Virex and the other perks are worth the price!

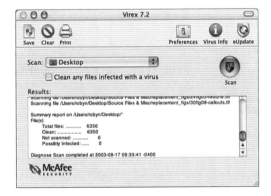

▶ VirusBarrier—A third contender, VirusBarrier, comes from Intego (www.intego.com), a fairly new software publisher in the Mac marketplace, but one that's attracting a lot of attention for its product line, which also includes Internet protection and security software. Similar to the virus protection applications, there's an automatic update feature so that your virus protection remains current.

Buying and installing virus software isn't necessarily a guarantee that you'll be protected.

New viruses are discovered all the time. The publishers of virus software share information, so everyone can be protected in case a new virus strain crops up. You'll want to check a publisher's Web site at least once a month for virus detection updates. The information on how to keep updated is usually included with the publisher's documentation. Using a program's capability to do automatic scheduled updates is a real plus.

Restoring the Administrator Password

If the Mac OS X administrator password is forgotten or misplaced, Apple provides a facility for restoring a password. Boot your computer from the Mac OS X install CD (hold down the C key while turning on your computer with the CD in the CD-ROM drive). When the Installer application starts, choose Reset Password from the Installer application menu.

Detected Mac OS X volumes are listed along the top of the window. To reset a password, follow these steps:

1. Click the main boot drive to load the password database for that volume.

2. Next, use the pop-up menu to choose the user account that you want to reset.

3. Fill in the new password in both of the password fields.

4. Finally, click Save to store the new password.

After rebooting your system, you can immediately log in with the new password.

Fixing Hard Drive Problems

Your computer comes with a tool that can check for and repair hard drive problems. The program is called Disk Utility, and you'll find a copy in the Utilities folder inside the Applications folder. (We looked at Disk Utility in Chapter 36, "Maintaining Your System," as a tool for making a disk image of your hard drive.

If you begin to see system errors related to denied permissions or failures to access needed components, you can run the First Aid component of Disk Utility to verify or repair file permissions. Simply open Disk Utility and then click the First Aid button. Finally, select the drive or drives whose permissions you want to verify or repair (see Figure 37.5). The process may take several minutes, but you can watch as Disk Utility lists all the files on your computer for which the current permissions don't match what they should be.

After you install software, you may want to use Disk Utility to repair file permissions—sometimes software installers make changes to file ownership or permissions that result in slower system performance or even failures by other applications.

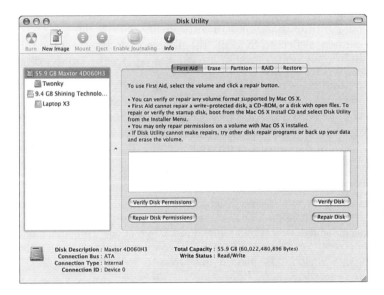

FIGURE 37.5
The First Aid component of Mac OS X's Disk Utility can check your drive for basic directory problems and fix them.

In addition to identifying and fixing permissions problems, Disk Utility can verify and repair drives. This feature can be used for preventive maintenance. If you repair your hard drive periodically, you may avoid the "sudden" appearance of a larger hard drive failure. (Hard drives, as storage devices that are continuously in use, can develop localized problems before a user becomes aware of them.)

Note, however, that you cannot repair directory problems on a startup drive (the drive from which the operating system is running) from the Disk Utility application on your hard drive. If you need to repair your main drive, you will need to boot from your system installation CD and run a version of Disk Utility from that disk. To do this, insert the CD and restart your computer while holding down the C key. When your system is booted, choose Open Disk Utility from the Installer application menu and run the repair.

The nice thing about Disk Utility is that it's free, but it's not a 100% solution. Several popular commercial programs offer to go beyond Disk First Aid in checking your drive and repairing catalog damage.

Here's a brief description of several hard drive diagnostic programs and what they do:

▶ DiskWarrior—This single-purpose program is from Alsoft (www.alsoft.com), a publisher of several Mac utility products. Its stock in trade is the capability to rebuild, rather than repair, a corrupted hard drive directory file. The original catalog is checked to locate the files on your drive and then that information is used to make a new directory to replace the damaged one.

▶ Norton Utilities—From Symantec, this is the oldest available hard drive maintenance and repair package. The centerpiece is Disk Doctor, which checks your hard drive and fixes problems. Additional components of the package can optimize your drive to speed up file retrieval and to recover your drive in the event a crash makes it inaccessible. The program can also help you recover the files you trash by mistake.

Watch Out!

> Older versions of Norton Utilities cannot work with the file system on your computer, which is known as HFS+ (or Mac OS Extended). At the very least, they might even make catalog damage worse, and the end result is that your computer's drive contents will become unavailable. In addition, you cannot scan disks running Mac OS X unless you use version 6.0 or later of this program.

▶ TechTool Pro—In addition to hard drive repairs, TechTool Pro (www.micromat.com) can optimize the drive and even run a wide range of diagnostic checks on all your computer's hardware and attached devices. One great feature is the capability to perform an extended test of your computer's RAM. This might be helpful if you suddenly face a lot of crashes after doing a RAM upgrade. To add to its bag of tricks, TechTool Pro can also do virus checks. To check a Mac OS X drive, you'll need to restart from your TechTool Pro CD.

▶ Drive 10—As the name implies, this is a special purpose utility from the publisher of TechTool Pro designed to diagnose hard drives running Mac OS X. Although it can run a pretty hefty suite of tests, you need to restart your Mac from the supplied CD to fix problems. Running a scan first is a real time-saver; you only have to restart if a problem is reported.

**Watch
Out!**

If you choose any of the disk repair packages, be sure to use them as directed in the instructions.

Optimizing Your Hard Drive

In the course of normal use of your Mac, the computer is constantly writing various files, deleting others, and fitting them into unallocated spaces on the hard drive. Over time, the hard drive becomes fragmented, where different parts of a single file are split into sections and spread out wherever they fit.

The demands that large files, such as digital video, place on the hard drive, can cause this fragmentation to have a significant impact in the length of time needed to read or save a file. *Defragmenting* basically takes the various parts of each file from different sections of the hard drive and reassembles them into one contiguous block. That allows the computer to read the file without having to jump around the hard drive.

**By the
Way**

There is some debate about whether optimizing drives running OS X is really beneficial for typical users. Although there may be some a small benefit immediately after optimizing a fragmented drive, crowding all the files together during optimization means that any subsequent changes to the files will result in new fragmentation that negates prior optimization. On the other hand, working with large files in iMovie or iDVD may benefit you enough to make disk optimization worth your while.

To defragment and optimize your hard drive, you must purchase a drive tool such as those mentioned previously.

Reinstalling System Software

Why do you want to reinstall system software? Perhaps your Mac is unstable, no matter what you do. At this point, all your efforts to clean up things have gone for naught.

There is a drastic method to fix everything, but it's not something you would do normally, and that's to run your Mac Restore CD (or CDs, because some models come with several). When you do that, however, you might lose all your custom program settings, and (if you opt for the erase disk option), all the files you created on your Mac. What's more, if you have updated your Mac Operating System, all that will be lost as well. So I mention it here as an option, but only as a last resort.

By the Way

Reinstalling Mac OS X does not necessarily replace your system accounts, information, or configuration. There are, however, a few drawbacks—most notably, the system updates are replaced by the original version of the operating system. After running the Mac OS X Installer to recover a damaged system, you must force an update on your computer by going to the Software Update setting of the System Preferences and clicking the Check Now button or by choosing Software Update from the Apple menu.

Here are the steps needed to reinstall OS X using your System Installer CD:

1. Get out your system Install CD, press the CD button, and insert the CD in your CD drive.

2. Restart your Mac. If need be, force a restart as described previously.

3. As soon as you hear the computer's startup sound, hold down the C key. This enables your computer to start from your system CD.

4. The installer launches automatically.

5. After your system installation is finished, go ahead and restart and check that everything is working properly.

Summary

System crashes and application quits can be inconvenient, but you learned in this chapter that you are not helpless against them. You learned to force quit unresponsive applications and to restart unresponsive computers. You discovered the secret of resetting your password with your system install CD. You also learned how to set up a preventive regime to defend against computer viruses. You learned about some disk repair options. Finally, you learned how to reinstall your operating system in case your computer begins to experience widespread failures.

PART VII

Advanced Topics

CHAPTER 38

Using Basic Unix Commands

In the past several years, an operating system known as Linux has sprung from obscurity to the front page of every IT publication in the world. Unix-based operating systems are powerful and stable, but many average computer users have been intimidated by their complexity. Also, traditionally, people had to access Unix systems from the command line, by typing text commands in a text-only window. As you found out way back in Chapter 1, "Introducing Mac OS X," Apple has harnessed that power and stability while maintaining the ease of a traditional Macintosh by designing Mac OS X with a Unix subsystem.

By creating Mac OS X, Apple has become the largest producer of Unix-based operating systems on the planet!

By the Way

If you've been using Mac OS X for a while now, you might be wondering what all this command-line talk is about—after all, you certainly haven't needed to type a command on your system, nor have any of your applications required you to access a command prompt. That's precisely what Apple intended when creating Mac OS X.

Beneath the veneer of Mac OS X's graphical interface lies the powerful BSD (Berkley Software Distribution) version of the Unix platform. This layer sits behind many of the tasks you perform on your machine and coordinates the actions that make using your Macintosh possible. Although you don't have to directly interact with this underlying system to complete your day-to-day tasks, you can—if you choose to do so.

Terminal: The Window to the Underworld

The Terminal application (/Applications/Utilities/Terminal) provides your point of access to the BSD subsystem of Mac OS X. Opening Terminal creates a new window with a beckoning command prompt, just waiting for some input, as shown in Figure 38.1.

FIGURE 38.1
Terminal opens a
window into the
Unix layer of Mac
OS X.

You can customize the appearance of the Terminal application in a number of ways, such as changing the font, resizing the window, and setting a title in the Window Settings, found in the Terminal application menu. One of the most important changes you can make, however, is setting an unlimited scrollback buffer.

As you use the Terminal program and begin to explore Unix, you will be able to "scroll back" to check on the output of commands that you've entered using the scrollbars. By default, the Terminal remembers 10,000 lines. This might seem like a lot, but those who use Terminal to do serious operations will quickly see that it isn't. To change to an unlimited scrollback buffer, follow these steps:

1. Open the Terminal application Window Settings, found in the application menu.

2. Click the Buffer option in the pop-up menu at the top of the window.

3. Select the Unlimited Scrollback radio button, shown in Figure 38.2.

4. Close the settings by closing the window or click Use Settings as Defaults.

5. Open a new Terminal window by choosing File, New Shell from the menu (Command-N).

6. The new window is ready for use with an unlimited scrollback buffer.

Now that you've found the command prompt, let's see what you can do with it. Whenever possible, I'll try to relate the command-line tools to their graphical Mac OS X alternatives.

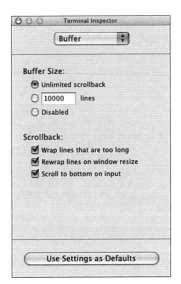

FIGURE 38.2
An unlimited scroll-back buffer helps you keep track of the things you've done.

Working with Files: Basic Commands

As you work with the Mac OS X Finder, you get to know a sequence of mouse commands for working with the files and folders on your system. These same actions can be carried out from the command line very easily. In some cases, you might find that the command line is actually faster for some tasks than the Finder.

Basic Commands

Let's start with some of the basic commands for listing, moving, and copying files. Obviously, you can't do much with your files unless you can see them, so we start with the ls (or list) function.

ls

Typing ls at the command prompt displays all the available files in the current directory (folder). Because the Terminal opens to your home directory and you haven't learned how to change directories, you probably see a list of the files inside your home that's similar to the list following list:

```
[client18:~john] john% ls
Desktop     Library    Music       Public
Documents   Movies     Pictures    Sites
```

As you know, your Mac OS X files also have permissions on them. To view the listing with permissions showing, use ls -l, and you see a list similar to the following:

```
[client18:~john] john% ls -l
total 94296

drwx — — —    9 john   john        306 Jul 25 01:11 Desktop
drwx — — —   49 john   john       1666 Jul 10 23:55 Documents
drwx — — —   41 john   john       1394 May 30 18:58 Library
drwx — — —    6 john   john        204 Mar 30 02:40 Movies
drwx — — —    3 john   john        102 Mar 30 02:40 Music
drwx — — —    6 john   john        204 Jul 10 23:55 Pictures
drwxr-xr-x    6 john   john        204 Mar 30 02:40 Public
drwxr-xr-x   16 john   john        544 Jul 10 23:55 Sites
```

For the most part, the listing is straightforward. The second column is a count of the number of files in a directory. The third and fourth columns are the owner and group, respectively. The fifth column contains the file size, whereas the sixth and seventh columns are the modification date and filename.

The first column, however, is filled with strange letters, such as drwx (repeated several times). The first character of this sequence of letters indicates what kind of file it is. In the listing example, the first characters are all the letter d—for directories. The rest of the nine letters represent read, write, and execute permissions for the user, group, and everyone, respectively.

By the Way

> The Mac OS X GUI doesn't provide a control over the execute permission of a file. This attribute, as its name suggests, controls whether the file can be executed or, in Mac terms, *run*.

For example, assume that you see a column with drwxr-xr—. Following the pattern we set up, the first letter, d, indicates that this is a directory, and the next three letters, rwx, tell us that the owner has read, write, and execute permissions. The middle three positions, r-x, show read and execute permission for everyone within the file's group, and the last three, r—, tell us that everyone else has read permission for the file.

Special "abbreviations" are used to represent two special files (you can see these when you use ls -al):

- ► .—A single period represents the current directory.
- ► ..—Two periods represent the parent directory of the current directory.

You can use this directory notation with the other commands we look at in this section.

cp

The next command we look at is the cp, or copy, command. Copy, as its name suggests, is used to copy files or directories of files. The syntax for cp is simply

```
cp <source file path> <destination file path>
```

For example, to copy the file test.txt to testcopy.txt, you would type

```
cp test.txt testcopy.txt
```

This does nothing more than create an exact duplicate of the file test.txt named testcopy.txt in the same directory. To copy a file to another directory, just include the full pathname of the file.

In the case of copying a directory, you must perform a *recursive* copy, which copies the contents of the folder and the contents of any folders within the source. Do this by supplying the -R option to cp. For example, if I want to copy the directory /Users/jray/testfiles and all of its contents to the folder /Users/robyn/otherfiles, I use the following command:

```
cp -R /Users/jray/testfiles /Users/robyn/otherfiles
```

Simple enough, isn't it? You might recognize this as the equivalent of Option-dragging a file within the Finder, or using the Copy contextual menu command.

If you play with cp, you might notice that it cannot copy Macintosh-specific files (applications, files with custom icons, and so on). To get around this, you can use the ditto command, which copies one directory to another, complete with all the information that makes a Macintosh file special.

Did you Know?

---

mv

"Moving" right along, the mv command can move a file or directory from one place to another or rename it. It uses the same syntax as cp:

```
mv <source file path> <destination file path>
```

This is the same as clicking and dragging an icon from one place to another within the Finder.

For example:

```
mv myfile.txt myoldfile.txt
```

This moves the file myfile.txt to myoldfile.txt, effectively renaming the file. Like copy (cp), you could move the file to another directory by using its full pathname.

For example:

```
mv myfile.txt /Users/robyn/robynsfilenow.txt
```

Here the file `myfile.txt` is moved to /Users/robyn and stored with the new name: robynsfilenow.txt.

rm

Now that you can list, move, and copy files, you should probably also learn how to delete them. The rm (remove) command erases a file from your system. It's extremely important that you pay attention to what you're doing with rm because no Undo command or Trash exists from which to remove a deleted file.

When using rm, I recommend using the -i option along with it. This forces the system to ask you before removing a file. The basic syntax for rm is

```
rm -i <filename>
```

If you want to remove an entire directory, you must also add the -r option to the mix to force rm to go through the directory and remove all the files within it. For example, suppose that you want to remove a directory called myjunkfiles, including all the files inside it. To do that, type the following:

```
rm -ri myjunkfiles
```

The rm command steps through each file in the directory and prompts you to confirm that the file should be deleted.

Wildcards

When working with files, you can use a few special symbols in place of characters in the filename. Specifically, the following sequences are available:

- ▶ *—Matches any number of characters in a filename
- ▶ ?—Matches a single unknown character
- ▶ [0-9]—Matches a range of characters

For example, if I want to list only the files in a directory that contain the letters memo anywhere in their names, I would type

```
ls *memo*
```

If, on the other hand, I want to be a bit more specific, such as listing all files that start with memo and end with exactly two characters that I don't know, I could use

```
ls memo??
```

Finally, to be even more exact, I could match a range of characters using the format [<start>-<end>]. Assume that I have a group of files, all named memo, followed by two extra characters—some of which are numbers. To list all the memo files followed by the numbers, I could enter

```
ls memo[0-9][0-9]
```

Wildcards make it easy to work with groups of files and directories without having to list each name separately.

Editing Files with `pico`

Creating and editing files is another important part of mastering the Mac OS X command line. This is a definite necessity for performing remote administration of the system, enabling you to make changes to your system's configuration from almost any terminal connected to the Internet.

A number of text editors are available that you can use from the Mac OS X command line:

▶ emacs — The emacs editor is a powerful editor that can be used for programming and basic editing tasks, and can even be programmed using the Lisp language.

▶ vi — vi is the choice editor for die-hard Unix fans. It's fast and omnipresent—it's available on just about any Unix machine that exists. (By the way, vi is pronounced *V-I*, not *Vee*.)

▶ pico—The pico editor is a modern editor for beginners. Like vi, it's fast, but it's much simpler to use and is the focus of our attention here.

To use pico, start it from the command line with the name of the file you want to edit or from a new file that you want to create:

```
pico <filename>
```

Figure 38.3 shows the `pico` editor running.

FIGURE 38.3
Pico is an easy-to-
use command-line
editor. (As you can
see, it can even be
used to make
changes to the
HTML for a Web
page.)

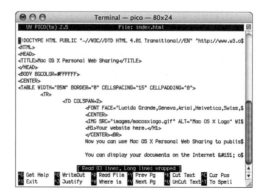

To operate `pico`, use the arrow keys on your keyboard to move the cursor around the screen. Typing enters new text, whereas pressing Delete removes existing characters. You can also use a number of control characters during editing:

- ▶ Control-G—Opens a help screen with basic usage instructions
- ▶ Control-O—Writes (saves) the file
- ▶ Control-R—Reads a new file into the editor
- ▶ Control-Y—Jumps to the previous page
- ▶ Control-V—Jumps to the next page
- ▶ Control-W—Searches the file for a given sequence of characters
- ▶ Control-X—Exits `pico`

> You can certainly use `pico` to read files as well as edit them, but if you just want to quickly scroll through a file, use `more <filename>` to move through the file a page at a time.

File Permissions

The final file operations that we look at are how to modify permissions. You've already discovered how you can tell what the permissions of a file are (using `ls`)—now let's see how you can change them.

```
chown
```

By default, you own every file that you create. That's fine, but you might want to change the owner of a file so that you can give it to someone else. The `chown` command (change ownership) performs this task with ease. Although you can also do this in the Finder, you can use the command-line `chown` command with filename wildcards to handle multiple files simultaneously.

To use `chown`, all you need is the name of the file you want to change and the username of the person you want to assign ownership to:

```
chown <username> <filename>
```

To change the ownership of a file called test.txt to the user jray, you would type

```
chown jray test.txt
```

You might need to prefix the line with the `sudo` command, which you learn about a bit later in this chapter.

```
chmod
```

The `chmod` command (change mode) modifies file permissions—the read, write, and execute attributes that you saw earlier when learning about the `ls` function.

The `chmod` command takes as its parameters a filename and the permissions that you want to assign to it. The permissions are given using a symbolic representation based on the letters u, g, o, and r, w, and x. The u, g, and o are user, group, and other, respectively. The letters r, w, and x represent the read, write, and execute permissions.

Combining these letters with + and -, you can add or subtract any permission from any type of access level:

```
chmod <permission> <filename>
```

For example, to remove write permission for the owner of a file named nowrite.txt, you would enter

```
chmod u-w nowrite.txt
```

Likewise, to add read permission for other users (the rest of the world), use this syntax:

```
chmod o+r nowrite.txt
```

As you can see, the Unix commands give you a much greater level of control than using the equivalent Get Info feature in the Finder.

Managing files in Unix is the same as managing files in Mac OS X's Finder, but instead of mouse actions, typed commands are used to tell your computer what to do. Before moving on, try editing a few files and using the basic mv and cp commands to move them around. When you feel comfortable with the process, move on to the next section, "Process Management." There you learn how the Unix side of your computer views running applications.

Process Management

As you use your Mac OS X computer, you create dozens of processes and support processes that you probably never realized existed. In Chapter 36, "Maintaining Your System," you learn about some of the GUI tools that enable you to manage these processes in a point-and-click manner. In this section, however, you see the commands that can provide the raw data of what is happening on your system.

Viewing Processes

To view the active processes on your computer, you can use one of two commands. The first command, ps, creates a process listing of whatever's running in the foreground (or, modified, everything that's running). The second command, top, shows a list of the applications using up the most resources on your computer.

ps

To use the ps command, all you need to do is type ps at the command prompt. This generates a list of the processes that you control on the computer. For example:

```
[localhost:~] jray% ps
  PID  TT  STAT     TIME COMMAND
  707 std  Ss    0:00.25 -tcsh (tcsh)
```

Here, the process is my command-line shell (tcsh), which isn't very interesting. To list *everything* that's running on a Mac OS X computer, add the argument -ax to the command, like this:

```
[localhost:~] jray% ps -ax
  PID  TT  STAT     TIME COMMAND
    1  ??  SLs   0:00.05 /sbin/init
    2  ??  SL    0:02.75 /sbin/mach_init
```

```
 41 ?? Ss    0:01.94 kextd
 68 ?? Ss    0:22.85 /System/Library/Frameworks/ApplicationServices.framew
 70 ?? Ss   40:38.78 /System/Library/CoreServices/WindowServer
 72 ?? Ss    0:07.96 update
 75 ?? Ss    0:00.01 dynamic_pager -H 40000000 -L 160000000 -S 80000000 -F
103 ?? Ss    0:00.61 /sbin/autodiskmount -va
127 ?? Ss    0:03.28 configd
185 ?? Ss    0:00.38 syslogd
218 ?? Ss    0:00.02 /usr/libexec/CrashReporter
240 ?? Ss    0:01.37 netinfod -s local
247 ?? Ss    0:04.32 lookupd
257 ?? S<s   0:05.72 ntpd -f /var/run/ntp.drift -p /var/run/ntpd.pid
270 ?? Ss    0:01.38 /System/Library/CoreServices/coreservicesd
277 ?? Ss    0:00.00 inetd
288 ?? S     0:00.00 nfsiod -n 4
289 ?? S     0:00.00 nfsiod -n 4
290 ?? S     0:00.00 nfsiod -n 4
291 ?? S     0:00.00 nfsiod -n 4
298 ?? S     0:00.27 DirectoryService
...and so on.
```

For each process, you'll notice a PID number in the listing. This is the process ID, and it uniquely identifies the program running on your computer. There's also a TIME field, which contains how much cumulative processor time the software has used on your machine.

> You might also notice the TT and STAT columns in the listing. These display the controlling terminal of a given process and its status. Unfortunately, these topics are beyond the scope of this book and are best addressed by an advanced book, such as *Mac OS X Unleashed* from Sams Publishing.

By the Way

Keep track of the PID values—you need them in a few minutes.

top

If you want a more interactive means of monitoring what's running on your system, try using the top command. The utility, shown in Figure 38.4, shows a listing of the most active and processor-intensive applications running on your machine. It can provide a good means of uncovering unusual activity on your computer and answering why your system is sluggish at a given point in time.

When running top, the most active processes are shown at the top of the listing. Usually the Mac OS X components rank very highly in the list (such as the Finder). Watching the CPU (percentage of CPU being used), TIME (total amount of CPU time the application has consumed), and RSIZE (amount of memory the application is using) columns gives you the most useful information about what your computer is doing. If you see an unusual piece of software that you didn't install (perhaps your coworker's copy of Seti@Home) in the listing, you can write down its PID and then force it to quit.

FIGURE 38.4
Use top to get an interactive view of the processes on your computer.

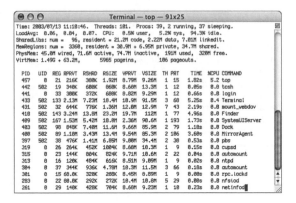

> **By the Way**
>
> To quit top, you'll need to type the key command Control-C. That returns Terminal to a command line where you can continue entering commands.

From the command line, you can use Unix to force any application to quit. Although powerful, this can also pose a danger to the system: Users can easily force important parts of the operating system to quit!

Killing Processes

As violent as it sounds, the action of forcing a running Unix process to quit is called *killing* it. Appropriately enough, this action uses a command called kill.

The kill command's actions don't need to be as drastic as forcing an application to quit. In reality, the kill command simply sends a signal to a process that can be interpreted in a number of ways. Some signals simply cause the software to reload its configuration, whereas others do indeed force it to exit.

The two most common signals you'll encounter are HUP (to force a reload) and KILL (to truly kill a process). Along with a signal, the kill command also requires a process ID (the numbers supplied in the PID column of the ps or top commands).

Armed with this information, you can kill a process using this syntax:

```
kill -<signal> <process id>
```

For example, to force a process with the ID of 1992 to quit, I would type

```
kill -KILL 1992
```

Killing a process with the KILL signal does not save any data that the application is processing. Use this as a last resort for gaining control of a piece of software.

Also be aware that indiscriminately killing processes on your system could make Mac OS X unstable or even crash the operating system.

The kill command can be used remotely to control what's running on your machine and shut down processes that shouldn't be active. In the next section, you learn how to gain complete control over the command line.

Server Administration

Although everything that you've learned so far in this chapter is valid, it isn't necessarily completely functional. For example, you can't change the owner of a file you don't own. In most cases, that's fine, but for complete control over the machine, you should be able to do whatever you want.

The command that makes this possible is sudo. When sudo is placed in front of any other command, it enables you to execute the command as the root user. Root has complete control over everything on your system, so be careful when using the command; you could end up removing all the files from your computer.

For example, to kill a process that you didn't create, you could use the following:

```
sudo kill <signal> <process ID>
```

sudo starts, asks you for your user password, and then executes the given command with root's permissions.

The commands themselves stay the same but gain a whole new level of capability. Using this technique, you can easily remove, copy, or rename files belonging to other users.

Don't let the power go to your head! Other people who use or store files on your system should have a right to privacy, unless you explicitly tell them otherwise. Reading files you don't own is unethical and, depending on the circumstances, may be illegal.

Getting Help with Manpages

Almost every function and utility that exists on your system includes a built-in help file called a *manpage* (manual page). The man command returns all the information you need to understand the arguments a given utility takes, how it works, and the results you should expect. Consider the more command, for example. Although this has been mentioned only briefly, you can quickly learn more information about it by typing

```
man more
```

For example:

```
[localhost:/etc] john% man more
man: Formatting manual page...

MORE(1)                                                          MORE(1)

NAME
     more, page—file perusal filter for crt viewing

SYNOPSIS
     more  [  -cdflsu  ] [ -n ] [ +linenumber ] [ +/pattern ] [
     name ...  ]

     page more options

DESCRIPTION
     More is a filter which allows examination of a  continuous
     text  one screenful at a time on a soft-copy terminal.  It
     normally pauses after each screenful, printing the current
     file name at the bottom of the screen or —More— if input
     is from a pipe.  If the user then types a carriage return,
     one  more  line  is  displayed.  If the user hits a space,
     another screenful is displayed.  Other  possibilities  are
     enumerated later.
...and so on...
```

This is only a tiny portion of the total manpage for the more command. There are more than five pages of information for this function alone!

Did you Know?

If you don't know exactly what command you're looking for, use apropos <keyword> to search through the manpage information for a given word or phrase.

Other Useful Commands

Thousands of other commands and utilities on Mac OS X could potentially be covered in a Unix chapter. Instead of trying to do the impossible and document them all in 15 to 20 pages, we finish the chapter by listing a few interesting functions that you can explore (remember to use man!) if you choose to do so.

- ▶ curl—Retrieves information from a given URL. Useful for downloading files from the command line.

- ▶ ncftp—A simple, yet surprisingly user-friendly FTP client.

- ▶ cat—Displays the contents of a file.

- ▶ file—Shows the type of a file (what it contains).

- ▶ locate—Quickly finds a file based on the text in its name.

- ▶ find—Locates files based on their size, modification dates, and so on. This is the Unix equivalent of the Finder's Find feature.

- ▶ grep—Searches through a text file for a given string.

- ▶ shutdown—Shuts down a Mac OS X computer.

- ▶ reboot—Reboots a Mac OS X computer.

- ▶ date—Displays the current date and time.

- ▶ uptime—Shows the amount of time your computer has been online and what the current system load is.

- ▶ passwd—Changes your Mac OS X password.

- ▶ df—Shows the amount of free and used space on all available partitions.

- ▶ du—Displays disk usage information on a directory-by-directory basis.

- ▶ tar—Archives and dearchives files in the Unix tar format.

- ▶ gzip/gunzip—Compresses and decompresses files.

Again, I want to stress that this should serve as a starting place for exploring the Unix subsystem. You will find commands that aren't listed in this chapter. However, with the documentation provided here, you're prepared for how they work and understand how to get more information about them.

If this chapter has whetted your appetite for using the command line, I highly recommend *Mac OS X Unleashed*, which covers many of the topics discussed in this book but with greater technical detail and much more attention to the Unix side of Mac OS X.

Summary

In this chapter, you learned some of the basics of the Unix command line. You should now be capable of performing many of the standard Finder functions from a command prompt. Although many gaps exist in what was covered, Unix is a broad topic and one that takes years to master. Hopefully you're on your way to becoming a future Unix guru!

CHAPTER 39

Introducing AppleScript

AppleScript has been referred to as Apple's best-kept secret—it is a command-line buried beneath many of the Mac's popular applications, including the Finder, that allows people to automate simple tasks.

To be controlled by AppleScript, an application must implement a *scripting dictionary*, which is a collection of commands and functions that can be invoked through AppleScript. Each application determines the features it makes available for scripting. The result of this approach is that applications can make their most useful functions available through a script so that complex actions can be run with ease.

It's also important to note the audience of Mac OS X's AppleScripting capabilities. AppleScript was intended to provide a means for normal, everyday Macintosh users to automate tasks on their computers. The syntax is surprisingly simple and can be understood even if you've never seen a programming language before. For example, take the following code:

```
tell application "Finder"
      activate
      close window "Applications"
end tell
```

It doesn't *look* like a programming language, but it is. This small example instructs Mac OS X to activate the Finder application and then close an open window with the title Applications.

Using a language that can almost be read aloud and understood, normal users can write scripts that combine the capabilities of multiple applications.

The Script Editor

The easiest way to get started with AppleScript is with the Script Editor. Besides being a programming editor that provides appropriate options for a given context, it also acts as a script recorder. You could open the Script Editor, click Record, and generate a simple program by simply interacting with an AppleScriptable application—the Script Editor records your actions and translates them into words.

By the Way

It's critical to note that AppleScript (and the AppleScript editor) should not be considered a macro system. Macros typically let you record keystrokes and "replay" them to re-create an action. Although this could be considered a limited form of programming, a macro doesn't "know" what it is doing. It can't make decisions or change what it is doing.

When AppleScript controls an application, the application understands what is happening. It can return error codes and extended status to the script, enabling it to react and adapt to changing conditions. AppleScript is a powerful tool and offers flexibility beyond simple macros.

Apple has made remarkable strides in making Mac OS X fully scriptable. Applications such s the Finder and iTunes are fully scriptable.

Basic Usage

Launch the Script Editor from the AppleScript folder inside the Applications folder to begin scripting. Figure 39.1 shows the basic editor window.

FIGURE 39.1
The Script Editor is used when editing or recording AppleScripts.

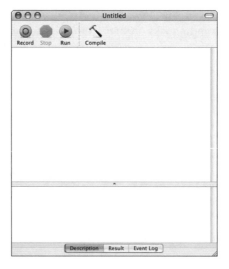

The Script Editor is composed of script recording and editing controls, which include

- ▶ Recording/playback—Similar to a tape deck, these buttons are used to control recording and playback of an AppleScript. Click the Record button (Command-D) to start monitoring your system for Apple events within scriptable applications. These events are then stored in a script. The Stop button (Command-.) is used to stop recording, whereas the Run button (Command-R) executes the actions.

▶ Compile—Reviews the syntax of the current script for errors and automatically reformats the script if needed.

▶ Content—The content area is used to compose and edit script content. It functions like any Mac OS X text editor but has the benefit of autoformatting code when syntax is checked or the script is run.

▶ Description/Result/Event Log—This area is used to display information from or about the script, depending on the active button at the bottom of the window.

Start using the editor by clicking the Record button, switching to the Finder, then opening and dragging a few windows around. As you work within the Finder, an AppleScript will build in the editor window. Click Stop to finish the code block and prepare it for execution. Figure 39.2 displays a script that has just finished generating.

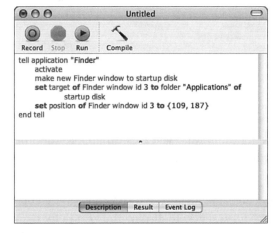

FIGURE 39.2
Click Record to monitor your actions and build an AppleScript and then click Stop to finish the script.

Scripting Dictionary

Obviously, the biggest draw to AppleScript is the capability to create scripts from scratch. Recording is a good way to get a quick start but can't be used to generate anything truly useful. The basic AppleScript syntax will be covered later in "Scripting Syntax.". Even basic syntax, however, is useless without knowledge of what commands an application can accept. You can view a scripting dictionary that shows the functions and properties offered by a given piece of software.

To access a scripting dictionary for any application, choose File, Open Dictionary from the menu. A list of the available scriptable applications is displayed, as demonstrated by Figure 39.3.

FIGURE 39.3
Choose from the available scriptable *applications.*

Be aware that some applications might not appear in this list—the Browse button at the bottom of the window opens a standard Open panel for choosing a file from an alternative location. After you pick an application from the default or browse view, a dictionary window appears, as shown in Figure 39.4.

Along the left side of the dictionary window is a list of the AppleScript functions provided. These functions are divided into categories, based on their purpose. These categories are called *suites*. To display the syntax for a given item, click its name in the list. Highlighting a suite name displays a description of the commands and classes within that grouping and a complete view of the syntax for each.

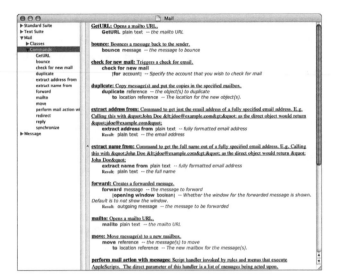

FIGURE 39.4
The dictionary doc-
uments the avail-
able AppleScript
functions.

Hold down Shift and select all the suite headings to create a master list of the available scripting functions. Choose File, Print (Command-P) from the menu to print a
hard-copy reference guide for AppleScripting your favorite applications.

Did you Know?

AppleScript abstracts the parts of an application into objects. An object represents
something you can work with, such as a file. Objects have properties that can be
set or modified to effect changes to the object. The properties can also be
retrieved with get to return results for evaluation. For example, the Finder has a
file object with a file type property. The following script gets and displays the type
for an arbitrary file:

```
1: tell application "Finder"
2:     set thisFile to (choose file with prompt "Pick the file to examine:")
3:     set theType to get the file type of thisFile
4:     display dialog theType
5: end tell
```

Line 1 indicates that instructions will be sent to the Finder. Line 2 sets a variable
called thisFile to point to a file. The choose command opens a file selection dialog box for visually selecting a file. Line 3 sets a variable called theType to the
results of a command that gets the file type of the file reference by thisFile. Line
4 displays a dialog box containing the contents of theType. Finally, line 5 stops
talking to the Finder.

This example introduces the structure you will see in most AppleScript programs. The `tell`, `set`, and `get` statements form the basis of scripts. The objects and the parameters that can be modified, however, will have to be looked up in the application's dictionary.

By the Way

> The `display dialog` command used in this script isn't even a function of basic AppleScript. It is provided by the Standard Additions scripting extension, automatically installed on Mac OS X. You can view additional functions offered by the Standard Additions by displaying its dictionary.

Results

When an AppleScript function returns a result, it is stored in a special temporary variable called `result`. This can be used to access a value without the need for additional variables. For example, lines 3 and 4 of the preceding script could be changed to

```
get the file type of thisFile
display dialog the result
```

To display the contents of the result container within the Script Editor, choose View, Show Result (Command-2) from the menu, or click the Result button at the bottom of the Script Editor window. Mac OS X displays the current value of `result` below the script.

Script Tracing

To trace the execution of a script as it runs, use the Event Log. This log keeps track of the events (commands) sent to an application and displays the results that are returned immediately. Click the Event Log button or press Command+3 to show the Event Log in the lower pane of the Script Editor window. Figure 39.5 shows the Event Log after replaying a simple script to get the location of a Finder window.

Saving

After creating a script that functions the way you want, you can save it for double-click execution whenever you want. Choose File, Save As or File, Save As Run-Only from the menu. The Run-Only option should be used to protect the script from future edits. Figure 39.6 displays the Save As panel.

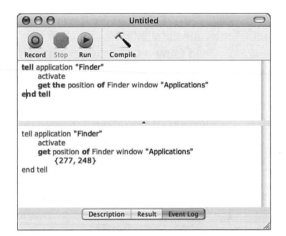

FIGURE 39.5
The Event Log can be used to monitor script execution.

FIGURE 39.6
Save a script for later execution.

There are four possible file formats for scripts:

▶ Compiled Script—Save the script as a compiled binary file.

▶ Script Document—A noncompiled binary form of the script.

▶ Script Text—Save the contents of the script in a plain-text file.

▶ Application—Save the script for double-click execution under Mac OS X.

In addition to the file format, you can also choose the line ending format if saving to a text file, and whether the file should be Run Only (not allow editing), display a Startup Screen, Stay Open (after it is finished executing), and whether it Requires Classic (Mac OS 9).

Scripting Preferences

The Script Editor automatically highlights and formats AppleScript as you type. To change the default font styles and formatting, choose Preferences from the application menu. Figure 39.7 shows the Formatting preference dialog box.

FIGURE 39.7
AppleScript Formatting controls enable the user to adjust the appearance of the Script Editor.

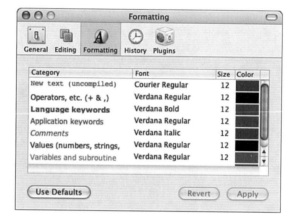

There are five categories of Script Editor preferences:

▶ General—The default scripting language to be used. AppleScript is the only language available without installing third-party software.

▶ Editing—Control line wrap settings, tab indentation, and enable/disable the Code Assistant—which attempts to autocomplete functions as you type them in the Script Editor.

▶ Formatting—Choose font size, color, syntax highlighting, and so on.

▶ History—Enable or disable a running history of AppleScript generated results and events.

▶ Plugins—Display any third-party plug-ins that have been installed.

Scripting Syntax

Describing the AppleScript syntax to a programmer familiar with a traditional language isn't as straightforward as you might think. AppleScript uses an entirely different programming model based on an English-like structure that, after a few minutes of use, leaves the programmer feeling as though he is having a deep, intellectual conversation with his computer.

tell

The basic building block of an AppleScript is the `tell` statement. `tell` is used to address an object and give it instructions to perform. A `tell` line is written in one of two common forms: a block or a single statement. The block format enables the programmer to send multiple commands to an application without stating its name each time.

Single:

```
tell <object> <object name> to <action>
```

Block:

```
tell <object> <object name>
        <action>
        <action>
        <action>
        ...
end tell
```

For example, the following two statements are identical but are structured using the simple and block forms of `tell`:

```
tell application "Finder" to empty trash
```

and

```
tell application "Finder"
        empty trash
end tell
```

Both of these short scripts cause the Finder to empty the Trash. Although the second form might seem more verbose, it is likely to be the most commonly encountered form. Most scripts interact with objects to perform complex compound operations rather than simple commands. In addition, the second version of the AppleScript is easier to read and view the functional components. Maintaining readable code is a good idea no matter what programming platform you're using.

Did you Know?

In addition to breaking up code with tell blocks, long lines are typically split using a code-continuation character. To break a single long code line across multiple lines, press Option-Return to insert a code-continuation character.

Variables: set/get

Variables are containers that can hold a value. In Applescript, variables can represent a number of things, such as the text "Hello" or the number "5" or more complex things such as files. To store a value in a container is called *setting*, and retrieving a value is *getting*.

In AppleScript, variables are automatically created when they are set. A variable name can be any combination of alphanumerics as long as the first character is a letter. No special prefixes are required to denote a variable within the code.

Variables can hold different types of data, and Applescript is smart enough to convert the data to the type it should be. For example, if you store "5" in a variable, AppleScript knows that when that variable is used in a calculation, it should be considered a number. Although type conversions happen automatically in many cases, a variable type can be explicitly given directly in the set statement:

```
set <variable/property> to <value> [as <object type>]
```

For example, both of the following lines set variables (thevalue and thevalue2) to 5, but the second line forces the variable to be a string (a piece of text):

```
set thevalue to 5
set thevalue2 to 5 as string
```

Variables can take on simple values, such as numbers or text, or more complex values in the form of lists. A *list* is a special variable that holds a number of pieces of information. For example, here is list called myGroceryList contains what I need to buy when I go to the grocery store:

```
set myGroceryList to {"peas","milk","soup","soap","jello"}
```

A list is represented by a comma-separated group of values, enclosed in curly brackets {}. Lists are often used to set coordinate pairs for manipulating onscreen graphics, such as windows but can be composed of any object. For example, the following line sets a variable, thePosition, to a list containing two values:

```
set thePosition to {50, 75}
```

To retrieve values from variables, or properties from objects, you would use the
get command. get, by itself, retrieves the value of an object or variable and stores
it in the result variable:

```
get the <property/variable> [of <object>]
```

Traditional programmers might feel uncomfortable with retrieving results into a
temporary variable (result); in that case, they can combine the get and set
commands to immediately store the results of a get in another variable or object
property:

```
set <variable/property> [of <object>] to
    get the <property/variable> [of <object>]
```

When dealing with list values, you can reference individual items within a list by
referring to them as just that: items. For example, assume that you've run the following command:

```
set myGroceryList to {"peas","milk","soup","soap","jello"}
```

To retrieve the value of the first item ("peas") in the list, you can use

```
get item 1 of myGroceryList
```

Again, the power of these commands is based in the dictionaries of AppleScript
applications. With products such as FileMaker Pro, your AppleScript can edit,
insert, and delete records.

if

A common programming construct is the If-then-else statement. This is used to
check the value of an item and then react to what it finds. The syntax for a basic
if statement is

```
if <condition> then
        <action>
end if
```

For example, the following code asks the user to input a value and check to see
whether it equals 5, and outputs an appropriate message if it does.

```
1: display dialog "Enter a number:" default answer ""
2: set theValue to (text returned of the result) as integer
3: if theValue = 5 then
4:     display dialog "Five is my magic number."
5: end if
```

Line 1 displays a dialog prompt for a user to enter a value. Line 2 sets a variable theValue to the text returned from the dialog and forces it to be evaluated as an integer. Line 3 checks theValue; if it is equal to the number 5, line 4 is executed. Line 4 displays an onscreen message, and line 5 ends the If statement.

The if statement can be expanded to include an else clause that is executed if the original condition is not met.

```
1: display dialog "Enter a number:" default answer ""
2: set theValue to (text returned of the result) as integer
3: if theValue = 5 then
4:     display dialog "Five is my magic number."
5: else
6:     display dialog "That is NOT my magic number."
7: end if
```

In this modified version of the code, line 6 contains an alternative message that will be displayed if the condition in line 3 is not met.

Finally, the else itself can be expanded to check alternative conditions using else if. This enables multiple possibilities to be evaluated within a single statement:

```
1: display dialog "Enter a number:" default answer ""
2: set theValue to (text returned of the result) as integer
3: if theValue = 5 then
4:     display dialog "Five is my magic number."
5: else if theValue = 3 then
6:     display dialog "Three is a decent number too."
7: else
8:     display dialog "I don't like that number."
9: end if
```

The latest version of the code includes an else if in line 5. If the initial comparison in line 3 fails, line 5 is evaluated. Finally, if line 5 fails, the else in line 8 is executed.

repeat

Another common programming construct is the *loop*. Loops are used to repeat a simple task, such as counting from 1 to 100. Sometimes instead of repeating a certain number of times, a loop repeats until something happens—such as a comparison becomes false.

AppleScript uses a single-loop type to handle a variety of looping needs. The repeat statement has several different forms that cover while, until, and other types of traditional loops.

There are six different forms of the `repeat` statement:

▶ Repeat indefinitely—Repeat a group of statements indefinitely, or until the exit command is called:

```
repeat
    <statements>
end repeat
```

▶ Repeat #—Using the second loop format, the user can choose the number of times a loop repeats:

```
repeat <integer> times
    <statements>
end repeat
```

▶ Repeat while—Loop indefinitely while the given condition evaluates to true:

```
repeat while <condition>
    <statements>
end repeat
```

▶ Repeat until—Loop indefinitely until the given condition evaluates to true. This is the inverse of the `repeat while` loop.

```
repeat until <condition>
    <statements>
end repeat
```

▶ Repeat with—Called a for/next loop in more traditional languages, this form of the repeat loop counts up or down from a starting number to an ending number. Each iteration updates a variable with the latest loop value.

```
repeat with <variable> from <starting integer> to
➥<ending integer> [by <increment>]
    <statements>
end repeat
```

▶ Repeat with list—Like the standard repeat with style loop, the repeat with list loop runs over a range of values, storing each value in a named variable during the iterations of the loop. The difference is the value range is specified with a list, rather than an upper and lower integer value. This enables the loop to operate over anything from numbers to strings, to lists of lists.

```
repeat with <variable> in <list>
    <statements>
end repeat
```

Subroutines

The final building block that we will cover in AppleScript is the subroutine. *Subroutines* help modularize code by breaking it into smaller, more manageable segments that can return specific results to a controlling piece of code. For example, if you have a specific application where you want to repeatedly perform a calculation on four values, rather than write out the equation each time, you could write a subroutine that accepts the four values as its input and then gives you back the response (called *returning* a value). Subroutines should be used any time you find yourself doing a common set of actions over and over.

The syntax of a subroutine is shown here:

```
on <subroutine name> ([<variable 1>,<variable 2>,<variable n>,...])
    <statements>
    [return <result value>]
end <subroutine name>
```

Although this might look confusing, it's easier to understand by looking at an actual piece of code. For example, the following beAnnoying routine takes a string and a number as parameters and then displays a dialog box with the message. The display will be repeated until it matches the number given.

```
1: on beAnnoying(theMessage, howAnnoying)
2:     repeat howAnnoying times
3:         display dialog theMessage
4:     end repeat
5: end beAnnoying
```

Line 1 declares the subroutine beAnnoying and its two parameters: theMessage and howAnnoying. Line 2 starts a loop that repeats for the number of times set in the howAnnoying variable. Line 3 displays a dialog box with the contents theMessage. Line 4 ends the loop, and line 5 ends the subroutine.

As expected, running this piece of code does absolutely nothing—it is a subroutine and, as such, requires that another piece of code call it. To call this particular routine, you could use a line such as

```
beAnnoying("Am I annoying yet?",3)
```

This causes the subroutine to activate and display the message "Am I annoying yet?" three times.

A more useful subroutine is one that performs a calculation and returns a result. For example, the following example accepts, as input, an integer containing a person's age in years. It returns a result containing the given age in days.

```
1: on yearsToDays(theYears)
2:     return theYears * 365
3: end yearsToDays
```

Because this subroutine returns a value, it can be called from within a set statement to store the result directly into a variable:

```
set dayAge to yearsToDays(90)
```

Scripting Additions

Enterprising developers who open the power of their software to the AppleScript model constantly expand AppleScript. The most common type of scripting addition is a new application. Applications that you install under Mac OS X may or may not be scriptable—be sure to check the documentation or try opening the software's dictionary using the Script Editor.

In addition, some developers may deliver extensions to AppleScript in the form of a scripting extension. These extensions are not applications themselves, but libraries of additional functions that can be used in any AppleScript.

Downloaded AppleScript extensions should be stored in ~/Library/ ScriptingAdditions or the system-level directory /Library/ScriptingAdditions for access by all users.

Script Menu

The Script Menu installer (path: Applications/AppleScript/Install Script Menu adds a menu extra to your menu bar that can be used to quickly launch AppleScripts from the /Library/Scripts folder, or ~/Library/Scripts.

Figure 39.8 shows the Script menu extra.

Any compiled scripts placed in either of the Scripts locations will become accessible from the menu. To create submenus for categorizing scripts, just create multiple folders within the Scripts folders. As with everything in Mac OS X, items stored in /Library/Scripts are accessible by all users, whereas those in your personal ~/Library/Scripts folders can be used only by you.

The Script menu can be used to access Perl and Shell scripts in addition to AppleScripts. Any script files placed in Scripts folders will be added to the list.

Did you Know?

FIGURE 39.8
The Script menu extra adds a menu bar launch point for all your scripts.

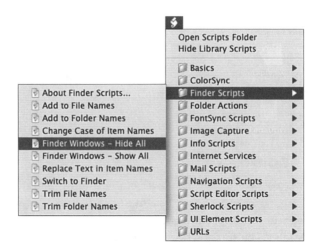

To remove the Script menu, Command-drag it from the menu bar, or use the Remove Script Menu utility included in the AppleScript folder.

Folder Actions

Folder actions are scripts that are executed when folders are opened, modified, or moved. Actions can be attached either via the Script menu's Folder Actions submenu or by selecting a folder in the Finder and choosing Enable Folder Actions from the folder's contextual menu, followed by dd Folder Action or Configure Folder Actions from the same menu. The Add Folder Action prompts you for a folder action script to attach to the highlighted folder, whereas Configure Folder Actions opens a window (Folder Actions Setup), shown in Figure 38.9, that provides access to *all* folder actions configured for your account.

Within the Folder Actions Setup window, use the Enable Folder Actions check box to globally enable or disable actions. To add a new action, click the "+" button below the left-hand column and choose a folder you want to attach an action to. When added to the folder list, highlight it and use the "+" button in the right-hand column to choose a folder action script that you want to attach to the folder. The "-" buttons can be used to remove folders and attached scripts, whereas the Open Folder and Edit Script buttons open the highlighted folder and open the selected script in Script Editor.

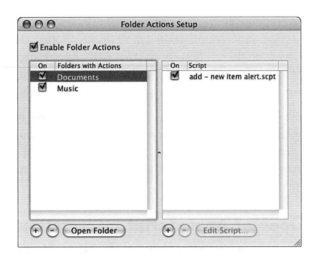

FIGURE 39.9
Configure Folder
Actions provides a
"control center" for
adding/removing
folder actions.

To get started with folder action scripts, Apple has include three basic scripts in /Library/Scripts/Folder Action Scripts:

- ▶ `close - close sub-folders.scpt`—Closes any open subfolders when the folder with the attached script is closed.

- ▶ `add - new item alert.scpt`—Displays an alert when new items are added to the folder with the attached script.

- ▶ `open - show comments in dialog.scpt`—Shows any comments stored when the folder with the attached script is opened.

Properly formed "Action" scripts should be placed in either /Library/Scripts/Folder Action Scripts or ~/Library/Scripts/Folder Action Scripts. Apple has provided an excellent tutorial on how to set up a folder action script at www.apple.com/applescript/folder_actions/.

AppleScript Studio

After you've familiarized yourself with basic AppleScript syntax, you might want to consider moving up to the "next level" of AppleScript development— AppleScript Studio. AppleScript Studio is Apple's integration of the AppleScript programming language with *XCode*.

Using XCode you can quickly create complete GUI applications powered entirely by AppleScript. Although not appropriate for real-time or graphically intense software, AppleScript Studio can quickly create a GUI around Unix-based commands. In fact, a number of popular Macintosh utilities (such as Carbon Copy Cloner) have been written in AppleScript Studio and have received rave reviews.

To get started with AppleScript Studio, install XCode and browse the examples in /Developer/Applications/AppleScript Studio. Apple has provided a simple tutorial along with PDF reference guides to get you started. Be warned; AppleScript Studio takes advantage of Apple's development tools—these, although powerful, have been known to take some time to master.

Other Sources of AppleScript Information

AppleScript is a capable language that offers many advanced features impossible to cover in the amount of space this title allows. What is provided here should be an ample start to creating scripts of your own and editing scripts included with Mac OS X. If you're interested in more information on advanced AppleScript syntax, we strongly suggest that you check the following resources:

AppleScript Language Guide— `http://developer.apple.com/documenta-tion/AppleScript/Conceptual/AppleScriptLangGuide/index.html`

AppleScript in Mac OS X—`http://www.apple.com/applescript/macosx/`

The AppleScript Sourcebook—`http://www.AppleScriptSourcebook.com/`

AppleScript in a NutShell, Bruce W. Perry, ISBN: 1565928415, O'Reilly, 2001

> AppleScript functionality has slowly been evolving with each revision of Mac OS X. If you're lagging a version or two behind, you're likely to notice serious limitations with the version of AppleScript you have installed. Panther's support far exceeds any of the previous releases.

Summary

AppleScript provides a powerful solution for automating tasks on your Mac. The Script Editor is the centerpiece of script development and offers even novice users the ability to record their interactions directly to an AppleScript. In the latest version of OS X, many applications can be recorded with AppleScript. Give it a try—you may be surprised by how easy the syntax can be.

CHAPTER 40

Exploring the Utilities Folder

Tucked inside the Applications folder is a folder called Utilities, which stores a treasure trove of helpful applications. Some of those "utilities" are employed by your system to carry out common tasks, whereas others are tools that you can use for specific purposes. In this chapter, we'll talk about each of these applications and, where appropriate, refer back to previous chapters where they were mentioned.

> Unlike the categorization structure used by the System Preferences, the items in the Utilities folder aren't in any particular order. However, for organizational purposes, we've grouped the applications in the Utilities folder into four categories: System Tools; Network Tools; Imaging, Font, and Audio Tools; and System Helpers.

By the Way

System Tools

You Mac is a complex machine that runs many processes and has many components, some of which you may not even know about! System Tools are useful for taking a in-depth look at your Mac, which you may want to do in case of system difficulties or merely as an interesting window into the workings of your Mac.

Activity Monitor

As discussed in Chapter 36, "Mantaining Your System," Activity Monitor reveals what processes are running on your system and how much CPU time they consume. This can be helpful for finding out which applications are monopolizing system resources if your computer seems bogged down.

Console

Console is a specialized window for reading system logs, which record events related to applications or even network activity. Refer to Chapter 34, "Creating and Hosting Your Own Website."

Disk Utility

Disk Utility is OS X's built-in hard drive repair tool—with the extra function of creating disk images of drives and allowing you to burn them to CD or DVD. We discussed the repair aspects in Chapter 37, "Recovering from Crashes and Other Problems," and the disk copy element in Chapter 36.

By the Way

> Disk Utility can also be run from your system installation disk. Use the version from the disk if you need to repair your main hard drive because drive repair can't be run from the currently booted drive.

System Profiler

System Profiler is a great utility to use if you ever need to call for technical support and are asked the exact system configuration of your computer. The System Profiler's sole purpose is to collect data on your computer, peripherals, and software and prepare a report of the results.

The information in the System Profiler is divided into four categories: Hardware, Software, Network, and Logs. (The Hardware and Software can be expanded by clicking their disclosure triangles.)

Hardware

The Hardware section, shown in Figure 40.1, displays general information such as the machine model, the amount of built-in memory, and your computer's serial number.

The additional items under Hardware give summaries of the devices connected to your computer (including internal disks and storage devices, video and sound cards, and modems). Here is a list of the information displayed in the Hardware section:

▶ Memory—Provides details about the location, type, and amount of memory installed in your computer.

▶ PCI/AGP—The Peripheral Component Interconnect (PCI) bus is a standard for connecting internal video cards, sound cards, and so on; AGP is another standard for video cards. This section of the Hardware information provides details about your video card and display.

▶ IDE/ATA—Integrated Drive Electronics (IDE) and Advanced Technology Attachment (ATA) refer to a standard for internal CD-ROM and disk storage; view details about your hard drive, such as model, capacity, and serial number.

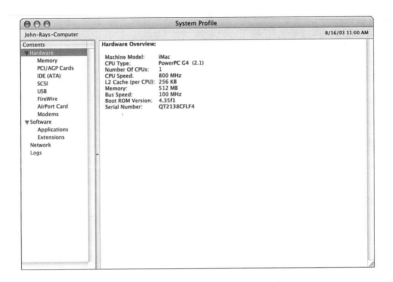

FIGURE 40.1
The main Hardware screen presents an overview of your system configuration.

▶ SCSI—The Small Computer System Interface is an older bus developed and used by Apple to connect storage devices and printers. (Most newer Macintoshes don't have SCSI buses, but there are SCSI adapters for people with SCSI devices they want to continue using.) If available, view any connected devices.

▶ USB—Universal Serial Bus is used for connecting external peripherals, such as scanners, printers, cameras, keyboards, and mice—as well as lower speed storage devices. View details about any USB devices connected to your computer, as shown in Figure 40.2.

Use of USB and FireWire peripheral devices are discussed briefly in Chapter 19, "Adding Peripheral Devices."

By the Way

▶ FireWire—An Apple-developed bus technology that supports speeds of 400Mbps, which is often used with high-speed storage and digital video cameras. (FireWire is also known as IEEE 1394 and, in Sony devices, as iLink.) If you have any FireWire devices connected, you can see details about them here.

FIGURE 40.2
Identify your keyboard, mouse, and any other USB peripheral.

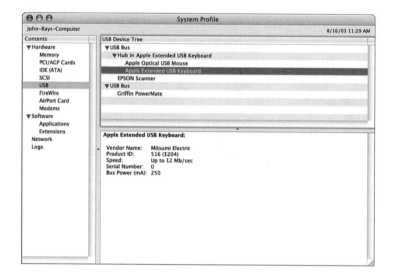

▶ AirPort Card—In Chapter 11, "Connecting to the Internet," you learned that one of the options for networking computers uses a wireless technology called AirPort. Most recent Apple computers come with a built-in card for connecting to existing wireless networks. View details about it, as well as about any wireless network currently accessed, in this section.

By the Way

Using a wireless connection requires special setup. If you don't have access to a wireless network signal, an AirPort card can't work its magic.

▶ Modems—Modems are a device used to connect to networks via phone lines—most modern computers come with them built-in. You can see information about your system's modem in this section. (For information about connecting to a network using your built-in modem, see Chapter 11.)

Software

The Software section displays general information about the version of the operating system, the computer name, and the user currently logged in. There are also two subsections—Applications and Extensions.

▶ Applications—The Applications section displays all the installed applications on your drive in alphabetical order, regardless of where they are installed. You can use the list to see what versions are installed and where an item is located.

▶ Extensions—Extensions help the operating system interact with hardware, such as network cards and peripheral devices. In this section, you can learn information such as the version, location, and developer about each extension.

Network

The Network category lists details about the hardware available to your computer for connecting to networks. (Configuration of these devices for network access is discussed in Chapter 11.)

Logs

Earlier in this chapter, we talked about the Console utility, which is used to view system logs. The Logs section of the System Profile also gives access to this information, which may include failed attempts by your system to access files or hardware that can give you clues about the source of problems with your system.

It's not unusual for errors and failure to be recorded in the console.log file and for you to have no idea that they occurred. If you haven't noticed anything strange with your system, don't worry about entries about elements not found or exceptions raised.

Watch Out!

The two types of logs available are console and system logs. The console.log item records errors having to do with the applications run on your computer. The system.log item reports events related to the operating system and networking, which are largely outside a user's control.

Terminal

Terminal is an application that provides a window, or shell prompt, into which you can type commands directly to the system. Chapter 38, "Using Basic Unix Commands," discusses some basic uses of Terminal.

Network Tools

Networking relates to how your computer interacts with other computers. The items in this section include setup assistants for various network-able devices as well as utilities for storing and looking up network information. The use of these applications is more advanced than those in the previous sections, and we'll describe their use only briefly here. However, if you are interested in learning more, you may want to pick up a copy of *Mac OS X Unleashed*, which discusses them thoroughly.

AirPort Admin Utility and Airport Setup Assistant

In Chapter 11 you learned that one option was a wireless connection called AirPort. Although at that time we talked about connecting to an existing AirPort network, the AirPort Admin Utility and the AirPort Setup Assistant are used to set up the wireless base station that conveys a wireless signal to computers.

Bluetooth Utilities

Three Bluetooth-related applications are located in the Utilities folder—Bluetooth File Exchange, Bluetooth Serial Utility, and Bluetooth Setup Assistant. Bluetooth refers to a wireless technology standard that allows compatible devices to interact with each other with little setup by the users—quite simply, Bluetooth devices send out signals that can be received by other Bluetooth devices.

The Bluetooth Setup Assistant allows you to configure a Bluetooth-enabled Mac to communicate with a Bluetooth-enabled mobile phone. (This would allow you to use a mobile phone that is not tethered to your computer to dial-in to your ISP.)

The Bluetooth Serial Utility is used to set up additional ports for your computer to use with Bluetooth devices.

Bluetooth File Exchange allows you to browse files on other Bluetooth computers, both Mac and Windows-based.

Directory Access

Directory Access is used to access directory servers, such as Window's Active Directory Server. It is used to configure where Mac OS X gets its account information. For example, in a computer lab, a server would contain a listing of all the accounts, and each user computer would be set up using Directory Access to get account settings from the server.

NetInfo Manager

The NetInfo Manager is a window into a database of information on your system about your computer's setup and files, its users, and its network.

For example, you can select the users folder (or directory) from the list and then choose your account. Among other things, you'll see your username, password hint, and the path to the user picture you chose as your login icon—which you can also access from the Accounts pane of the System Preferences.

In the other categories are more advanced settings related to the Unix underpinnings of OS X, many of which you don't have the option to change from the graphical interface.

> For an average user, it's not wise to make system changes with NetInfo Manager. The information it accesses is vital to the operation of your computer, and mistakes made may be difficult to fix. (Even experienced system administrators are advised to make duplicates of the original information before changing settings here.)

**Watch
Out!**

Network Utility

Also in the Utilities folder is something called Network Utility. This collection of functions, shown in Figure 40.3, is commonly used by people who manage or work with networks. Most of these functions display information or are used to test network connections.

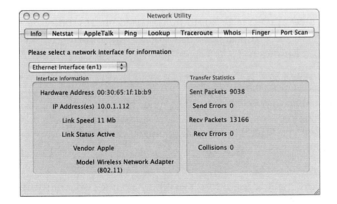

FIGURE 40.3
Network Utility collects several network administration tools into a single resource.

Following is a brief description of the options available:

▶ Info—Lets you see information about the installed network cards, including whether they are connected and to which IP address. It also lists any errors in transmission that have occurred.

▶ Netstat—Shows all the connections to and from your computer. It is of most use to server operators who need to see who is connected to the computer at a particular instant.

▶ AppleTalk—Shows AppleTalk zone details as well as statistics and errors.

▶ Ping—A function that enables you to test whether a remote machine is responding and how fast the connection is. (Essentially, this is a low-level contact between machines that is used to see whether a machine is online.)

▶ Lookup—Translates between IP addresses and hostnames.

▶ Traceroute—Shows the path required to connect to a given IP address or hostname.

▶ Whois—Enables you to look up who owns and administers a domain name. Note that when using the default whois server options, you may be directed to another host for more detailed information.

▶ Finger—Lets you look up information on a specific user on systems that have this service enabled. Finger was traditionally a feature of Unix-based systems that, when supplied with a username, returned information about a user, such as a real name and whether the user was currently logged in. (Large institutions, such as universities, often offer this service.)

▶ Portscan—Used to test which services (such as FTP and file sharing) are running on a computer, but should not be used on any but your own computers. This feature was discussed in Chapter 35, "Sharing Files to Windows and Unix Computers."

Watch Out!

Portscan is nothing to play with. Scanning other people's networks can be interpreted as suspicious behavior—it's one of the ways malicious hackers find vulnerable systems to hack into—and if portscans are being performed by your computer, your ISP may receive letters of complaint.

For the most part, typical users won't need to use Network Utility. It is a powerful tool for network administrators to diagnose network problems.

ODBC Administrator

ODBC stands for Open Database Connectivity. The ODBC Administrator is an application that can be used with the appropriate database drivers to provide database access to ODBC-aware applications, such as FileMaker.

Imaging, Font, and MIDI Tools

The applications discussed here are related to imaging, character-based language fonts, and MIDI composition. For imaging, Mac OS X includes applications to measure onscreen color and to calibrate your display as well as to create screen captures. It also includes a digital music composition tool. For those who write in character-based Asian Languages, there is also a special set of tools in the Asia Text Extras folder.

Asia Text Extras

The Asia Text Extras item is a folder of utilities for people who use character-based Asian languages. It includes Chinese Text Converter, which performs encoding conversions between Traditional and Simplified Chinese as well as other conversions.

Audio MIDI Setup

The Audio MIDI Setup utility allows you to view and customize settings for audio and MIDI devices.

In the Audio Devices section, you can view which peripheral devices and built-in hardware are available—and, with selected devices—change their configuration.

MIDI, an acronym for Musical Instrument Digital Interface, is a protocol for creating music with electronic devices. If you connect MIDI hardware to your Mac and launch the Audio MIDI Setup, you can check for device drivers or customize your MIDI setup in the MIDI Devices section.

ColorSync Utility

ColorSync Utility helps you calibrate your display. You learn about monitor calibration in Chapter 18, "Working with Monitors and ColorSync."

DigitalColor Meter

The next application, DigitalColor Meter, measures and reports the color of an onscreen pixel, or the average color of a group of pixels. It comes in handy when trying to find an exact match for any color appearing on your display.

When launched, DigitalColor Meter opens the window shown in Figure 40.4.

FIGURE 40.4
Use DigitalColor
Meter to get the
RGB values for any
onscreen color.

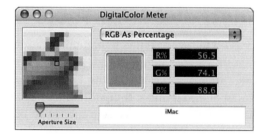

The section at the left of the window displays an enlarged view of whatever is currently under the mouse cursor. Immediately to the right of the enlarged view is a color well that contains the sampled color. Adjusting the aperture slider controls the number of pixels sampled from 1×1 to 16×16. (For apertures greater than 1×1, the displayed color is the average of several pixels of image surrounding the mouse cursor.)

To the right of the color well is a numeric representation of the currently selected color. The pop-up menu at the top of the window determines the color model being used.

> **By the Way**
>
> To match an onscreen color with a Web color, select RGB As Hex in the DigitalColor Meter's pop-up menu. The three sets of letter/number combinations describe the color.

Grab

Mac OS X offers the ability to make a screen capture, or an exact snapshot of your screen at the current moment, by pressing Shift-Command-3 for full-screen captures or Shift-Command-4 for partial screens. The Grab application can do things that are not possible with the built-in screenshot function. Grab can capture screen information in four different ways:

> **By the Way**
>
> Screen captures created with Shift-Command-3, or partial screen captures created with Shift-Command-4, are in PDF format. They appear on the desktop as "Picture #." Although this method works for quick screen captures, Grab offers a few more features.

▶ Selection (Shift-Command-A)—Captures a portion of the screen, determined by the user drawing a rectangle.

▶ Window (Shift-Command-W)—Captures a selected window, determined by which window is clicked after the Grab capture is initiated.

▶ Screen (Command-Z)—Captures the entire screen.

▶ Time Screen (Shift-Command-Z)—Captures the screen with a 10-second delay. That gives you time to position your windows, pull down (or pop up) menus, and so on. You can take screenshots with menus in the down position in Mac OS X!

No matter what method you use, Grab displays a window with short instructions on how to proceed. This window is *not* included in the final screenshot, despite appearing onscreen as the shot is taken.

For example, to capture a timed screenshot:

1. Choose Capture, Timed Screen from Grab's menu. Grab displays the window shown in Figure 40.5.

FIGURE 40.5
Timed screenshots give you a chance to get things in order.

2. Click the Start Timer Button.

3. As the clock counts down, change your screen into the arrangement you want. At the end of 10 seconds, Grab captures the screen and opens the image in a new window.

4. Choose File, Save from the menu to save the image in Tiff format.

Grab saves images in Tiff format. If another image format would be more appropriate, you can open the image in the Preview application, discussed in Chapter 6, "Using Calculator, Stickies, Preview, and TextEdit," and select File, Export from the menu. You can then choose from a number of common image formats.

Did you Know?

When taking a screenshot, you can choose to superimpose a cursor of your choice over the screen; by default, no cursor is shown at all. Choose Preferences under the Grab application menu to change the cursor that will be used. Figure 40.6 shows the preferences.

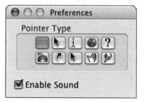

In the Pointer Type section, click the button for the cursor your want to use.

The preferences can also toggle the camera shutter noise that is played when an image is captured. Select or deselect the Enable Sound check box as you see fit.

System Helpers

At the start of this chapter, you learned that the Utilities folder is home to several applications that help your computer perform necessary tasks. Let's take a quick look at them.

Installer

The Installer utility is used by many applications when they are installed. It essentially provides the wizardlike interface that appears with many of Apple's applications.

Java

Java is programming language specifically written to create programs that can be run on any operating system, or even from Web pages, easily. Inside the Utilities folder is a Java folder containing several applications for installing and running with Java-based applications, or applets.

Keychain Access

Keychain Access is the utility that maintains all your application passwords. It was discussed in Chapter 8, "Working with Address Book, Keychain Access, iSync, and Ink."

Printer Setup Utility

As covered in Chapter 20, "Printing, Faxing, and Working with Fonts," the Printer Setup Utility allows you to configure available printers and choose your default.

StuffIt Expander

To reduce their size, files are often compressed, especially those distributed via email or Web site. StuffIt Expander uncompresses these files so that you can read them. We talked about StuffIt Expander in Chapter 9, "Installing Additional Software," as used when installing downloaded software.

Summary

In this chapter, we've examined the contents of the Utilities folder located inside the Applications folder. Several utilities can be used to monitor system functions. Others relate to networking options. A few are useful, targeted applications, such as Grab and DigitalColor Meter. There are also several applications used by your system for specific purposes.

Index

titles

DVDs, 547-548

movies, 443, 446-447

   adding, 450

   Bounce In To Center, 444

   Centered Multiple, 445-446

   color, 453

   editing, 452-453

   over black, 448

   overlay, 448

   selecting, 448-452

   text size, 452-454

   video clips, 480

Titles palette (iMovie), 450

To Do Lists (iCal), 315

Tool Mode buttons (Preview toolbar), 107

toolbars

   Finder, 25-28

   Keynote, 172-175

tools

   AppleWorks, 168

      Arc, 169

      Bezier, 169

      cutter, 170

      drawing, 169

      eraser, 170

      Eyedropper, 169

      fills, 170-171

      Freehand, 169

      Lasso, 170

      Line, 169

      Magic wand, 170

      Oval, 169

      Paint, 168

      paint bucket, 170

      paintbrush, 170

      painting, 170

      pen strokes, 170-171

      pencil, 170

      Polygon, 169

      Rectangle, 169

      Regular Polygon, 169

      Rounded Rectangle, 169

      spray can, 170

      Spreadsheet, 168

      table, 170

      Table creation, 168

      table editing, 170

      tables, 170

      Text, 168

      text color, 170-171

   Network, 695

      AirPort Admin Utility, 696

      AirPort Setup Assistant, 696

      Bluetooth Utilities, 696

      Directory Access, 696

      NetInfo Manager, 696

      Network Utility, 697-698

      ODBC Administrator, 698

   Selection rectangle, 170

   System, 691

      Activity Monitor, 691

      Console, 691

      Disk Utility, 692

      System Profiler, 692-695

      Terminal utility, 695

transitions, 454-455

   Cross Dissolve, 455-456

   deleting, 461

   editing, 459-461

   Fade In, 457-458

   multiple clips, 458

   speed, 459

   video clips, 478

Transport layer (TCP/IP protocol), 447-448, 463

Trash, 53-54

   Dock, 48

   emptying, 62

   files, 54-55

   iMovie, 420

   iPhoto, 398

   opening, 56

   retrieving files from, 62

   secure empty trash, 56

Trash mailbox, 262

troubleshooting

   printing, 350

   Safari status bar, 196

   viruses, 648-649

   Web sites, 198

Twirl movie title, 448

Typewriter movie title, 448

typography, 358

How can we make this index more useful? Email us at indexes@samspublishing.com

How can we make this index more useful? Email us at indexes@samspublishing.com